Animal Patents

The Legal, Economic and Social Issues

Editor
William H. Lesser

M
stockton
press

Published in the United States and Canada by
STOCKTON PRESS, 1989
15 East 26th Street, New York, N.Y. 10010

ISBN 0-935859-64-0

First published in the United Kingdom by
MACMILLAN PUBLISHERS LTD (Journals Division), 1989
Distributed by Globe Book Services Ltd
Brunel Road, Houndmills, Basingstoke, Hants RG21 2XS

British Library Cataloguing in Publication Data

Animal patents: the legal, economic and social issues.
   1. Genetic engineering. Patents. Legal aspects
   I. Lesser, William
   342.64'86

   ISBN 0-333-49012-6

Printed in Great Britain

Contents

Contents

Economic Issues

Users' Perspectives

PART TWO: APPENDIXES

News release announcing the internal US Patent Office decision on higher animal
life as patentable subject matter.

The first patent granted for a multi-celled animal (April 12, 1988), commonly called
the Harvard or Leder mouse patent.

House passage of animal patent Bill HR 4970: passed the House of Representatives
but died in the Senate due to lack of action prior to adjournment (1988).   173

HR 1556: revision and reintroduction of HR 4970 (1989).   181

Staff report of the Subcommittee on Courts, Civil Liberties and the Administration
of Justice accompanying the Transgenic Animal Patent Reform Act, including a
synopsis of the congressional testimony at the hearings of June, August and
November 1987.

List of Tables in Part One

List of Figures in Part One

Contributors

Stephen Bent is a partner in Foley and Lardner, Schwartz, Jeffery, Schwaab, Mack, Blumenthal and Evans, Alexandria, Virginia. He is perhaps best known as the lead author, with R. Schwaab, D. Conlin and D. Jeffery, of the influential book *Intellectual Property Rights in Biotechnology Worldwide* (New York: Stockton Press, 1987).

Baruch Brody is the Leon Jaworski Professor of Biomedical Ethics at Baylor College of Medicine and is a professor of philosophy at Rice University.

R. Stephen Crespi is widely known for his far-reaching writing on the application of patent law to living organisms, most recently with the textbook, *Patents: a Basic Guide to Patenting in Biotechnology* (Cambridge: Cambridge University Press, 1988). Formerly with the British Technology Group, he is presently a private patent consultant.

Karl Ebert received his doctoral degree from the University of Massachusetts, Amherst in the animal science department. He received his postdoctoral training under Dr Ralph Brinster at the University of Pennsylvania and is presently an assistant professor in the Department of Anatomy and Cellular Biology at the School of Veterinary Medicine, Tufts University. His research focuses on preimplantation embryo development in laboratory and livestock species, with major emphasis on the production of transgenic animals.

Robert Foote is Professor of Animal Psychology and Jacob Gould Schurman Professor in the Department of Animal Science at Cornell University. He has worked extensively in the areas of egg and sperm interaction and embryo development, and has produced with colleagues and students over 400 articles on the subject.

William Hansel, who has spent most of his professional career at Cornell University, has held the distinction since 1983 of being named the Liberty Hyde Bailey Professor of Animal Physiology in the College of Veterinary Medicine. His many distinctions include Guggenheim and National Science Foundation Fellowships, the Morrison Award from the American Society of Animal Science, the Carl Hartman Award from the Society for Study of Reproduction, and the Borden Award from the American Dairy Science Association.

William Lesser, an agricultural economist by training, has been evaluating the implications of patents on agriculture for the past eight years. Studies completed include analyses of the Plant Variety Protection Act, utility patents for seeds, international coordination of statutes for plants, and the implications of plant patents in the UK and Canada, as well as several other approaches to the animal patent issue. He is currently an Associate Professor of Agricultural Economics at Cornell University.

Patrick Luby, who has a PhD in agricultural economics from Purdue University, has been with Oscar Mayer Foods Co. for most of his professional career. He currently holds the position of Vice President and Corporate Economist and is responsible for forecasting and procurement.

Robert Milligan specializes in farm management issues as Professor of Agricultural Economics at Cornell University. He is a specialist in management of large farms and the implications of managerial ability on farm size. In recent years his research has dealt with biotechnology products applied to commercial agriculture, especially animal agriculture.

Kevin O'Connor is a legal analyst with the Office of Technology Assessment of the US Congress. He is concerned with the biological applications area, and, most recently, was director of the study *Patenting Life* (1989).

A. Ann Sorensen, who holds a PhD in entomology from the University of California at Berkeley, has been the Assistant Director of the Natural and Environmental Resources Division of the American Farm Bureau Federation since 1986. Her work covers environmental issues which affect farmers, and, among other subjects, she specializes in biotechnology, pesticide issues, integrated pest management and groundwater pollution. She is in frequent contact with farmers and a wide range of audiences to whom she presents the perspectives of the Bureau membership on issues affecting farming. She is also a skilled artist, having contributed scientific illustrations to numerous publications.

Joseph Straus is known internationally for his scholarly work on intellectual property law, especially on patent law for biotechnology products and processes. In the latter field he has acted as a consultant for the Organization for Economic Cooperation and Development (OECD) in Paris and the World Intellectual Property Organization (WIPO) in Geneva. He recently contributed substantially to the *Proposal for a Council Directive on the Legal Protection of Biotechnological Inventions* of the Commission of the European Communities. He is head of Department at the Max Planck Institute for Foreign and International Patent, Copyright and Competition Law and Professor of Intellectual Property Law at the Faculty of Law, University of Ljubljana.

Preface

The subject of animal patents is, at the time of writing, a current one with an antecedent of barely a year and a half. It is perhaps the last major class of products to which patent protection is to be extended, and in many ways is the most complex. The complexity stems from the legal issues associated with anything as individual as a multicellular animal: from the complexity of the science involved with such sophisticated life forms, and from the mammoth size of the potentially affected industries. Medical research, which relies heavily on laboratory animals, is a multibillion dollar undertaking. In 1986 livestock agriculture provided $71.6 billion in sales. But beyond these statistics and economic considerations, tampering, as some would have it, with animals is an enormously sensitive moral and ethical issue with many people.

The papers presented in this volume were prepared for a symposium of the same name held at Cornell University in Ithaca, New York on December 5–6, 1988. The symposium was structured to touch upon each of the relevant issues associated with patenting complex animals by having an expert address each topic.

Organizationally, the papers are presented under four headings—Legal Issues, Technical Issues, Economic Issues, and Users' Perspectives—the final heading including input from farm organizations and agribusiness as well as an overview of the moral and ethical issues associated with the genetic altering of higher animal life. Today it is not sufficient to limit the scope of analysis to single nations for the research under way has worldwide applicability. Certainly with national economies as interlocked as they are, the effects will be felt across major portions of the world even if only selected countries actually put the technologies to use. Several of the papers are directed to the international dimension of animal patenting although, of course, much more could be done on this topic.

Each presentation at the symposium was followed by a lively debate which it has not been feasible to capture within the bounds of this volume. However, the edited papers presented here have incorporated the major issues identified during the discussion.

The credit for this work goes to the authors of the papers. They, in the quality of their work and the punctuality of response, made the editor's job an easy one. Also to be recognized are the two sponsoring agencies which made the symposium possible by covering the expenses of the speakers. They are, for the international contingent, the Cornell University Western Societies Program and for US agricultural issues the Farm Foundation. The employers of a number of the speakers generously contributed transportation which greatly facilitated the operation of the symposium. I would also like to recognize Jennifer Wyse for her major contribution in bringing the raw texts to publishable form.

WILLIAM LESSER

Abbreviations

AI	artificial insemination
AIDS	Acquired Immune Deficiency Syndrome
AIPPI	Association for the Protection of Industrial Property
ATCC	American Type Culture Collection
bGH	bovine growth hormone
BSCC	Biotechnology Science Coordinating Committee
c	centigrade
CAST	Council for Agricultural Science and Technology
cDNA	copy (cloned) DNA
CMV	cytomegalo virus promoter
CPC	Community Patent Convention
D	Democrat
DHHS	Department of Health and Human Services
DNA	deoxyribonucleic acid
EC	European Community
EEC	European Economic Community
EPA	U.S. Environmental Protection Agency
EPC	European Patent Convention
EPO	European Patent Office
FDA	Food and Drug Administration
FSH	follicle stimulating hormone
FY	Fiscal Year
GATT	General Agreement on Tariffs and Trade
hCG & eCG	chorionic gonadotropins
hGH	human growth hormone
IIC	International Review of Industrial Property and Copyright Law
LH	luteinizing hormone
mRNA	messenger RNA
MT	metalloth ionine promoter
NCDHIP	National Cooperative Dairy Herd Improvement Program
NCDP	National Commission on Dairy Policy
NER	National Environmental Resources Division, American Farm Bureau Federation
NIH	National Institutes of Health
NSF	National Science Foundation
OECD	Organization for Economic Cooperation and Development
OSHA	Occupational Safety and Health Administration

Abbreviations

OSTP	Office of Science and Technology Policy, U.S. White House
OTA	Office of Technology Assessment, U.S. Congress
PA	Patent Act (U.S.)
pGH	porcine growth hormone
PHS	Public Health Service, U.S. Department of Health and Human Services
PTO	U.S. Patent and Trademark Office
PVPA	Plant Variety Protection Act (U.S.)
R & D	Research and Development
R	Republican
rDNA	recombinant DNA
RNA	ribonucleic acid
SS	somatostatin
SV40	semian virus signal sequences
TDA	Texas Department of Agriculture
TGF-B	transforming growth factor -B
tPA (or TPA)	tissue plasminogen activator
TSH	thyroid stimulating hormone
UPOV	International Convention for the Protection of New Varieties of Plants
USDA	U.S. Department of Agriculture
WIPO	World Intellectual Property Organization

PART ONE
ISSUES AND PERSPECTIVES

LEGAL ISSUES

Introduction

The concept of a patent is a complex legal invention directed initially to mechanical/industrial devices. The carefully drawn system of the 18th and 19th centuries came under strain as life-based inventions began the ascent in patentability status during the 20th century. Two basic means exist for extending patent protection to living organisms:

(1) Existing law can be amended or interpreted to enfold it.
(2) New legislation can be adopted.

Many countries with extensive patent statutes have simultaneously chosen both of these approaches.

The following five papers attempt to make clear what may seem from the outside extremely complex. **Bent** reviews the history of legislation in the USA up to the *Ex parte Allen* decision, which in April 1987 extended patentability status to higher animals. Working from the position that the US Patent Act is fully flexible and hence encompassing, he discusses the interpretation of the key requirements for patentability, novelty, non-obviousness, and enablement in light of the technical characteristics of higher animals.

Once granted, patents are exclusionary, that is, they allow holders to limit the use of their invention. This raises the problem of whether the patent holder can prevent another from using the invention for the purposes of improving it. It is a most significant matter for living organisms where much non-unique genetic material is incorporated in an animal. **Bent** is reassuring on this point, arguing that there is no binding dictum in the case law to limit such experimental use of patented products.

Straus undertakes the ambitious task of contrasting European law with that of the US as it would apply to higher animals. Europeans (via the Federal Republic of Germany) made the first significant stride in this area in the "Red Dove" case of 1969, but a parallel law adopted earlier in the decade prohibited the patenting of an "animal variety." **Straus** discusses the complexity of interpreting the term, including a recent effort by the Commission for the European Communities to codify these and other pertinent interpretations so as to maximize the patentability scope under existing law without the necessity for a lengthy revision process. **Straus** is optimistic about the potential for animal patents, noting they are possible "in principle," but the routine treatment of animal patent applications is clearly sometime off. It will be interesting to see if Convention Internationale pour la Protection des Obtentions Vegetales (UPOV), the prevailing system for protecting plant-based inventions, is extended to cover all animals, or at least animals developed through "traditional breeding" practices.

Crespi continues from this point in his evaluation of international coordination possibilities. He cites numerous examples of the need for and signs of flexibility regarding the patenting of animals, but notes the uncertainty of the role of UPOV. Since several restrictive clauses of the UPOV agreement, and associated terminology in European patent law, are contrary to a basic thrust of US law, this factor will have significant ramifications for eventual international harmonization.

Not to be outdone by the legal debate in Europe, several bills directed at limiting, to one degree or another, the scope of patent protection allowable in the USA have been put forward in Congress. These are discussed by **O'Connor** in the context of the regulatory role exercised at the national level. To date, none of the bills has become law (one did pass the House, but was not acted upon in the Senate as the term expired), but the more basic message is clear.[1] The period of full autonomy by the US Patent Office is drawing to a close; the public is demanding a greater voice.

Underlying these legal discussions are the technical aspects, and **Foote**, an animal scientist rather than a lawyer, is the appropriate person to answer the technical issues regarding deposit. Stated succinctly, patents must be repeatable and, other methods failing, an example placed on deposit is an acceptable solution for the repeatability requirement. But can higher animals be deposited? Yes, says **Foote**, as frozen embryos for which the method is both proven and economical. In this respect, higher animals fit easily within existing US Patent Office practices.

---

[1] As of date of publication, one additional bill has been introduced into the House of Representatives (see Appendix 3).

Issues and Prospects in the USA

Stephen A. Bent

INTRODUCTION

As participants in this convocation on animal patenting, we share the rare opportunity to study a nexus between modern technology and the law at a most opportune time—*before* either legislators or judges have had a real chance to occupy the field and put us all on the defensive!

In initiating this survey of the patenting of animals, I am inclined to paraphrase Sir Winston Churchill: never has so much been said and written about so little so soon. After all, the world still awaits its *second* animal patent, the first having been issued in April 1987 on an invention developed by Harvard researchers working on transgenic, cancer-prone rodents.[1] Even now there are probably fewer than three dozen animal patent applications pending before the US Patent and Trademark Office (PTO). Yet already Dr. Michael W. Fox of the Humane Society of the United States has said that, by virtue of the issuance of animal patents, "the wholesale industrialized exploitation of the animal kingdom will be sanctioned, protected and intensified," accelerating the "transformation of life and of the creative process to serve purely human ends, and as many see it, the end of the natural world" (Atlanta Journal, 1987).

A BRIEF HISTORY

In the face of apocalyptic declarations like that of Fox, it should not be forgotten that there is a fairly long history to the patenting of multicellular life forms in the USA. In 1930, the US Congress passed the Plant Patent Act, principally to reward the much-publicized innovative activity of the horticulturist Luther Burbank. Limited to the protection of asexually propagated varieties, the institution of plant patenting flourished for 40 years before Congress responded to public pressure and established a protective scheme, under the auspices of the US Department of Agriculture (USDA), which also encompassed sexually propagated plants[2] (see Bent *et al.*, 1987: pp. 448–59).

---

[1] US Patent no. 4,736,866: Transgenic Non-Human Mammals, issued April 12, 1988 (see Appendix 2).

[2] The Plant Variety Protection Act of 1970 (PVPA) empowered the Secretary of Agriculture to issue to breeders a "certificate of plant variety protection" embodying a patent-like exclusive right over the propagation and sale of a sexually propagated plant variety which is distinct from existing varieties, uniform and stable. (7 US Const §§2321 *et seq.*). There are significant qualifications to the exclusive right under the PVPA that do not have a statutory counterpart in the patent system.

By the mid-1970s, intimations of a revolution in the applied biological sciences were evident in the patent arena. In 1975, a French company failed on a technicality in its attempt to patent a "dwarf, egg-laying chicken hen produced by a [breeding] process" that exploited a "sex-linked recessive dwarfism gene" (*In re Merat*).[3] Then, in 1980, a series of appeals culminated in a landmark decision of the US Supreme Court which held that an invention could not be treated as unpatentable in principle simply because it was comprised of living matter (*Diamond v. Chakrabarty*; *In re Bergy*).

For a time after that, the PTO made it known that a so-called "doctrine of preemption" would be applied to preclude patent protection for plant-related inventions that were covered, at least in theory, by the plant protection laws previously mentioned. That policy was repudiated in 1985 by the PTO's own Board of Appeals (*Ex parte Hibberd*),[4] which followed in short order with another decision upholding the patentability, in principle, of a genetically altered form of Pacific oyster (*Ex parte Allen*).[5] Confronted with such a precedent, the Commissioner of the PTO issued a formal pronouncement of the patentability, in principle, of "non-human" multicellular organisms, be it plant or animal, that were not "naturally occurring" (Quigg, 1987) (see Appendix 1).

With that official notice came a firestorm of controversy over whether there should be a delay or even a cessation of the PTO's further consideration of patent applications claiming animals. Despite the fact that federal legislation precluding patent protection for a particular technology was virtually unheard of,[6] an *ad hoc* coalition of animal protection, farm, and religious groups proved itself a very effective lobbyist of the anti-patent perspective during a series of congressional hearings (Merges, 1989).

As a result, several bills were introduced with proposals ranging from an outright ban of animal patenting (S 2111) to a waiver of infringement liability under such patents for certain activities (HR 4971), including a small farmer's production through normal breeding procedures of animals covered by trans-genic animal claims. Although these initiatives ultimately stalled during the last session, animal-patenting provisions of various stripes are almost certainly going to be on the congressional agenda again in 1989.

As the legislative mill grinds on, word has come that DuPont will soon

---

[3] The court in *Merat* ultimately upheld an "indefiniteness" rejection, based on an alleged inconsistency in appellants' use of the term "normal" in the application; the question of whether the claimed invention was statutory subject matter was expressly reserved, however.

[4] A tryptophan-overproducing corn plant constitutes statutorily acceptable subject matter for patent claims.

[5] The Board of Appeals also concluded that the claimed "polyploid Pacific oyster" was unpatentable in light of prior developments in the relevant art. The Board's disposition on this point was upheld by the US Court of Appeals for the Federal Circuit (Washington, DC) in an unpublished decision.

[6] Congress has prohibited patents on nuclear-related inventions having only military applications. Atomic Energy Act of 1954, codified as amended at 42 US Const §1281 (1982). But the goal of this provision is to enforce the military norm of secrecy, for national security reasons, not to retard the development of the affected technology.

begin marketing genetically engineered mice under the Harvard patent (*Chemical and Engineering News*, 1988).[7] On the other hand, the brouhaha over animal patenting has prompted the USDA not to seek patent protection for a disease-resistant chicken or a pig that expresses the human growth hormone gene, both transgenic animals having been developed through government-funded research (Gladwell, 1988; W. Talent, USDA, personal communication).

DIMENSIONS OF THE PATENT SYSTEM

Given the continuing controversy, it must be acknowledged that the future of animal patents is not yet settled. In the meantime, valuable insight on the dispute may be gained if agreement is reached on what a patent is and, more importantly, what it is not.

A US "letters patent" is the legal document issued by US Patent and Trademark Office (PTO). It is important at this point to focus on the right the document embodies: a right, which the federal law recognizes in the patent holder, to *exclude others* from making, using or selling an invention that is described in the patent specification and delimited by the language of a patent claim.

In one sense, a patent is a key to the federal courthouse. It gives the patent holder access to a federal district court where he may seek redress for an alleged unauthorized use of technology which might otherwise be protected, if at all, under state trade secrecy law. A patent can also be a valuable tool for the orderly transfer of technology, as well as for signalling one's intentions to a particular market.

A patent, however, does not in itself permit the patent owner actually to do anything with the claimed invention which he could not do before the patent was issued. The uses (or abuses) to which subject matter claimed in a patent may be subjected are circumscribed by applicable regulations and the evolving case law, both federal and state, but not by the patent law. By the same token, the existence of a patent compels no one to exploit the patented invention, which must compete on its merits with products or processes already accepted in the market-place. A patent can facilitate the creation of new products and methods; it cannot nullify the economic forces that determine whether a patented item is commercialized.

With these thoughts in mind, let us review the objections that have been raised in the USA to the patenting of animals (Dresser, 1988):

(1) The availability of patent protection for animals will foster excessive interference with the "natural" world.
(2) Animal patenting will devalue human life.
(3) The issuance of patents on animals will contribute to the suffering of

---

[7] The product is now being marketed under the name OncoMouse. (Ed.)

animals in both research and agricultural contexts.
(4) The patenting of animals will lead to a decline in the genetic diversity in commercialized species.
(5) Animal patenting will accelerate the trend toward commercialization of academic research.
(6) The patenting of animals will undermine the family farm.

Objections (1) and (2) are premised on value judgments, such as what degree and kind of human intervention is deemed an "interference" with nature, and what amount of such interference is "excessive." Questions like these are really not patent legal in nature and, hence, are better left for the other contributors to this symposium to ponder. Still, it is not surprising that people who are convinced of the moral reprehensibility of animal research should find the patent system an attractive target for collateral attack, since the availability of patent protection in this context will surely foment animal research. But activists pressing this point should remember that the alternative to patenting—trade secrecy—can lead to redundant usage of experimental animals by researchers who would otherwise be fully aware of each other's work in a pro-patent/pro-disclosure environment.

Underlying objection (3) are two assumptions. One, just alluded to, is that patenting will spur research and development in animal-related technologies. The other is that such research and development will engender inhumane treatment of animals. The first assumption incorporates the *raison d'être* for a patent system that is entering its second century in 1990; its validity, therefore, has been well tested. The second assumption is the focus of an ongoing political debate between the research community and so-called "animal rights" advocates (Kaplan, 1988).

In one guise or another, objection (4) has been raised whenever the possibility is considered of a proprietary right in any multicellular organism, be it plant or animal. The staying power of this argument is surprising given the paucity of credible evidence supporting a correlation between the existence of such a right and a decline in genetic diversity not otherwise occasioned by monoculture farming practices. To the contrary, the patent system actually provides both an incentive (by promoting the value of naturally occurring organisms used as raw material by breeders and molecular biologists alike) and a means (via patent-related deposits of biological material) for preserving the broadest possible genetic base (Bent *et al.*, 1987: p. 139).

Objections (5) and (6) relate, respectively, to controversies of differing ilk which have sociopolitical and economic overtones. No doubt, other contributors to this symposium will examine whether these implications are real or, as I tend to believe, largely ephemeral. At the outset, however, let us take note again of the fact that the patenting of an invention, whatever its constituency, in no way affects the range of uses the patent holder may make of that invention. Whether he be a traditional breeder or a molecular biologist, the "creator" of a new animal form already exercises dominion over it, pursuant to the ancient principles of property law. He may sell the animal outright or license its use under restrictive contract; he may employ the animal in research, process it to obtain some product, or keep it as a pet. Each of these activities is regulated by local, state, and federal laws that implement, in piecemeal fashion, a hodgepodge of legislative directives having absolutely nothing to do with fostering innovation, and vice versa.

There is good reason to expect, therefore, that revisions to the patent system would be ineffective in altering, even indirectly, practices subsumed either under the general property law or under more specialized regulatory schemes concerned with environmental protection, the curtailing of animal abuse, and the like. In a similar vein, it should be acknowledged that the economic forces driving a family farm into liquidation, or an academic institution into embracing some corporate suitor, operate quite independently of patents. The reason for this is simple: the promoting of progress in the useful arts, according to the constitutional mandate upon which the US patent system is founded, is essentially neutral as to oligopolistic trends that may be at work in the present economy.

If there are oligopolistic trends, and if you view them as undesirable, think twice before turning to the patent system for a means to alter their course. Attacking animal patents in order to address a perceived social or economic ill is about as likely to succeed as a ban on patents concerning tobacco-processing technology would be expected to ameliorate the epidemic of nicotine addiction!

SPECIFIC LEGAL ISSUES OF ANIMAL PATENTING

Given this overview of what can and cannot be achieved via the patent system, let us look more closely at what using the system to protect an animal-related invention really involves.

There is an inescapable tendency for an explanation of patenting to lapse into jargon. For present purposes, though, only three items of legalese need concern us: novelty, non-obviousness, and enablement. The first of these pertains to a requirement of US law that the subject matter of a patent claim must be new under the sun. The requirement for "non-obviousness" is a little more difficult to summarize, but essentially it means that some aspect or property of an invention claimed in a patent must not have been predictable *a priori* from what was known before the invention was made. The third requirement for "enablement" is satisfied when a patent teaches a person of ordinary skill in the relevant technical field to make and use the claimed invention without having to undertake what would be considered an undue amount of experimentation.

The close relationship between enablement and non-obviousness is reflected in the fact that the patentability of many biological inventions turns on the inventor's having been the first to "enable" an endeavor that, beforehand, was of uncertain outcome. Thus, the inventors of the "transgenic non-human mammal" claimed in the Harvard patent were considered, by the PTO at least, to have led the field in describing a reproducible method for obtaining such mammals from starting material accessible to the interested public.[8] Where means for producing an animal form are alleged already to have been available, as happened in the case of the "polyploid Pacific oyster" at issue in the *Allen* appeal (see Bent, 1987), the patent applicant may have to argue that the manipulations described in the specification, when applied to identified starting material, yield an end-product (as claimed) having unexpected properties.

The paradigm for a patent-related description of any biological invention, including a new animal form, can be depicted in Figure 1.

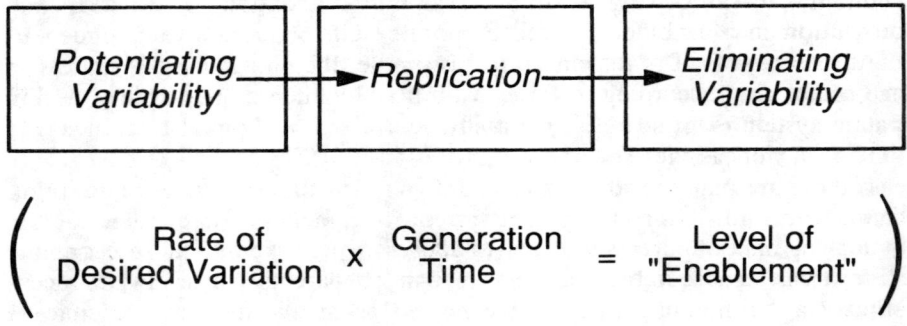

Fig. 1 A paradigm for a patent-related description of any biological invention, including a new animal form

According to this view, a biological system is first perturbed—this could involve, for example, genetic transformation, cell fusion or a cross-fertilization—in order to potentiate variability in the system, say, with regard to resistance to a particular disease. This variability is made manifest in a population of variant forms (plasmids, cell cultures, offspring) when the system is replicated. A selection criterion, such as the display of disease resistance beyond a predetermined level, is then applied to eliminate those segments of the variant population that are deemed non-characteristic of the invention.

---

[8] The PTO was also convinced that a person of ordinary skill in the embryonic discipline of animal genetic engineering could still follow the patent disclosure and, thereby, be able without undue experimentation to produce a reasonable diversity of different transgenic "mammals" within the claimed invention. Although that disclosure actually exemplified only transgenic mice, the patent refers to "any species of transgenic animal," stating that, "for instance, it may be desirable to use a [primate] species . . . such as the rhesus monkey, which is evolutionarily closer to humans than mice" (column 9, lines 28–32). The PTO apparently could not shoulder the burden, imposed on it under US law, of marshalling factual grounds to challenge the accuracy of the inventors' assertion regarding the use of "any species." Thus, the applicants were required only to change "transgenic animal" in the original claims to "transgenic mammal" in the allowed claims.

In conceptual terms, whether the invention is "enabled" is determined: (1) by the rate at which desired variation arises in the system, as manipulated, and (2) by the time it takes to replicate a testable population (i.e. "generation time"). According to this model, a written patent description would be enabling if the rate at which desired variation occurs (e.g. once in 10,000 variants) is associated with a generation time that permits a third party, by following the description, to produce the claimed invention *de novo* within a "reasonable" period of time.

For many commercially important animals, generation time has been measured in months or even years, as opposed to hours or days for most microorganisms. Since this tremendous difference in generation time is not usually matched by a compensatingly higher rate of desired variation for animals versus microorganisms, it has seemed more difficult, in theory, to provide an enabling patent disclosure for animal inventions.

At least two factors, however, have changed this picture. First, advances in gene transfer, cell culture, and cloning technologies are bringing about dramatic reductions in both the rate of desired variation and the generation time for animal inventions in general. As a consequence, it is becoming easier to write enabling patent disclosures in support of broader claims to animal inventions. Second, the PTO has recognized that a public deposit of biological material, representative of either the invention or the starting material, is an acceptable adjunct to a written patent disclosure which might otherwise be non-enabling (US Department of Commerce, Patent and Trademark Office, 1987; 1988) (see Appendix 5). (The technology of animal-related deposits is the object of considerable research interest these days: see Professor Foote's paper.) With the deposit option, patenting becomes a tenable alternative to trade secrecy even in instances where the balance of variation rate and generation time is unfavorable to a written disclosure, or where starting material is not readily available to the public.

Unless there is prohibitive legislative intervention, therefore, it can be expected that animal patent claims will issue from the PTO at an accelerating pace. Even if Congress does intercede, there is not likely to be wholesale proscription of patenting animal-related inventions, a broader category of technology which is exemplified by the following list of the issued and pending patent claims.

US Patent No. 4,607,388 Method of Incorporating DNA into Genome of Drosophila.

A method for incorporating a desired foreign . . . DNA sequence into the genome of a Drosophila insect, comprising:

(1) producing a transposable element of DNA . . . derived from the P element isolated from *Drosophila melanogaster* [and containing]

11

... a fragment of foreign exogenous DNA located between [two] sets of target DNA sequences;

(2) incorporating the transposable element ... in[to] a germ cell of a Drosophila insect;

(3) causing the transposable element to be ... inserted into the genome of the recipient Drosophila insect so as to become part of the heritable genome of the ... insect ...

International Application WO 87/00864   Insertion into Animals of Genes Coding for Interferon-Induced Proteins.

A method of protecting an animal against viral infection, comprising inserting into an animal a gene coding for an interferon-induced protein which is capable of protecting said animal against said viral infection.

US Patent No. 4,775,630   Transcriptional Control Element Adapted for Regulation of Gene Expression in Animal Cells.

A hybrid DNA plasmid including a functional adenovirus transcriptional regulator region containing DNA sequences controlling expression of an adenovirus E1A gene ...

(The "transcriptional regulator" element is said to be useful in regulating expression of a selected gene in animal cells.)

US Patent No. 4,736,866   Transgenic Non-Human Mammals.

A transgenic non-human mammal all of whose germ cells and somatic cells contain a recombinant activated oncogene sequence introduced into said mammal, or an ancestor of said mammal, at an embryonic stage.

International Application WO 88/01648   Expression of Heterologous Proteins by Transgenic Lactating Mammals.

A recombinant expression system comprising a lactogen-inducible mammalian genomic regulatory region and a structural region encoding a heterologous protein.

A transgenic mammal having mammary secretory cells incorporating a recombinant expression system [as defined above].

International Application WO 88/00239   Peptide Production.

A genetic construct comprising a DNA sequence encoding a polypeptide incorporated into a gene of a mammal that codes for a milk whey protein in such a way that the DNA sequence is expressible in the mammary gland of the adult female mammal.

An animal whose genetic material includes a genetic construct as claimed [as above].

What will patent claims like these mean to the industries influenced by them? First and foremost, there will be heightened intensity and diversity of research, leading to improvements in the quality and efficiency of technology for production of food, fine chemicals, and pharmaceuticals. To the extent that these improvements are cost-effective relative to existing products and processes, there will be a demand for the dissemination of the technology by means of licensing and other arrangements which are much easier to effect with patents than without.

This pattern of events has pertained whenever patent protection was available, even when the nature of the technology has complicated the task of patent valuation and enforcement. Based on this record, there is no reason to conclude, in advance, that a particular segment of the industrial or agricultural sectors is incapable of accommodating the use of patents as tools for the protection and transfer of technology.

Much has been made, for example, of the possibility that the owner of an animal patent may require farmers to pay a royalty for each offspring of a patented animal (Schneider, 1988; Merges, 1989). Some have assumed that the sale of a patented animal "exhausts" all patent rights in it, freeing the purchaser to use the animal for any purpose, including the production of additional animals (progeny) which may themselves satisfy the recitations of the patent claims. A more closely reasoned analysis, however, shows that propagation of any patented life form from a purchased embodiment, be it animal or otherwise, may avoid infringement of the patent only to the extent that the propagation is necessary to maintain that quantity of the life form necessary for its continued use *as intended*, under what the law refers to as an "implied license" (Bent *et al.*, 1987: pp. 279–85).

Thus, the implied license accompanying the purchase of a patented animal would be delimited by the nature of the intended use of the animal. To the extent that the intended use entails periodic breeding, say, to build up and sustain a herd, the sale price of the animal could reflect the patent owner's expectation of a cumulative adverse effect such "maintenance" reproduction may have on his potential market share. Alternatively, the farmer/purchaser and the patent owner/seller may negotiate the sort of arrangement mentioned above, where a payment is made for each offspring.

Exacting a per unit royalty in this manner is only one of the ways that a patent owner can be compensated, and need not (indeed, surely will not) be employed where doing so renders the patented animal non-competitive with accepted life forms. For example, the farmer and patent holder could

13

negotiate an arrangement whereby a percentage royalty is calculated based on some measure of production (e.g. gallons of TPA-containing milk per unit time), the percentage being commensurate with the farmer's projected increase in realized value for the milk of his transgenic herd. (For a discussion of tissue plasminogen activator (TPA) production by transgenic animals see Van Brunt, 1988.)

In closing, I would like to offer a personal opinion as to one thing I believe the issuance of animal patents will *not* mean, and that is an up-swing in infringement suits against those who use a patented animal for experimentation. By "experimentation" I do not mean the testing of an animal as a preamble to its commercialization, for example, in seeking regulatory approval for its sale. Rather, I refer to experimentation that represents an investigation of a patented invention to some end, even "designing around" the invention, that is other than making or selling the invention itself.

Like royalties applied to each offspring of patented animals, the specter of unscrupulous patent owners exacting tribute from those who engage in experimentation of this sort has haunted the debate on animal patents in the USA; so much so, in fact, that a "research exemption" applicable to experimentation with patented transgenic animals was made a part of one of the bills (HR 4971) alluded to earlier. Much of the concern in this regard stems from a single opinion, in *Roche Products v. Bolar Pharmaceutical Co.* (Fed. Cir., 1984), in which the US Court of Appeals for the Federal Circuit held that an accused infringer's intended use of a patented drug for premarketing tests mandated by federal law did not fall within traditional limits of what is called the "experimental use" defence to infringement.

Since the use in question was clearly an overture to marketing the very drug covered by the patent in question, *Roche* is not an experimental use case; the court's extended commentary on the boundaries of the experimental use defence must therefore be considered non-binding dicta. In fact, a diligent search of the US case law reveals hardly one unambiguous instance where someone was sued for patent infringement alleged to have occurred in the context of a true experimental use, regardless of the degree of commercialism affecting that use. Dicta in the *Roche* opinion, suggesting that infringement liability attaches even to experimental use of a patented invention, so long as that use has any commercial dimension, are so clearly at odds with the essential purpose of the patent system—to promote technological progress—that I believe it should be, and will be, distinguished when a true experimental use case is finally decided.

In the meantime, we should not be fooled into thinking that the choking off of experimentation, for example, in the context of a progressive breeding effort, is a legitimate objection to the patenting of animal-related inventions. If impatience with the courts prompts some of us to turn to Congress for a statutory pronouncement on the experimental use defence, then Congress should address how the defence applies to *all* patented inventions.

14

To do otherwise is to invite the conversion of a generally unified system for protecting such inventions into a patchwork of exceptions, exemptions, and prohibitions wheedled from the legislature by special interests.

References

The Atlanta Journal & Constitution (1987), May 25: 15.

Bent, S. A. (1987) Stan Allen's Invention—The World His Oyster? *J. Chartered Inst. Patent Agents* (UK), Nov.: 30.

Bent, S. A., R. L. Schwaab, D. G. Conlin, and D. D. Jeffery (1987) *Intellectual Property Rights in Biotechnology Worldwide.* New York: Stockton Press.

Chemical and Engineering News (1988) Nov. 21: 6.

Dresser, R. (1988) Ethical and Legal Issues in Patenting of New Animal Life. *Jurimetrics J.*, **28**: 399–410.

Gladwell, M. (1988) USDA's Chicken Feat: A Resistant New Breed. *Washington Post*, Aug. 11: E3.

Kaplan, R. (1988) The Use of Animals in Research. *Science*, **242**: 839–40.

Merges, R. P. (1989) Intellectual Property Rights in Higher Life Forms: The Patent System and Controversial Technologies. *Md. L. Rev.*, **47**: 1051.

Quigg, D. J. (1987) *Off. Gazette*, **24**: 1077.

Schneider, K. (1988) Farmers to Face Patent Fees to Use Gene-Altered Animals. *New York Times*, Feb. 1: 1.

US Department of Commerce, Patent and Trademark Office (1987) Deposit of Biological Materials for Patent Purposes: Advance Notice of Proposed Rulemaking. *Fed. Reg.*, **52** (Sept. 9): 34080–93.

—— (1988) Deposit of Biological Materials for Patent Purposes; Notice of Proposed Rulemaking. *Fed. Reg.*, **53** (Oct. 6): 39420–32.

Van Brunt, J. (1988) Molecular Farming: Transgenic Animals as Bioreactors. *Bio/Technology*, **6**: 1149–54.

LEGAL REFERENCES

Ex parte Allen, 2 USPQ2d 1425 (Bd. Pat. App. Int. 1987).

In re Bergy, 563 F.2d 1031, 195 USPQ 344 (CCPA 1977).

Diamond v. Chakrabarty, 447 US 303 (1980).

Ex parte Hibberd, 227 USPQ 443 (Bd. Pat. App. Int. 1985).

In re Merat, 519 F.2d 1390, 186 USPQ 471 (CCPA 1975).

Roche Products v. Bolar Pharmaceutical Co., 733 F.2d 858, 221 USPQ 939 (Fed. Cir. 1984).

The Development and Status of European Law

Joseph Straus

INTRODUCTION

At present the overall superiority of US biotechnology in science and industry is beyond all doubt. In the field of animal biotechnology, however, some US authors have suggested an apparent lead of two European countries, namely of the UK and the Republic of Ireland (Raines, 1988). Since during this symposium only US scientists will report on their achievements, a comparison between developments in Europe and the USA in the field of interest will not take place. Thus, it is not possible to find out whether or not such a statement is pure calculated pessimism in order to mobilize more intellectual and financial resources, and to provide a more favorable legal and social environment for animal biotechnology. Nonetheless, it seems to come close to the truth that at least some research groups in Europe are more or less keeping pace with US scientists in animal biotechnology (Brem et al., 1986; Clark et al., 1987; Land and Wilmut, 1987; McEvoy et al., 1987; Brem et al., 1988; Brem, 1988a; 1988b). This observation, however, could also indicate that scientists on both sides of the Atlantic are equally far away from their targets (Jaenisch, 1988).

Apart from the status of European law concerning the protection of results of animal biotechnology, which will be discussed more in depth below, Europe is, no doubt, lagging behind the USA in respect to investigations into the economic effects of biotechnology in agriculture in general, and more specifically in the field of animals and animal patenting. Until now Europe has completely relied on the work performed in the USA either by governmental[1] or private institutions (Board on Agriculture National Research Council, 1984; Teich et al., 1985; Committee on a National Strategy for Biotechnology in Agriculture, 1987) or by such distinguished scientists as the organizer of this symposium (Lesser, 1987; 1988). (For a more general discussion see Ruttan, 1982.) Whether Europe can afford such an indolence in the medium and long term seems doubtful in view of the fact that conditions governing the field of agriculture in Europe differ considerably from those in the USA. It is to be hoped, however, that free riding

---

[1] All studies prepared under the auspices of the US Congress, Office of Technology Assessment (OTA) have formed the basis and starting point for nearly all pertinent European considerations.

on the part of the Europeans will not provoke any new US action in the GATT.

Even if the Europeans were to lead in the field, this should not be a cause of serious concern. The USA should have learned from experience that a leading position in research in Europe in a particular scientific field does not necessarily result in its lead in innovation. One reason is the lack of patent protection for the processes and products in question. The most prominent example was the case of penicillin, where the more favorable patent situation in the USA, notwithstanding the previous UK lead, eventually resulted in the successful engagement of the US industry and in the necessity for royalty payments overseas for the national production of penicillin in the UK (Clark, 1985). If nothing happens in due time, Europe could well face a similar situation in respect to results of research into animal biotechnology.

PECULIARITIES OF PAST EUROPEAN DEVELOPMENTS

In order to provide for a better understanding of the main existing differences between the US patent law, as presented by Stephen Bent in his paper, and the European legal framework, as well as the problems arising from the protection of animal biotechnology results, it seems appropriate to reflect briefly on past developments.

Although neither the US patent law nor those of European countries originally provided for special provisions concerning inventions in the field of living matter, it was commonly understood that such inventions could not, as a rule, form patentable subject matter. Patent offices and courts in Europe, as well as in the USA, only gradually departed from that idea. Eventually, at least as far as the Federal Republic of Germany (FRG) is concerned, they expressly declared all inventions in the field of living matter, including animal-breeding processes and even animals *per se*, patentable (Beier *et al.*, 1985: p. 22 *et seq.*; Straus, 1985: p. 51 *et seq.*). It is worth while mentioning that it was the German Federal Supreme Court which took the lead internationally when in 1969 it decided the well-known "Red Dove" (*Rote Taube*) case.[2] The key statement of this decision was that a technique in the field of biology could be considered patentable if it was shown to utilize controllable natural forces to achieve a causal, perceivable result. It was further required that this technique should meet the general patentability requirements and should be repeatable (i.e. it could be readily duplicated by others skilled in the art). Since the animal-breeding process claimed in the "Red Dove" case was not repeatable merely on the basis of a written description no patent was issued. Apart from the generally criticized repeatability requirement, this decision was well received. This was because it particularly broadened the concept of a patentable invention to encompass animal-breeding methods and animals *per se*. Unlike the 1980 *Diamond v. Chakrabarty* decision of the US

[2] 1 IIC 137(1970)

Supreme Court and the recent grant of the Leder transgenic mouse patent by the US Patent and Trademark Office (Raines, 1988), the "Red Dove" decision was not followed by discussions devoted to either the ethical and moral aspects of patenting animals or to the possible economic effects of such patenting. Why this was not the case is difficult to answer, but it is probably due to the techniques used. In the "Red Dove" case the classical cross-breeding methods were employed, whereas in *Diamond v. Chakrabarty*, and even more so in the Leder case, a universally applicable technique (i.e. also applicable to humans) was at issue, namely that of recombinant DNA. It is primarily this collection of universally applicable new techniques labelled as genetic engineering, together with the lack of understanding of how the patent system works, that has created concern among the public when discussing the patenting of higher living organisms, especially animals.

The situation in the USA remained virtually unchanged until the introduction of the Animal Patent Bill (HR 4970) (*Patent, Trademark and Copyright Journal*, 1988a; 1988b): it was governed by case law with patent office practice following suit. In Europe, however, problems started to develop in the late 1950s and early 1960s when countries decided to establish a special type of protection for new varieties of plants and to unify their patent laws. The first initiative resulted in the well-known International Convention for the Protection of New Varieties of Plants (UPOV Convention), signed in Paris in 1961. In Article 2 it introduced the so called prohibition of double protection (i.e. barring access to protection by plant variety rights and patents for one and the same botanical genus or species) (Straus, 1984; Adler, 1986). In view of current discussions in UPOV, Article 2 in the future could also play a role with regard to animals (UPOV, 1987). The second phase ended in the Convention on the Unification of Certain Points of Substantive Law on Patents for Inventions, established in 1963 (the Strasbourg Convention). That Convention in Article 2b made it mandatory to protect microbiological processes and their resulting products, but left it to the discretion of the signatories as to whether or not to protect new plant or animal varieties and essentially biological processes employed in their production (Straus, 1985: para. 54; Commission of the European Communities, 1988: par 21 *et seq.*).

When the European Patent Convention (EPC) was adopted in 1973, it was decided that it could not impose obligations on contracting states other than those provided for under the Strasbourg Convention. The principles governing the UPOV and Strasbourg Convention were, therefore, introduced into the EPC without any serious reconsidering of developments which, in the meantime, had taken place in various areas of biotechnology, and which clearly demonstrated the distinction between micro- and macrobiology as an artificial one. Since that difference serves as the dividing line between mandatory patentable and discretionary patentable inventions in the Strasbourg Convention it is no longer tenable (Commission of the European Communities, 1988: Memo, part I, para. 25).

ACTUAL STATUS OF EUROPEAN LAW

Resulting from the historical development in Western Europe, Article 53(b) of the EPC excludes from patent protection plant or animal varieties, as well as essentially biological processes for the production of plants or animals. Microbiological processes and their resulting products, however, are explicitly protected. In addition to Article 53(b), provisions of Articles 53(a) and 52(4) of the EPC are of decisive importance in this context. There is no disagreement that the exclusion by Article 53(a) of inventions, the publication or exploitation of which would be contrary to *ordre public* or morality is both necessary and useful. It guarantees that social and ethical considerations can be taken into account in the patent law system, which is otherwise neutral in its judgement and entirely devoted to the technological appreciation of inventions (Beier and Straus, 1986). In view of more recent developments in animal biotechnology (e.g. embryo recovery, embryo transfer, etc.), there is increased questioning of the general and undifferentiated exclusion of methods for treatment not only of the human, but also of the animal body by surgery or therapy, as laid down in Article 52(4) of the EPC (Straus, 1985: para. 73; Bent *et al.*, 1987: pp. 162–63).

The situation that initially existed under the EPC was a logical and, at least in part, understandable consequence of previous international developments. It was aggravated and apparently made definitive when European countries, in the course of harmonizing their national patent laws with the EPC in the 1980s, took over the wording of Article 52(4) as well as that of Articles 53(a) and 53(b) of the EPC. This step left inventors in the field of traditional animal breeding without any possibility of protection. Other national issues such as in the FRG led to a questioning of the present status on constitutional grounds (von Pechmann, 1987: p. 347; Benkard, 1988: p. 205; Moufang, 1988: p. 218).

Although this paper is aimed at presenting the legal situation in Western Europe, for the sake of completeness it should be mentioned that a number of Eastern European countries expressly offer some sort of protection to ("traditional") animal breeders. Hungarian Patent Law of 1969 (as amended in 1983) provides for a UPOV-type protection for animal varieties under the conditions that they are:

(1) *new* in the sense of being different from known breeds in at least one essential characteristic (morphologically, physiologically, or in some other respect);
(2) *homogeneous*, i.e. identical in essential characteristics of their members;
(3) *relatively stable*, i.e. they may not deviate from their essential characteristics, as described in the patent, in the course of propagation by natural or artificial means or in the course of a propagatory cycle (Article 67 in connection with Article 31) (Cooper, 1985, pp. 6–14).

Bulgaria, Rumania, and the USSR, on the other hand, issue so-called inventors' certificates to animal breeders. These certificates, however, do not secure for the inventor an exclusive right to exploit. Instead they only provide some moral rights and a title for remuneration (Pretnar, 1982: pp. 6–49; Moufang, 1988: p. 217).

PROTECTION OFFERED UNDER THE EPC AND HARMONIZED EUROPEAN PATENT LAWS

Prior to discussing the protection of the results of animal biotechnology offered under the EPC and the harmonized patent laws of Western European countries, it should be made quite clear that the EPC, although providing a system for granting European patents, does not secure uniform effects in designated states. Rather, European patents have, in each of the contracting states for which they are granted, the effect of—and are subject to the same conditions as—a national patent granted by that state (Articles 1 and 2 of the EPC). As is correctly stated in the Commission of the European Communities (1988) Memo on the Draft Directive, which will be considered later on (Beier, 1984: p. 54):

> A European Patent is granted, defined and revoked in applying rules of the EPC, and to this extent, represents a collection of "European patents". For all other purposes, such as the scope of protection, European patents represent patents with national effects, subject to national laws, although certain minimum standards are prescribed in Articles 64(2) and 67 EPC.

It follows that the role of the European Patent Office (EPO) is to focus on the important but limited task of granting European patents. The interpretation and revocation of these patents are the responsibility of national authorities, who are not bound by the EPO practice, including its examination guidelines. Whatever the EPO and its executives decide, the patentability of the results of animal biotechnology will not necessarily remain valid in the contracting states. Past experience is, however, encouraging, since the case law in the FRG, Sweden, and the UK indicates that national courts are inclined to accept the EPO practice.[3]

Following the concept of the language of Article 53(b) of the EPC with

---

[3] Following the practice of the EPO, the German Federal Supreme Court in 1987 revised its long-standing case law as regards the effects of deposits of microorganisms as substitute for enabling written disclosure: claims directed to biological material *per se* can now be based on deposits (Decision of February 12, 1987, 18 *IIC* 396 [1987]—Rabies Virus [Tollwutvirus] with comment of Geissler). Similarly the UK High Court of Justice, Patents Court (Decision of July 4, 1985, [1985] R.P.C. 545 = [1986] *Off. J. EPO* 175—Second Medical Use/Wyeth and Schering) and the Swedish Court of Patent Appeals (Decision of June 13, 1986, [1987], NIR 248 = [1988] *Off. J. EPO* 196—Hydropyridine/SE) decided the question of patentability of inventions concerning a second medical use in the same way as the Enlarged Board of Appeals of EPO.

regard to patentability of inventions in animal biotechnology, it seems advisable to distinguish between the following categories of inventions:

(1) animals and animal varieties *per se*;
(2) animals and animal varieties as products of a process;
(3) processes for the production of animals;
(4) animal material *per se*;
(5) processes for the production of animal materials.

Although there is no case law applying to the patentability of animals under the EPC, it has long been assumed that, in view of the parallel language for plant and animal varieties in Article 53(b), plants and animals are to be treated in exactly the same way. Since in respect to animals the problem of the prohibition of double protection dces not exist, more flexibility exists in applying the patent system in a way that fulfills the legitimate interests of inventors (Teschemacher, 1987). Nonetheless a press release in June 1988 entitled "Patents for Living Matter?" indicated for the first time that the EPO, for ethical reasons, might view inventions in animals as being excluded from patentability under Article 53(a), the "morality" clause. Thus, it was said that Professor Leder, whose transgenic mouse application is pending with the EPO, might not be granted a patent.[4]

This general reference to Article 53(a) of the EPC and the idea that inventions in animals could be excluded from patentability for ethical reasons in general came as a surprise and are neither well founded nor in accordance with the original intention of the contracting states, at least as far as the European Community member states are concerned. During discussions on the draft of Article 29(c) of the Community Patent Convention (CPC), which deals with the prohibition of direct uses of inventions involving products directly obtained by a patented process, it became evident that although Article 53(b) excluded plant and animal varieties as such from patent protection, this exclusion could not be interpreted in a way as to leave unprotected plant and animal varieties as products directly obtained by a patented process.[5] An interpretation of Articles 53(a) and (b) of the EPC in the way that would lead to a general exclusion of inventions in animals for ethical reasons car therefore hardly be correct.

Regarding the patentability of claims directed to animal varieties as such, as well as animal varieties produced by a patentable process, the solution is clear: both are excluded from patent protection. The latter are excluded, notwithstanding the fact that protection conferred by a patent for a process for the production of animals according to Article 64(2) of the EPC extends

[4] The same concerns are expressed in a unpublished EPO document of September 6, 1988 (CA/H 6/88-III).
[5] Preparatory documents no. 11 and 17, published in *Records of the Luxembourg Conference on the Community Patent 1975*, Luxembourg, 1981: pp. 32, 40, 41. See also Straus, 1987: p. 439.

to animals, and even to animal varieties obtained by such process (Moufang, 1988: pp. 380, 381).

For the patentability of claims directed generally to animals and animal material, provided that the invention complies with all other patentability requirements, the answer should be in the affirmative. The problem, however, is with the notion of an "animal variety," which seems to be much more difficult to define both on a legal and a scientific basis, than with that of a "plant variety." Yet this issue is critical for it is this distinction which draws the dividing line between patentable and non-patentable animal kingdom inventions in Europe. In the absence of any practice, it is impossible to foresee what approach could be chosen by the EPO in the future. It is not known whether it will be influenced by the legal term of "variety" as applied in breeders' right systems, or if it will try to solve the problem scientifically. In Switzerland the Federal Office for Intellectual Property in its Examination Guidelines, as amended in March 1986,[6] has chosen the first alternative by generally drawing a parallel to plant varieties, as defined in Swiss Plant Variety Law (SR 232.16). According to No. 3.3 of the Swiss Examination Guidelines, in connection with No. 3.2, one can assume that product claims directed to whole animal species and genera (e.g. a mouse) are allowed, as well as claims directed to animal material, be it either propagating material in which a variety is not yet fixed[7] or "building blocks" such as animal cell lines, modified cells, genes, or plasmids, which are not capable of regenerating into whole animals. The problem remains: when can an animal with new characteristics be viewed as distinguishable from others while being stable and homogeneous enough so as to form a new animal variety? Simple parallelism with plant varieties does not seem appropriate and possible (Teschemacher, 1987: p. 98). Doubts may also be expressed as to whether science could help lawyers in this area. If an animal variety (race) is understood as including (Kruger, 1961: p. 25; Herre, 1961: p. 2):

> Those animals of a given species that—whilst having the same genetic traits—differ from all the other animals of the same species and—by the means of these genetic traits (characteristics)—can be viewed as a population.

and

> Varieties (races) are open genetic populations within the closed genetic population of a species and can undergo changes more rapidly than species.

This does not really solve the problem that we are faced with.

---

[6] SchwPMMl. 36-38 (1986) = 1986 GRUR Int. 541.
[7] In the sense of being distinguishable from other varieties, homogeneous, and stable.

Under the case law of the EPO Board of Appeals, exclusions from patentability in the EPC must be narrowly construed.[8] Following this rule of interpretation, EPC product protection should, in principle, be available for most results of modern animal biotechnology along the lines indicated by the Swiss Examination Guidelines, beginning with animal biological material of all kinds, such as genes, transfer vectors, cell lines, modified cells, etc., and ending with transgenic animals (Moufang, 1988: p. 215). In other words, in my understanding of Articles 53(a) and 53(b), in principle, all twelve claims of the US Leder patent for "transgenic non-human mammals" should be allowable.[9] The same should apply for the invention of "transgenic animals secreting desired proteins into milk," which is also pending at the EPO,[10] because none of the claims of concern is directed to a specific "animal variety."[11] Furthermore, such transgenic animals as the newly reported quail chick chimeras should be viewed as, in principle, patentable subject matter (Balaban et al., 1988; Barnes, 1988).

The words "in principle" are used here to indicate that all the product claims mentioned may well face some problems: for instance, the problem of the enabling written disclosure according to Article 83 of the EPC,[12] which in many animal biotechnology inventions could presumably be met only by a deposit of pertinent animal material in a depository as provided for in Rule 28 and 28(a) of the EPC. Although the deposit of animal genes, plasmids, and cells and cell lines should not, as a rule, produce any specific problems, it is at present completely uncertain whether any animal propagating material deposit, if technically practicable, would be accepted under the EPC and the harmonized European patent laws (Savignon, 1985: p. 85; Straus, 1985: para. 94; von Pechmann, 1987: p. 486).

Because of the possible problems of enabling written disclosure, and taking into account possible negative effects of the release of deposited material, the importance of claims based upon modern biotechnological processes becomes evident. Recent advances in genetic engineering have considerably improved the ability of inventors to disclose in sufficient detail the methods employed. This fact, combined with the language of Article 53(b) of the EPC, clearly favors the modern animal biotechnologists over traditional animal breeders. As already noted, Article 53(b) declares that "essentially biological processes" for the production of animals are unpatentable, but at the same time it explicitly allows protection for microbiological processes in general, and implicitly allows for non-biological

---

[8] Technical Board of Appeals 3.3.1 of March 27, 1986, 1986 Off. J. EPO, **301** (at 304)—Appetite suppressant/DUPONT; see also decision of the Technical Board of Appeals of July 26, 1983, 1984 Off. J. EPO, **112** (at 116)—Propagating Material/CIBA-GEIGY.
[9] US Patent no. 4,736,866 (issued April 12, 1988).
[10] EP publication no. 0264166—A 1 (April 20, 1988).
[11] Neither the rodent of claim 11 nor the "rodent being a mouse" of claim 12 in the Leder patent can be viewed as an animal variety.
[12] Article 83: "The European Patent Application must disclose the invention in a manner sufficiently clear and complete for it to be carried out by a person skilled in the art."

processes for the production of animals. According to the EPO Examination Guidelines (Part C-IV 3.4):

> The question whether a process is "essentially biological" is one of degree depending on the extent to which there is technical intervention by man in the process; if such intervention plays a significant part in controlling the result it is desired to achieve, the process would not be excluded.

As examples of essentially biological processes the Guidelines enumerate methods of crossing, interbreeding or selectively crossing (EPO Examination Guidelines, Part C-IV 3.4). It is commonly understood that any method of genetic engineering (e.g. recombinant DNA, microinjection, etc.) is regarded as being "non-biological" (i.e. technical in character) (Beier and Straus, 1986: p. 456; Teschemacher, 1987: p. 95; von Pechmann, 1987: p. 348). When, in a process for the production of animals, biological as well as technical elements are present, then, as Teschemacher has correctly pointed out, one has to find out where the core of the invention lies. In other words, it has to be determined whether the human intervention plays only a supporting or a determining role in the invention. If the product could not have been created naturally, the human intervention was decisive. It is clear that some examples of that art, especially when multistep processes are involved, can create problems. For example, the method of inducing polyploidy in Pacific oysters of the species *Crassostrea gigas* in *ex parte Allen* could have presented a borderline case.[13] In my opinion, however, the steps of inducing oysters to spawn, the fertilizing of the eggs with sperm to form zygotes, and, especially, the applying of hydrostatic pressure to zygotes at a predetermined intensity for a predetermined duration after a predetermined time following formation of zygotes to induce polyploidy made human intervention the determining or controlling factor in producing the desired result. As a consequence, the method of producing these oysters is patentable in the sense of the EPO Examination Guidelines.

UNRESOLVED PROBLEMS UNDER THE EPC

Notwithstanding the general attitude of the EPO to interpret exclusionary provisions as restrictively as possible and to grant the broadest possible protection, a number of questions raised by the language of Article 53(b) of the EPC remain unclarified. This is specifically true for the necessary application of the notions of "microbiological" or "essentially biological" processes, as well as of "animal varieties." These form a grey area and represent a factor of constant uncertainty. Although the EPO Examination Guidelines offer some reasonable solutions, application is faced with

[13] Decided by the Board of Patent Appeals and Interferences on April 3, 1987.

difficulties, and the final outcome of patents granted in this area is uncertain.

Less satisfying and clear are the areas not covered by the EPC, namely scope or extent and exhaustion of protection. Until the competent courts of contracting states resolve such questions as how to interpret the notion of "products directly obtained by a process," inventors and industries will remain without any reliable guidance as to the purposefulness of their investments. The scope of protection is of decisive importance for determining the value of process patents in this area, and until now it is a point of controversy in the literature (Moufang, 1988: pp. 382–3). A similar statement can be made regarding the exhaustion of rights conferred by a product patent (e.g. for an animal gene inserted into a host organism and transferred to its progeny) (Moufang, 1988: pp. 384–5).

APPROACH OF THE EEC COMMISSIONS

Although the potential to protect biotechnological inventions under the EPC cannot be claimed as particularly bad,[14] the procedures clearly fall short compared with those available in the USA. But the overall situation in Europe is far worse if one takes into account the fact that not all EEC member states are party to the EPC and that the practice of EPO could well be questioned by national courts when deciding on infringement and revocation of European patents. Widely differing outcome of national case law could also be imagined in respect to the scope and extent of the rights conferred by European patents.

In order to establish harmonized, clear, and improved patentability standards as well as greater certainty regarding the scope of protection, the Commission of the European Communities presented a *Proposal for a Council Directive on the Legal Protection of Biotechnological Inventions* on October 17, 1988. This draft directive will, no doubt, be the main object of discussions among governments and interested circles in the near future. Since it is of decisive importance also for inventions in animal biotechnology, I shall try to introduce briefly its main characteristics, as well as some provisions of specific interest.

The main characteristic, but possibly also the main handicap, of the draft is its intention not to interfere with exclusionary provisions existing under the EPC and the national patent laws. It is aimed at establishing as narrow an application of those provisions as possible on the one hand, as well as a firm and appropriate scope of protection on the other. A more radical approach, which would certainly make the life of patent lawyers easier and would be welcomed especially in the field of animals, did not seem feasible for political reasons. Although the proposed directive neither directly nor legally affects

---

[14] It has to be noted, however, that possible negative positions of the EPO towards patenting in specific fields are controlled only by its Board of Appeals, which is deciding in the last instance. Applicants are so far facing a quite badly balanced system. For details see Beier (1989).

either the EPC or the practice under the EPC, it will indirectly have substantial effects in both areas. By means of correlation with the existing patent-granting practice based on the EPO Examination Guidelines and by providing for solutions to problems not yet resolved in the Examination Guidelines of the EPO, the directive is aimed at supporting the EPO in its ongoing efforts to establish its Examination Guidelines (Directive, Part 1, para. 40–46) on a firmer basis.

As regards the patentability of products of animal biotechnology, the draft directive ensures the patentability of living matter in general and clarifies the point that any exclusion of animal varieties shall not extend to the patenting of parts of animal varieties. Claims for classifications higher than varieties (e.g. for species, genera, etc.) are allowable (Article 3(1)), as are patents for uses of animal varieties and processes for the production thereof (Article 4).

Definitions clarifying expressions such as "microbiological process" or "essentially biological process" are of great value. According to Article 5, "a microbiological process is one which is carried out with the use of or is performed upon or resulting in a microorganism." In addition, a process consisting of a succession of steps is regarded a microbiological process if the essence of the invention is incorporated in one or more microbiological steps of the process (Article 6). A process in which human intervention consists of no more than selecting between available biological material and letting it carry out an inherent biological function under natural conditions is not regarded as essentially biological (Article 7). Finally, the draft directive clarifies that surgical or diagnostic methods practiced on an animal body are excluded from patent protection only if practiced for a therapeutic purpose (Article 18). Thus such methods as embryo recovery and transfer employed for animal production should be patentable in the European Community member states in the future.

Provisions concerning the scope of protection incorporate the introduction of the clear rule that process protection of self-replicable matter extends to the identical or differentiated products of first as well as of subsequent generations, notwithstanding the fact that such products may be excluded from patent protection as such (Article 12). In other words, the draft directive provides explicitly for the protection of animals and animal varieties produced by a patented method (e.g. genetic engineering) and extends such protection to products of subsequent generations. Moreover, protection for a product comprising or consisting of genetic information (e.g. a gene coding for a specific animal trait) as an essential characteristic of the invention is extended to any products in which that genetic information has been incorporated and is of essential importance for its industrial applicability or utility (Article 13; Directive Part 2). For the sake of completeness, it should be added that the draft directive is also introducing the reversal of the burden of proof in cases of infringement of process patents for obtaining new as well as known products. This provision of Article 17 could play an important role in the field of animal biotechnology.

CONCLUSIONS

With regard to the scientific development in the field of interest, in Europe there is a situation comparable with that in the USA. With regard to the ability of the courts and legislation to react to new technological developments, the differences are considerable. Whereas both the courts and legislation of the European Community member states are preempted or bound either by narrow limits of the law or by existing, expressed or assumed international obligations,[15] US legislation, courts, and administration do not have such constraints. Scientific achievements in modern animal biotechnology, the exclusionary provisions of the EPC and harmonized national patent laws do prevent patenting of traditional animal-breeding results, but do so while allowing the patenting of all kinds of animal material and of transgenic animals, as long as claims are not directed to animal varieties. For the time being, the situation has not been clarified by the courts or by patent office practice. The national patent offices, as is the case of the EPO, are hesitant to exploit existing opportunities. The adoption of the European Community draft directive would improve the situation considerably and make the legal status of European law comparable to that of the USA.

References

Adler, R. G. (1986) Can Patents Coexist with Breeders' Rights? Developments in US and International Biotechnology Law. *Int. Rev. Ind. Property Copyright Law*, **17**: 195–227.

Balaban, E., M.-A. Teillet, and N. LeDouarin (1988) Application of the Quail-Chick Chimera System to the Study of Brain Development and Behaviour. *Science*, **241**: 1339 *et seq.*

Barnes, D. (1988) Bird Brain Switch Leads to New Song. *Science*, **241**: 1434.

Beier, F. K. (1984) Das europäische Patentsystem. *Europäisches Patentübereindommen*, ed. Beier, Haertel, and Schricker. Münchner Gemeinschaftskommentar, Cologne.

—— (1989) Die Rechtsbehelfe des Patentanmelders und seiner Wettbewerber im Vergleich: eine rechtsvergleichende Untersuchung zur Chancengleichheit im Patentverfahren. *GRUR Int.*: 1 *et seq.*

Beier, F. K., R. S. Crespi, and J. Straus (1985) *Biotechnology and Patent Protection: An International Review*. Paris: OECD.

Beier, F. K. and J. Straus (1986) Genetic Engineering and Industrial Property. *Ind. Prop.*, **11**: 447–9.

Benkard, G., K. Bruchhausen *et al.* (1988) *Patentgesetz Gebrauchsmustergesetz*, 8th edn. Munich: C. H. Beck Verlag.

Bent, S. A., R. L. Schwaab, D. G. Conlin, and D. D. Jeffery (1987) *Intellectual Property Rights in Biotechnology Worldwide*. New York: Stockton Press.

Board on Agriculture, National Research Council (1984) *Genetic Engineering of*

---

[15] The exclusion of animal varieties and essentially biological processes for the production of animals as introduced in national laws of European countries does not directly result from any international treaty.

Plants—Agricultural Research Opportunities and Policy Concerns. Washington, DC.

Brem, G. (1988a) Aspects of the Application of Gene Transfer as a Breeding Technique for Farm Animals. *Biologisches Zentralblatt*, **108**: 1–8.

—— (1988b) The Development of Gene Transfer in Farm Animals. *Pro Veterinario*, **8** (Feb.): 1 *et seq.*

Brem, G., B. Brenig, H. M. Goodman, R. S. Selden, F. Graf, B. Kruff, K. Springmann, Hondele, J. Meyer, E. L. Winnacker, and Kräusslich (1986) Gene Transfer in Rabbits and Pigs, *3rd World Congress of Genetics Applied to Livestock Production*, July 16–22, 1986, Lincoln, Nebraska, Part XII, p. 45 *et seq.*

Brem, G., B. Brenig, G. Hörstgen-Schwark, and E. L. Winnacker (1988) Gene Transfer in Tilapia (*Oreochromis niloticus*). *Aquaculture*, **68**: 209 *et seq.*

Clark, A. J., J. P. Simons, I. Wilmut, and R. Lathe (1987) Pharmaceuticals from Transgenic Livestock. *Trends Biotec*, **5**: 20 *et seq.*

Clark, R. W. (1985) *The Life of Ernst Chain: Penicillin and Beyond*. London: Weidenfeld and Nicolson, p. 56.

Commission of the European Communities (1988) *Proposal for a Council Directive on the Legal Protection of Biotechnological Inventions*. COM (88) 496 final–SYN 159, Brussels, Oct. 17, 1988.

Committee on a National Strategy for Biotechnology in Agriculture, National Research Council (1987) *Agricultural Biotechnology: Strategies for National Competitiveness*, Washington DC.

Cooper, I. P. (1985) *Biotechnology and the Law*, 2nd edn. New York: Clark Boardman.

Herre, W. (1961) Der Art- und Rassebegriff. *Handbuch der Tierzüchtung*, ed. J. Hammond *et al.* Hamburg: Parey.

Jaenisch, R. (1988) Transgenic Animals. *Science*, **204** (June): 1468 *et seq.*

Krüger, L. (1961) Geschichtliche Entwicklung der Rassen in der europäischen Tierzucht. *Handbuch der Tierzüchtung*, ed. J. Hammond *et al.* Hamburg: Parey.

Land, R. B. and I. Wilmut (1987) Gene Transfer and Animal Breeding. *Theriogeneology*, **27** (Jan.): 169 *et seq.*

Lesser, W. (1987) Applying Animal Patents in Agriculture: Lessons for Farmers and the Patent Office for Self-Reproducible Animals. *World Intellectual Property Organization, Proceedings, Symposium on the Protection of Biotechnological Inventions*, June 4–5, 1987, Ithaca, NY, pp. 134–54.

—— (1988) *Animal Patents in the USA: Are the Concerns Justified?* Lecture given at World Intellectual Property Organization, Geneva, Sept. 1988.

McEvoy, T. G., M. Stack, T. Barry, B. Keane, F. Gannon, and J. M. Sreenan (1987) Direct Gene Transfer by Microinjection. *Theriogeneology*, **27** (Jan.): 258 *et seq.*

Moufang, R. (1988) *Genetische Erfindungen im gewerblichen Rechtsschutz*. Cologne: Heymans.

Patent, Trademark and Copyright Journal (1988a) House Passage of Animal Patent Bill (HR 4970). **36** (Sept. 15): 499–502.

—— (1988b) House Judiciary Committee Report on HR 4970. **36** (Sept. 15): 503–542.

Pretnar, S. (1982) Inventors' Certificates, Rationalization Proposals and Discoveries. *Copyright and Industrial Property*, International Encyclopedia of Comparative Law, vol. 14. Tübingen: J. C. B. Mohr (Paul Siebeck).

Raines, L. J. (1988) The Mouse That Roared. *Iss. Sci. Technol.*, **70** (summer): 64 *et seq.*

Ruttan, V. W. (1982) *Agricultural Research Policy*. Minneapolis: University of Minnesota Press.

Savignon, F. (1985) Die Natur des Schutzes der Erfindungspatente und seine Anwendung auf lebende Materie, *GRUR Int.*: 83 *et seq.*

Straus, J. (1984) Patent Protection for New Varieties of Plants Produced by Genetic

Engineering: Should "Double Protection" Be Prohibited? *Int. Rev. Ind. Property Copyright Law*, **15**: 426 *et seq.*

—— (1985) *Industrial Property Protection of Biotechnological Inventions, Analysis of Certain Basic Issues.* Geneva: World Intellectual Property Organization, BIG 281 (July).

—— (1987) The Principle of "Dependence" under Patents and Plant Breeders' Rights. *Ind. Prop.*, **12**: 433 *et seq.*

Teich, A. M. *et al.* (eds.) (1985) *Biotechnology and the Environment.* Washington DC: AAAS.

Teschemacher, R. (1987) Patentable Subject Matter under the European Patent Convention (EPC) in the Field of Biotechnology. *World Intellectual Property Organization, Proceedings, Symposium on the Protection of Biotechnological Inventions*, June 4–5, 1987, Ithaca, New York, p. 87 *et seq.*

UPOV (1987) *Possible Consequences of Biotechnology in the Field of Intellectual Property Protection.* Doc. IOM/III/2 (July 9), p. 7, para 9.

von Pechmann, E. (1987a) Ausschöpfung des bestehenden Patentrechts für Erfindungen auf dem Gebiet der Pflanzen- und Tierzüchtung unter Berücksichtigung des Beschlusses des Bundesgerichtshofs-Tollwutvirus. *GRUR Int.*: 475 *et seq.*

—— (1987b) Ist der Ausschluss von Tierzüchtungen und Tierbehandlungsverfahren vom Patentschutz gerechtfertigt? *GRUR Int.*: 344–7.

Prospects for International Cooperation

R. Stephen Crespi

INTRODUCTION

At present, any assessment of the prospects of international cooperation towards the establishment of a legal system of protection for novel animal breeds is bound to be speculative and exploratory. In most countries outside the USA, the preparatory debate on this subject has not yet been launched in an open and public manner. In official circles responsible for agriculture, the desirability of some system of protection comparable to the plant variety right or the patent right is still at an early stage of consideration and, in view of the apparent sensitivity of the subject, most representatives of official patent circles are not keen to force a conclusion.

Patent authorities outside the USA have only recently come to terms with the possibility of patents for plants. Until this issue has been properly settled, the corresponding question of animal protection will be kept on the back burner unless pressure from industry brings it to the forefront. Industry itself is only now beginning to mobilize opinion and is in the process of clarifying its own ideas as to the type of system most appropriate to its needs and for which it is prepared to campaign. The international patent professional community, ever zealous to ensure that no area of technology is deprived of the caring concern of the patent law, will be an ardent group in the lobby for animal patents, and its voice will become stronger as more and more inventions flow from the laboratories of the animal molecular biologists.

Before tackling the specific issues of this symposium, it would be instructive to glance briefly at the related question of plant patents and consider the problems that have arisen in Europe and elsewhere in that connection in case they should resurface in the animal field. There is still a rearguard action from certain sections of the agricultural community against plant patents. This has held up issuance of the long-awaited, recently published proposal for a European Community directive to member states of the EEC to put their national houses in order on a whole range of questions bearing upon the patent law relating to inventions in biotechnology. The agricultural community, or industry as it is now known, has been generally much more cautious towards strong systems for the legal protection of innovation compared with the "smoke stack" industries and those of the new sunrise. Thus the plant variety right was framed deliberately less strongly than the patent system, which was thought to go too far in granting monopolies of wide scope and potential significance to the industry. Although this attitude has softened somewhat with the admission that the plant variety right is not well adapted to the technology of plant genetic manipulation, there is still concern that basic commodities, such as bread, could become the subject of patents. The same disquiet may be expressed over the patenting of eggs, milk, and meat! Common to both spheres are the fears of small firms that the large science-based companies will swamp the industry with their technology and their patents.

In addition to the reservations of industry, the attitudes of patent offices and other departments of state to this question should be noted. Although the patenting of microorganisms has become commonplace, the patenting of the larger and more visible of life forms still appears to involve a feeling of unease on the part of many. The very idea of a patent for an intact animal, which can scamper around the farmyard, may be difficult to accept, in spite of the fact that these animals have been articles of trade from primitive times. In the last analysis, the question is a legal one, but public policy cannot be ignored and government officials must consider public opinion when faced with enthusiasts of the new technology. With this note of caution let us review the present law.

PRESENT LEGAL SITUATION IN EUROPE

Among the differences between the patent laws of other countries and that of the USA, the existence of various statutory exclusions from patentability must first be noted. In a major study on the possible international harmoniz-ation of patent laws the World Intellectual Property Organization (WIPO) has prepared a survey of technological fields excluded from patent protection (World Intellectual Property Organization, 1988a). Nineteen such fields have been identified, among which the prohibition of patents for animal varieties is found in the law of no fewer than 45 countries throughout Europe, Africa, and Asia. For Europe the prototype provision is Article 53(b) of the Euro-pean Patent Convention (EPC) which states that European patents shall not be granted for

plant or animal varieties or essentially biological processes for the production of plants and animals; this provision does not apply to microbiological processes or the products thereof.

In Europe, and elsewhere, most discussion of this provision has concen-trated upon the plant aspect of the clause. Their country cousins—the animals—are having to wait patiently in their pens for their case to be heard. The prohibition of patents for plant varieties is said to be justified because of the fact that they can be protected under the plant variety right (i.e. Certifi-cate of Variety Protection). No parallel system, however, exists for the protection of animal varieties and, so far, no justification has been advanced for the lumping together of the two fields of breeding in this negative way.

31

Article 53(b) of the EPC itself derives from the first international attempt at harmonization in the Strasbourg Convention of 1963, and it has also been adopted in European national patent laws and is therefore in an entrenched position that will not be easily assailed. The statutory exclusions in the EPC affecting inventions in the biological sciences reflect attitudes prevalent in official circles three decades ago, before the potential of the new techniques of gene manipulation had become fully apparent. The European Patent Office (EPO) is alive to the scientific advances that have since been made and gives the impression of being sympathetic to the problems of the users of the European system. One hopeful sign is the attitude of the Appeal Board towards these exclusions as seen in three notable decisions.

(1) The discovery of biological activity in a known substance can be protected by a "product for use" claim, but for some time it was considered impossible to protect the discovery of a second or subsequent utility ("second indication"). In the *Bayer* (Nimodipin) case, the Board of Appeal allowed a new type of patent claim to be formulated to cover the use of the substance in the manufacture of a medicament for the new biological application. This type of claim has now become standard.

(2) In the *Ciba-Geigy* case, the claim was for a plant-propagating material treated with a particular chemical compound to protect the material against certain herbicides. The Examiner rejected this claim under Article 53(b), but the Board of Appeal overruled the objection, holding that the exclusion must be construed narrowly so as to deny only a claim directed to the "genetically fixed form of the variety."

(3) In the *Bruker* case, the exclusion under consideration was that related to methods of diagnosis which are denied patentability under Article 52(4) in so far as the method is practiced on the human or animal body. The claim in suit was to a method of examining the intact body by magnetic resonance imaging, a method that could hardly have any other purpose than in diagnosis. In a remarkable decision, the Board of Appeal held that the only diagnostic methods to be excluded are those whose results make it immediately possible to decide on a particular medical treatment. So if the diagnostic conclusion is not part of the claim the exclusion does not apply! The real significance of the case is the positive ruling that an exclusion clause must be narrowly interpreted.

The policy of the highest authority in the European patent jurisdiction is thus designed to ensure that the EPC will not be judged as an emasculated system, but will be assessed as giving value comparable to that of the US or Japanese system; this trend must be welcome to all. The problem of protecting genetically modified plants and animals may after all be solved, at least for the present, by the interpretative solution thus leaving for future attention the much greater problem of amending the Convention. So long, therefore, as the patent claim is not directed to a variety as such, be it plant or animal, it ought to be acceptable provided the specification as a whole complies with the overriding requirement of being a repeatable disclosure.

In the case of plant varieties, there are numerous examples of the descriptions typically used in connection with the grant of variety rights. They tend mostly to be of a qualitatively descriptive and rather imprecise nature such as would receive rough treatment from patent examiners if presented as a patent claim. The type of claim used in the Canadian patent application seeking to protect an improved soyabean variety developed by crossbreeding and selection techniques is a good example.[1] But, in the development of new types of plant or animal using gene technology, it is likely that the patent attorneys will be painting with a much broader brush and will be presenting claims in terms of generic protection so long as the data justify such breadth.

The *Ciba-Geigy* case mentioned above encourages us to believe that this approach will succeed (i.e. not to claim varieties as such but to cover them in an all-embracing claim to the biological type—genus or species—in which the characteristics of the new genetic complement are specified). The Patent Offices of Switzerland and the UK have also given such encouragement. This trend is likely to spread. These official or informal statements, however, have been made primarily in connection with plants; there has been more reticence with regard to animals. Nevertheless, the WIPO document mentioned above refers to the UK position in the following terms (World Intellectual Property Organization, 1988a):

> The exclusion of animal and plant varieties is applied only to varieties which are characterised by purely biological features.

The *Ciba-Geigy* case must be an important precedent for its animal counterpart. The Technical Board of Appeals held that Article 53(b) prohibited only the patenting of plants or their propagating material in the genetically fixed form of the plant variety. In the case before them, the claimed propagating material was not the result of an essentially biological process for the breeding of plants, but the result of a protective treatment (i.e. using a seed dressing agent to protect seeds against certain herbicides).

Two important passages in the decision are as follows.

> The skilled person understands the term "plant varieties" to mean a multiplicity of plants which are largely the same in their characteristics and remain the same within specific tolerances after every propagation or every propagation cycle. This definition is reflected in the International Convention for the Protection of New Varieties of Plants of 2nd December 1961, which is intended to give the breeder of a new plant variety a protective right (Article 1(1)) extending both to the

---

[1] Pioneer Hi-Bred Ltd application. Canadian Patent Office decision 11 CPR (3d) 311, Appeal Court decision 14 CPR (3d) 491 (appeal to Supreme Court pending).

reproductive or vegetative propagating material and also to the whole plant (Article 5(1)). Plant varieties in this sense are all cultivated varieties, clones, lines, strains and hybrids which can be grown in such a way that they are clearly distinguishable from other varieties, sufficiently homogeneous, and stable in their essential characteristics (Article 2(2) in conjunction with Article 6(1) (a), (c) and (d)). The legislator did not wish to afford patent protection under the European Patent Convention to plant varieties of this kind, whether in the form of propagating material or of the plant itself.

and

It is immaterial to the question of patentability that the propagating material which is treated can also be, or is primarily, a plant variety. If plant varieties have been excluded from patent protection because specifically the achievement involved in breeding a new variety is to have its own form of protection, it is perfectly sufficient for the exclusion to be left restricted, in conformity with its wording, to cases in which plants are characterised precisely by the genetically determined peculiarities of their natural phenotype. In this respect there is no conflict between areas reserved for national protection of varieties and the field of application of the EPC. On the other hand, innovations which cannot be given the protection afforded to varieties are still patentable if the general prerequisites are met.

On the other side of the world, the Japanese and Australian Patent Offices have taken an open position, declaring that no obvious objection exists, in principle, to animal patents provided the disclosure requirements of patent law are met. It is notable that the laws of these countries have no inhibitory provision comparable to Article 53(b) of the EPC.

ESSENTIALLY BIOLOGICAL PROCESSES

Before leaving Article 53(b) something further must be said of this lawyer's feast. The meaning of an "essentially biological process" has so far defied clear explanation, but it can be surmised that the intention of this term was to exclude traditional breeding methods from patentability. The EPO Examination Guidelines contrast an essentially biological process with one involving technical intervention. This is helpful up to a point, but the traditional breeders would be surprised to learn that their intervention in the handiwork of nature is not technical. It has also been suggested that "essentially biological" means "non-reproducible" (i.e. from a written description). What the European draftsman was striving for was presumably to exclude the ordinary reproductive processes of nature, which operate either unaided or with the assistance of the breeder who acts as an intermediary in bringing

34

together the mating elements in a suitable environment and then letting nature take its course. This kind of mediation is distinguishable from the direct manipulation of cells or parts of cells by a biochemical interaction that does not or cannot occur naturally. Perhaps this latter activity is what is meant by the term "microbiological process" in Article 53(b).

If the above analysis is correct, there may be further cause to be optimistic that the law permits the possibility of patents for animal genetic manipulation processes and "the products thereof" (i.e. the genetically modified animal). Official circles may require convincing of the correctness of this sanguine conclusion.

INTERNATIONAL COOPERATION

The prime instrument of international cooperation in the intellectual property field on a world scale is WIPO, based in Geneva. There is also an ongoing collaboration between the patent offices of the USA, Japan, and the EPO that is styled "trilateral cooperation." On a more restricted scale there is cooperation between the contracting states of the EPC and of the European Economic Community (EEC). These are the vehicles for change and improvement, and some motion has taken place, but the destination still lies distant in the biotechnology field and no more so than in relation to the topic of this symposium.

WIPO works through a system of committees of experts, these being spokesmen primarily for the national industrial property offices. The Committee of Experts on Harmonization should be noted first because it aims at the conclusion of an international treaty. However, it has barely begun to consider the problems of particular technologies, and it is doubtful whether it could come to grips with the animal patent issue in the short term. Secondly, there is a Committee of Experts on Biotechnological Inventions which has had four meetings in as many years. No treaty will emerge from this project, but a series of "suggested solutions" of the special problems of patent law relating to biotechnology will be formulated. So far, the animal issue has taken a low profile in the agenda of these meetings. At its recent session in Geneva, this committee discussed WIPO documents covering the whole range of inventions in biotechnology that are too complex to summarize, although the specific suggestion relevant to animal patents is commendably brief, namely (World Intellectual Property Organization, 1988b; 1988c),

An invention shall not be excluded from patent protection for the mere reason that it concerns a plant or a part of a plant, an animal or a part of an animal or a micro-organism (or a plant or animal variety or a strain of micro-organism).

The committees of experts represent official circles. Industry and the professions, known collectively as "interested circles," send observers to these meetings. Observers can express their views, but proper consideration of such views depends on their adoption by one or more official representatives, or by the WIPO Secretariat. Many of the suggested solutions have been based on the views of interested circles, but these meetings seem to be more a forum for discussion rather than an occasion for taking positive decisions.

INTERESTED CIRCLES

The largest of the various groups of interested circles is the worldwide patent fraternity known as the Association for the Protection of Industrial Property (AIPPI). The April 1988 resolution of AIPPI on this subject is as follows.

> All prohibitions on the patentability of living things, be they plants, animals or other organisms, or of processes for obtaining them which exist in national laws and international treaties, especially the European Patent Convention, should be abolished as soon as possible.
>
> Since such a change will take time to achieve, during the interim period the present provisions should be interpreted so as to provide the minimum limitation on patent protection. AIPPI endorses the proposals of WIPO in suggested Solutions 1 and 9 of Document BIOT/III/2, dated 8th April 1987, which are to the effect that patent protection should be allowed for all plants or animals when produced by patentable processes and for plants, plant materials or animals other than plant or animal varieties as such; it being understood that the effects of such patents are not affected by any existing exclusion of plant or animal varieties from patent protection.

The same fundamental standpoint is taken by almost all the other groups representing industry and the professions, which are too numerous to mention individually.

Trilateral cooperation, as gauged by the document drawn up by the US Department of Commerce, Patent and Trademark Office (USPTO) in January 1988, has begun by identifying the differing practices of the three patent offices (US Department of Commerce, 1988). Dealing with the question of animals, the document notes that there is no clear understanding of the term "animal variety" under the EPC and that it is an open question whether animals (as opposed to animal varieties) are patentable. After mentioning the position of the USA, the document briefly records that there is no special law in Japan for protecting animals so that animals and animal-breeding methods seem to be patentable in that country. However, there has not yet been any grant of a patent for an animal in Japan. The trilateral cooperation group has met again recently and hopefully real progress may now have begun.

PROSPECTS OF CHANGE

As mentioned earlier, the extension of patents into the field of agricultural processes and products of the kind under discussion has met with resistance. This has come in the first place from the custodians of the International Convention for the Protection of New Varieties of Plants (UPOV). The UPOV spokesmen wish to minimize the effect on agriculture which, it is thought, will result from such patents. It has also been suggested that the UPOV Convention should be expanded not only to strengthen plant variety protection but also to incorporate animal variety rights. So far no progress towards this end has been made.

The possibility of introducing national systems of animal variety rights has been canvassed in some countries. At present, this movement is no more than a ripple. In the UK, it is highly doubtful whether the government would wish to create the bureaucracy that such a system would entail. Pressure for such a system is far from uniform over the whole range of animal breeding, and the producers of certain types of animal seem to be content with the control they possess over the parent stock from which breeding takes place. It would be much more complicated apparently to introduce such a scheme for animals as compared with that for plants. For example, the tests of distinctiveness, uniformity, and stability, which are the keystones of the plant variety right system, may be inappropriate or more difficult to apply in the case of animals. Judgement on these particular issues must be left to experts in the biology of animal breeding.

The absence of any existing system of animal protection relieves us of the problem of conflict with any corresponding establishment. It would therefore seem appropriate to consider whether the patent system could give all that is required in the way of protection. On this issue, however, official patent circles may be influenced at present more by public attitudes than by the potential of existing law. The wisdom of the Boards of Appeal of the EPC and of other patent offices may well be called upon once more.

Patents for gene technology in the animal field will be able to control commercial application of that technology from the gene construct stage through all subsequent stages up to the final product (the intact animal). The same can be said of corresponding patents in the plant field, although the strategy of UPOV now appears to be to restrict the dominance of a plant patent or a plant gene patent over subsequent plant variety rights obtained for new varieties produced with the aid of the patented technology. The enthusiasts for animal patents do not have to contend with any organization as influential as UPOV, but they may still not have an easy ride. What real difference to anyone would result from the possibility of animal patents remains to be determined. A throughput royalty based on the input to or output of the slaughterhouse is one possibility that the industry might have to contemplate. In devising exploitation strategies in both the plant and animal fields, the structure of these industries must be taken fully into account. In particular, the commercial chain reaction between innovative laboratory, specialist biotechnology company, animal breeding company, and farmer will require careful consideration of the legal principle of exhaustion of rights when licensing and royalty-bearing transactions are formulated. These questions take us into waters that have yet to be charted.

References

International Association for the Protection of Industrial Property (1988) *Resolution on Question 93*. Sydney, April 15.

US Department of Commerce, Patent and Trademark Office (1988) *Comparative Study of Patent Practices in the Field of Biotechnology Related Mainly to Microbiological Inventions*. Project No. 12.3, Washington, DC.

World Intellectual Property Organization (1988a) *Exclusions from Patent Protection*. Document HL/CE/IV/INF/I.

—— (1988b) *Industrial Property Protection of Biotechnological Inventions*. Document BioT/CE/IV/2.

—— (1988c) *Revised Suggested Solutions Concerning Industrial Property Protection of Biotechnological Inventions*. Document BioT/CE/IV/3.

LEGAL REFERENCES

Bayer AG (1985) *EPO Off. J.*, **4**: 60.

Bruker Medizintechnik GmbH (1988) EPO Technical Board of Appeal 3.4.1. Decision of September 25, 1987. *EPO Off. J.*, **8**: 308.

Ciba-Geigy (1984) EPO Technical Board of Appeal 3.3.1. Decision of July 26, 1983. *EPO Off. J.*, **3**: 112.

Enlarged EPO Board of Appeal (1985) Decision of December 5, 1984.

Congressional Perspectives

Kevin W. O'Connor

INTRODUCTION

Legal, economic, ethical, and social issues relating to animal patents were the subject of hearings and legislation during the 100th US Congress. The purpose of this paper is to explain why Congress is interested in the topic of animal patents, to highlight the legislative activities of the 100th Congress related to this issue and to describe the role of the Office of Technology Assessment (OTA) in advising Congress on issues raised by animal patents.

BACKGROUND TO CONGRESSIONAL CONSIDERATION

Patents

The US Congress, through its constitutional powers, has jurisdiction over matters relating to animal patents. Article 1, Section 8 of the Constitution allows Congress "to promote the progress of science and the useful arts, by securing for limited times to authors and inventors the exclusive right to their respective writings and discoveries." The first patent act was enacted by Congress in 1790. It embodied Thomas Jefferson's philosophy that "ingenuity should receive a liberal encouragement." The first patent act provided protection for "any new and useful art, machine, manufacture, or composition of matter, or any new and useful improvement [thereof]." Subsequent patent statutes, enacted in 1793, 1836, 1870, and 1874, employed the same broad language as the 1790 act. The Patent Act of 1952 replaced "art" with "process" as patentable subject matter. The committee reports accompanying the 1952 act demonstrated that Congress intended patentable subject matter to include "anything under the sun that is made by man."

In 1970, the Supreme Court, in a five-to-four ruling, held that a live, human-made microorganism is patentable subject matter as a "manufacture" or "composition of matter" (*Diamond v. Chakrabarty*). In reaching its decision, the Court noted that arguments against patentability based on potential hazards that may be generated by genetic research should be addressed to the Congress and the executive for regulation or control, not to the judiciary.

Commerce

In addition to its authority to grant patents and to designate what constitutes patentable subject matter, Congress has the authority under the "commerce clause"[1] to regulate the research, testing, approval, and marketing of new animals that may or may not be patented. Under the commerce clause, for example, Congress can enact statutes that govern the approval and marketing of pharmaceuticals, the slaughtering and labelling of meat products, and the control of plant pests.

The development of recombinant DNA techniques during the 1970s raised concerns about potential hazards posed by the new technologies. Recognizing a need to establish consensus, scientists became involved in discussing recombinant DNA technology and its potential risks. The International Conference on Recombinant DNA Molecules (better known as the Asilomar Conference) convened 140 scientists in February 1975 to address self-regulation of research involving recombinant DNA technology until its safety could be assured. Recommendations were issued assigning risk categories to various recombinant DNA experiments and containment levels for each.

Federal regulation of genetically altered organisms began in 1976, when the National Institutes of Health (NIH) adopted "Guidelines for Research Involving Recombinant DNA Molecules." These stringent guidelines established containment standards and review procedures to be applied by institutional biosafety committees at each institution.

In 1984, the White House Office of Science and Technology Policy (OSTP) published a "Proposed Coordinated Framework for the Regulation of Biotechnology" in order to ensure the safety of biotechnology research and products. This document proposed policies for federal agencies responsible for reviewing the research and products of biotechnology. It also proposed the establishment of a new, centralized advisory committee within the Department of Health and Human Services (DHHS) to coordinate responses to scientific questions raised by applications received by the various federal agencies.

Following a period for public comment, OSTP (1985) decided against establishing a committee within DHHS. Instead, a Biotechnology Science Coordinating Committee (BSCC) was formed "to monitor the changing scene of biotechnology and serve as a means of identifying potential gaps in regulation in a timely fashion, making appropriate recommendations for either administrative or legislative action." In the same notice, OSTP published an index of laws conferring authority that could be used to ensure the safety of biotechnology-related products. Many elements of the proposed coordinated framework were incorporated into the Coordinated Framework published by OSTP on June 26, 1986.

The coordinated framework includes separate descriptions of the regulatory policies of the Food and Drugs Administration (FDA), Environmental Protection Agency (EPA), Occupational Safety and Health Administration (OSHA), and the US Department of Agriculture (USDA), as well as the

---

[1] US Constitution, Article 1, Section 8, Clause 3, the commerce clause, gives Congress the power to regulate interstate commerce, which has been interpreted to mean transactions across state boundaries and also any activity that affects commerce in more than one state.

research policies of NIH, the National Science Foundation (NSF), EPA, and USDA. The coordinated framework mandates both the agencies responsible for approving commercial biotechnology products (see Table 1) and the jurisdiction for biotechnology research proposals (see Table 2).

Table 1 Agencies responsible for approval of commercial biotechnology products

Biotechnology products	Responsible agencies
Foods/food additives	FDA,* FSIS[a]
Human drugs, medical devices and biologics	FDA
Animal drugs	FDA
Animal biologics	APHIS
Other contained uses	EPA
Plants and animals	APHIS,[b] FSIS,[a] FDA[c]
Pesticide microorganisms released in the environment	
All	EPA,[d] APHIS[b]
Other uses (microorganisms):	
intergenetic combination	EPA,[d] APHIS[b]
Intrageneric combination	
Pathogenic source organism	
Agricultural use	APHIS
Non-agricultural use	EPA,[d] APHIS[b]
No pathogenic source organisms	EPA report
Non-engineered pathogens:	
Agricultural use	APHIS
Non-agricultural use	EPA,[d] APHIS[b]
Non-engineered non-pathogens	EPA report

* Designates lead agency where jurisdictions may overlap; FDA, Food and Drug Administration.

[a] FSIS, Food Safety and Inspection Service; under the Assistant Secretary of Agriculture for Marketing and Inspection Services responsible for food use.

[b] APHIS, Animal and Plant Health Inspection Service: involved when the microorganism is plant pest, animal pathogen, or regulated article requiring a permit.

[c] FDA involved when in relation to a food use.

[d] EPA requirement will only apply to environmental release under a "significant new use rule" that EPA intends to propose.

(Source: 51 *Fed. Reg.* (1986) **51** 23304)

It is important to note that the powers of Congress over patents and commerce are substantively different from each other. Patents are designed to encourage inventiveness by granting to inventors a limited property right—the right to exclude others from practicing the invention for a period of 17 years. A patent, however, does not grant the inventor any affirmative right to make, use or sell an invention. The affirmative right to make use of an invention may be regulated by federal, state or local law.

LEGISLATIVE RESPONSE TO THE PATENT AND TRADEMARK OFFICE DECISION

In April 1987, the US Patent and Trademark Office (PTO) announced that it "now considers nonnaturally occurring non-human multicellular living organisms, including animals, to be patentable subject matter within the scope" of

41

Table 2 Jurisdiction for biotechnology research proposals

Proposed research	Responsible agencies
Contained research, no release in environment	
Federally funded	Funding agency[a]
Non-federally funded	NIH or S&E voluntary review, APHIS[b]
Foods/food additives, human drugs, medical devices, biologics, animal drugs	
Federally funded	FDA,[c] NIH guidelines and review
Non-federally funded	FDA,[c] NIH voluntary review
Plants, animals and animal biologics	
Federally funded	Funding agency,[a] APHIS[b]
Non-federally funded	APHIS,[b] S&E voluntary review
Pesticide microorganisms	
Genetically engineered	
Intergeneric	EPA,[d] APHIS,[b] S&E voluntary review
Pathogenic intrageneric	EPA,[d] APHIS,[b] S&E voluntary review
Intrageneric non-pathogen	EPA,[d], S&E voluntary review
Non-engineered	
Non-indigenous pathogens	EPA,[d] APHIS
Indigenous pathogens	EPA,[d] APHIS
Non-indigenous non-pathogen	EPA
Other uses (microorganisms) released in the environment	
Genetically engineered	
Intergeneric organisms	
Federally funded	Funding agency,[a] APHIS,[b] EPA[d]
Commercially funded	EPA, APHIS, S&E voluntary review
Intrageneric organisms	
Pathogenic source organisms	
Federally funded	Funding agency,[a] APHIS,[b] EPA[d]
Commercially funding	APHIS,[b] EPA[d] (if non-agricultural use)
Intrageneric combination	
No pathogenic source organisms	EPA report
Non-engineered	EPA report,* APHIS[b]

* Designates lead agency where jurisdictions may overlap.
[a] Review and approval of research protocols conducted by NIH, S&E, or NSF.
[b] EPA jurisdiction to research on a plot greater than 10 acres.
[c] APHIS issues permits for the importation and domestic shipment of certain plants and animals, plant pests and animal pathogens, and for the shipment or release in the environment of regulated articles.
[d] EPA reviews federally funded environmental research only when it is for commercial purposes.

APHIS: Animal and Plant Health Inspection Service; EPA: Environmental Protection Agency; NIH: National Institutes of Health; S&E: United States Department of Agriculture Science and Education.

(Source: 51 (1986) *Fed. Reg.* 23305)

the utility patent statute.[2] Subsequent to this announcement and a congressional brief (US Congress, Congressional Research Service, 1987), several legislative actions occurred.

[2] 35 USC 101, which says that: "whoever invents or discovers any new and useful process, machine, manufacture, or composition of matter, or any new and useful improvement thereof, may obtain a patent . . ."

(1) Senator Mark Hatfield (R-OR) introduced an amendment to HR 1827, a supplemental appropriations bill for FY 1987, to prohibit funding for the patenting of genetically altered or modified animals.

(2) Representative Charlie Rose (D-NC) introduced HR 3119 to prohibit the patenting of animals for a two-year period.

(3) Senator Hatfield introduced S 2111 to prohibit the patenting of genetically altered or modified animals.

(4) The House Judiciary Subcommittee on Courts, Civil Liberties, and the Administration of Justice held four hearings on patents and the constitution: transgenic animals.

(5) Representative Robert Kastenmeier (D-WI) introduced HR 4970, the Transgenic Animal Patent Reform Act.

Supplemental Appropriations Amendment (HR 1827)

The first action, Senator Hatfield's amendment to the FY 1987 supplemental appropriations bill, was introduced on the Senate floor on May 28, 1987. A supplemental appropriations bill is a mechanism by which Congress provides funding for federal programs after the passage of an initial appropriations bill. Senator Hatfield's amendment read as follows:

> Notwithstanding any other provision of law, none of the funds appropriated for fiscal year 1987 shall be used for the purpose of granting any patent for vertebrate or invertebrate animals, modified, altered, or in any way changed through engineering technology, including genetic engineering.

In introducing his amendment, Senator Hatfield said that the PTO decision "signifies a technological and ethical leap which I believe we are not prepared to take." He expressed concern regarding economic, environmental, religious and ethical questions, as well as animal suffering and the use of genetic human traits in animals (*Congressional Record*, 1987). The amendment was approved by the Senate by a voice vote, but was not reported out of conference committee subsequent to Senate passage of the supplemental appropriations bill.

Moratorium on Patenting Animals (HR 3119)

Representative Charlie Rose (D-NC) introduced HR 3119, a bill to amend the patent statute to prohibit the patenting of animals altered by genetic engineering technology for a two-year period, and to revoke previously granted patents for such animals. This bill was introduced on August 5, 1987, and subsequently had 67 co-sponsors. The bill stated four Congressional findings:

(1) The patenting of genetically engineered invertebrate and vertebrate animals, including animals engineered with human genetic traits, raises

profound economic, environmental, and ethical questions which Congress has not had the opportunity to address fully.

(2) Untimely action on this issue could unnecessarily expose patent holders to revocation of their patents and expose the government to financial liability for their restitution.

(3) Vertebrate and invertebrate animals have never been patented under the patent laws of the USA.

(4) Such monumental decisions about the fate of animal life should not be left solely to the PTO.

HR 3119 was a subject of hearings held by the House Judiciary Subcommittee on Courts, Civil Liberties and the Administration of Justice. On July 13, 1988, the subcommittee voted eight-to-six against reporting HR 3119 to the full committee on the judiciary. The subcommittee instead approved HR 4970 (see discussion below).

Prohibition on Patenting Animals (S 2111)

S 2111, a bill to prohibit the patenting of genetically altered or modified animals, was introduced by Senator Hatfield on February 29, 1988.[3] This bill was similar to HR 3119. One notable difference, however, was the absence in the Senate bill of any time limit for the proposed patent moratorium. The bill, which had two co-sponsors, was referred to the Senate Judiciary Committee, Subcommittee on Patents, Copyrights and Trademarks. No further action occurred on this bill.

The House Judiciary Subcommittee Hearings

The House Committee on the Judiciary, Subcommittee on Courts, Civil Liberties and the Administration of Justice held four hearings[4] on *Patents and the Constitution: Transgenic Animals*. These hearings produced a 931-page record of testimony and materials, and preceded subcommittee mark-ups on HR 3119 and HR 4970 (US Congress, Committee on the Judiciary, 1987).

Transgenic Animal Patent Reform Act (HR 4970)

HR 4970 was introduced by Representative Robert Kastenmeier (D-WI) on June 30, 1988 (see also US Congress, House Report, 1988). The bill addressed patent infringement, specification for a patent application and the patentability of human beings. The bill was amended and approved by the Subcommittee on Courts, Civil Liberties and the Administration of Justice (July 13, 1988) and the Committee on the Judiciary (August 2, 1988). The amended bill was approved by the House of Representatives by voice vote on September 13, 1988.

---

[3] For Senator Hatfield's statement accompanying the introduction of S 2111, see *Congressional Record* (1988), S1620-21.
[4] June 11, July 22, August 21, and November 5, 1987.

The major provisions of the bill, as amended and passed by the House, are as follows:

(1)   It shall not be an act of infringement for a person whose occupation is farming to reproduce a patented transgenic farm animal through breeding, to use such animal in the farming operation, or to sell such animal or the offspring of such animal. It shall be an act of infringement, however, for a person to sell the germ cells, semen or embryos of a patented transgenic farm animal.

(2)   The Commissioner of the PTO may accept a deposit of biological material to satisfy specification for a patent application.

(3)   The patent statute is amended to specify that human beings are not patentable subject matter.

The House-passed bill was referred to the Senate on September 14, 1988 and was referred to the Committee on the Judiciary, Subcommittee on Patents, Copyrights and Trademarks. The Senate took no action on HR 4970 prior to the end of the 100th Congress in October 1988.

OFFICE OF TECHNOLOGY ASSESSMENT REPORT ON PATENTING LIFE

The Office of Technology Assessment (OTA) is a non-partisan analytical support agency that serves the Congress by providing objective analyses of major public policy issues related to scientific and technological change. OTA prepares assessments at the request of committees of Congress and the approval of the Technology Assessment Board (the 12-member bipartisan congressional board that governs OTA).

At the request of several committees, OTA has been conducting an assessment of new developments in biotechnology. To date, this assessment has resulted in four reports: *Ownership of Human Tissues and Cells*; *Public Perceptions of Biotechnology*; *Field-Testing Engineered Organisms: Genetic and Ecological Issues*; *US Investment in Biotechnology*. The fifth report, *Patenting Life*, is expected to be released in early 1989. This report will review US patent law as it relates to the patentability of microorganisms, plants, and animals; as well as recent specific areas of concern, including deposit requirements and international considerations. Several staff papers on this latter topic have been released (US Congress, Office of Technology Assessment, 1988a; 1988b).

SUMMARY

The Congress has legislative authority to grant patents and regulate commerce. Under this authority, Congress has enacted a patent code and enacted laws that now make up the Coordinated Framework for the Regulation of Biotechnology.

45

The announcement by the US Patent and Trademark Office in 1987 that animals are patentable subject matter resulted in a public policy debate regarding the appropriateness of such patents. The 100th Congress considered several legislative proposals relating to animal patents. Although both the Senate and House approved legislative proposals (the Senate approved a supplemental appropriations amendment prohibiting the use of funds for the issuance of animal patents, and the House approved a Transgenic Animal Patent Reform Act), no bill relating to animal patents was enacted into law.

The Office of Technology Assessment, as part of its assessment of new developments in biotechnology, is currently preparing a special report, *Patenting Life*. This report will be released in early 1989.

References

Congressional Record (1987)   **133** (May 28): S7268-9.
Congressional Record (1988)   **134** (Feb. 29): S1620-21.
US Congress, Committee on the Judiciary, Subcommittee on Courts, Civil Liberties, and the Administration of Justice (1987)   *Patents and the Constitution: Transgenic Animals*. Hearings, 100th Congress, Serial No. 23.
US Congress, Congressional Research Service (1987)   *Patenting Life*. Issue Brief, IB87222.
US Congress, Office of Technology Assessment (1988a)   *Transgenic Animals*. Staff Paper, Biological Applications Program.
—— (1988b)   *Federal Regulation and Animal Patents*. Staff Paper, Biological Applications Program.
US Congress, House Report (1988)   *Transgenic Animal Patent Reform Act*. No. 100-888, to accompany HR 4970.
White House, Office of Science and Technology Policy (1984) Proposed Coordinated Framework for the Regulation of Biotechnology. *Fed. Reg.*, **49**: 50856 *et seq.*
—— (1985)   Coordinated Framework for Regulation of Biotechnology; Establishment of the Biotechnology Science Coordinating Committee. *Fed. Reg.*, **50**: 47174–6.
—— (1986)   Coordinated Framework for Regulation of Biotechnology; Announcement of Policy and Notice for Public Comment. *Fed. Reg.*, **51**: 23301 *et seq.*

LEGAL REFERENCE

Diamond v Chakrabarty, 447 US 303 (1980).

The Technology and Costs of Deposits

Robert H. Foote

INTRODUCTION

This topic is a broad one and the discussion will be limited to mammals, primarily mice and farm animals. Clearly, the world of biotechnology is moving rapidly in various sectors of plant and animal biotechnology (Council for Agricultural Science and Technology, 1986; US Congress, Office of Technology Assessment, 1987; Jaenisch, 1988). The benefits to agriculture of genetic engineering techniques could be enormous in terms of increasing the quantity and quality of food (Council for Agricultural Science and Technology, 1986). The world population will probably double in the next 40 years. If this happens, the food required during that time will equal all the food produced in human history. Animal products will continue to be an important part of a nutritious and appetizing diet. Animals utilizing forages compete less with humans for plant sources in the diet. They can indirectly harvest a virtually inexhaustible source of energy—sunlight—acting through photosynthesis, plant growth, and animal conversion to produce high quality proteins.

Other applications are emerging in human and veterinary medicine. The adoption of various procedures can cause major social and economic problems, along with the benefits. In humans, the adoption of various reproductive technologies alone has resulted in major unresolved controversy (Ashwood-Smith, 1986; Ethics Committee, 1986). Other contributors to this symposium will deal with these and legal issues. The focus of this paper is on the technology or state of the art(s) that may make deposits possible in one form or another, depending upon the type of deposit required.

METHODS OF PRODUCING GENETICALLY DIFFERENT ANIMALS BESIDES "TRANSGENIC ANIMALS"

It is important to recognize that in livestock breeding and the production of laboratory animals, different strains have evolved through selection. This selection has been effective in changing gene frequency and in producing many subpopulations. With extensive inbreeding many strains of mice, essentially homozygous, have been established. Mutant stocks have been established as a result of mutations occurring spontaneously or induced by a variety of techniques. These have occurred historically in a somewhat random fashion.

An example of the major impact of selective breeding is dairy cattle, in which the genetic ability to produce milk has increased greatly through the use of superior sires in artificial breeding. This has brought about a genetic change in dairy cattle in the past few decades that exceeds all previous history.

Other reproductive technologies, such as superovulation, estrous cycle regulation and embryo transfer, have permitted outstanding females to contribute to more progeny. Such techniques as sexing of sperm and/or embryos and the dividing of embryos into at least two parts with full developmental potential have further enhanced the potential application of reproductive technologies. Of special interest is the possibility of cloning, to be discussed more later.

Practical livestock breeding programs were enhanced by the discovery that bull sperm could be preserved by freezing in the presence of glycerol. Using glycerol and other cryoprotectants, the field of cryobiology has grown to encompass embryos and many types of cells, tissues, and organs. None of the techniques listed here have been patented; any attempted patent applications were unsuccessful. However, the ability to preserve living animal material, such as embryos, by freezing is especially germane to the discussion of deposits.

TRANSGENIC ANIMALS

Animals for which patents are likely to be sought are food-yielding animals capable of producing meat, milk, eggs, and other animal products more efficiently, animals that produce pharmaceutical compounds, particularly for human use such as transgenic sheep capable of synthesizing factor IX (important in treating hemophiliacs) and the production of tissue plasminogen activator (TPA) (used to treat humans to minimize heart attacks). Other transgenic animals will be produced as models for studying human diseases. One such strain of mice useful as a model in cancer studies is the Harvard mouse (Raines, 1988) which has been patented (US Patent No. 4,736,866). Since that patent was issued there has been considerable discussion about a moratorium (Adler, 1988) on animal patents, and currently only the Harvard mouse, of the many applications pending, has been approved.

PATENTS

Many pros and cons are being expressed concerning animal patents. Those for patenting point out that patenting of genetically engineered animals is important both economically and legally. The private sector is investing a greater proportion of the effort in the USA to pursue fundamental and applied research in agriculture. Without patent protection there would be less incentive for the private sector to invest in this type of research. Many other countries are producing transgenic animals, and it is not clear what the patent status will be there in the future (see Straus's paper).

At the 1988 Annual Meeting of the American Society of Animal Science the following resolution was passed:

WHEREAS, the American Society of Animal Science is concerned that restrictions on patenting of genetically engineered animals or removal of incentives for return on research investments would reduce such research in this country and make us noncompetitive with other countries where those restrictions and disincentives might not exist:

THEREFORE BE IT RESOLVED the American Society of Animal Science supports patenting of genetically engineered animals so as to provide incentive for research and development of methods to produce such animals, and

BE IT FURTHER RESOLVED that we encourage legislators to consider deviations from usual patent policy so as not to be a financial or a paperwork burden on producers of animals by considering the following guidelines:

(1) To have an exemption for non-commercial researchers who are trying to develop further genetically engineered animals from those already patented.
(2) To have limits of not more than two generations on animals destined for sale as breeding animals so that multiple royalties do not continue over the usual 17-year period.
(3) To have an exemption for commercial breeders, which allows them to perpetuate offspring of patented animals for their own use without royalties.

The definition of "commercial breeders" will have to be refined. As it applies to relatively small enterprises patents without exclusions may be counterproductive; the incomplete record-keeping systems, low numbers of animals involved and movement of animals are not conducive to collection of royalties. Some type of policing and testing system to collect royalties will be necessary, and the cost may make application prohibitive.

Those opposed to the patenting of animals are often part of a group which feels that any sort of genetic engineering is unethical and causes animal suffering. Any requirements for deposits would simply add to the concerns of these groups. Others point out that patenting of animals may cause researchers to be driven more by selfish economic rewards than by the goal of producing animals useful in alleviating human suffering and the solving of other problems. Does the pursuit of patent protection seriously retard advancement of science by restricting free exchange of information?

There is little doubt that animal patents will be issued in many countries, including the USA. In the Congressional Record of 9/13/88 HR 4970 on the

Transgenic Animal Patent Reform Act, a portion of this bill reads as follows:

(g) (1) It shall not be an act of infringement for a person whose occupation is farming to reproduce a patented transgenic farm animal through breeding, use such animal in the farming operation, or sell such animal or the offspring of such animal.

(2) Notwithstanding the provisions of paragraph (1). It shall be an act of infringement for a person to sell the germ cells, semen, or embryos of a patented transgenic farm animal.

(3) For purposes of paragraphs (1) and (2)

(A) the term "transgenic farm animal" means a farm animal whose germ cells contain genetic material originally derived from another animal other than the parent of the farm animal; and

(B) the term "farm animal" means any animal used or intended for use as food or fiber.

It is interesting to note here the use of the phrase "other than the parent of the farm animal." "Parent" usually is understood to mean the immediate ancestor. Is "parent" used here ambiguously or incorrectly to indicate any animals in the ancestral line? As written, it would appear that patent protection is limited to one generation. This may be all that would be feasible for farm animals. For example, if a genetically engineered sire is used in dairy cattle breeding with sons and daughters in thousands of herds, can all animals realistically be accounted for? Bulls that carry the engineered gene construct might be turned out on pasture to breed heifers, including those on the other side of an old fence. Owners of progeny of the engineered parent are likely to use or sell (often for slaughter) their own animals without necessarily recognizing the source. Would the owner of the patent find it profitable to send a representative to each farm with kits to test each animal to determine which ones carry the engineered genetic component?

Also in HR 4970 it states that Section 112 of title 35, US Code, is amended by adding at the end the following new paragraph.

With respect to an invention involving biological material, the Commissioner may accept a deposit of biological material to satisfy any requirement of this section if made accessible under such conditions as the Commissioner may require.

Incidentally but importantly, the Bill indicates that "human beings are not patentable subject matter."

DEPOSIT REQUIREMENTS

In the *Federal Register*, the Patent and Trademark Office proposed the following concerning deposits of biological material for patent purposes.

> Every patent must contain a written description of the invention sufficient to enable a person skilled in the art to which the invention pertains to make and use the invention. Where the invention involves a biological material and words alone cannot sufficiently describe how to make and use the invention in a reproducible or repeatable manner, the required biological material must either be known and readily available and likely to continue to be available or be deposited in a suitable depository to obtain a patent. Access to a deposit during the pendency of a patent application relying upon it will be governed by the same criteria used to consider access to the patent application. Samples of the deposited material must become publicly available upon issuance of the patent. The deposit will be considered part of the patent disclosure.

Discussion in the *Federal Register* continues, noting that guidelines will be clarified as to the conditions under which a deposit must be made, the kinds of materials in the deposit and various obligations of where, and for how long, the deposit should be maintained. Timing is clearly stated. The deposited material "must become publicly available upon issuance of the patent." The interpretation of availability is discussed (see also *Fed. Reg.*, **52** (174): pp. 34080 *et seq.*).

Relative to animals the following quotation is relevant: ". . . it is anticipated that inventions relating to the development of animals having new and otherwise patentable characteristics will rely on the identification and description of a known and readily available animal that will be treated in a reproducible process to obtain the new animal variety. The PTO is presently not aware of any organization that is willing and able to undertake the responsibilities of a suitable depository for live animals." (*Fed. Reg.*, **52** (174): p. 34081)

TYPE OF DEPOSIT REQUIRED

A patent disclosure must provide a description and whatever else is necessary (US Congress, Office of Technology, 1984) to enable anyone "skilled in the art to practice the claimed invention without undue experimentation" (Van Horn, 1987). There are many factors considered in determining what is "undue experimentation," such as:

(1) the amount of experimentation required;
(2) the amount of guidance required;

(3) the availability of samples;
(4) the nature of the invention;
(5) the state of the prior art;
(6) the relative skill of those in the art;
(7) the predictability of the art;
(8) the breadth of the claims.

This would seem to indicate that animals, or embryos capable of producing animals, would be the required form of the deposit. In the case of the Harvard mouse, however, I believe that only the plasmid and an oncogene had to be deposited. The patent application covered a wide range of conditions and many species. Because of species differences, and many other factors of unpredictability, whether the material deposited really would allow even skilled persons to achieve the desired result from the deposit made is uncertain. Until such time as it is possible repeatably to insert a prescribed number of gene constructs into a specific chromosomal locus, many strains of animals from the same construct would exist.

If a deposit is required some of the requirements are as follows (Proposed Rules, 35 USC Sec. 1.204, 1.205, 1.206).

(1) Deposit is viable initially.
(2) Deposit is maintained in an acceptable depository for at least 30 years.
(3) Replenishment of the original deposit if the original deposit is no longer viable.

ANIMAL DEPOSITS

Obviously it is not feasible to maintain live animals over a period of many years. This is very difficult even in a facility such as the Jackson Laboratory, a resource for many strains of mice. Attempts have been made to freeze whole animals, but this has not been successful. Testes (Deanesly, 1954) and ovaries (Parkes, 1956) have, however, been frozen with some success.

EMBRYO CRYOPRESERVATION

Preserving embryos obtained from established strains of transgenic animals clearly is one of the possible solutions.

(1) What is involved?
(2) What is the state of the art and science?
(3) What does it cost?

Superovulation

For most laboratory animals (mice, hamsters, rats, and rabbits) treatment of females with gonadotrophins (Foote, 1987) to yield a large number of oocytes is routine in many laboratories. Following mating or artificial insemination, a large number of fertilized eggs or young embryos can be collected surgically at various stages of development. The cow, pig, sheep, and goat (Armstrong, 1983; Foote, 1987) can also be superovulated by gonadotrophin treatment. The mare does not respond well to superovulation. The young embryos collected can then be evaluated for normal morphology and those which appear to be normal can be frozen.

Embryos of many species have been cryopreserved (Whittingham *et al.*, 1972; Whittingham and Wood, 1984; Mazur and Schneider, 1986; Schneider, 1986; Massip *et al.*, 1987; Prather *et al.*, 1987). In 1986 Leibo reported that live-offspring from frozen-thawed embryos of ten species had been produced (Leibo, 1986). Species included were mouse, rat, rabbit, cow, sheep, goat, horse, antelope, human, and baboon. Frequently, there are new reports of successful freezing of embryos of additional species.

Principles and Practice of Cryopreservation

(1) Embryos require a medium that is physiological plus a cryoprotectant. The cryoprotectant usually used is glycerol, dimethylsulfoxide or propanediol.
(2) Cooling from room temperature to about 0°C can be fairly rapid.
(3) Embryos are frozen in a programmed freezer.
(4) As embryos are cooled below the freezing point of the suspending solution the embryos are held for a few minutes to equilibrate. Touching the surface of the container holding the embryos with a metal object kept at −196°C causes ice crystals to form quickly at the point of contact. This prevents the sample from undergoing substantial supercooling below the temperature of the solution before ice crystals form. If substantial supercooling occurs, the temperature will rise quickly with a rapid change in salt concentration as the water freezes out. This is damaging to the embryo.
(5) Embryos are then slowly cooled to about −35 to −40°C and are allowed to equilibrate for a few minutes.
(6) Embryos can then be transferred to liquid nitrogen at −196°C for long-term storage. Liquid nitrogen refrigerators properly resupplied with liquid nitrogen can efficiently maintain these low temperatures.
(7) At the appropriate time embryos can be thawed rapidly and transferred to suitable recipient females for development.

Cloning and freezing of cloned embryos can be used to increase the number of embryos per female. This may not be of major value in mice where homozygous strains of animals can be readily developed. In domestic animals most of the transgenics will be heterozygous, and the embryos that carry the gene can be identified if up to 20 embryonic cells are available. It is expected that amplification systems will soon be perfected, permitting expressed genes to be detected in a single cell. This is sufficient to test for the presence of the inserted gene construct. Only such embryos could then be cloned and cryo-preserved. At the present time it is known that in cattle embryos past the 32-cell stage retain totipotency.

Viability of Cryopreserved Embryos

The most extensive results are available for mouse and cattle embryos. In a large center in the UK, where many stocks of mutant mice are maintained, about 30 percent of all embryos frozen result in live young upon thawing and embryo transfer (Glenister and Lyon, 1986). About 200 frozen embryos must be maintained in storage to reestablish a line. Some strains are only maintained in the frozen state. Stocks have been reestablished for embryos stored in liquid nitrogen for periods up to 11 years. Studies have also been carried out on irradiated embryos. No damage was detectable in embryos exposed to the equivalent of 2000 years of background radiation (Glenister, 1986). Minor chromosomal damage, however, was reported in cryopreserved oocytes (Glenister *et al.*, 1987).

At the Jackson Laboratory 500 strains of mutant mice have been preserved in liquid nitrogen (Mobraaten, 1986). About 500 embryos per strain are frozen if the parents are both homozygous, and 1000 embryos when one is heterozygous. This is more than sufficient even for certain inbred mutants in which only 8–10 percent of the embryos initially frozen result in live young. No change in fertility has been noted for embryos stored for up to nine years. One strain was reconstituted from a bank of 28 embryos.

There is no indication that freezing mouse embryos affects the mutation rate (Mobraaten and Bailey, 1987). A group of mice resulting from radiated embryos, however, had a higher mutation rate.

In cattle, tens of thousands of frozen-thawed embryos are inovulated yearly. Frozen embryos make export of genetic material reasonably simple while preventing the spread of disease. Pregnancy rates of 50–70 percent with frozen embryos are usually about 10 percent below results obtained using unfrozen embryos. There are no good experimental data on survival during long-term storage of bovine embryos, but the life of well-frozen embryos probably exceeds several hundred years (Leibo, 1986). Thus this appears to be the best way to maintain the integrity of strains of animals, as spontaneous mutations occur in control lines maintained for many generations.

COSTS OF EMBRYO DEPOSITS

No attempt will be made here to determine the cost of producing transgenic animals. This cost may be only a few thousand dollars for mice and hundreds of thousands of dollars to establish a strain of domestic animals. Even with the best techniques many animals must be injected to obtain the necessary incorporation, integration, and expression. With the same gene construct positive animals will have different numbers of copies of the construct inserted at different locations in the chromosomes, thus forming multiple strains. To establish a strain it is desirable to breed animals and establish a stock homozygous for the gene construct. This is obviously very costly. Should heterozygotes be useful and cloning become practical, germ plasm might be distributed that way.

A very encouraging aspect is the success of embryo cryopreservation, making possible many practical breeding programs and the preservation of germ plasm whether or not it is in a legally required deposit. Based on results at the Jackson Laboratory (Dr Larry Mobraaten, 1988: personal communication) it costs about $600 per year to maintain a bank of 500–1000 embryos in two locations. This includes a small cost of about $15 per year for liquid nitrogen, equipment, labor for tank checking, and refilling and miscellaneous items.

OTHER TYPES OF DEPOSITS

It is possible that the requirements for a deposit will only be that the material for making a transgenic animal, along with instructions for making one, as in the case of the Harvard mouse, is all that is required. That issue may be settled in the courts. Starting with the raw materials it is much less likely that a transgenic animal identical to the one patented will result. The Office of Technology Assessment is studying this question and will soon issue a report with recommendations. This will be a recommendation only, and the type of deposit required is likely to be the center of long discussions.

If the deposit becomes non-viable then it must be replaced. If sufficient embryos are stored under proper conditions this should not be necessary. If it does become necessary, molecular techniques are available to determine the composition of the new transgenic animals relative to the gene construct.

LOCATION OF STORAGE

The American Type Culture Collection (ATCC) at 12301 Parklawn Drive, Rockville, MD 20852 accepts cell lines (including hybridomas), plasmids, various types of tissue culture and other materials. The ATCC is approved as a depository for strains of material involved in US patent applications. They recommend that the strain be tested for viability upon deposit. The fee for 30 years of storage is $570. If other services are required, such as viability testing, the fee depends upon the nature of the material. Likewise, the amount of material stored varies with the type. If embryos were to be stored the cost presumably would be somewhat higher as the $570 covers a maximum of 25 ampoules of cell culture. However, an ampoule or straw could contain 10 embryos, and 25 ampoules each with 10 embryos would be enough to reestablish the strain. At the Jackson Laboratory 28 embryos have been shown to be enough to reestablish one strain (Mobraaten, 1986). The freezing and storage system in place for organisms and tissue culture at ATCC is also well suited for storing embryos.

The ATCC also offers a cryopreservation service for a fee. They are equipped to follow a variety of freezing procedures and have on their staff scientists well trained in cryopreservation of embryos. Placing appropriate embryos on deposit would seem to be a reliable, inexpensive, stable, and practical method for meeting the requirements of a deposit.

References

Adler, R. G. (1988) Controlling the Applications of Biotechnology: A Critical Analysis of the Proposed Moratorium on Animal Patenting. *Harvard J. Law Technol.*, **1**: 1–61.

Armstrong, D. T. and G. Evans (1983) Factors Influencing Success of Embryo Transfer in Sheep and Goats. *Theriogenology*, **19**: 31–42.

Ashwood-Smith, M. J. (1986) The Cryopreservation of Human Embryos. *Human Reprod.*, **1**: 319–32.

Council for Agricultural Science and Technology (1986) *Genetic Engineering in Food and Agriculture*. Report no. 110.

Deanesly, R. (1954) Spermatogenesis and Endocrine Activity in Grafts of Frozen and Thawed Rat Testis. *J. Endocrinol.*, **11**: 201–6.

Ethics Committee, American Fertility Association (1986) Ethical Considerations of the New Reproductive Technologies. *J. Fert.*, **46** (Suppl.): 1S–94S.

Foote, R. H. (1987) *In vitro* Fertilization and Embryo Transfer in Domestic Animals: Applications in Animals and Implications for Humans. *J. In Vitro Fert. Embryo Transfer*, **4**: 73–88.

Glenister, P. H. and M. F. Lyon (1986) Long-Term Storage of Eight-Cell Mouse Embryos at −196°C. *J. In Vitro Fertil. Embryo Transer*, **3**: 20–27.

Glenister, P. H., M. J. Wood, C. Kirby, and D. G. Whittingham (1987) The Incidence of Chromosome Anomalies in First-Cleavage Mouse Embryos Obtained from Frozen-Thawed Oocytes Fertilized *in vitro*. *Gamete Res.*, **16**: 205–16.

Jaenisch, R. (1988) Transgenic Animals. *Science*, **240**: 1468–73.

Leibo, S. P. (1986) Cryobiology: Preservation of Mammalian Embryos. In: *Genetic Engineering of Animals*. Plenum Pub. Press, New York, pp. 251–72.

Massip, A., P. Van Der Zwalmen, and F. Ectors (1987) Recent Progress in Cryopreservation of Cattle Embryos. *Theriogenology*, **27**: 69–80.

Mazur, P. and U. Schneider (1986) Osmotic Responses of Preimplantation Mouse and Bovine Embryos and their Cryobiological Implications. *Cell Biophys.*, **8**: 259–84.

Mobraaten, L. E. (1986) Mouse Embryo Cryobanking. *J. In Vitro Fert. Embryo Transfer*, **3**: 28–32.

Mobraaten, L. E. and D. W. Bailey (1987) Effect of Freezing Mouse Embryos on Mutation Rate. *Cryobiology*, **24**: 586.

Parkes, A. S. (1956) Survival Time of Ovarian Homografts in Two Strains of Rats. *J. Endocrinol.*, **13**: 201–10.

Prather, R. S., M. F. Spire, and R. R. Schalles (1987) Evaluation of Cryopreservation Techniques for Bovine Embryos. *Theriogenology*, **28**: 195–204.

Raines, L. J. (1988) The Mouse that Roared. *Iss. in Sci. Technol.*, **70** (summer): 64–8.

Schneider, U. (1986) Cryobiological Principles of Embryo Freezing. *J. In Vitro Fert. Embryo Transfer*, **3**: 3–9.

US Congress, Office of Technology Assessment (1987) *Technologies to Maintain Biological Diversity*. OTA-F-330. Washington, DC, pp. 137–65.

—— (1984) Intellectual Property Law. In: *Commercial Biotechnology: An International Analysis*. OTA-BA-218. Washington DC, pp. 383–406.

Van Horn, C. (1987)   Recent Developments in the Patenting of Biotechnology in the United States. *Symposium on the Protection of Biotechnological Inventions*. Cornell University.

Whittingham, D. G., S. P. Leibo, and P. Mazur (1972)   Survival of Mouse Embryos Frozen to −196°C and −269°C. *Science*, **178**: 414.

Whittingham, D. G. and M. Wood (1984)   Bibliography on Low Temperature Storage of Mammalian Embryos. *Biblio. Reprod.*, **43**(5): A1–A112.

TECHNICAL ISSUES

Introduction

Biotechnology as a scientific endeavor has progressed more rapidly than many knowledgeable individuals expected. Just how rapidly is evidenced in the two papers on applications to laboratory animals and agricultural animals. Complex animals are an extremely demanding area for research and development, demanding because of the inherent complexity of the subjects and the exacting techniques required for the insertion of foreign genomes into the ova and the rearing of a viable animal.

The papers by **Ebert** and by **Hansel** divide the realm into small and large mammals. The division, although somewhat artificial, does make some sense in terms of the technical requirements and the market for the products. Small mammals, notably mice, are a more tractable research target and have the added benefit of being thoroughly studied in the past so that a number of strains with documented and stable traits are available to work with. These strains are, of course, laboratory research animals. A practical outcome of much of this research is indeed the development of further strains of animals, or disease models, specifically adapted for particular lines of research. The recipient of the first animal patent—the "Harvard mouse"—is such a disease model for cancer research (see Appendix 2). Other development work is directed to *in vivo* testing and, of course, basic research.

Ebert reviews the developments to date in laboratory animals, including target hereditary diseases such as dwarfism and Down's syndrome, prototype development for large mammals, and *in vivo* testing of suspected carcinogens. Several impediments to research and patenting in this area of endeavor are identified, including particularly the efficacious placement of the inserted fusion genes and the complexity inherent in making those traits inheritable. The success rates of current gene transfer technologies are far too low, always in the single-digit percentages, and sometimes a fraction of a percent, for it to be economically viable to produce each specimen through direct genetic transfer. Despite these significant challenges, **Ebert** predicts products will be ready for the market in three to five years. This is in addition to the 20-odd animal patent applications currently on file with the US Patent Office, but not all of these products necessarily have practical uses. The achievement of a cherished goal—the development of a disease model for AIDS—is regrettably further off.

Hansel divides the period of applications for larger mammals, that is livestock, into pre- and post-2000. The pre-2000 era will, in his judgement, be dominated by embryo splitting and transfer. These procedures will enhance the availability of progeny from genetically superior females and hence accelerate the selective breeding process, which is the cornerstone of the livestock sector. Embryo transfer is a biotechnology in its broader connotation, but does not involve the transgenetic approach commonly associated with biotechnology.

Transgenetic livestock, **Hansel** projects, will not become widely available until after the year 2000. One of the reasons for this relatively long development period is the limited gene mapping that has been carried out for domestic animals. Thus experiments to date have typically been done using genetic material from rats and mice, or humans. At this time it is unclear if such "foreign" genes will be appropriate for solving the problems that limit the economic components of livestock production: growth, reproduction, lactation, and disease/stress resistance. Despite gaps in knowledge, imaginative approaches have led to advances at the research level in all of the areas of economic significance. Nonetheless the systemized production of commercially viable strains awaits, among other developments, the ability to target the location of the introduced gene sequences. Recent advances in that area of research are very encouraging.

Mammals do not constitute the entire animal kingdom, and it is worth noting that successful transgenic experimentation has been carried out in poultry (disease resistance), fish (growth), and even caterpillars (production of pharmaceuticals). Each application has its own characteristics and difficulties, but procedures and outlook are generally as described herein.

Prospective Developments in Laboratory Animals

Karl M. Ebert

INTRODUCTION

The debate over the patenting of mammalian species was recently spear-headed by the ability to alter the genetic constituents of individual animals through the revolutionary technology of direct transfer of genes into the mammalian embryos immediately following fertilization. Genetic engineering of animals has resulted in phenotypic changes in these "transgenic" animals which can be used as prototypes for the improvement of agricultural livestock species, models for various human and animal diseases, and/or used as the ultimate in *in vivo* testing for the regulation of specific genetic elements through normal regulatory signals or environmental substances that act as mutagens or toxins. The opportunities that are envisioned have stimulated the commercial enterprises to identify a market for these valued animal systems. Securing proprietary rights for the protection of their investments may necessitate the patenting of these animals. This paper will describe how transgenic animals are produced and, through specific examples, outline some of the important areas in biology that are using transgenic laboratory animals.

TRANSGENIC ANIMALS AND PATENTING

Transgenic animals are animals that have received foreign genes directly into the genome, usually by microinjecting the DNA into the nucleus of the embryo shortly after fertilization and prior to the first cell division (Figure 2). The foreign genetic material will generally consist of (1) a structural gene and (2) regulatory sequences necessary for proper transcription of the introduced genes (fusion genes). Introduced into the genome, the foreign gene will be appropriately replicated during cell division and thus will be found in each cell of the developing animal. These genes can ultimately be transferred to its progeny.

A typical outline of the production of transgenic mice is shown in Figure 3. Essentially, zygotes are collected from superovulated female mice. During the microinjection procedure, the zygote is stabilized with a holding pipette and either the male or female pronucleus is injected with approximately 2 pl DNA solution. Of the injected zygotes 50–70 percent survive and are transferred to the oviduct of pseudopregnant females. Young are born and weaned by three weeks of age.

Transgenic Mice

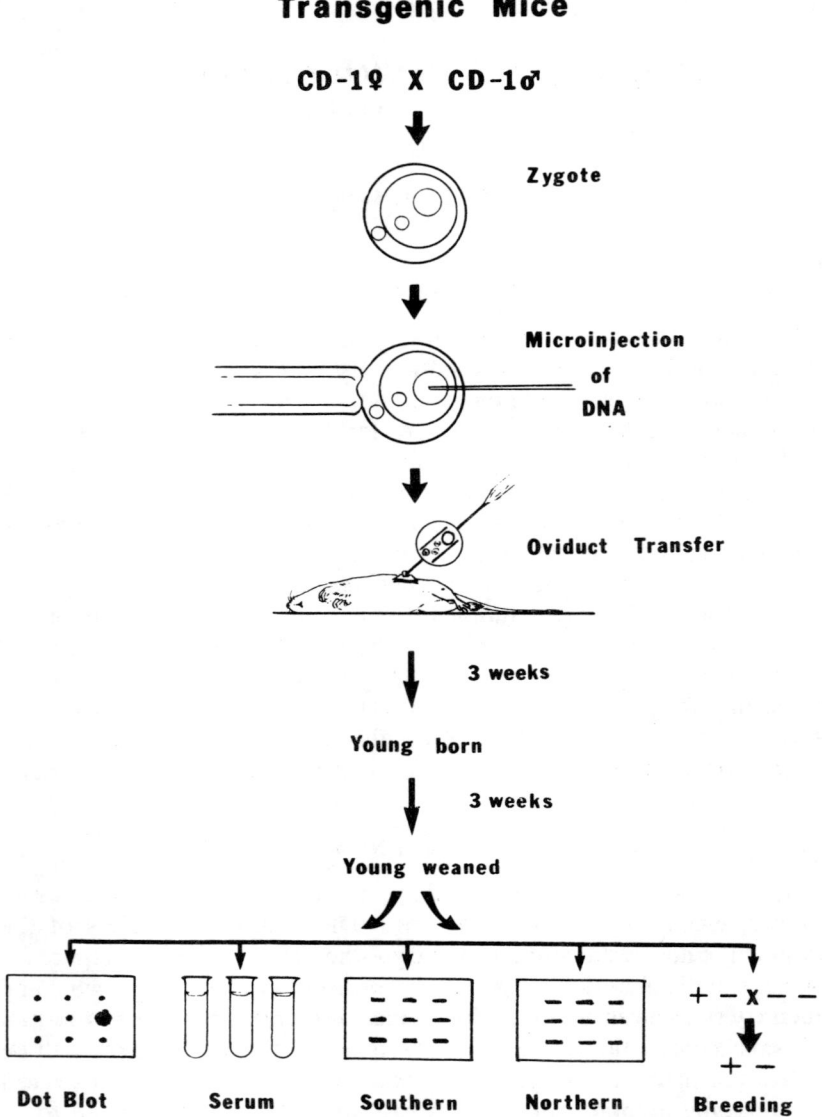

Fig. 2 Production of transgenic mice (Illustration by Thomas E. Smith)

A small section of the tail is used for DNA extraction. Employing that material, transgenic animals are identified by positive Southern dot blot analysis using an appropriate probe that hybridizes specifically to segments within the foreign gene. Southern analysis is performed to determine the arrangement of the foreign gene and whether there was more than one integration site. Northern analysis on various tissues will indicate whether the

WHAT IS A TRANSGENIC ANIMAL ?

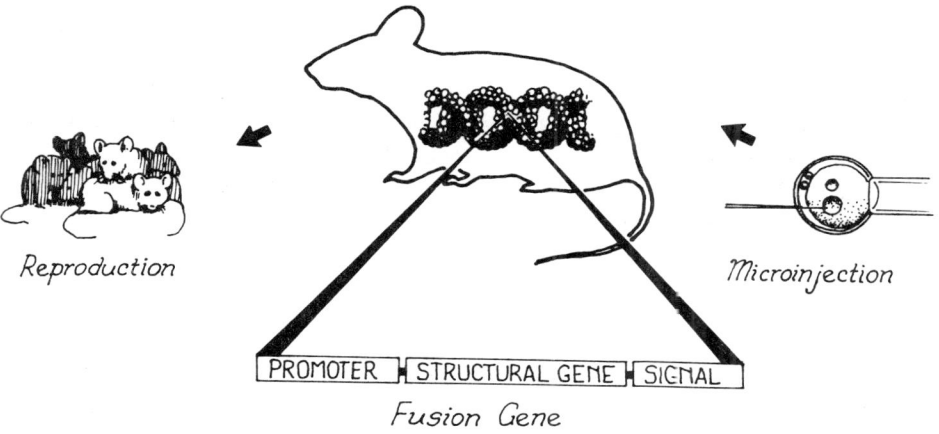

Reproduction

Microinjection

| PROMOTER | STRUCTURAL GENE | SIGNAL |

Fusion Gene

PATENTABLE ?

Fig. 3 What is a transgenic animal? (Illustration by Thomas E. Smith)

fusion gene is transcribed and whether there are specific tissues that selectively transcribe the foreign gene. After using these techniques to identify the
suitable gene-carrying parents, breeding programs are established to develop
lines of similar transgenic animals and to produce homozygous animals for
use or sale.

There are several important features of transgenic animals that may ultimately affect the patentability of these animals.

(1) Each founder animal is a unique animal, and many transgenic animals
that carry the same fusion gene can have dramatic differences in their
expression patterns. Generally, the expression pattern of a given transgenic founder animal will be passed from one generation to another so
that the utility of progeny can vary substantially based on differences in
parentage.

(2) Fusion genes are randomly inserted and, thus, can either enter the
genome in an innocuous location and have no effect on the flanking
genetic elements, or they may become integrated into a vital gene
sequence resulting in a lethal or mutagenic condition. The proportion of
insertions that result in the proper location of the fusion genes for the
expression of the desired traits is very small.

(3) The fusion genes that are engineered for insertion consist of three basic elements: (a) the promoter, (b) the structural gene, and (c) the signal sequences for proper translation. Using a host of restriction endonucleases, researchers have an unlimited number of ways of rearranging these genetic elements. It is often said the major ingredient in the construction of fusion genes is imagination.

(4) The most important element in transgenic animals is the ability to pass the fusion gene and expression patterns to their offspring. This is essential for the development of a subpopulation of animals that may be commercialized at an acceptable cost. The inheritability of this gene and patterns is affected by a number of factors including their location within the genome.

USES OF TRANSGENIC ANIMALS

In order to appreciate the usefulness of transgenic animals, reference will be briefly made to specific examples, and attempts will be made to categorize them according to potential commercial applications.

Basic Research

The majority of the transgenic animals have been produced to study the genetic elements that make up specific genes. Using various combinations of elements within a fusion gene, the investigator can isolate those regions important to the regulation of a gene product. In a major study, Low et al. (1986) have demonstrated that genes containing the metallothionein promoter (MT) and either the somatostatin (SS) cDNA or human growth hormone (hGH) structural gene was expressed in the gonadotrophs of transgenic mice when the genes were fused to identical 3' hGH flanking sequences. These experiments suggested that either the MT promoter sequences or an element within the 3'-hGH fragment was responsible for the identical expression of two independent reporter genes.

Further experiments by Low et al. (1989) have been designed to determine which of the two fragments was responsible for gonadotrophin specific expression. Two additional gene constructs were prepared and transgenic animals produced. Both fusion genes had the SS cDNA as the reporter gene. One gene had the MT promoter replaced by the cytomegalovirus (CMV) early immediate promoter, and the other gene had the 3'-hGH terminal sequences replaced by the semian virus (SV40) signal sequences. When transgenic animals that expressed these genes were compared to the original fusion gene, only the CMV-SS-hGH gene was found to be specifically expressed in gonadotrophs while the MT-SS-SV40 fusion gene was expressed primarily in liver tissue. These experiments suggest that the 3'-hGH fragment contains an unidentified element that confers cell-specific expression to gonadotrophs within the pituitary.

Similar forms of experiments are used routinely to identify the various types of genetic elements that have been isolated (i.e. promoters, enhancers, introns, silencers). Although there is little commercial value in the resultant transgenic animals, very important discoveries identifying combinations of good promoters and active enhancer elements have been made. The maximization and direction of tissue-specific expression are extremely important in the development of commercialized transgenic animals.

Disease Models

Transgenic animals can be used as laboratory models for various diseases. Certain genetic diseases such as hypogonadism, Down's syndrome, thalassemia, and diabetes can be studied in more detail if animal models with similar genetic mutations, duplicated by molecular biological techniques, can be created. A few examples will illustrate the usefulness of transgenic animals for human disease models.

Dwarfism   One of the first genetic disorders that was partially corrected by using transgenic animal models was dwarfism caused by the deficient production of growth hormone mRNA, resulting in reduced serum growth hormone. Hammer *et al.* (1984) inserted the human growth hormone gene into embryos of a genetically deficient mouse strain with a dwarf phenotype. The transgenic dwarf animals grew significantly larger than the normal phenotypic dwarf mutants.

Hypogonadism   Another common hereditary disorder in mammalian species is hypogonadism, which is correlated with failure of pituitary gonadotrophin release. A hypogonadal mouse has been used as an animal model for this disorder for over 10 years. Recently, Mason *et al.* (1986a; 1986b) from Genetech Inc. isolated the normal and abnormal gonadotrophin releasing hormone genes from mice and have identified a deletion in the hypogonadal genes that results in a translationally incompetent mRNA. Proving that this disorder can be corrected requires introduction of the normal gene into these deficient mice and showing that their fecundity was reestablished. Scientists at Genetech produced transgenic mice that, due to their mutant phenotype, would normally not reproduce. The transgenic mice containing the intact normal gonadotrophin-releasing hormone fusion gene expressed this gene, resulting in the complete reversal of the hypogonadal phenotype (Mason *et al.*, 1986b).

It may be difficult to envision a commercial application for these particular experimental designs. However, such experiments do document a potential use for gene therapy for correcting disorders manifested by mutated genes.

Down's syndrome   Another use for transgenic laboratory animals is the development of models that simulate the symptoms or pathogenesis of the disease. The generation of a line of animals that can be thoroughly studied for

65

potential therapeutic testing could result in a valuable model for extrapolation to other species. An example of this line of research is the development of a transgenic animal model for Down's syndrome. Epstein *et al.* (1987) have introduced a gene containing the human Cu/Zn superoxide dismutase sequences into transgenic mice. The expression of the gene increases the activity of the superoxide dismutase, as in the case in Down's syndrome individuals. Thus, these transgenic animals offer a unique model to study the correlation of increased dosage of Cu/Zn superoxide dismutase to clinical symptoms that occur in patients with Down's syndrome.

PROTOTYPES

A second major role for transgenic animals is their ability to document the feasibility of developing livestock species with improved qualities or for use in an alternative capacity aside from food production. Transgenic mice, therefore, can serve as prototypes of potential commercially important livestock species. Two examples that received considerable publicity in the last few years are mice engineered to grow faster and larger, and mice able to produce pharmaceuticals in their milk.

Palmiter *et al.* (1982) developed mice that expressed a fusion gene containing the rat growth hormone gene. Specimens with high levels of rat growth hormone in their serum grew significantly larger than their non-transgenic littermates. These exciting experiments had implications for studying the complex biological effects of growth hormone, as well as for developing livestock species with accelerated growth. Subsequent work has shown that transgenic animals expressing growth hormone, growth hormone releasing factors, or the insulin-like growth factor I will cause mice to grow at an accelerated rate. Success with these animals suggests that similar phenotypic alterations can be achieved in economically important domestic species and, moreover, can be used to validate a potential patent on this process. To date, transgenic swine that contain and express the rat growth hormone or the porcine growth hormone genes have been produced (Ebert *et al.*, 1988). These animals did not grow at an accelerated rate, but did exhibit dramatic changes in their carcass composition with a significant decrease in body fat deposition.

Another potential use for transgenic animals is in the production of large quantities of biologically important drugs or pharmaceuticals secreted in their milk. These substances can be separated from the milk in quantities that would be more economical than *in vitro* culture systems. With the production of transgenic mice prototypes, Pittius *et al.* (1988) demonstrated the feasibility of this alternative method of producing and harvesting pharmaceuticals, in this case tissue plasminogen activator (TPA). Subsequently, similar experiments have been carried out in sheep by Simons *et al.* (1988).

IN VIVO TESTING

Finally, transgenic laboratory animals may be extremely useful for *in vivo* mutagenesis and carcinogenesis testing. The present *in vitro* mutagenesis tests, such as the mouse lymphoma cell L5178Y (Myer *et al.*, 1985) or Sister chromatid exchange induction in Chinese hamster ovary cells may not correlate well with rodent carcinogenicity tests (Galloway *et al.*, 1985). Transgenic animals designed to express a reporter gene as a result of a mutagenic event could be extremely valuable in the detection of the early effects of suspected carcinogens. This approach will be feasible if appropriate fusion genes can be designed whose products are detected early during development and localized by *in situ* analysis in organs or tissues that are likely to be affected by the mutagenic substance.

As the fusion genes that would effectively produce this mutagenic model are under patent application, these genes will not be further discussed. However, some recent experiments carried out in Dr Malcolm Low's laboratory at the New England Medical Center, Boston, Massachusetts, in collaboration with the laboratory at Tufts University, School of Veterinary Medicine in Grafton, Massachusetts show how transgenic animals can be used for early detection of the expression of fusion genes and *in situ* localization of reporter products. The β-galactosidase gene is being used as a reporter to detect the tissue-specific elements that are responsible for somatostatin expression. Although, at present, there is no complete correlation between the expression of the reporter gene and the appropriate tissues that normally produce somatostatin, the method of analysis of the expression of this fusion gene is a good example of the usefulness of this approach to study the early detection of mutagenic events in transgenic animals.

Transgenic mice containing the putative somatostatin promoter elements fused to the β-galactosidase reporter gene have been generated. Adults incorporating the transgene were bred to normal mice. At various times during gestation, whole fetuses were removed and analyzed for the expression of β-galactosidase. Expression was then correlated with anatomically distinct organs and tissues. In addition, further analysis of selective organs and tissues allows the identification of the cell type that is producing the reporter gene product. This type of analysis of gene regulation during development offers a powerful tool for studying normal and abnormal genetic events at the cellular level and, more importantly, in an *in vivo* test system.

CONCLUSION

Although the transgenic mouse model is not the only prospect for patenting animals, it certainly is the most contemporary example of how biotechnology will influence the establishment of the need to patent animal species. The award of the patent on transgenic non-human mammals to Drs Leder and Stewart, and the recent announcement that transgenic mice which develop breast cancer are to be marketed by Charles River Laboratories under contract with DuPont, underlines the certainty that transgenic animals will have commercial application. Genetically engineered models, such as the OncoMice and similar animals that produce other diseases such as AIDS, are obvious candidates for commercialization. Also, during the next few years commercially important modified animal species may be produced that will provide us with a more accurate and sensitive sentinel strategy for mutagenic and carcinogenic testing. These two areas may represent potential commercialization of laboratory species. However, the most promising commercial application of biotechnology may reside in our domestic species. The production of pharmaceuticals that are difficult to produce in large quantities with the current culture systems may be produced in the milk of transgenic livestock more efficiently and thus more economically. In addition, genetically altered livestock may be developed such that they will be resistant to the common diseases that pose an economic drain on our agricultural species or increase their feed conversion ratios so significantly to be economically important. Although the latter examples are more long-term possibilities, it is expected that commercially viable livestock species will be available within the next three to five years. The potential uses of transgenic animals are many. The commercialization, although speculative, remains realistically viable.

References

Ebert, K. M., M. J. Low, E. W. Overstrom, F. C. Buonomo, C. A. Baile, T. M. Roberts, A. Lee, G. Mandel, and R. H. Goodman (1988) A Moloney MLV-Rat Somatotropin Fusion Gene Produces Biologically Active Somatotropin in a Transgenic Pig. *Mol. Endocrinol.*, **2**: 277.

Epstein, C. J., K. B. Avraham, M. Lovett, S. Smith, O. Elroy-Stein, G. Rotman, C. Bry, and Y. Groner (1987) Transgenic Mice with Increased Cu/Zn-Superoxide Dismutase Activity: Animal Model of Dosage Effects in Down Syndrome. *Proc. Natl Acad. Sci.*, **84**: 8044.

Galloway, S. (1985) Development of a Standard Protocol for *in vitro* Cytogenetic Testing with Chinese Hamster Ovary Cells: Comparisons of Results for 22 Compounds in Two Laboratories. *Environ. Mutagen*, **7**: 1.

Hammer, R. E., R. D. Palmiter, and R. L. Brinster (1984) Partial Correction of Murine Hereditary Growth Disorder by Germ-Line Incorporation of a New Gene. *Nature*, **311**: 65.

Low, M. J., R. H. Goodman, and K. M. Ebert (1989) Cryptic Sequences in the Human Growth Hormone Gene Direct Gonadotroph-Specific Expression. (submitted.)

Low, M. J., R. M. Lechan, R. E. Hammer, R. L. Brinster, J. F. Habener, G. Mandel, and R. H. Goodman (1986) Gonadotroph-Specific Expression of Metallothionein Fusion Genes in Pituitaries of Transgenic Mice. *Science*, **231**: 1002 *et seq.*

Mason, A. J., J. S. Hayflick, R. T. Zoeller, W. S. Young III, H. S. Phillips, K. Nikolics, and P. H. Seeburg (1986a) A Deletion Truncating the Gonadotropin-Releasing Hormone Gene is Responsible for Hypogonadism in the Mouse. *Science*, **234**: 1366.

Mason, A. J., S. L. Pitts, K. Nikolics, E. Szonyi, J. N. Wilcox, P. H. Seeburg, and T. A. Stewart (1986b) The Hypogonadal Mouse: Reproductive Functions Restored by Gene Therapy. *Science*, **234**: 1372.

Myer, B., L. Bowers, and W. Caspary (1985) Report of the International Program on Chemical Safety's Collaborative Study on *in vitro* Assays in *Evaluation of Short-Term Tests for Carcinogens*. Progess and Mutation Research Series, vol. 5, ed. J. Ashby *et al*. Amsterdam: Elsevier, p. 555.

Palmiter, R. D., R. L. Brinster, R. E. Hammer, M. E. Trumbauer, M. G. Rosenfeld, N. C. Birnberg, and R. M. Evans (1982) Dramatic Growth of Mice that Develop from Eggs Microinjected with Metallothionein-Growth Hormone Fusion Genes. *Nature*, **300**: 611.

Pittius, C. W., L. Henninghauser, E. Lee, H. Westphal, E. Nicols, J. Vitale, and K. Gordon (1988) A Milk Protein Gene Promoter Directs the Expression of Human Tissue Plasminogen Activator cDNA to the Mammary Gland in Transgenic Mice. *Proc. Natl Acad. Sci.*, **85**: 5874.

Simons, J. P., I. Wilmut, A. J. Clark, A. L. Archibald, J. O. Bishop, and R. Lathe (1988) Gene Transfer into Sheep. *Biotechnology*, **6**: 179.

Prospective Developments in Animal Agriculture

William Hansel

INTRODUCTION

Technology has made US agriculture one of the world's most productive and competitive enterprises. Animal agriculture represents a large part of this enterprise, contributing nearly two-thirds of the protein, one-third of the energy, and a major portion of the essential minerals and vitamins in the daily US diet (Gerrits *et al.*, 1979). Animal products also supply nearly half of the fat in our daily diet, and the linkage of cholesterol and saturated fats of the type that predominate in animal products to the development of athero-sclerosis and cardiovascular problems has resulted in a decline in the average daily consumption of meat and eggs. Thus, the objectives in genetic engineer-ing research on domestic animals are not only to produce more efficient animals, but to change the nature of the products they produce to meet better consumer demands.

Three basic physiological processes—growth, reproduction, and lact-ation—are responsible for most of the animal traits that have economic value. These include the production of meat, milk, hides, and glandular products. Additionally, disease resistance and resistance to non-specific stresses are traits of great economic importance. Nearly all of the current activities in animal genetic engineering are focused in these five areas.

In 1986, 92 firms in the USA were known to be engaged in some form of animal biotechnology and development; nearly two-thirds were new companies and one-half of them were engaged in producing genetically engineered products. However, 35 percent of these companies were develop-ing animals or products for improvement of growth, reproduction, and lact-ation. The animal component of the biotechnology industry is characterized by extensive interaction between and among public and private sector organ-izations. The Cornell Biotechnology Program, which integrates the efforts of New York State, several large corporations, and a federal agency, is an excellent example of such cooperative activities.

GENETIC ENGINEERING FOR IMPROVED REPRODUCTIVE PERFORMANCE

In 1986 it was stated that by the year 2000 an animal breeding system will have been developed in which natural breeding and artificial insemination will be replaced, at least in part, by a system of artificial inembryonation (Hansel,

1986). In this system bovine embryos, produced by fertilization of ova from genetically superior females will be fertilized *in vivo* or *in vitro* with sperm from selected males, the embryos will be split (two for one) and stored frozen until needed. Later, these embryos will be transferred by non-surgical techniques into the uteri of groups of recipient cattle whose estrous cycles have been synchronized with the stage of development of the embryos. As a result of development of new methods for selecting embryos and reducing early embryonic death losses, conception rates of these "inembryonated" animals will likely be higher than those now being obtained by either artificial or natural matings.

Beginning at about the year 2000, genetically engineered embryos containing genes that will result in faster growth rates, leaner carcasses, greater disease resistance, improved lactational performance and other desirable traits are likely to become available.

A series of remarkable biotechnological advances involving embryo manipulations has occurred in recent years. When coupled with the already established techniques of superovulation and estrous cycle synchronization, these advances will likely result in a number of important changes in the animal industries before the year 2000. Non-surgical collection of embryos from superovulated cattle has become a well-established practice, and non-surgical transfers to recipient animals result in pregnancy rates only slightly lower than those resulting from surgical transfers. Systems for estrous cycle regulation that allow successful insemination of cattle at predetermined times without checking for estrus have been developed (Hansel and Convey, 1983).

A successful technique for sexing bovine embryos has been reported (Anderson, 1986) and several workable methods for freezing and storing embryos have been reported (Leibo, 1986). The feasibility of transferring frozen embryos into the uteri of groups of cycle-synchronized heifers is now being tested. Splitting of single seven-day blastocysts into two identical twin half embryos has been achieved (see Donahue, 1986) and may soon become a routine procedure in embryo transfer operations. All of these techniques, and especially the methodology for superovulation, need to be improved and adapted for use in the field. However, it is expected that these improvements will occur rapidly. It appears likely that these biotechnological advances, along with increased use of hormones and drugs produced by recombinant technology, will occur during the next decade. We will probably have the capability to transfer significant numbers of genetically engineered embryos by the year 2000, or perhaps sooner.

Traits such as reproductive performance in domestic animals are influenced by a number of genes. For the most part we do not know the number of genes involved in expression of a given quantitative trait, how each gene contributes, or where it is located on the chromosomes. Modern methods of gene mapping have generally not been applied to domestic animals. Indeed, most gene maps for domestic animals consist of only a few linkage groups and, in most cases, are not assigned to specific chromosomes.

71

Nevertheless, recombinant DNA techniques and the development of embryo transfer techniques have opened the way for the introduction of specific genes into animals. As a result of a series of pioneering studies by Gordon *et al.* (1980), Brinster *et al.* (1981), Wagner *et al.* (1981), and Gordon and Ruddle (1981), among others, Palmiter *et al.* (1982) were finally able to alter the phenotype of an animal by the introduction of recombinant DNA. In this series of experiments, the rat growth hormone gene was fused to the same mouse metallothionein I regulatory promoter sequence that had been used in their earlier studies of the Herpes simplex thymidine kinase gene. The introduction of the growth hormone fusion gene to transgenic mice resulted in animals that grew faster and for a longer time than litter mates which did not possess the fusion gene.

The commercial possibilities of this achievement were obvious, and attempts to produce transgenic animals having improved reproductive capacities, increased growth rates, improved lactational performance, and increased disease resistance were initiated throughout the world. A variety of methods for producing transgenic animals are available. These include microinjection of recombinant DNA into the pronuclei of recently fertilized eggs, introduction of the gene construct into fertilized ova or blastocysts by retroviral infections, and introduction of the gene in embryonic stem cells or primordial germ cells, which are then recolonized and introduced into an embryo.

Selection of the genes of choice for producing domestic animals having improved reproductive performance is a difficult task and is best approached in terms of solving the major problems limiting reproductive efficiency. These problems may be characterized as follows:

(1) low ovulation rates;
(2) limited breeding seasons;
(3) delayed puberty;
(4) prolonged postpartum anestrus, often associated with lactation or suckling;
(5) high early embryonic death losses.

Attempts to increase ovulation rates in ewes, cows, and sows have generally involved administration of combinations of the pituitary gonadotrophins follicle-stimulating hormone (FSH) and luteinizing hormone (LH). These are the hormones that control follicle growth, ovulation, and corpus luteum formation and function in the ovary (Figure 4). Techniques that reduce the negative feedback of the ovarian steroids on secretion of these hormones may also be used to increase ovulation rate. For example, immunization of animals against testosterone and estradiol is an effective way to increase ovulation rate in sheep and cattle.

All of the glycoprotein reproductive hormones (FSH and LH), as well as thyroid-stimulating hormone (TSH), consist of two dissimilar non-covalently

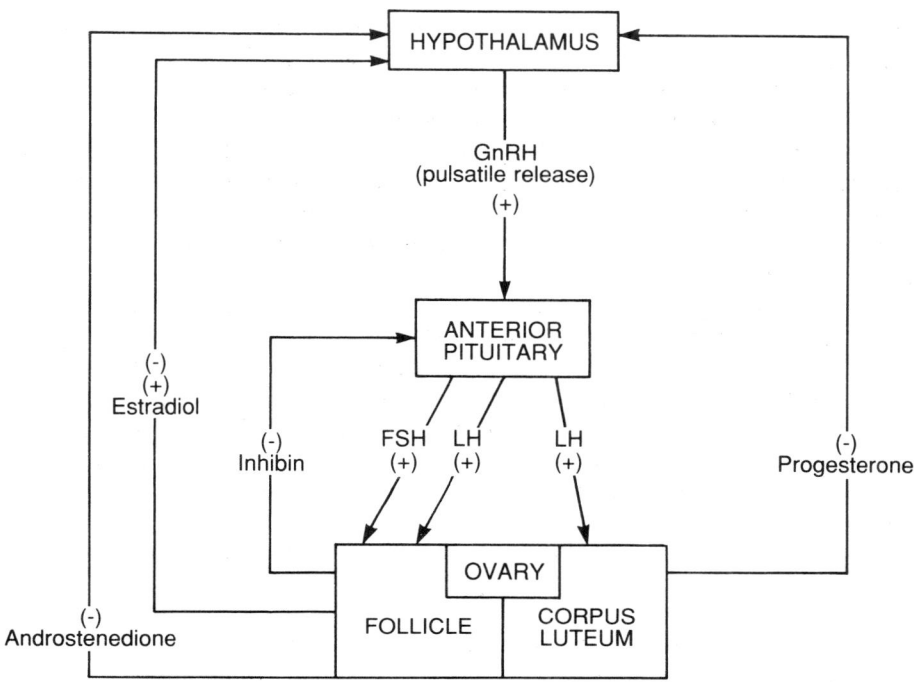

Fig. 4　A diagrammatic representation of the hormonal control of ovarian function

associated subunits (α and β). Within a species, these hormones share a common α-subunit; the β-subunits are unique and confer hormone specificity. The chorionic gonadotrophins (hCG and eCG) are synthesized by placental cells, and the β-subunits of these hormones have glycosylated COOH-terminal extensions of approximately 30 residues that are not present in the β-subunits of other pituitary glycoprotein hormones. The genes for all of the glycoprotein β-subunits have now been cloned, and the possibilities for introducing one or more of them into animal embryos are being explored. The genes controlling production of the placental gonadotrophins hCG and eCG are of particular interest, since these hormones differ in their relative FSH and LH potencies, and introduction of these genes could alter the relative proportions of FSH and LH secreted by the transgenic animals. The structural features of the genes for α- and β-subunits of bovine LH have been described, and expression vectors for each have been made and introduced into ovarian cell lines (Nilson and Kaetsel, 1987).

One of the most exciting possibilities for increasing ovulation rate involves manipulation of the levels of inhibin produced by the granulosa cells in the ovarian follicle. The purification and characterization of inhibin have been described in detail by, for example, de Jong (1987) and Findlay and Clarke (1987), and it appears that three genes code for the subunits of inhibin present in the ovary. Cloning and sequencing of a DNA for inhibin have confirmed the similarity of the genes coding for inhibin among different species and underlined the extensive homology of the subunits among species. In addition, there is significant homology between the β-subunit of inhibin and transforming growth factor B (TGF-B). TGF-B specifically stimulates FSH secretion. The molecule responsible for this stimulation was found to consist of a homo- or hetero-dimer of inhibin β-subunits. It is not known whether this dimer of inhibin (sometimes referred to as activin) can reach the circulation in quantities large enough to affect FSH secretion.

These findings point to the need to devise methods to inhibit or decrease the function of certain specific genes in order to influence physiological responses in desirable ways. In a sense, the Booroola ewe (a highly prolific strain of Merino sheep in Australia) may be considered to be a natural example for genetic engineering. These ewes have developed a mechanism (the F gene) for suppressing one or more of the inhibin genes in order to achieve a higher ovulation rate. Booroola ewes have been shown to produce less inhibin and, consequently, more FSH than less prolific breeds of sheep.

Simons and Land (1987) have suggested that neutralization of an inhibitor gene, such as the inhibin gene might be achieved by "anti-sense" gene expression. The first step in gene expression is transcription or synthesis of messenger RNA (mRNA), using one of the gene's strands, the coding strand, as a template; the mRNA is a "sense" transcript. Normally, the complementary strand is not transcribed. By rearranging the gene, expression of the complementary strand can be obtained. This transcribed anti-sense RNA and the mRNA from the coding strand are complementary and thus can hybridize forming a double stranded RNA that will interfere with subsequent steps of gene expression, including RNA processing, export from the nucleus and translation. A large excess of anti-sense RNA over mRNA is required. Thus, anti-sense methods may result in a reduction of gene expression, rather than total inhibition. In the case of inhibin, this would likely be a desirable result.

Factors that control initiation of the estrous cycle at the time of puberty, at the beginning of the breeding season in seasonal breeders, and following parturition in lactating animals are thought by some to be of even more economic importance than factors that control the ovulation rate. Obviously, initiation of cyclicity is influenced by many genes, but a common denominator in all of the research results presented to date is an increase in the frequency and amplitude of pulsatile LH secretion which occurs before initiation of cyclicity. This increase in the frequency of the LH pulse is directly attributable to increases in the frequency of gonadotrophin-releasing hormone (GnRH) pulses (Figure 4). Although the factors controlling the GnRH "pulse generator" are not yet well understood, the potential for manipulating the GnRH gene is obvious.

A single gene encodes the precursor protein for the decapeptide GnRH and an associated 56-amino acid peptide (GnRH-associated peptide, GAP). These peptides are released at intervals into the portal circulation between the hypothalamus and the pituitary, where they cause release of both LH and FSH, and inhibit prolactin secretion. Failure of this system leads to hypogonadism, in several species, often associated with increased blood levels of prolactin. A strain of hypogonadal mice has been identified in which the failure of the ovaries or testes to develop normally has been linked to a failure of expression of the GnRH gene. Mason *et al.* (1986) showed that this condition is due to a mutation resulting in deletion of at least 33.5 kilobases, encompassing the distal half of the gene for the common biosynthetic precursor of GnRH and GAP. These workers then introduced an intact GnRH gene into the genome of these mutant mice and completely reversed the mutant hypogonadal genotype. Transgenic hypogonadal homozygotes of both sexes were capable of mating and producing offspring; pituitary and blood concentrations of LH, FSH, and prolactin were restored to normal. The hypogonadal mouse is an excellent model for hypogonadism in man and domestic animals.

Nett (1987) has shown that the high circulating levels of estradiol and progesterone which occur during pregnancy result in inhibition of the synthesis of LH by the anterior pituitary, resulting in a depletion of pituitary stores of LH. These steroids inhibit GnRH secretion by the hypothalamus; however, the mechanism for releasing LH remains functional throughout pregnancy. Removal of the fetoplacental unit at parturition results in a dramatic decrease in the levels of estradiol and progesterone in the circulation, and removal of this negative feedback influence on the hypothalamus allows a gradual recovery of gonadotrophin production. Nett (1987) has also shown that, in sheep, the first detectable change during the postpartum period is an increase in pituitary concentrations of the mRNA for the α- and β-subunits of LH. Thus, animals that produce higher concentrations of GnRH during the early postpartum period have shorter postpartum intervals. These results suggest that manipulation of the GnRH gene through transgenic animals is indeed a promising tool for producing animals that undergo earlier puberty, have longer breeding seasons or return to estrus sooner after parturition. These are only a few examples of ways in which genetic engineering is being used to manipulate the hormones controlling reproduction in domestic animals.

GENETIC ENGINEERING FOR IMPROVED GROWTH RATES AND CARCASS CHARACTERISTICS

As is the case for reproduction, the major developments in improving efficiency of growth and carcass characteristics in meat animals between now and the year 2000 will probably come about as a result of the use of genetically engineered products. However, by the year 2000, and perhaps earlier, significant numbers of genetically engineered animals with improved feed efficiencies and that produce carcasses which are lower in fat, higher in protein and contain a much greater proportion of lean meat will reach the market. These changes will occur in response to consumer demands for leaner meat; fortunately, they will also result in improved efficiencies in the conversion of feed to product.

An insight into the nature of these developments can be gained by examining the results of recent experiments in which the growth hormone and the growth hormone-releasing factor, both of which can be produced by recombinant DNA technology, have been administered to growing sheep, cattle, and swine. In order to appreciate fully the significance of these results, one must understand some of the interactions between the major hormones that control the growth process. The hormones involved are growth hormone itself, produced by the pituitary gland, two hormonal factors of hypothalamic origin—growth hormone-releasing factor and somatostatin, which stimulate and inhibit, respectively, the secretion of growth hormone—and a factor produced by the liver, called somatomedin, which is directly responsible for a number of the growth hormone effects (Figure 5). The genes for all of these

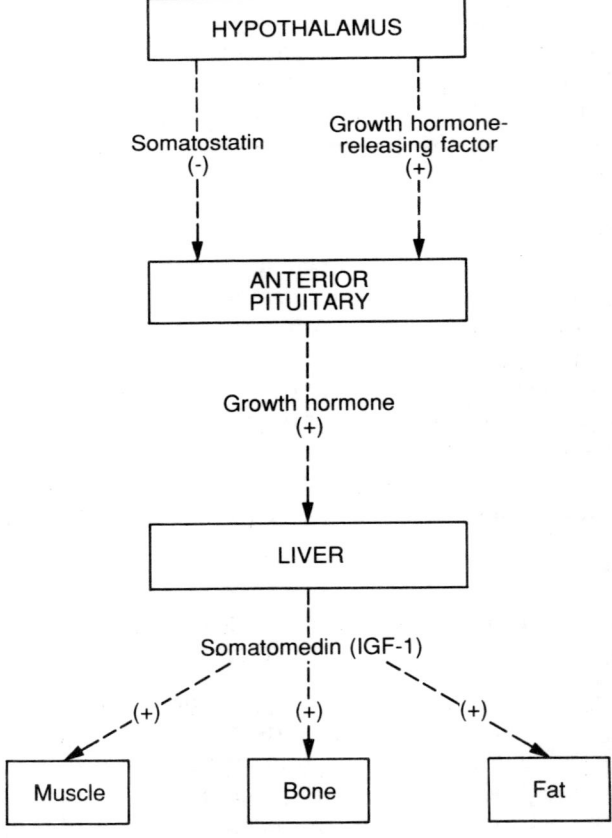

Fig. 5 A diagrammatic representation of the hormonal control of growth hormone secretion and its effects on various tissues

hormones or factors have now been cloned; both porcine and bovine growth hormone are produced by recombinant DNA technology, and it is expected that they will be marketed in the near future.

In a recent experiment (Boyd *et al.*, 1986), crossbred pigs were allotted to five treatment groups receiving 0, 30, 60, 120, and 220 μg/kg body weight of porcine growth hormone daily. Pigs receiving the growth hormone grew up to 19 percent faster and were 29 percent more efficient in feed conversion. This increase in efficiency was due to a marked decline in carcass lipid (−55 percent), and a marked increase in nitrogen retention (+27 percent). These remarkable decreases in fat and increases in muscle mass are illustrated in Table 3.

Table 3 Effect of growth hormone dose on carcass measures and selected ham muscle weights

	Dose[a] (μg/kg)				
Item	0	30	60	120	200
Number of Pigs	8	8	8	8	8
Backfat[b] (cm)	2.74	2.51	2.39	2.13	1.83
Loin eye area (cm^2)	33.7	34.6	35.3	37.0	37.8
Semimembranosus[c] (g)	889	877	949	1011	1013
Semitendinosus[c] (g)	406	418	415	474	466

[a] Treatment period between 45 and 100 kg.
[b] Average of first, last rib and last lumbar vertebra. Linear effect ($P<0.01$).
[c] Treatment linear and quadratic ($P<0.05$).

(Source: Boyd *et al.*, 1986)

Similar effects have been reported for cattle and sheep treated with bovine growth hormone produced by recombinant DNA techniques. "Slow-release" vehicles that extend the effects of single treatments over several weeks have now been developed, but further improvements in methods for administering the hormone are needed.

Similar experiments in which domestic animals have received frequent injections of the growth hormone-releasing hormone have also been carried out. Results of these experiments indicate that injection of this hormone at intervals of approximately four hours causes treated animals to release growth hormone in amounts sufficient to cause gains in feed efficiency, and increased lean meat and decreased fat in the carcass, as described for growth hormone itself. These desirable changes occurred in the treated animals, despite the fact that blood concentration of the growth hormone were elevated for only about one hour after each injection of the growth hormone-releasing factor. Improvements in growth rates and carcass characteristics have also been reported for domestic animals that had been immunized against somatostatin, the hypothalamic hormone that normally inhibits growth hormone secretion.

Genes for all of these growth regulating hormones have been cloned and all are candidates for gene transfer. Transgenic pigs, sheep, goats, and chickens that express the transferred growth hormone gene have been produced in a number of laboratories in Australia, Europe and the USA (Hammer *et al.*, 1985; Michalska *et al.*, 1986). Although relatively little information has been published, some of these animals clearly show growth characteristics similar to those that occur in response to the growth hormone treatments described above. In many of these transgenic animals the metallothionein gene has been used as a "promoter" for the growth hormone gene. Since the metallo-thionein gene is activated by certain heavy metals (most notably zinc), it may be possible to regulate the secretion of growth hormone by controlling the animal's intake of the appropriate heavy metals. Clearly, better methods for regulating the transferred genes are needed. In all cases, the growth hormone is produced by tissues other than the pituitary gland (mainly the liver), and thus is not susceptible to the normal feedback control mechanisms. As was the case for inhibin, the production of transgenic animals that produce less somatostatin by use of the "anti-sense" technique described above is a possibility.

Unfortunately, the success rate in producing transgenic domestic animals is quite low and many problems concerning factors that regulate expression of the transferred genes remain to be solved. However, it is estimated that most of these problems will be solved by the year 2000 and that significant numbers of transgenic animals in which the growth-related genes are regulated will become available by that time.

GENETIC ENGINEERING FOR IMPROVED LACTATIONAL PERFORMANCE

Like growth and reproduction, lactation is controlled by a number of gene products. However, it has been known since about 1950 (Folley, 1956) that growth hormone is the major pituitary factor controlling milk yield. Recently, daily recombinant growth hormone (somatotrophin) injections have been

Table 4 Effect of exogenous somatotrophin on yield and composition of milk

Variable[a]	Pituitary bovine somatotrophin		Recombinant bovine somatotrophin			
	Control	(27.0mg/day)	(13.5mg/day)	(27.0mg/day)	(40.5mg/day)	SE
Cows (*n*)	6	6	6	6		
FCM (kg/day)[b]	27.9[c]	32.5[c,d]	34.4[d,e]	38.0[e]	39.4[e]	1.8
Milk fat (%)	3.6	3.3	3.8	3.6	3.6	.1
Milk protein (%)	3.4	3.4	3.4	3.4	3.4	.1
Milk lactose (%)	4.8	4.8	4.9	4.8	4.9	.1

[a] Treatment period was 188 days commencing at 84 ± 10 days postpartum. Response data (weekly means) were adjusted by covariance analysis using each individual cow's response during the excipient period.
[b] FCM = 3.5 percent fat-corrected milk.
[c,d,e] Means in same row different superscripts differ ($P < 0.05$).

(Source: Bauman *et al.*, 1985)

shown (Table 4) to increase milk yield in high producing Holstein cows from 23 to 41 percent over control animals (Bauman *et al.*, 1985).

Transgenic animals containing additional copies of the growth hormone gene, the growth hormone-releasing hormone gene, or insulin-like growth factor may also have increased milk yields. However, transfer of the growth hormone gene into cattle has not yet been reported. The gene for prolactin, another pituitary hormone that is primarily involved in lactogenesis (the initiation of milk secretion), is yet another candidate for gene transfer. Animals bearing twin or triplet fetuses develop larger mammary glands during pregnancy than animals bearing single fetuses. This is thought to be an effect of the higher levels of placental hormones, such as placental lactogen, produced by animals with multiple pregnancies. Accordingly, attempts will be made to inject placental lactogen during pregnancy and to produce transgenic animals containing the placental lactogen gene in an attempt to develop larger mammary glands during pregnancy and increase milk production after parturition.

Attempts are also being made to transfer the genes that control expression of enzymes in the mammary gland that desaturate lipids in order to produce milk with a higher proportion of unsaturated fats and lower proportion of saturated fats. Although the major milk protein, casein, is nutritionally one of the highest-quality proteins found in nature, genetic engineering of the major casein polypeptide families may be used to alter the proportion of the various caseins to yield novel dairy products.

In addition to using genetic-engineering techniques to alter the normal constituents of milk, there is the possibility of introducing genes controlling the production of highly specific compounds that are difficult or expensive to produce by recombinant DNA technology. Some compounds that might be produced in this way are the interferons, growth factors, such as epidermal growth factor, fibroblast growth factor and transforming growth factor, and enzymes. These animals would be "living factories" and, in contrast to the proteins produced by transformed bacteria, the protein molecules they produce would probably not require further processing before use. It may even be possible to produce certain pharmaceutical drugs in this way.

GENETIC ENGINEERING TO IMPROVE DISEASE RESISTANCE AND RESISTANCE TO STRESS

Recombinant DNA and monoclonal antibody techniques are being widely used to develop new types of vaccines to supplement and, in some cases, supplant conventional ones. Similarly, the application of recombinant DNA, monoclonal antibody and immunoassay techniques to develop improved methods for disease diagnosis is proceeding rapidly. However, relatively few attempts appear to have been made to produce transgenic animals with increased disease resistance. The interferon genes are obvious candidates and attempts to introduce them into laboratory and farm animals to enhance resistance to viral infections are under way. Relatively little is known of the genes that impart resistance to stress in farm animals, but this is clearly an area of great economic importance.

SOME NEW DEVELOPMENTS

Until recently, it has not been possible to control where transferred genes would be incorporated into the genome. However, recent advances in targeted gene expression may solve this problem. Direction of transferred genes to a specific site in the genome requires that the vector used to introduce the new gene into cells carry nucleotide sequences identical to those of the DNA at the site where the new gene is to be integrated. In some fashion, these shared nucleotide sequences assist the vector in finding the desired location and in exchanging its genetic material with the DNA there. This process is called homologous recombination (Marx, 1988).

Although the frequency of targeted gene transfer is low, improved methods for selecting the cells that acquire the transferred gene in the correct location have recently been developed. These methods of targeted gene transfer can be used to introduce foreign DNA into a gene to either inactivate it or repair it in cells in which it is defective. By the use of embryonic stem cells, it is possible to produce chimeric animals that contain the gene of interest which has been inserted or modified by targeted gene transfer. The targeted gene transfer is carried out in cultured embryonic stem cells, which are then transferred back into embryos in which both the normal embryo cells and the stem cells contribute to the developing tissues. If the embryonic stem cells contribute to the production of germ cells in the chimeras, it will be possible to develop pure lines of animals bearing the altered genes. The potential to inactivate genes such as those for inhibin and somatostatin by gene targeting in embryonic stem cells may be of particular significance for domestic animals. The ability to carry out targeted gene transfers is likely to have a great impact on the production of transgenic domestic animals.

References

Anderson, G. B. (1986) Identification of Sex in Mammalian Embryos. In: *Genetic Engineering in Animals*, ed. J. W. Evans and A. Hollaender. New York: Plenum Press, pp. 242–50.

Bauman, D. E., P. J. Eppard, M. J. DeGeeter, and G. M. Lanza (1985) Responses of High-Producing Dairy Cows to Long-Term Treatment with Pituitary Somatotropin and Recombinant Somatotropin. *J. Dairy Sci.*, **68**: 1352–62.

Boyd, R. D., D. E. Bauman, D. H. Beerman, A. F. Deneergard, L. Souza, and H. T. Kuntz (1986) *Proc. Cornell Nutrit. Conf.*, Ithaca, NY, pp. 24–8.

Brinster, R. L., H. Y. Chen, M. Trumbaueer, A. W. Senear, R. Warren, and R. D. Palmiter (1981) Somatic Expression of Herpes Thymidine Kinase in Mice Following Injection of a Fusion Gene into Eggs. *Cell.*, **27**: 223–31.

de Jong, F. H. (1987) Inhibin—Its Nature, Site of Production and Function. *Oxford*

Reviews of Reproductive Biology, vol. 9. New York: Oxford University Press, pp. 1–53.

Donahue, S. E. (1986) A Technique for Bisection of Embryos to Produce Identical Twins. In: *Genetic Engineering of Animals*, ed. J. W. Evans and A. Hollaender. New York: Plenum Press, pp. 163–73.

Findlay, J. K. and I. J. Clark (1987) Regulation of the Secretion of FSH in Domestic Ruminants. *J. Reprod. Fert., Suppl.*, **34**: 27–37.

Folley, S. J. (1956) *The Physiology and Biochemistry of Lactation*. Springfield: Charles C. Thomas Publisher, pp. 47–72.

Gerrits, R. J., T. H. Blosser, H. G. Purchase, C. E. Terrel, and E. J. Warwick (1979) Economics of Improving Reproductive Efficiency in Farm Animals. In: *Beltsville Symposia in Agricultural Research (3) Animal Reproduction*. Montclair, NJ: Allenheld, Osman.

Gordon, J. W. and F. H. Ruddle (1981) Integration and Stable Transmission of Genes Injected into Mouse Pronuclei. *Science*, **214**: 1244–6.

Gordon, J. W., G. A. Scangos, D. J. Plotkin, J. A. Barbosa, and F. H. Ruddle (1980) Genetic Transformation of Mouse Embryos by Microinjection of Purified DNA. *Proc. Natl Acad. Sci.*, **77**: 7380–84.

Hammer, R. E., V. B. Pursel, C. E. Rexroad, Jr., R. J. Wall, D. J. Bolt, K. M. Ebert, R. H. Palmiter and R. L. Brinster (1985) Production of Transgenic Rabbits, Sheep and Pigs by Microinjection. *Nature* 318: 680–3

Hansel, W. (1986) *Animal Agriculture for the Year 2000 and Beyond*. William Henry Hatch Memorial Lecture. United States Department of Agriculture, Cooperative State Research Services.

Hansel, W. and E. M. Convey (1983) Physiology of the Estrous Cycle. *J. Anim. Sci.*, **58** (Suppl. 2): 404–24.

Leibo, S. P. (1986) Cryobiology: Preservation of Mammalian Embryos. In: *Genetic Engineering of Animals*, ed. J. W. Evans and A. Hollaender. New York: Plenum Press, pp. 251–72.

Marx, J. L. (1988) Gene Transfer is Coming on Target. *Science*, **242**: 191–2.

Mason, A. J., S. L. Pitts, K. Nikolics, E. Szonyl, J. N. Wilcox, P. H. Seeburg, and T. A. Stewart (1986) A Deletion Truncating the Gonadotropin-Releasing Hormone Gene is Responsible for Hypogonadism in the *hpg* Mouse. *Science*, **234**: 1366–71.

Michalska, A., P. Vize, R. J. Ashman, B. A. Stone, P. Quinn, J. R. E. Wells, and R. F. Seamark (1986) Expression of Porcine Growth Hormone cDNA in Transgenic Pigs. In: *Proc. 18th Animal Conf. Aust. Soc. for Reprod. Biol.* Brisbane, p. 13.

Nett, T. M. (1987) Function of the Hypothalamic-Hypophysial Axis During the Post-Partum Period in Ewes and Cows. *J. Reprod. Fert., Suppl.*, **34**: 201–13.

Nilson, J. H. and D. M. Kaetsel (1987) Expression of the Genes Encoding Bovine LH in a Line of Chinese Hamster Ovary Cells. *J. Reprod. Fert., Suppl.*, **34**: 227–36.

Palmiter, R. D., R. L. Brinster, R. E. Hammer, M. E. Trumbauer, M. G. Rosenfeld, N. C. Birnberg, and R. M. Evans (1982) Dramatic Growth of Mice that Develop from Eggs Microinjected with Metallothionein-Growth Hormone Fusion Genes. *Nature*, **300**: 611–15.

Simons, J. P. and R. B. Land (1987) Transgenic Livestock. *J. Reprod. Fert., Suppl.*, **34**: 237–50.

Wagner, T. E., P. C. Hoppe, J. D. Jollick, D. R. Scholl, R. L. Hodinka, and J. B. Gault (1981) Microinjection of Rabbit β-Globin Gene into Zygotes and its Subsequent Expression in Adult Mice and their Offspring. *Proc. Natl Acad. Sci.*, **78**: 6376–80.

ECONOMIC ISSUES

Introduction

In this section I, together with my colleague **Bob Milligan**, attempt to anticipate the impacts of transgenic livestock on the farm sector. The *Ex parte Allen* decision (see Appendix 1) allowing animal patents in the USA is based, ultimately, on an interpretation of the Constitution. Practical considerations, including the impacts of that decision on farmers, or certain groups of farmers, do not enter these decisions, at least not directly. Many individuals are, nonetheless, very concerned by these matters, individuals including not only farmers, but also their governmental representatives and other rural (and not so rural) groups whose welfare depends directly on agriculture.

Current indications are that some transgenic alterations of livestock will have some dramatic impacts on production and productivity on livestock farms. Whenever productivity improvement has come about as the result of previous new technologies the effect has been fewer and larger farms. In the case of transgenic livestock, we feel the impact on farm structure will be relatively limited (compared to, say, the introduction of tractors) and indirect—not due to the technology itself, but associated with managerial ability to make maximum use of the enhanced productive potential of these animals. Farmers are probably not concerned with the fine points of causality but rather with the outcome, which is toward larger and fewer farms. This perspective appears to motivate the several farmer-backed efforts to weaken or block altogether the patenting of animals. Causality, though, is important, for, in our opinion, the driving force for this technology is the promised efficiencies of the new transgenic animals. Improved strains are likely to be invented and used even in the absence of patents, but the control mechanisms used are likely to induce more concentration in farm numbers than would occur under patenting.

The situation regarding the implications of patents on the livestock-breeding sector, the producers of inputs for animal agriculture, is even more complex. This sector must be analyzed by species, by product (meat or milk, eggs, or meat), and by sire selection procedures. With that number of variable factors, no really legitimate general summary of probable implications can be made. What does seem to be a likely outcome is that breeding practices for beef cattle will become increasingly sophisticated, and that the number of breeders will be dramatically reduced. Other species and classes have already reached a near lower limit of firm numbers, so that a slight threat of monopoly exists in response to patents.

Less easy to resolve are the complexities inherent in collecting royalties for patented animals. We believe that royalties are a critical component of the incentive role of patents for animals, but royalties will be counterproductive if the costs of collection are so high as to absorb much of the productive enhancement of the transgenic animals. Further thinking is urgently needed on practical means of royalty collection.

Some mention must be made of the omission of laboratory animals from this analysis. Certainly the specter of "monopoly prices" exists for those products; prices that could affect the costs of research and treatment of human disease. The announcement that the first patented animal would be sold under the name of OncoMouse for $50 a specimen heightened these concerns, although the price is not unprecedented for highly specific strains. The scale of the issue is, nonetheless, very different: research animals are a small component of the cost of medical research, whereas livestock is a major cost (if not the major cost) of livestock agriculture. The two sides also seem better balanced—the likes of the Cornell Medical School and the National Institutes of Health are more influential customers than is the individual farmer. Research institutions are also more convenient sources from which to collect royalties. In short, the problems foreseeable with livestock—and they appear limited—would seem to be even less for laboratory animals. Further analysis is, however, needed to substantiate that point.

Implications for Breeders

William Lesser

INTRODUCTION

Consumers of animal protein in the USA and elsewhere in the world continue to benefit from ongoing cost-reducing breed improvements. Most dramatic of these have been in dairy cattle, where the output per cow has doubled over the past 20 years, so that output is comparable, but herd size is roughly half what it was in the 1960s. In the poultry industry an essentially new product was created with the advent of the "broiler" in the pre-World War II era. Much of these and other less obvious efficiency improvements are attributable to the breeding sector, that group of firms which identifies and combines desirable traits of existing strains to provide new variants that are superior in one or more characteristics. The efficiency of animal agriculture then depends heavily on the functioning of these firms so they assume an importance, and visibility, far in excess of their dollar value of sales.

This paper considers the implications of animal patents on the organization and operation of this important sector. Many of the practical concerns raised about patenting agricultural animals relate to the implications for livestock breeders, especially regarding possible monopolization of the sector (e.g. see review in Dresser, 1988: pp. 417–18). Thus it is important to evaluate if animal patents will abet or hinder the efficient and competitive operation of these firms, be they in the public or private sector. As a corollary, the role of these firms as producers of the new, potentially patentable innovations and/or their functioning as the introducers of major new innovations into commercial varieties must be appraised.

A review of the likely role of agricultural livestock breeders under animal patents is undertaken here. The paper begins by reviewing the current structure and operation of breeding firms in each of the major livestock species and classes in the USA: beef cattle, dairy cattle, hogs, and poultry, and then proceeds to incorporate that material into a projection of likely responses to patented animals.

STRUCTURE OF THE LIVESTOCK BREEDING SECTOR

Even before mankind moved from hunting and gathering to agriculture, domesticated animals had become important to his safety and well-being. The origins of domestication are lost, but a component most certainly was the selection of animals for mating. Initially this was probably done unintentionally

85

with the more compatible animals being selected over the less adaptive ones. Gradually, and it took a considerable time, it became apparent that producers were better off with fewer, higher-quality animals than with numerous ill-fed and inefficient ones. From that profound insight the science of animal breeding was born (Acker, 1983: chapter 21).

The cornerstone of the contemporary breeding sector is the purebred. A breed may be defined as a group of animals possessing certain characteristics that are common to the individuals within the group and that distinguish them from other groups of animals within the same species. "Purebred" is a rather imprecise term, but it is widely understood to mean a group of individuals that share certain common characteristics like size, shape, and coloration (Campbell and Lasley, 1985: pp. 43–44). The number of major pure breeds that make up the bulk of the US livestock sector is quite limited in many instances. For beef cattle there are some 70 breeds in use, but only six dairy breeds and but one predominate breed for laying hens, where sub-breeds predominate (Table 5).

Table 5   Major breeds of North American livestock

Dairy Cattle	Hogs
Ayrshire	Berkshire
Brown Swiss	Cheshire White
Guernsey	Duroc
Holstein	Hampshire
Jersey	Poland China
Milking Shorthorn	Spotted
	Tamworth
Beef Cattle	Yorkshire
Angus	Landrace
Brahman	
Brangus	*Poultry*
Shorthorn	White Plymouth Rock (broiler)
Limousin	Leghorn (eggs)
Charolais	New Hampshire
Hereford	Barred Rock
Santa Gertrudis	Rhode Island Red
Polled Hereford	
Simmental	
Chianina	

(Source: Campbell and Lasley, 1985)

Typically, production herds are not purebred (although it is estimated the Holstein herd, the major milk breed, is 90 percent pure). Instead, commercial producers use crossbred stock which has the benefit of heterosis or "hybrid vigor." Access to the pure lines then determines what firms are able to participate in the breeding sector.

Related to this is the means by which hybridization is maintained in a commercial herd. The most straightforward procedure is for the farmer to buy (or use artificial insemination as a source) purebred breeding stock, generally males, to mate with the crossbred females in the herd. Depending on the number of breeds and the size of the herd, a rotation of two or three or more breeds might be used (Koch, 1974; see also Sorensen's paper). This practice, for the purposes of this paper, shall be called "traditional breeding."

The limitation of traditional breeding is its unscientific nature in the selection of sires. The farmer may identify some desirable traits in a sire, such as disease resistance or a greater milk production potential (see Table 6), but with the low inheritability of many traits (Table 7) it is extremely difficult for the farmer to predict the characteristics of the progeny. When multiple or non-economic traits are being sought simultaneously, both the rate of generational advance and the likelihood of inheritance decline (Van Vleck, 1987). Traditional breeding is then largely a random matter.

Table 6 Example of characteristic description of a dairy bull

*High repeatable, Tri-State young sire graduate
*High-test Pete son
*Outstanding pedigree
*Used extensively in ET programs and as a sire of sons

USDA Sire Summary (1/88)

63 Daus. (48 herds)   19,666 3.7 734
PRED. DIFF.
+$185   +1,559M   +.01%   +58F   Rept. 77%
PROTEIN
+$168   −.08%   +34 Lbs.   Rept. 76%
CHEESE YIELD +$160

HFA Type Summary (1/88)

42 Cl. Daus. Avg. 77.1   Age Adj. 79.5
PRED. DIFF./TYPE +1.25   Rept. 73%
TOTAL PERFORMANCE INDEX (TPI) +760

Table 7 Approximate percent heritability of selected livestock and poultry traits

Trait/Species	Dairy cattle	Hogs	Beef cattle	Poultry
Number born	—	10	5	—
Weight of weaning	—	10	25	—
Mature weight	60	—	—	50
Milk produced	25	—	—	—
Feed efficiency	—	30	40	—
Egg production	—	—	—	35
Thickness of fat	—	50	55	—
Tenderness	—	—	60	—

(Source: Acker, 1983: Table 18-1)

Alternatively, producers may buy crossbred animals that have been pre-selected for desirable characteristics. In order for these to breed true to type it is necessary that the traits be stabilized through repeated inbreeding. Such a process shall be called for the purposes of this paper "synthetic breeding."

The benefit of synthetic breeding is the use of trained geneticists with superior knowledge of the traits of the parent stock to make the breeding selections and test the offspring prior to release of an improved line. The use of these synthetic breeds ranges from zero for dairy and beef cattle to virtually 100 percent for broiler and laying chickens. Pigs fall in a middle ground with some traditionally bred and some (about 20–25 percent) synthetically bred animals. The reason for the differences in breeding practices between cattle, on the one hand, and pigs and poultry, on the other, is not immediately clear. Contributing factors are the slow maturation of cattle and their low reproduction rate—one calf per year—which make breeding slow and costly.

The reliance on traditional breeding for cattle means that purebred stock must be widely dispersed in ownership. Indeed, there are tens of thousands of producers of purebred beef cattle for breeding purposes. The Polled Hereford Association, representing a single popular breed, has membership above 10,000. Similarly there are some 20,000 estimated breeders of Holstein dairy cows. Many of these are part time farmers or producers of breeding stock in conjunction with milk or meat sales. Thus, purebred production is a dispersed, fragmented industry.

The use of artificial insemination on about half of all dairy cows differentiates that sector from the production of beef-breed bulls. Only 1.5 percent of beef-breed cows are bred artificially because of the difficulty of detecting estrus and inseminating animals that spend a large portion of their time in pasture (Gilliam, 1984).

Producers of purebred breeding boars operate similarly to those for beef-breed bulls with an estimated 10,000 farms in this sector. Like beef cattle, hogs are bred naturally with only a small percent of sows artificially impregnated (Van Arsdall and Nelson, 1984). Continuing the parallel, most marketing is done locally, often with the assistance of a breed association or university-run bull- or boar-testing program. Under these programs, progeny and their offspring are evaluated and described to potential buyers as guides to the value of the male as a sire (Gillespie, 1983: pp.137–9). Overall, the sectors producing purebred bulls and boars may be described as very unconcentrated and decentralized with relatively easy access by new firms. Profits in such industries are typically modest.

At the opposite extreme in terms of numbers of firms and concentration of control are producers of chicken breeding stock. There is a total of 11 major ones, but effectively the number is even fewer as firms specialize in sex and class (i.e. egg or meat production) and even color of egg.

The production of synthetic hogs is similarly limited in terms of number of firms (Table 8).

Entry into synthetic hog breeding could be classified as moderately difficult due to the initial expense of acquiring pure lines and delays in developing marketable varieties (Hayenga et al., 1985). Further impediments are the development of a sales force and specialized customer service in the areas of health care and feeding. Considerable practical experience and scientific

Table 8 Numbers of major producers of breeding stock, by species and class, US and world

Species/Class	No. of firms[a]	Market share	Source
Beef cattle	10,000s of thousands (e.g., 11,198 in Polled Hereford Assn.)	Tiny	—
Dairy cattle	Cows: approx. 20,000 Bull semen: 4 AI producers in USA	Tiny 80% for top 4	Dr Bean, Eastern AI Corp., personal commn
Hogs			
Purebred	over 10,000	Tiny	Hayenga *et al.* (1985)
Synthetic-bred	4	20–25% total of boar market 50% of synthetics by largest	Dr David, PIC, personal commn
Poultry (major firms only)[b]			
Egg-type			
white	7	40%	Mr Myers, ISA/
brown	5	Unavailable	Babcock, personal commn
Broiler-type	8	substantial	

[a] Subsidiaries are counted as single firms.
[b] Total number of major chicken breeders is 11.

knowledge have been developed by the major firms, a basis which would be expensive and time-consuming for a new entrant to duplicate. Thus entry would appear to be possible, but expensive. With poultry, entry is further inhibited by the tight control over ownership of pure lines, without which no breeding program is possible. With the exception of a few universities, pure lines are owned, and carefully guarded, by private firms (Marion and Arthur, 1973). Entry would then probably involve buying out an existing firm, raising costs, and effectively limiting the number (but not the size) of firms in the sector.

Economists have generally found that sectors with high concentration of control and difficult entry by new firms have relatively higher profits (e.g. Scherer, 1980 chapter 9). Nonetheless, there is reason to believe the potential problem is not as severe with animal breeding as with other sectors. This is because breeding stock is price based on readily evaluated productive merit, as contrasted with non-objective image and taste factors predominating with many consumer goods. Hence the relationship between concentration and profits and prices is generally not as strong with producer as with consumer goods. Moreover, profits in the poultry sector, especially egg production, have been depressed in recent years. This factor has been shown to provide a restraint on prices charged by input suppliers (for a discussion of a roughly parallel situation with seeds see Butler and Marion, 1985). Specific studies of these industries are, however, lacking. (For a broader review see Marion, 1986: chapters 3 and 4.)

IMPLICATIONS OF BIOTECHNOLOGY

With this background, it is apparent that the US livestock breeding sector is composed of two quite distinct segments. One is a highly unconcentrated and decentralized industry whereas the other is quite the opposite—concentrated and centralized. About the former there is little basis for concern about price performance as economists define it; the latter may be problematical, but that is not certain and most assuredly has not been documented. These two subcomponents also produce quite distinct products. The more concentrated industries produce something closer to a finished product, whereas the unconcentrated ones provide inputs for farmer breeding decisions.

It is reasonable to expect that these differences will influence strongly the implications of, and for, patented animals. Three issues form the core of these potential differences:

(1) Who will make (invent) the biotechnical advances for livestock, and what will the relationship be to the breeding sector?
(2) Who will introduce those inventions into existing breeds so as to produce a commercially viable line?
(3) How will the structure and operation of the breeding sector be affected as a result?

These matters will first be explored for the traditional breeding sector, followed by a consideration of the synthetic breeding one.

Traditional, Purebred Producers

This group includes virtually all beef and dairy cattle producers and breeders of purebred hogs. Firms predominating in this sector are relatively small and are largely lacking in technical expertise in genetics. Marketing of live animals is generally localized and relies, in part, on assistance from universities and other public organizations. It seems highly unlikely that these companies will be able to carry out the biotechnological research necessary for a patentable invention in this area. This research will probably be done by government, universities, and/or private companies, which will be the patent holders.

Traditional breeders will likely license patents from the holder and introduce the patented trait into commercial purebred lines for sale to farmers. Operating in such a way, purebred breeders will have a dual function, partly acting as propagators of the patented trait and partly continuing as breeders who have provided ongoing, if small, annual improvements in breeding stock. This will be a complex activity, and since the product is a joint one it will be complex to price.

When breeding is natural, as now predominates in the case of beef cattle and hogs (Table 3), relatively large numbers of breeding stock are required, even if only males are purchased. For hogs, for example, one boar services 14–20 sows, so that the annual market is about 200,000–300,000 breeding boars (Hayenga *et al.*, 1985). This is a large market which could be expensive to serve if indeed it proves difficult to incorporate the engineered traits into commercial varieties. Artificial insemination is an effective means of greatly expanding the productive potential of a sire—a single bull can potentially impregnate 100,000 cows—but it is expensive for meat-type animals. Any development necessitating artificial insemination of red-meat animals would require a large production enhancement to justify the cost.

It can be expected that private biotechnology firms working on animal genetics will integrate with existing breeders as a means of acquiring expertise and a means for commercializing their inventions. Much the same thing happened with plant breeders, raising some statements of concern about the competitiveness of the sector (e.g. see Doyle, 1988; Butler and Marion, 1985). Several factors differ which suggest that the situation would not be as pronounced with animals. Few animal breeders have the expertise and brand image of the major seed companies, and the multiplication rate with seeds is far greater than with animals. Moreover, the principal acquiring firms were large agribusiness enterprises such as Olin/Royal Dutch-Shell and Sandoz which clearly were looking for marketing outlets for agrichemicals and other existing products. The same relationship could exist between animal breeders and say animal pharmaceutical companies, but those roles would seem to oppose rather than compliment each other. This all suggests that inventors of patented animals will rely more on contracts than ownership of breeders for the commercialization of their inventions.

The situation is likely to be a little different for dairy cows where artificial insemination is more prevalent. Here firms are larger, potentially better capitalized, and have more in-house expertise. But the sector is influenced by producer cooperatives—two of four major US dairy AI firms—and it is unclear if the farmer-owners would be interested in a substantial expansion of the activities of the cooperatives into a far more risky and capital-intensive area. Certainly farmers could be expected to proceed cautiously. However, the largest firm, American Breeders Service owned by W. R. Grace Co., has the potential to develop its own biotechnological innovations.

Synthetic Breed Producers

The situation for synthetic breed producers is substantially different from that of purebred producers because in this subsector firms are larger, have more in-house expertise, and work more intensively with customers. Several firms have, or will be establishing, internal biotechnology departments which potentially have the expertise to produce patented animals. Yet developments in this area are so labor-intensive and uncertain that no firm would wish to rely solely on internal developments, preferring rather to contract with biotechnology firms either for directed research or for licence rights of patented animals (Dr Emsley, Director of Research, ISA/Babcock: personal communication). Viewed in this light, the internal biotechnological capability is as much to monitor general developments in the field as to generate patentable inventions. But as owners or licensors of the inventions, it is highly probable that the existing breeders in this subsector will play a major role in the commercialization process, the incorporation of the invention into commercial lines.

The uncertainties of invention in this area are such that it is unlikely that breeding firms will wish to acquire biotechnology research firms. Biotechnology companies may wish to acquire an animal breeder as an avenue to commercializing inventions, but most research firms at this time are not well capitalized for such a takeover. The large agribusiness companies have the financial wherewithal, but are not heavily involved in the animal biotechnology area. Indeed, the trend, if anything, is in the opposite direction, with Monsanto recently spinning off Farmer's Hybrid as an independent swine-breeding operation (Hayenga *et al.*, 1985). Therefore, biotechnological inventions would seem to be incorporable within the existing poultry- and synthetic hog-breeding industries without major changes in industry structure and practices. There could be some further concentration, but the current system is quite highly concentrated, so the opportunities are restricted.

IMPLICATIONS OF PATENTS FOR ANIMAL BREEDERS

With this background on the implications of biotechnology for the animal-breeding sector, it is possible to consider what, if any, additional impacts animal patents may have. It is assumed that what is patented is some special attribute of an animal such as heightened levels of growth hormone (and hence greater milk production and/or growth potential) or resistance to a disease of major economic significance. (For more detail see Hansel's paper.) With a patented animal, this attribute will be embedded in a particular example, but the claim will possibly cover the species and class (i.e. all dairy cows or all Holstein cows), and possibly several species (cattle and hogs). The discussion will again follow the division into purebred and synthetic-bred producers.

Purebred Producers

This sector appears unlikely to make the inventions or hold any subsequent patents. Their role therefore is a secondary one of licensing and other arrangements with the patent holders. In the short term this implies no major impact on the sector. In the longer term, it is likely that full benefit from the invented attributes can be realized only through more systematic breeding decisions than are feasible on individual farms using pure breeds (see also Smith, 1987). Patent holders will be interested in maximizing the productive value of the commercial varieties as a means of maximizing the return on their research and development investment. Thus the existence of biotechnology, and secondarily patents, will likely push the purebred sector to become more like the synthetic-bred one. This will, in my estimation, result in the loss of numerous small, many part-time, breeders and the rise of a more specialized breeding industry.

During a transitional period when inventors are likely to be licensing breeders, it is questionable if animal patents will be sought at all. Rather, the preferred option might be to patent the altered gene sequence and license it to the breeders. The sequence would express the desired traits and may be more easily identified for the purpose of licensing and royalty agreements.

Overall, the existence of animal biotechnology will probably hasten the movement of this sector into the production of synthetic breeds, but the role of animal patents in that process will be limited. Conversely, animal patents will have a limited incentive impact in investments on this class of animals. In the case of beef cattle, this is an unfortunate situation as the feed conversion efficiency of these animals is far lower than for poultry and pork, making beef more costly than those other products, a major reason beef has lost market share. (For further information refer to Luby's paper.)

Synthetic-Bred Producers

Unlike the purebred producers, those firms providing synthetic breeds are likely to be deeply involved in the production of potentially patentable inventions. At issue is whether those firms are likely to patent these inventions, and, conversely, whether animal patents will provide an incentive to invest in research and development.

It can, and has been argued that biotechnological inventions are different only in process from what is being done now (Dr David, Pig Improvement Co.: personal communication). A series of ongoing improvements are presently being offered, each with a limited commercial life as it is superseded by further advances. Due to the rapid rate at which each new variety becomes outmoded, the breeder has no reason to attempt to claim rights following the first sale. Will not, it is argued, biotechnology-based improvements be treated the same way? Improvements can be made in, say, the area of growth rate (production of growth hormone), but no single improvement will be the final one. Rather, constant enhancements will be sought in the genes selected, their placement and the form of regulation of expression. Under this scenario, no single development has great or long value, and would likely not be patented.

Two factors may, nonetheless, differ which would change the complexion of the scenario. First is the matter of regulation. To date, the several regulatory agencies with jurisdiction have been very conservative about approving engineered animals for release into the environment (e.g. Adler, 1988; House Judiciary Committee Report, 1988). This regulatory oversight raises the cost of developing a commercial product by requiring detailed test results, as well as extending the period from laboratory to market. As a result, only more significant developments will be submitted for testing, making each enhancement less frequent and, consequently, more valuable to the breeder. The incentive to use patents to protect these commercialized inventions will be increased.

Second is the matter of altered genes already introduced into the commercial red-meat herd. As I have argued elsewhere (Lesser, 1987), the only viable enhancements for these animals are those which are inherited on a relatively high level. This would mean an altered gene sequence would be dispersed relatively widely in say the swine herd. If those genes controlled growth hormone production, subsequent innovators with growth hormone genes would have to consider not only their change in isolation but also its interaction with other altered genes already in the gene pool of the commercial herd.

For these reasons, it appears likely that genetically altered farm animals will be released only occasionally onto the market, and then only when the economic benefits to producers are substantial. Recovery of the required investment will likely require the imposition of royalties, if that is permitted, since producers can not be expected to pay the entire cost of the innovation upon the first purchase of breeding stock. Presently, poultry breeders favor the sale of parent, as opposed to grandparent, breeding stock because customers are unwilling to pay for the multiplier inherent in grandparent stock. Thus, if parent stock can produce 100 commercial chicks and grandparent 1,000, then grandparent birds should be worth roughly 10 times parent stock, but the market will not support that price (Dr Emsley, Director of Research, ISA/Babcock Breeders: personal communication). Similarly, payment for patented innovations would likely have to be spread out to maximize income.

Alternatively, breeders of synthetic animals could rely on contracts as substitutes (or supplements) to patents. That, too, has a current precedent with sales of breeding hogs sold on condition that they be used for breeding only and not resold (Dr David, Pig Improvement Co.: personal communication). Poultry breeders selling to commercial hatcheries operate with similar conditions (Mr Myers, General Manager, ISA/Babcock Breeders: personal communication). The use of contracts may, nonetheless, not suffice for some genetically improved animals because of the cost and complexity of signing contracts with every possible buyer. Moreover, if the engineered trait did enter the public domain, contract law would be largely ineffective in curtailing its further unauthorized use. Contracts apply only to the signatories, not to third parties. For these reasons, breeders are likely to use patents, alone or in conjunction with contracts, to protect genetically altered animals.

As the holder of patents, breeders would be responsible for collecting any royalties imposed. Royalty collection will be a costly and complex matter, as I have previously emphasized (Lesser, 1987). If all of a producer's animals were known to possess the trait, then the royalty could be attached to a readily observable number, such as pigs farrowed or eggs sold. More involved is the mixed herd/flock with several patented traits, owned by multiple breeders, intermixed throughout. Under these circumstances, the only equitable way to levy royalties would be to test each animal—an enormously costly practice. Alternatively, some form of the system used to collect royalties under a compulsory licensing system for jukeboxes could be developed and applied based on a sample testing of a herd. (For a description of the Copyright Royalty Tribunal see Henn, 1988: chapter 23; Strong, 1984: pp. 104–8). The "royalty collection tribunal" seems to have compelling economies and could well become the procedure used. These bodies could possibly be operated by the breed associations which have in-place systems for registering animals, but the volumes described here would be far greater than are currently handled.

Several factors, nonetheless, argue against using the tribunal approach. It raises serious antitrust concerns, as was accommodated in the Copyright Law, 1976, which established certain antitrust exemptions for the Tribunal (PL 94-553 sec. 116(c)). At best it will be slow in developing, and it will leave producers in some uncertainty regarding royalty payments, making financial planning difficult. The tribunal approach does facilitate entry by new breeders as each firm need not develop its own royalty collection system. Also a centralized testing system may be sufficiently efficient that sales can be made to small producers on equivalent terms. Otherwise the possibility exists that breeders will sell patented animals only to large producers who can be relatively easily monitored (see also Sorensen's paper). In any case, the organization required to collect royalties could have a major impact on the structure of the breeding industry itself. It should be emphasized that an application of the "tribunal" collection procedure to patented animals would be purely voluntary; no suggestion is made that licenses should be compulsory as they are under the non-exclusionary copyright statutes.

Legality of Reproduction

The US patent laws make it an act of infringement for "whoever without authority makes, uses or sells any patented invention . . ." either directly or through active inducement (35 USC sec. 271(a), 271(b)). Since the reproduction of a patented animal is in fact "making" the invention, concern has been expressed that such an act would require permission in order to avoid infringement of the patent. Livestock farmers are understandably concerned about such a direct invasion of their activities, and these concerns are in part responsible for the "farmers' exemption" from royalties proposed in HR 4970, sec. 2 (see Appendix 3). This matter is involved because it invokes the patent law concepts of exhaustion of rights and implied licenses. These are defined by case law rather than by statutory authority, leaving them open to considerable interpretation and evolution.

The implied license doctrine says, in essence, that the purchaser of a patented product has the right to use it for its intended purpose. Thus, a farmer has the right to plant a patented seed as that is the purpose for which the seed was purchased. This right is not imperiled by the coincidence that the act of growing the seed can lead to the replication of the patented invention (i.e. production of more seed) (e.g. see Bent *et al.*, 1987: chapter 6). In a parallel manner the purchasers of breeding stock appear to have the legal right to mate these animals. Indeed, the mating of a potential dairy cow is essential for her to achieve her economic purpose—the production of milk. With poultry, the purchased synthetic breeding parent stock is used for the production of all chickens raised in commercial operations. When grandparent stock is sold it is done with a license for the production of parent stock so that the legality of breeding does not appear to be a concern with the first sale of breeding stock by the patent holder or licensee.

More problematic are the matters of the legal use of the progeny, especially the subsequent breeding of animals inheriting the patented trait. Take the case of a producer of beef-breed calves for feeding and eventual slaughter for meat, a so-called cow-calf operator. Suppose he buys a patented bull from the patent holder or licensee to mate with his cows? The mating appears to be legal, and as the law does not distinguish the technical means of mating, artificial insemination appears acceptable (or embryo transplant for a patented cow). However, the sale of semen would probably be an infringement. The resulting calves could probably be sold for feeding and slaughter without permission. However, the farmer typically holds some cows (or sows) as brood animals. If these animals carry the patented trait, are bred to a non-patented bull or boar and produce offspring with the patented trait, that would appear to infringe the patent holder's rights. This is roughly equivalent to a farmer saving and replanting seed from patented seed stock (Bent *et al.*, 1987: chapter 6).

The patent holder appears to have the legal right to prohibit such use of his/her invention. Although this is a right which would likely not be invoked, for two reasons. First, it would be impossible to enforce. Second, and more significantly, patent holders typically want their inventions to be used as widely as possible. Therefore, rather than prohibiting the reproduction through breeding of their inventions, patent holders are much more likely to encourage breeding *provided that* royalties are paid. As a matter of expediency, royalties can be expected to be imposed (if permitted by law) on *all* offspring, not only those produced by stock not sold expressly by the patent holder (or licensee) for breeding purposes. Since the legality of these distinctions is cloudy, breeding stock will probably be sold by the patent holder/licensee with a side contract specifying the requirement to pay royalties on offspring. Livestock farmers nevertheless need not be overly concerned about the outright prohibition by patent holders of breeding any animals in their herds.

SUMMARY AND CONCLUSIONS

The material in this paper may be summarized and concluded with the following points:

(1) The livestock breeding sector may be divided into two quite distinct components: a very decentralized segment producing purebred stock for beef and dairy cattle and some hogs, and a highly concentrated sector providing synthetic breeds of hogs and poultry.

(2) The concentration in synthetic breeding occurred long before animal patents appeared. Although firm concentration at those levels is often of concern to economists, the reliance of breeders on easily measured performance factors as well as the general low profitability of agriculture mitigates that concern to a large degree.

(3) Purebred producers in the main are ill-equipped to "invert" patentable animals. That work will likely be done by other public or private entities with the breeders acting under license to incorporate the new trends into existing lines and propagate the stock. Thus this sector will play a relatively minor role in animal patenting.

(4) Inventors of the patentable traits may find it more practical to patent a series of engineered genes than an animal that contains those genes. Thus, in the short run, animal patents are expected to have only a minor incentive effect on traditional animal breeding.

(5) In the longer term, larger new firms may arise that replace many of the smaller purebred breeders by providing more sophisticated products and services, including some in-house biotechnology research. The existence of animal patents may hasten that development but it is unlikely to be a critical factor for or against.

(6) Synthetic breeders often have in-house biotechnology expertise and could potentially generate patentable animals. Uncertainties are, however, such that contracts and licenses with research firms and universities are likely to be used to supplement internal research.

(7) Synthetic breeding firms may be takeover targets for other companies in the livestock business, but the potential does not appear to be as great as occurred with seed breeders. Overall, animal patents could lead to a modest further increase in firm concentration in this subsector.

(8) Federal regulation of releasing genetically altered animals is likely to change the operation of synthetic breeders from annual sales of incremental improvements to occasional sales of more major improvements. These improved animals will have longer commercial lives and patents will be instrumental in recovering the investment made.

(9) Streamlining of the regulatory process seems necessary if the breeding sector is to make full benefit of the efficiency-improving opportunities offered by biotechnology.

(10) The responsibility for royalty collection will fall to the patent holder, here identified as the synthetic breeder. This will be a complex and costly process, especially over time as multiple patented traits intermix irregularly into commercial herds. Some testing for the presence of a trait will likely be needed.

(11) A "royalty collection tribunal," similar to that used currently for

recordings played on jukeboxes (but not involving compulsory licenses) could well develop for the collection and distribution of royalties. Such systems are not without substantial problems, but they can facilitate entry by new breeders, and sales to smaller farmers, and therefore be of major public benefit. The "tribunal" may operate under the auspices of existing breeders' associations.

(12) Expressed concerns about the legality of reproducing patented animals appear misplaced. Even if the legal interpretations are not absolutely clear on this point, it is generally to the benefit of the patent holder that the invention be practiced as widely as possible. Thus breeding will probably be encouraged, provided that royalties are paid. Ambiguities of interpretation for initial sale of breeding stock can be clarified with the use of contracts.

References

Acker, D. (1983) *Animal Science and Industry*. Englewood Cliffs, NJ: Prentice-Hall, 3rd edn.

Adler, R. G. (1988) Controlling the Applications of Biotechnology: A Critical Analysis of the Proposed Moratorium on Animal Patenting. *Harvard J. Law Technol.*, **1**: 1–61.

Bent, S., R. Schwaab, D. Jeffery, and D. Conlin (1987) *Intellectual Property Rights in Biotechnology Worldwide*. New York: Stockton Press.

Butler, L. J. and B. W. Marion (1985) *The Impact of Patent Protection on the US Seed Industry and Public Plant Breeding*. University of Wisconsin Monograph, NC-117, no. 16.

Campbell, J. R. and J. F. Lasley (1985) *The Science of Animals that Serve Humanity*. New York: McGraw-Hill, 3rd edn.

Doyle, J. (1988) Testimony before the House Judiciary Subcommittee on Courts, Civil Liberties, and the Administration of Justice. In: *Hearings, Patents and the Constitution: Transgenic Animals*, Committee on the Judiciary, serial no. 23.

Dresser, R. (1988) Ethical and Legal Issues in Patenting New Animal Life. *Jurimet. J.*, **28**: 399–435.

Gillespie, J. R. (1983) *Modern Livestock and Poultry Production*. Albany, NY: Delmar Publishers, 2nd edn.

Gilliam, H. C., Jr. (1984) The US Beef Cow-Calf Industry. *US Dept. Agr., Econ. Res. Service, Agr. Econ. Rpt.* no. 515.

Hayenga, M. G., V. J. Rhodes, J. A. Brandt, and R. E. Deiter (1985) *The US Pork Sector: Changing Structure and Organization*. Ames, Iowa: Iowa State University Press.

Henn, H. G. (1988) *Copyright Law: A Practitioner's Guide*. New York: Practising Law Institute, 2nd edn.

House Judiciary Committee Report on HR 4970 (1988) In: *BNA's Patent, Trademark and Copyright J.*, **36**: 503–81.

Koch, R. M. (1974) Breeding for Meat Production. In: *Animal Agriculture*, ed. H. H. Cole and M. Ronning. San Francisco: W. H. Freeman and Co.

Lesser, W. (1987) Applying Animal Patents in Agriculture: Lessons for Farmers and the Patent Office for Self-Reproducible Animals. In: *World Intellectual Property Organization Proceedings, Symposium on the Protection of Biotechnological Inventions*, June 4–5, 1987, Ithaca, NY, pp. 135–54.

Marion, B. M. (1986) *The Organization and Performance of the US Food System.* Lexington, Mass.: Lexington Books.

Marion, B. M. and H. B. Arthur (1973) Dynamic Factors in Vertical Commodity Systems: A Case Study of the Broiler System. *OARC Res. Bull.*, no. 1065.

Scherer, F. M. (1980) *Industrial Market Structure and Economic Performance.* Chicago: Rand McNally, 2nd edn.

Smith, C. (1987) Potential for Animal Breeding, Current and Future. In: *Proceedings of the Second International Conference on Quantitative Genetics*, ed. B. S. Weir, E. J. Eisen, M. M. Goodman, and G. Namkoong. Sunderland, Mass.: Sinauer Associates, 2nd edn.

Strong, W. S. (1984) *The Copyright Book: A Practical Guide.* Cambridge, Mass.: MIT Press, 2nd edn.

Van Arsdall, R. N. and K. E. Nelson (1984) US Hog Industry. *US Dept. Agr., Econ. Res. Service, Agr. Econ. Rpt.*, no. 511.

Van Vleck, L. D. (1987) Observations on Selection Advances in Dairy Cattle. In: *Proceedings of the Second International Conference on Quantitative Genetics*, ed. B. S. Weir, E. J. Eisen, M. M. Goodman, and G. Namkoong. Sunderland, Mass.: Sinauer Associates, 2nd edn.

Implications for Agriculture

Robert Milligan and William Lesser

INTRODUCTION

Although a number of individuals oppose animal patents on moral or ethical grounds (see Brody's paper), a large portion of the expressed concerns is based on economics. This is true in particular of owner/managers of small farms who have been buffeted by change in the farm sector to the degree that US farm numbers have declined by some 60 percent from 1950 to 1984 according to the US Department of Agriculture. Virtually all of this loss has been among the groups of smaller farms, and most studies project further attrition of small farms for the predictable future (US Congress, Office of Technology Assessment, 1986). It is no surprise therefore that among farmers the "family farm" advocates are the most vocal opponents of patenting animals (Huber, 1988; see also Sorensen's paper).

In this paper we attempt to project the implications of animal patents for livestock producers in the USA. In particular we address the fundamental issues of potential impacts on farm size, farm numbers, farm location, and profitability, all interrelated factors.

Such an analysis is, in some regards, a compounded groping into the future. First an appraisal must be made of what technological innovations are likely to come along, and then an extrapolation of the implications for individual farms and, in summation, the agricultural sector. Although this is an uncertain undertaking, it is done within a backdrop of decades of prior analysis of the impact of technological change on agriculture. We begin with a brief review of the technological change literature and follow with several "scenarios" of patented livestock. These scenarios will be used as a basis for projecting the impacts of patents on different components of the livestock sector.

OVERVIEW OF TECHNOLOGY ADOPTION IN AGRICULTURE

The adoption of new technology has had a profound impact on US agriculture and, in fact, is the basis for the economic growth that has made the USA a world leader. This transformation has been the basis from which the USA moved from a 44 percent rural, largely farming population in 1930 to the present day, when less than 5 percent of the population produces too much food for the 240 million-plus inhabitants (US Department of Commerce, 1975).

The Office of Technology Assessment (OTA) describes this transformation as follows (US Congress Office of Technology Assessment, 1986: pp. 91–3):

Perhaps the best known characteristic of U.S. agriculture is the trend toward fewer and larger farms . . . The number of farms reached a peak of about 6.8 million farms in 1935 and is now approximately 2.2 million. The rate of decline has slowed since the late 1960s with a loss of about 100,000 farms since 1974.

Employment in farming began a pronounced decline after World War II, when a major technological revolution occurred in agriculture. The replacement of draft animals by the tractor began in the 1930s and was virtually complete by 1960, releasing about 20 percent of the cropland, which had been used to grow feed for draft animals.

The increased mechanization of farming permitted the amount of land cultivated per farm worker to increase fivefold from 1930 to 1980. The amount of capital used per worker increased more than 15 times in this period. Total productivity (production per unit of total inputs) more than doubled because of the adoption of new technologies such as hybrid seeds and improved livestock feeding and disease prevention. The use of both agricultural chemicals and fuel also grew very rapidly in the postwar period. Agricultural production began to rely heavily on the nonfarm sector for machinery, fuel, fertilizer, and other chemicals. These, not more land or labor, produced the growth in farm production. The resultant changes have greatly increased the capital investment necessary to enter farming and have generated new requirements for operating credit during the growing cycle.

A somewhat different situation followed the development of corn hybrids, following their discovery in 1908. The production benefits were so enormous that adoption in the corn belt jumped dramatically from 0.2 percent of acreage in 1933, to 83 percent in 1944, to virtually 100 percent in 1955. Hybrid corn alone is attributed with increasing yields by about 20 percent (Leibenluft, 1981).

The impacts of these major yield increases can be seen by examining US acreage and yield data. In 1933, 110 million acres were planted to corn, with an average yield of 23 bushels per acre. In 1957, acres planted had declined to 73 million, a full third reduction, but total production was up over 40 percent due to a 100 percent yield increase (US Department of Agriculture, 1967: table 38). Not all of these increases can be attributed to hybridization due to major policy changes, production technology, and weather. But hybridization did have a major impact on the location of production. In 1945 the South Central states planted 17.1 million acres to corn, declining to 4.7 million 20 years later. Clearly, even in the mid 1940s, states like Texas were no longer efficient in corn production with a 3 percent penetration of hybrids, compared with 99.8 percent in Iowa (US Department of Agriculture, 1945: tables 45 and

48; 1965, table 39). Farms with such major cost disadvantages soon left the sector, although some survived by switching to alternative crops.

Synopsis of Analysis

From this brief overview and additional materials, a brief summary of the past implications of new technology can be presented. These are offered under four topic headings as follows:

Cost of production and profits   Benefits from new technology accrue to society by way of a decrease in the total cost of production or in economic terms in a shifting of the supply curve to the right, resulting in a lower market price. This decline in cost of production can result from an increase in productivity, thereby spreading fixed cost over more units of output, from a decrease in cost, or from a combination of the two. Although much has been made of the difference between "productivity-enhancing" and "cost-reducing" technologies, the distinction is rather insignificant from an economic viewpoint with the important question being the impact of the new technology on cost of production.

In the long term in a competitive sector like farming, cost savings are passed along to consumers in the form of lower prices. Thus in the days of the $400 Ford "Model T" a bushel of wheat cost $1.30 (US Department of Commerce, 1975: E123-34). Today an equivalent amount of wheat costs $4.05 (no. 2 hard winter) whereas a new Ford costs at least $7000. Farmers who do not adopt the cost-reducing innovation or adopt it late do not benefit; indeed, adoption is often essential for farmers to remain in business. Early adopters, however, can gain in the short term with lower costs before market prices fall.

Adoption   For significant new technologies, it is generally expected and true that eventual adoption is virtually 100 percent. However, the period of time required to reach that level varies considerably depending on a number of economic and non-economic factors. Very rapid adoption, such as experienced with hybrid corn in some US "corn belt" states (Griliches, 1957) is unusual, but has a dramatic impact on supplies and prices. More common is the slow adoption experienced with machinery and other innovations.

Studies of adoption have found five controlling factors (Rogers, 1962; Agriculture Canada, 1984). *Relative advantage* is the preferability of the new technology, usually measured in terms of higher profit potential or lower risk. *Compatibility* is the extent to which a new innovation is consistent with the existing norms, values, and prior experience of prospective adopters. *Complexity* refers to the degree of difficulty of understanding a new technology and its consequences. *Desirability* is the extent to which a technology can be adopted on a partial basis, or if full adoption is required from the onset. *Communicability* describes the ease with which knowledge of an innovation can be passed along to prospective users.

Management quality   Management is a broad, complex, and difficult topic, but at its core it is the application of processes to define, analyze, execute, and evaluate plans for continuing the improvement of the business. Management includes both the acquisition of technical knowledge through education, hired employees, or consultants, and the organization of staff to utilize that technical expertise. The best test of the level of management is current productivity and profitability levels, and usage of up-to-date technologies. If a business is not using current technologies and obtaining reasonable levels of productivity, there is very little reason to anticipate an interest in trying or ability to utilize effectively many new technologies.

Related to this issue of management is the apparent trend that productivity and profitability differences between "top" farm businesses and "average" farm business are increasing. This trend, which is really a hypothesis, is difficult to test empirically because time series data for "top" producers are rarely available. However, to cite one example, data from the New York dairy sector shows that over the past decade the top 10 percent of farms had an annual average increase in milk production of 2.18 percent, compared to a statewide average of only 1.16 percent (Smith *et al.*, 1988; New York Agricultural Statistics Service, 1987). A generalization of new technologies is that they will accelerate this divergence between "top" and "average" managers.

Farm size and number of farm businesses   The impact of new technology has direct and indirect impacts on farm size and number of farm businesses. The direct impact is related to economies of size, and the indirect impact is associated with factors correlated with farm size.

The direct impact of hybrid corn, for example, is limited as it can be planted on any size farm. This may be compared with a tractor, which requires a minimal acreage to be used a sufficient number of hours to be economical. More recently, computers and other forms of "information technology" are most efficient on the largest farms because the cost of set up and operation are largely fixed. Thus, the larger the farm then the lower the unit cost.

The indirect effects of technology are not as clear and may be represented by experiences with New York dairy farms. There both productivity and profitability increase with size (Table 9). In part this is attributable to the size economics of some innovations, including on-farm computer use. In part it is a ramification of the simple fact that successful managers generate greater income and have more opportunities to grow. Thus, when combined with varying management ability, even size-neutral new technologies can lead to increases in farm size and reductions in farm numbers.

SCENARIOS OF PATENTED LIVESTOCK

In order to place the following discussion of probable impacts of patented animals on a more concrete basis, several potential developments will be

103

Table 9 Productivity and profitability of New York State dairy farms by farm size, 1987

No. of cows	No. of farms	Milk sold per cow (lbs)	Labor and management income per operator ($)
under 40	32	15,234	1,228
40 to 54	69	15,380	4,429
55 to 69	74	15,816	1,362
70 to 84	71	15,982	6,573
85 to 99	41	16,098	12,999
100 to 149	70	15,915	10,501
150 to 199	31	16,217	12,241
200 to 299	27	16,710	27,968
300 and over	11	18,808	99,693

(Source: Smith *et al.*, 1988)

outlined in some detail. One of these is a technology, here represented by the use of growth hormone (somatotrophin) as a growth stimulant, that affects the supply curve by allowing the production of a product at lower cost. The second, and less well researched at this time, is the altering of the animal itself so that the meat is changed. This latter technology affects the demand curve. These two changes, depending on how they are introduced, can have very different impacts on agriculture (see Figure 6).

Growth Hormone[1]

Although it was recognized in the 1940s that injections of growth hormone could enhance milk production, the expense of extracting hormone from natural sources made this practice prohibitively costly. More recently, the use of engineered bacteria to produce a chemically identical product has altered these costs to the point that the use of injected hormones seems highly profitable in the case of milk production (Kalter *et al.*, 1984). One of the goals of genetic engineering is to alter animals to enhance the natural production of growth hormone. If the effect is similar to results from injected hormone then current research results give an indication of likely effects. At this point, none of these products is authorized for sale, but approval is anticipated soon, possibly within a year (Kalter and Milligan, 1986).

Research trials using bovine growth hormone (bGH) in lactating dairy cows have the longest history of the animal growth hormones. Milk yield improvements have reached 25 percent and, based on use over the full lactation, could achieve 30 percent on individual cows. Increases in feed efficiency, defined as total energy input per unit of milk output, have been somewhat variable (Bauman *et al.*, 1985; Baird *et al.*, 1986; Chalupa *et al.*, 1986; Soderholm *et al.*, 1986; Hutchison *et al.*, 1986) at least partially due to the small numbers of cows in the experiments. Results, however, indicate that the increases are at least as great as can be explored by spreading the feed maintenance requirements for the cow over a larger amount of milk production. If feed efficiency

[1] This section is drawn from Kalter and Milligan (1986).

were to increase due only to the dilution of maintenance requirements, a 25 percent increase in milk production from a cow producing 6500 kilograms of milk per year would result in a corresponding feed efficiency increase of 8.7 percent.

Magrath and Tauer (1986) have estimated that the use of bGH could lead to an 11 and 20 percent reduction in cow numbers in New York, resulting from a 10 and 20 percent production response, respectively. The decline in cow numbers is projected to be 7 and 12 percent, respectively. Small farms are expected to exit first, hence farm loss exceeds reductions in cow numbers. Actual losses, however, will depend on a number of factors, including federal milk price policy and regional competition among crops.

With meat animals, since the output of growing and finishing beef, swine, and broilers is the animal itself, an improvement in feed efficiency is a direct response to use of growth hormones. Meltzer (1987) concluded that, based on early research in swine, improved feed/gain ratios of 10–20 percent are attainable. More recent research has achieved feed efficiency improvements of from 30 to 50 percent during the last 60 days of the fattening cycle (Beermann, Cornell University Animal Science: personal communication; Etherton, Pennsylvania State University Animal Science: personal communication). Gains of this magnitude did, however, require higher protein rations than have been considered optimal in commercial practice. Tests on beef cattle have been far fewer, but early results have shown increased growth efficiency with gains of up to 21 percent (Fabry et al., 1985). Of equal interest for both swine and beef cattle is the fact that these efficiency gains were achieved in conjunction with major reductions in back fat (in swine reductions have reached as high as 70 percent). Results for broilers have been the most disappointing to date with less than a 5 percent improvement in efficiency.

The use of the hormones will result in a decreased cost of production due to improved efficiency and productivity. Kalter and Milligan (1986) estimated the impact of commercial production of animal growth hormone on the cost of production for milk, beef, and hogs using several levels of response. The reduction is greatest for milk (10.8–15.7 percent, excluding hormone cost) and least for beef (5.0–8.6 percent, excluding hormone cost). Since the actual hormone cost upon commercialization is expected to be comparatively small, the impact these technologies will have on cost of production is large. The cost reduction results through spreading the overhead and maintenance feed cost over more units of output in the case of milk and less time in the case of hogs and beef.

For all species, the above summary must be treated with caution. All experimental results to date are from carefully controlled tests usually conducted under ideal conditions. Achievement of the efficiency gains reported will be far more difficult when new products are employed in commercial herds.

ANIMAL CHARACTERISTICS

Recent changes in the age structure of the population and in food habits are providing considerable opportunity to alter the composition of livestock to be more desirable to consumers (see Luby's paper). The best example currently under study is the use of porcine growth hormone (pGH) which reduces both surface and intramuscular fat (see above). Red meats lower in saturated fats will be more appealing to the growing health-conscious component of the population.

It is easy to imagine a number of more specialized developments along these lines. Pork processors may favor larger hams or thicker bellies, whereas turkey producers are always seeking larger breasts. The increasing popularity of prepared, microwaveable foods makes meats that retain texture or flavor better under those conditions very attractive to processors. Alternatively, the attribute may be purely cosmetic and used as a visual distinguishing factor for a brand, as Purdue Farms now feeds marigold petals and other natural substances to give birds a flavorless yellow color.

Such changes are notable because they can cause shifts in the demand curve through the production of a new product (or at least the perception of a new product). If the shift is positive (to the right) the same quantity of product can be sold at a higher price than previously. Productivity-improving innovations, for their part, shift the supply curve to the right, leading to a lower market price (Figure 6).

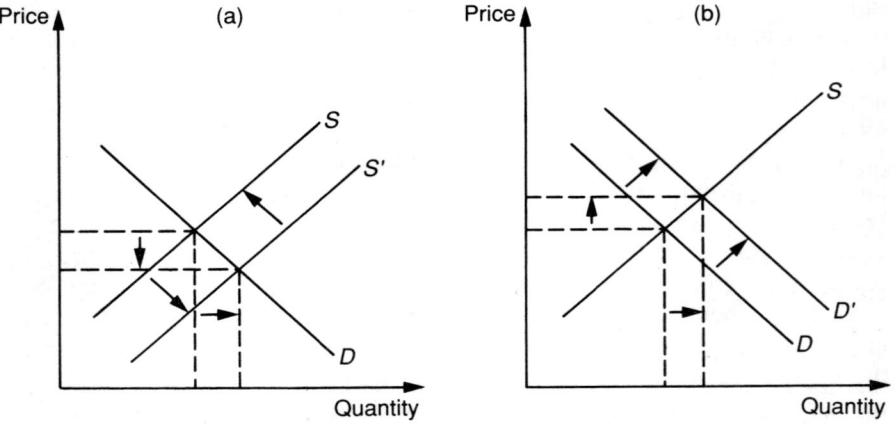

(a) Supply shifting: more at a lower price; (b) demand shifting: more, but at a higher price

Fig. 6   Comparison of price effects of demand-shifting and supply-shifting innovations

IMPLICATIONS OF BIOTECHNOLOGY

As discussed in a general way above, the direct impact of patentable technologies is related to economies of size. If the patentable technologies are marketed so as to be available to all producers, the direct impact of the new technologies is expected to be minimal because the technologies are generally size neutral. The currently discussed biotechnologies, like the growth hormones, result in changes in variable costs that are constant on a per-unit basis and are expected to be captured by all producers.

As the patentable biotechnologies become more sophisticated, they will probably become less size neutral. One reason for this is the increased costs associated with purchasing breeding stock. Larger, better managed, and better capitalized farms typically have more ready access to capital and can adopt new technologies more rapidly. This increases the opportunity to benefit financially before widespread adoption pushes price and profits down. If better managers are able to make more productive use of those new livestock strains, then they can gain a substantial and ongoing business advantage over small competitors.

There is already some evidence that many smaller farms may not be able to make the best use of the new animal technologies. In New York, for example, a number of typically smaller farms are producing below 10,000 pounds of milk annually per cow, far below the state average of 12,000 pounds and the genetic potential of around 20,000 pounds annually (Kelleher, 1988). Increasing through biotechnology the genetic potential of cows on those farms could only damage further a weak profitability position.

Among hog feeders, it is the larger operations that pay the most for breed boars, such that producers with the largest operations pay two to three times as much for boars as do those with small operations. As the researchers note, "These price differences may not be a proportional reflection of differences in quality and performance, but they are a strong indication of the levels of producer commitment to improving performance." (Van Arsdall and Nelson, 1984: p. 23) If the same differential commitment to improving performance continues with genetically altered livestock, larger producers will have even a greater productivity and cost advantage over small competitors.

The authors, therefore, argue that the new technologies will accelerate the longstanding trend toward larger and fewer farms due to the stress placed on the management requirements of farm businesses that do not have access to the new technology or are unable to adopt successfully that technology. Profitability of these unsuccessful farms will be severely eroded, increasing the probability of business failure. Since such failures are expected to predominate among smaller farms' businesses, the trend toward fewer and larger farms will be accelerated.

It is important to note that the discussion on this point refers to the impacts of bioengineering of livestock, and not to patents *per se*. Therefore much of the concern expressed by the small farm group seems misdirected. The basis for any major change is the emergence of a new technology itself, a process in which patents appear to play a relatively minor role. Certainly that was the situation with hybrid corn for which patents were neither available nor sought.

The expected attrition in farm numbers associated with livestock biotechnology will create personal hardship and community dislocation, but is unlikely to cause major public concern over food prices and availability. For example, if all hog-finishing operations reach the size of 100,000 annually, the USA would require nearly 1000 of them. That is down very sharply from a total of 315,000 in 1982 but still a substantial number (US Department of Commerce, 1975: table 30). In fact, the current total is misleading as by 1984, 6 percent of farms (about 25,000 according to one count), had over half of the total number of hogs (Van Arsdall and Nelson, 1985: p. 39). Within the broiler sector, concentration of control is already very high, with some 11 "integrators" owning 90 percent of the chickens produced. Yet it has been said about this sector, "Net returns from production and marketing activities, while somewhat variable from year to year, have not been high. The technological and organizational changes that have transformed these sectors over the last three decades have wrought important benefits to consumers but have had little effect on the cyclical pattern of fortune in these subsectors." (Marion, 1986: pp. 145–6) Thus there seems little basis for general public concern about the implications of animal biotechnology provided that the innovations are distributed widely.

Quite a different scenario could develop if the animal-based inventions were not made universally available. With efficiency-improving developments it is generally advantageous to have them used as widely as possible provided some form of charge or royalty can be levied (see Lesser's paper). Hence the cost-reducing inventions are likely to be dispersed broadly. What may not be is something conferring a particularly desirable attribute to the product, such as a thicker belly producing wider and leaner bacon. A single firm—to pick on one, let it be Armour—may increase the profit potential by making that strain proprietary, that is by not allowing access by competing firms. If that new form of bacon were truly desirable, Armour could increase its share of the market at the expense of competitors, and may raise prices in accordance with a stronger market position (Connor et al., 1985). The implications of such an arrangement are difficult to comprehend as they are dependent in part on the relationships between producers, packers, and processors, all dynamic factors. In general, however, the public will not be as well off, in terms of price and product supply, as would be the case if the invention were more widely dispersed.

IMPLICATIONS OF PATENTS

Above we argued that much of the impact of animal biotechnology is associated with the technology itself, and that the ramifications can be predicted with reasonable confidence based on experience with over a century of technological change in agriculture. But the situation under consideration here is somewhat different as it potentially involves patents for self-reproducible animals. Here we explore whether patents, beyond the technology itself, are likely to affect the structure and functioning of animal agriculture.

Certainly a key, if not the key, issue is the incentive impacts of patents. Will the existence of patents for animals increase research funding for livestock? That was the experience with seeds in the aftermath of the adoption of the Plant Variety Protection Act (Butler and Marion, 1985; Perrin *et al.*, 1987; Brim, 1987), but will it apply to animals?

The excitement about the potentials of biotechnology has resulted in major expansion in funding of agricultural research through increased private funding, the establishment of biotechnology centers at many universities, and increased corporate funding of university research. The additional funds have come from the private sector and from outside of the traditional agricultural research system (National Research Council, 1987). Major research support for studies of growth hormones, for example, has come from such agribusiness giants as Monsanto, American Cyanamid, and Ciba-Geigy. These monies have been made available as traditional research support for agriculture, in the form of Hatch allocations, has been in a long-term decline. Concurrently, many universities have been using patents as a means of generating ongoing research support. (For the case of Cornell University see Lesser, 1987.)

The continuation of this private support is dependent on the realization of the expected returns from research expenditures. It is here that patents play a crucial role for they allow the collection, through royalties, of payments over a sustained period. In our judgment, it is not practical for producers in the low-margin business that farming is to pay the full value of many new innovations at the first sale. The use of artificial insemination (AI) is a means of raising the productive value of male breeding stock and of collecting a higher return than the outright sale of the animal for natural breeding would allow. In the cases of hogs and beef cattle, however, the use of AI would impose a major technical inefficiency on the system, which would reduce the value of the invention and the profits of the inventor.

In the absence of royalties, inventors are likely to use contracts as an alternative means of recovering costs. Such contracts could be administered most efficiently with large farms, meaning that small farms may not have access to the new technologies no matter how efficient and well managed they were. This could create a far greater decline in small farm numbers if their larger competitors had a major and permanent efficiency advantage through access to the improved animals.

The use of royalties are then regarded as being essential to encourage research and development investment in this critical area and to maintain access to the new animals across the spectrum of farm size. It is for these

109

reasons that we oppose HR 4970, which in Section 2 bars the use of royalties for "a person whose occupation is farming."

There are other more technical and practical reasons for our opposition to the bill. Earlier laws which contain such general references to farming have been all but impossible to enforce equitably. The Capper–Volstead Act of 1922 (7 USC sec. 291 and 292), for example, refers in section 291 to "persons engaged in the production of agricultural products as farmers, planters, ranchmen . . . ," but it has not been clear just who is a farmer (e.g. *Case-Swayne Co., Inc. v. Sunkist Growers, Inc.*, 389 US 384 (1967); discussed in Manchester, 1980). The Plant Variety Protection Act (7 USC sec. 2321 *et seq.*) in Section 2543 provides an exception for a person "whose primary farming occupation is . . ." This too has evaded judicial definition as it requires identifying not only what is farming, but also what constitutes "primary" (e.g. *Asgrow Seed Co. v. Kunkle Seed Co., Inc., et al.*, Appeal No. 87-1402 (Court of Appeals for the Federal Circuit)). Under HR 4970 there is a distinct possibility that breeders could develop with the purpose of propagating patented livestock, but claiming exemptions from royalty payment as "a person whose occupation is farming." At best, litigation would be complex and costly, a further disincentive to researchers and legitimate farmers not knowing the practical bounds of the exemption.

If royalties then are to be collected they can have an indirect impact on the structure of agriculture. Again, if the collection point is the individual farm, patent holders will favor release only to larger farms. That would be disadvantageous to small farmers, to the public, and, in many cases to the patent holder. More research is required on an efficient royalty collection system (see Lesser's paper). Particularly critical will be the long transition period for red-meat animals as the patented stock becomes slowly infused into the national herd.

A second possible negative component of patents is their potential use to exclude some from the use of the invention. Since it is an infringement to recreate a patented invention through breeding without expressed permission, farmers could be prevented from using certain patented animals. As discussed above this is likely to occur more frequently with characteristic-changing innovations ("demand shifting") than with efficiency enhancement ("supply shifting"). This situation would create modest public concerns about food prices, but with, for example, regular pigs serving as competition for a thick-bellied hog there is only a limited amount of price enhancement possible for the thicker-bellied variant. More complex would be the case of the farmer who contracted for production of those new hogs, only to have the contract terminated.

At that point the genes could be widely disseminated in the herd, but the farmer would technically be infringing by breeding his sows which carried the altered gene sequence. This would be a real dilemma for the farmer and one which could not be averted by any simple amendment to the Patent Act. In our judgment, any alteration in the wording would either be too broad or would create interpretation problems greater than the problem that was being rectified. As an alternative we recommend contract language which allows the farmer breeding rights to his sows for a specified period (say five years) following the termination of the agreement. The offspring could be sold for slaughter only, not for breeding.

This scenario does, however, suggest that the use of contracts as a coordination and control mechanism is likely to increase with use of animal patents in agriculture. Contract production has been growing slowly from low levels with red meats and patents are likely to accelerate the trend. (For more on contract coordination see Luby's paper.)

SUMMARY AND CONCLUSIONS

This analysis of the potential impacts of animal patents on agriculture separates the implications of the technology of genetically altered animals from the legal issue of patents. The biotechnology of animals has a strong potential of causing major changes in the livestock sector. These changes may be supply-shifting, due to efficiency improvements in animals, or demand-shifting, a term relating to the form of animals or meat produced. Presently, most effort seems directed to supply-shifting technologies, especially those related to enhanced growth. Yet it is the demand-shifters that perhaps will have a major effect on the sector in the long term.

The impact of the new animal-based technology can be inferred from over a century of technological change in US agriculture. Based on knowledge gained over that period, we anticipate that this new technology will follow familiar lines. In particular, livestock biotechnology is expected to lead to some acceleration of the ongoing trend to fewer, larger farms. Animal-based technologies themselves are largely size neutral so that the causal factor is an indirect one with superior managers better able to benefit from the technology, and hence more likely to grow. Stated simply, better managed farms tend to get bigger. There is little indication that the loss in farm numbers will have a significant effect on food prices.

Under this scenario, patents themselves will have a limited additional impact on the agricultural sector. The major implication is for the facilitation under patenting of the collection of royalties. We conclude that royalties are necessary to encourage the needed investment in animal biotechnology research. In their absence, investment will be curtailed and/or access to these promising new technologies denied to small farms because of the cost of contract enforcement. The latter case would have a potentially greater impact on farm size distribution than the imposition of royalties. For these and other more pragmatic reasons, we are opposed to the current bill (HR 4970) which would ban royalty collection from farm operators.

The required organization to collect royalties could in itself affect farm structure as an operational inefficiency. More research is required to develop an efficient and equitable system. The one potentially disadvantaged group would be those farmers who produce patented livestock under contract, only to have the contract end, and with it permission to breed animals within the herd capable of passing the patented gene sequence on to offspring. This scenario is more likely with demand-shifting than supply-shifting innovations where the patent holder has the incentive to practice the invention as widely as possible. There is no obvious amendment to patent law which would rectify that situation so we recommend a clause in any contract for using potential animals which allows a limited post-contract period for continued breeding of patented animals.

References

Agriculture Canada, Regional Development Branch (1984) *Technology Transfer in Agriculture: What It Is and How It Occurs.*

Baird, L. S., R. W. Hemken, R. J. Harmon, and R. G. Eggert (1986) Response of Lactating Dairy Cows to Recombinant Bovine Growth Hormone (rbGH). *J. Dairy Sci.*, **69** (Suppl. 1): 118.

Bauman, D. E., P. J. Eppard, M. J. De Geeter, and G. M. Lanza (1985) Responses of High Producing Dairy Cows to Long Term Treatment with Pituitary- and Recombinant-Somatotropin. *J. Dairy Sci.*, **68**: 1352.

Brim, C. (1987) Plant Breeding and Biotechnology in the United States of America: Changing Needs for Protection of Plant Varieties. Symposium on the Protection of Biotechnological Inventions, Ithaca, NY, June 4–5, 1987.

Butler, L. J. and B. W. Marion (1983) *Impacts of Patent Protection in the US Seed Industry and Public Plant Breeding.* University of Wisconsin, NC-117, Monograph no. 16.

Chalupa, W., B. Vecchiarelli, P. Schneider, and R. G. Eggert (1986) Long-Term Responses of Lactating Cows to Daily Injections of Recombinant Somatotropin. *J. Dairy Sci.*, **69** (Suppl. 1): 151.

Connor, J. M., R. T. Rogers, B. W. Marion, and W. F. Mueller (1985) *The Food Manufacturing Industries: Structure, Strategies, Performance and Policies.* Lexington, Mass.: Lexington Books.

Fabry, J., L. Ruelle, V. Claes, and E. Ettaib (1985) Efficacity of Exogenous Bovine Growth Hormone for Increased Weight Gains, Feed Efficiency and Carcass Quality in Beef Heifers. *J. Anim. Sci.*, **61** (Suppl. 1): 261–2.

Griliches, Z. (1957) Hybrid Corn: An Exploration in the Economics of Technological Change. *Econometrica*, **25**: 501–22.

Huber, S. (1988) Testimony in Hearings before the Subcommittee on Courts, Civil Liberties, and the Administrator of Justice of the Committee on the Judiciary. *Patents and the Constitution: Transgenic Animals.* Washington, DC, serial no. 23.

Hutchison, D. F., J. E. Tomlinson, and W. H. McGee (1986) The Effects of Exogenous Recombinant or Pituitary Extracted Bovine Growth Hormone on Performance of Dairy Cows. *J. Dairy Sci.* **69** (Suppl. 1): 152.

Kalter, R. J. *et al.* (1984) *Biotechnology and the Dairy Industry Production Costs and Commercial Potential of the Bovine Growth Hormone.* Cornell Univ., Dept. Agr. Econ., A.E. Res. 84-22.

Kalter, R. J. and R. A. Milligan (1986) Emerging Agricultural Technologies: Economic and Policy Implications for Animal Production. National Academy of Sciences Conferences on Technology and Agricultural Policy, December 11–13, 1986.

Kelleher, M. (1988) Cornell University, Agricultural Economics, unpublished data.

Leibenluft, R. F. (1981) *Competition in Farm Inputs: An Examination of Four Industries*. US Federal Trade Commission, Office of Policy Planning.

Lesser, W. (1987) Financing University Research through Patenting and Licensing: Recent Policies and Practices at Cornell University as an Example. *Int. Rev. Indust. Property Copyright Law*, **18**: 360–71.

Magrath, W. B. and L. W. Tauer (1986) The Economic Impact of bGH on the New York State Dairy Sector: Comparative State Results. *NE J. Agric. Res. Econ.*, **15**: 6–13.

Manchester, A. C. (1980) *Agricultural Marketing Cooperatives and Antitrust Law: A Discussion Paper*. Unpublished monograph, US Dept. Agriculture, Econ., Statistics and Cooperatives Service.

Marion, B. W. (1986) *The Organization and Performance of the US Food System*. Lexington, Mass.: Lexington Books.

Meltzer, M. I. (1987) *Repartitioning Agents in Livestock: Economic Impact of Porcine Growth Hormone*. Master's thesis, Cornell University.

National Research Council (1987) *Agricultural Biotechnology Strategies for National Competitiveness*, Report Prepared by Committee on a National Strategy on Biotechnology in Agriculture, Washington, DC.

New York Agricultural Statistics Service (1988) *New York Agricultural Statistics 1987*. Albany, NY.

Perrin, R. K., K. A. Hunnings, and L. A. Ihnen (1983) *Some Effects of the US Plant Variety Protection Act of 1970*. North Carolina State Univ., Econ. Res. Rpt. 46.

Rogers, E. M. (1962) *Diffusion of Innovations*. New York: Free Press.

Smith, S. F., W. G. Knoblauch, and L. D. Putnam (1988) *Dairy Farm Business Summary, New York, 1987*. Cornell University, Dept. Agricultural Economics, A.E. Res. 88-8.

Soderholm, C. G., D. E. Otterby, F. R. Ehle, J. G. Linn, W. P. Hansen, and R. J. Annexstad (1986) Effects of Different Doses of Recombinant Bovine Somatotropin (rbSTH) on Milk Production, Body Composition, and Conditions Score in Lactating Cows. *J. Dairy Sci.* **69** (Suppl. 1): 152.

US Congress, Office of Technology Assessment (1986) *Technology, Public Policy, and the Changing Structure of American Agriculture*. Washington, DC: US Government Printing Office, OTA-F-285.

US Department of Agriculture, Crop Reporting Board, Statistical Reporting Service (various years) *Crop Production Summary*.

US Department of Commerce, Bureau of the Census (1975) *Historical Statistics of the US: Colonial Time to 1970*, part 1.

US Department of Commerce, Bureau of the Census (1982) *1982 Census of Agriculture*, vol. 1, part 51, US: Summary and State Data.

Van Arsdall, R. N. and K. E. Nelson (1984) US Hog Industry. *US Dept. Agr., Econ. Res. Service, Ag. Econ. Rpt.*, no. 511.

—— (1985) Economics of Size in Hog Production. *US Dept. Agr., Econ. Res. Service, Tech. Bull.*, no. 1712.

USERS' PERSPECTIVES

Introduction

The following material reflects the perceptions of various professional groups involved, in one way or another, in the production or commercialization of transgenic animals. The opinions of these groups, although complex, are also comprehensible given their roles. Far more intricate are the perspectives of those who are passive, and sometimes unwilling, recipients of this new technology. For our purposes, this amorphous group of the "public" can be divided into three subgroups: (a) producers of transgenic livestock (i.e. farmers); (b) users of products of transgenic livestock (i.e. agribusiness); and (c) the public, which opposes, on moral or ethical grounds, the extension of patents to this class of living organisms.

In the following three papers noted spokespersons for each group present their perspectives. They are quick to note that no one can present the views of an entire sector so that some caution should be used in interpreting their comments. They do, however, provide powerful insights into the differing opinions on patented animals and, hence, on the outlook for their functioning in the economy and society in general.

Sorensen, who works closely with farmers as an employee of the largest farm organization, the American Farm Bureau Federation, reports on the positions taken by her and other farm organizations. Farmers are discussing and forming opinions on this subject even though it lacks the immediacy of many other issues. As a general matter, support for patents seems to increase with organization size so that full opposition appears to be limited to a rather small percentage of farmers.

Luby comments on the likely future role of agribusiness in the area of patented and transgenic animals. Agribusiness has in the past taken a very strong role in the adoption of new technologies, most notably broiler (meat-type) chickens. A similar active role by agribusiness in the adoption of transgenic (and possibly patented) animals would dramatically change the complexion of the issues. **Luby** argues, however, that major firms will rely first and foremost on the pricing system to induce the desired products. Alterations in pricing have been used in recent years to adjust product volumes and characteristics to rapidly evolving consumer preferences, and that approach will likely be continued with transgenic animals.

Brody possibly has the most difficult task: to offer an appraisal of the moral and ethical objections to animal patents. As a philosopher and ethicist he is not one to raise concerns in his own right or to summarize the positions of

115

other groups. Instead he uses the logic of philosophy to scrutinize the objections raised by several religious, farm, and environmental groups according to their implications and consistency with Western thought. Using that approach he finds the objections lacking in consistency with prevailing values and sometimes radical in their implications. Some readers will find an inherent dichotomy in this effort to apply logic to an inherently emotional matter. Logic may not resolve these issues to everyone's satisfaction, but it does establish a basis for a meaningful discussion.

Perspectives of Farmers

A. Ann Sorensen

INTRODUCTION

The issue of whether or not transgenic animals should be patented and what the effect will be on US agriculture has been actively debated for over a year. At first, the idea of transgenic animals caught many by surprise. Although genetic improvement of livestock is an important component of production agriculture, the idea of inserting a foreign gene successfully into an animal and subsequently having a novel trait expressed was difficult to grasp. In addition, the concept of patents, what they do and don't do, was also novel. Just thinking about the sheer mechanics of collecting royalties on offspring was staggering. But now, after we have had a chance to collect our breath, agriculture is speaking out, although not always with a united voice.

I have been asked to summarize how farmers feel about animal patents. Chances are, if you put 200 farmers in a room, you would get 200 different answers. What I propose to do is this. First I will review the current livestock production systems that make collection of patent royalties such a challenge. Then I will review the viewpoints of those farm groups that have spoken out on this issue. Finally, I will address current controversies and possible future outcomes.

LIVESTOCK AGRICULTURE

In the USA about 17 percent of the land area is used for crop production. An additional 30.6 percent is grassland pasture and range, and 8.7 percent is forest land suitable for grazing. Thus, of the 2264 million acres of land in the USA, only about 56 percent is suitable for any kind of agricultural purposes (Lasley, 1981). And of this land area, 70 percent can be used only for grazing livestock (Dikeman, 1983).

Animal products account for fully one-half of all US agricultural revenues and involve more than two-thirds of all farms. Livestock farms are defined as those farms where sales of livestock products constitute more than half of total cash receipts. The number of dairy farms in the USA was 164,500 in 1982 with nearly 40 percent located in the Lake states. These farms averaged 304 acres, with total assets of $401,189.00 (excluding inventories of crops and livestock), 59 dairy cows, and a cash return of $112.00 per acre (Reimund *et al.*, 1986).

There were 41,900 poultry farms in 1982, of which nearly half were located in the Southeast. They averaged 117 acres, with total assets of $243,043.00 and cash returns of −$535.00 per acre. Poultry was the only commodity with negative cash returns in 1982. This is not uncommon in the poultry industry. It is highly competitive and can increase production rapidly in response to higher prices. Other livestock farms (farms producing cattle and calves, hogs and pigs, and sheep and lambs) numbered 905,800, averaged 524 acres, had $294,824.00 in assets, averaged 73 cattle and calves, and had a net cash return of $18.10 per acre. It is the net cash returns that will decide how much farmers are willing to pay for transgenic livestock.

Cattle Production

Cattle and calves account for about 26 percent of farm cash receipts (Council for Agricultural Science and Technology, 1979). No other single agricultural enterprise exceeds this level of importance in the US food supply. The beef industry supplies US consumers with 12 percent of their food energy and 23 percent of their protein. In 1982, there were 116 million beef cattle in the USA (US Department of Agriculture, 1982).

Beef cattle production is split into calf production and cattle feeding. Calf production occurs principally in Texas, the Dakotas, Oklahoma, and the Southeast. After 18 months, calves are sold to feedlot operations, where they are grain-fed and fattened for slaughter. The feedlot operations are concentrated in areas where feed grains are readily available: the western corn belt states, the Texas high plains, Arizona, and California. Some of these operations are enormous. About 5 percent of the feedlots accounted for about 61 percent of the cattle slaughtered in 1982. Because producers are widely scattered and removed from feedlot locations, most cattle pass through the hands of several brokers and are sold several times between birth and slaughter. This makes it extremely difficult to track individual animals.

The production of cattle is regional in nature. Beef herds remain relatively small, averaging fewer than 100 cows in most states. For many farms, beef cattle represent supplementary income. These farms tend to average 20 head or less. Beef cattle herd-size per owner is increasing, but large corporations are not heavily involved in the change (Council for Agricultural Science and Technology, 1980). Beef cattle, particularly breeding cattle, are required to graze and to utilize roughages in a variety of environments, usually without shelter. Thus, different breeds must be matched to the feed resources and climate. In the Southeast and South, there is abundant grass and forage production, but relatively low grain production. The winters are very mild and the grazing season is quite long, whereas the summers are hot and humid. Much rangeland is located in the Southwest where vegetation varies from good to very sparse. Where water is available and topography permits, grain sorghum is grown to feed cattle for slaughter. Many of the commercial feedlots are located in these areas because of the suitable climate and availability of feed. In the West, rangeland varies from mountains to deserts and the severity of the winter also varies considerably. In the Midwest, North, and

Northeast, forage and grain production are abundant. Extensive farm feeding of cattle for slaughter occurs in these regions where winters are moderately severe.

Most calves in the USA are born in the spring, although in the South and Southeast, a significant portion of calves are born in the fall. Most are weaned at seven to ten months, held through the winter, and either grazed the following spring and summer or placed in a feedlot for finishing on a high-concentrate diet. The practice of weaning calves and placing them directly in the feedlot without backgrounding and grazing is increasing because of the need to reduce overhead costs. Cattle are generally fed a high-concentrate diet until they are considered ready to slaughter.

Genotypes of beef cows are basically matched to the environment and food resources. There is moderate use of crossbreeding, and the use of terminal sires is increasing. Purebred cattle breeders are essentially the seed stock producers for the industry. Each breed has its own breed association which receives and approves applications for registration according to certain requirements and issues registration certificates. It has been estimated that 10–15 percent of US beef cattle producers have registered cattle (A. Keating, personal communication). Only 5 percent of US beef cattle are artificially inseminated (H. Hawk, personal communication).

The goal of genetic improvement is to optimize beef production. This is generally done by selecting breeding females on the basis of fertility, mothering ability, and foraging ability (Notter *et al.*, 1979). These breeding females are then mated to sire genotypes selected for growth rate, muscling, and reduced body fat. Sire breeds that already have the germ plasm for these traits such as Charolais, Limousin, or Simmental are the most common breeds used for terminal crossbreeding. Hereford and Angus breeds form the base for breeding female genotypes. Hereford females are more popular in regions where vegetation is more sparse, Angus females where feed is more abundant. Sometimes, Angus–Hereford reciprocal crossbred females are mated to the imported breeds to achieve the goals of increased growth rate, feed efficiency, and decreased carcass fatness.

In the South and extreme Southeast, Zebu genotypes (e.g. Brahman, Santa Gertruis, Brangus, Simbrah) are popular because they are much more tolerant of the heat, humidity, and insects. In these regions, productivity can be increased by crossbreeding with these breeds (Cartwright *et al.*, 1964).

This type of crossbreeding system optimizes use of feed resources, increases efficiency of lean meat production, and meets consumer demands for lean beef that is acceptable in palatability. However, this system requires a higher level of management and has not yet become the predominant production system in the USA. Maintaining separate sire and dam genotypes is not as easy as crisscrossing or rotational breeding. In addition, there is some cattle feeder and meat packer discrimination against these large, muscular breed types. They will not achieve the same percentage of USDA Choice carcasses as Angus–Hereford reciprocal crosses unless fed to considerably heavier weights. If the producer complies, the advantage in feed efficiency is eliminated.

Beef production centers around finishing steers and heifers for slaughter. Males are castrated because they are easier to manage, although bulls grow 15–20 percent faster than steers. Because of this, and the fact that they are 25–30 percent leaner, bulls are more efficient in feed conversion than steers (Oltjen, 1982). There is only limited production of young, intact males (bullocks). Even if research reveals improved production and processing systems for bulls, the transition from feeding steers to feeding bulls will be slow (Dikeman, 1983).

Most fed cattle are sold directly to the meat packer on a live weight basis; some are still sold through stockyards or commission markets. The majority of US cattle are fed to reach a quality-grade endpoint, namely USDA Choice. Grading is voluntary, and costs of grading are paid by the packer; approximately 75 percent of fed beef is graded in the USA. Last year, the four largest meat-packing firms accounted for 66 percent of the finished beef cattle slaughtered and 82 percent of boxed beef sales. Some producers fear that this concentration of buying power may have serious effects on competition for beef cattle, price discovery, and price reporting.

Approximately 5 million male offspring are produced annually from nearly 11 million dairy cows, and these males are also fed and slaughtered for meat. Dairy steers receive a lower price than beef steers because they have lower dressing percentages and lower muscle-to-bone ratios (Callow, 1961).

Swine Production

US swine production occurs largely in the Midwest where most of the corn and grain sorghum are produced. In this region, swine are commonly referred to as "mortgage lifters" (Lasley, 1978). 75 percent of US hogs are produced by farrow-to-finish operations. Their goal is to market the maximum number of offspring per sow in the shortest time possible. Economic pressures have forced producers to become larger and more intensified in their production systems. In 1982, 315,000 farms produced hogs, with 10 percent of the largest farms producing 50 percent of the total production. The 1988 herd size has been estimated at 53.8 million head. Large corporations, especially feed and grain companies, have had continued interest in swine feeding operations, but few have entered the business on a successful basis (Council for Agricultural Science and Technology, 1980).

Most producers utilize crossbreeding extensively for hybrid vigor (approximately 85–90 percent of all hogs slaughtered). Most crossbreeding programs include either crisscross or rotational crossbreeding. However, the development of separate female and sire genotypes is increasing. Here, females are selected for reproductive performance, prolificacy and mothering ability, whereas sires are selected for growth rate, muscling, and reduced body fat (Dikeman, 1983, p. 4). This system optimizes efficiency, but is more difficult for producers to utilize than either rotational or crisscross breeding systems.

120

Yorkshires are the most popular breed in the USA, while Durocs, Hampshires, and Chester Whites are also used extensively. Most market hogs are marketed on a live weight basis, either through buying stations or directly to meat processors. Price differentials for different grades are minimal. Because pork is not merchandised on a grade basis, pork processors use grading primarily to evaluate the accuracy of hog buyers and to predict cut-out yields. Because of modified environments, improved management, and improved breeding stock, market hogs now are generally slaughtered before six months of age. The four largest packing firms accounted for 37 percent of the hogs slaughtered last year.

Sheep Production

The sheep industry in the USA is quite small. In 1982, 100,000 farms raised a total of 12.4 million sheep, half with fewer than 50 head. In the Southwest and West, large flocks account for approximately 80 percent of all sheep, and about 38 percent are managed in flocks of over 2500 head (Council for Agricultural Science and Technology, 1982). In the Midwest and Northeast, sheep are managed in smaller farm flocks that do not represent a major income source to owners. Both large and small sheep flocks are owned by farmers and ranchers. Large corporations have shown little interest in this segment of animal agriculture (Council for Agricultural Science and Technology, 1980). The small size of the industry, poor consumer demand for lamb, predation problems, infectious diseases and parasites, noxious range weeds, seasonal breeding, and lack of skilled labor are significant limitations to growth of the industry (Council for Agricultural Science and Technology, 1982).

About 78 percent of the gross income from sheep is from meat production. The single most important factor affecting profitability for the commercial lamb producer is number of lambs weaned per ewe bred (Dickerson, 1970). Twinning is important, and white-faced breeds are more prolific than black-faced breeds. The sheep industry has been the leader in utilizing dam breeds and sire breeds to maximize lambs marketed per ewe. White-faced dam breeds also have higher-quality fleeces, but slower growth rates and less muscling than black-faced sire breeds. White-faced breeds are utilized almost exclusively in large range flocks and make up most of the breeding females used in Midwest farm flocks. The Suffolk breed is the most common sire breed used in crossing with these white-faced ewe breeds.

Some attempts have been made to accelerate lamb production, but more intensive and specialized management is required. One approach is to use ewe breeds that will breed out of season, so that more than one lamb crop can be marketed in one year. This involves such ewe breeds as Dorset, Rambouillet, and Merino (Schwulst, 1982).

Lambs are born in the winter or early spring. Some range flock lambs are marketed for slaughter at the end of the grazing season without supplemental feed. Those not heavy enough for slaughter at that time are shipped to the

Midwest for finishing on high-energy diets. Lambs born in farm flocks are fed moderately high-energy diets from weaning to slaughter. Large meat-packing companies feed some lambs and contract other lambs from farmer feeders to assure a year-around supply for slaughter. There are only 14 sheep packers in the USA. Last year, the four largest firms accounted for 75 percent of the sheep and lamb processed.

Lambs are marketed almost entirely on a live weight basis. Ram lambs bring lower prices than ewes or wethers, even though they are more efficient to produce, have leaner carcasses, and are essentially equal in palatability. Grading is voluntary.

Poultry Production

Large corporations dominate the poultry industry. Integrated firms are responsible for production of 99 percent of the nation's broilers, 80 percent of the market eggs and 80 percent of the turkeys (Rogers *et al.*, 1977). They supply the feed, grow the birds themselves or under contract, and process the products. A typical integrated poultry firm includes one or more hatcheries, hatching-egg flocks, feed mills, production farms, slaughter plants, and plants to process feathers and viscera for recycling. Currently, 11 major integrated firms dominate the broiler market. Concentration is higher among breeders who sell chicks to the integrators. Three firms control 90 percent of the market in female birds, whereas four firms control 90 percent of the market in male birds. Broiler or meat production largely utilizes two breeds: the White Plymouth Rock hen, good in both egg and meat production, is crossed with the white Cornish male, a breed noted for heavy muscling but poor egg production (Lasley, 1978). This single one-way cross produces most of the broilers all over the world.

Most of the broiler chickens are raised in the Southeast and South Central states where food supplies are plentiful and the winters are mild. It takes about seven weeks to raise broilers to a live weight of about 4 lb, with each pound of live weight being produced with slightly less than 2 lb of feed. The broiler industry operates on very narrow profit margins, with feed accounting for 60 percent of the costs. Americans consume about 13.7 million broilers a day.

The egg production industry has not developed as dramatically. About 60 percent of all eggs produced come from smaller producers. Commercial egg production utilizes the crossing of certain inbred lines developed within the egg-laying breeds, such as the Leghorn.

The turkey industry is also highly organized. Most turkey breeder hens are kept under controlled light so that they will lay eggs at a specified date. The toms (males) are also kept under controlled light so they will reach sexual maturity at a specified time. All matings in turkeys are by artificial insemination. Hens lay eggs for about 20 weeks and produce about 85 eggs per laying period. From the hatcheries, the young turkeys (poults) are shipped to growers who grow them out for market. The edible meat on the oven-ready carcass of a male turkey ranges from 74 to 80 percent of the total weight (Council for Agricultural Science and Technology, 1980). This is the highest yield of edible product for any domestic meat-producing species.

Dairy Industry

There are currently about 11 million dairy cows in the USA. Dairying has grown from a one-cow or small-herd operation used to supplement the family food supply to a specialized farming business. It remains primarily a family enterprise. However, dairy farming does require considerable capital. For example, to establish a 100-cow herd, a minimum investment of $250,000 would be required, not including the cost of land or the cost of replacement animals (Council for Agricultural Science and Technology, 1980). The average dairy farm has approximately 59 head (National Commission on Dairy Policy, 1988). Dairy production occurs in all states, in part due to the Federal milk marketing order system (National Commission on Dairy Policy, 1988). The leading milk-producing states are California, Minnesota, New York, and Wisconsin.

More attention has been given to the improvement of performance of dairy cattle through breeding than to any other class of farm animal except poultry. One reason for this is that performance can be measured relatively easily and accurately by weighing the milk produced and by testing for butterfat content at certain intervals during lactation. Consumer demands have remained fairly consistent so there has been no need to revise selection objectives (as there has been with swine and now beef, with demand shifting towards leaner meat).

The traits of greatest economic importance in dairy cattle breeding are reproduction, milk production, butterfat production, type, and productive life span. Crossbreeding in dairy cattle has not been commonly practiced because of the great differences among breeds in milk and butterfat production. Approximately 90 percent of the US herd is Holstein–Friesian. Other breeds include Jerseys, Guernseys, Ayrshires, and Brown Swiss. Virtually all dairy operations breed their own replacement stock. Approximately 65 percent of the total dairy cattle are artificially inseminated, at an average cost of $9.00–$10.00 per unit (H. Hawk, personal communication).

Over the last 50 years, the dairy industry has used test records of individual animals to help in genetic improvement. The National Cooperative Dairy Herd Improvement Program (NCDHIP) is a nationwide program for collecting, analyzing, and disseminating information on the performance of dairy cattle. It is a voluntary program and involves individuals, state and federal agencies, breed associations, and professional and scientific societies. It is almost totally financed by dairy farmers. Approximately 36,000 herds with 2.8 million cows were enrolled in 1979. These cows outproduced cows not enrolled in the program by 52 percent more milk per lactation (US Congress, Office of Technology Assessment, 1982). The increases in production per cow were a result of improved management techniques and genetic producing ability.

Currently, some 60,000 farmers participate in the improvement program, which involves recording milk production of each cow for one day every month. Information on each animal is compiled and sent to the Animal Improvement Program Laboratory in Beltsville. In July 1989, the US Department of Agriculture (USDA) will release a new system, called the "Animal Model," which takes into account more of the cow's relatives when evaluating the animal's ability to pass on high milk production capability to its offspring.

FARM ORGANIZATIONS AND THE ANIMAL PATENT ISSUE

As I mentioned in my introduction, several farm organizations have now gone on record as being either for or against animal patents. Others are taking a wait-and-see attitude, remaining somewhat neutral, but voicing some concerns. Most of these concerns are economic. In addition to the farm organizations, some commodity groups and a state department of agriculture have also adopted policies regarding transgenic animals.

It is difficult to obtain membership figures for most US farm organizations. Some farmers belong to more than one organization, and some are unaffiliated. However, rough estimates can be made and are quite useful for the purposes of weighting testimony. The very first farm organization was the Grange, established in 1867. It now represents about 12 percent of US farmers in about 37 states. The next organization to be established was the National Farmers Union in 1902. This currently represents about 5–10 percent of farmers in 20 states. The American Farm Bureau Federation was established in 1919, and is now the largest general farm organization in the world. Approximately 80 percent of farmers belong to one of 2759 county farm bureaus. The county farm bureaus, in turn, make up the membership of the state farm bureaus. All states except Alabama have a state farm bureau and the Commonwealth of Puerto Rico is represented by the Puerto Rico Farm Bureau. The state farm bureaus are members of the American Farm Bureau Federation.

In 1955, the National Farmers Organization was set up. It represents less than 2 percent of US farmers in 17 states. About seven or eight farm organizations were created between 1977 and 1983 as a result of the farm crisis. They still exist, and their membership includes about 5 percent of farmers in 30 or so states. Some farmers belong to more than one farm organization; most also belong to commodity organizations. Approximately 5 percent of US farmers are non-aligned.

American Farm Bureau Federation

The American Farm Bureau Federation supports the granting of animal patents. The Federation argues that patents will act as an incentive for the commercialization of genetically improved animal breeds. They point out that the option of deliberately delaying technological progress to avoid anticipated social or economic problems does not exist for very long in one part of the world if others refuse to follow this strategy. The Federation is generally supportive of any legislation that will encourage research on and commercialization of new agricultural products. The continuing decrease in availability of funds in the public sector for agricultural research makes this policy even more essential. They highlighted some of the benefits of genetic engineering in their testimony. These include more rapid and precise changes in breeding, increased efficiency of food utilization, disease resistance, improved reproductive performance, and the opportunity to produce non-food products such as protein pharmaceuticals from livestock. Comparing patents to trade secret protection, the Federation concluded that patents, which allow access to the process, were preferable. Addressing some of the ethical implications, the Federation contended that the trend towards vertical integration in food production and the possibility of more farm failures are not appropriate to the issue of whether or not patents should be granted. These issues are covered by other laws. The Farm Bureau did not think farmers would be "forced" into buying transgenic breeds, thus decreasing genetic diversity. The number of breeds is solely a function of market demand. Animal welfare concerns were similarly dismissed on the basis of market pressures ruling out transgenic breeds with traits that would subject them to stress.

They did, however, raise some concerns over how the system would work. They called for a set of guidelines for the Patent Office to follow concerning issues such as determining if animals meet patent requirements, defining the scope of patent coverage, and detailing enforcement procedures of animal patent law. Collection of royalties on offspring was seen as a logistical nightmare of paperwork in those few cases where it would be feasible. A one-time fee was suggested in lieu of royalty payments. Recently, the American Farm Bureau Federation submitted an alternative proposal for consideration by industry and other farm and commodity organizations. This proposal, which uses purebred associations to collect fees on offspring of transgenic livestock used for breeding purposes, appears in the Addendum at the end of this paper.

Policy Development in the Farm Bureaus

Every year, the American Farm Bureau Federation undergoes a unique process that allows all of its farmer members the opportunity to participate in setting policy for the upcoming year. At the county level, some 2759 county farm bureaus begin by reviewing all of their policies in small committees and deciding whether to change, delete, or add to them. These changes are then voted on at the county Farm Bureau Annual Meeting. Each county sends delegates to the state Farm Bureau Annual Meeting with their recommendations. The state delegates review policies at both the state and national levels. Recommendations for national policy are then sent on to Chicago where the Resolutions Committee (composed of the presidents of the state farm bureaus) meet to consider them.

It is these revised policies that are voted upon by state delegates to the national meeting. Up until the final vote, any delegate can amend or suggest new policy provided that the voting delegates agree to the change. The whole process takes most of the year.

If questions on policy come up in the meantime, the American Farm Bureau Federation Board of Directors (all of whom are farmers or ranchers) has the authority to interpret policies. The farm bureau system has a tradition of encouraging its farmer and rancher members to participate in the policy development process and to run for elective office within the farm bureau. In this manner, the farm bureau is assured that its policies truly represent the viewpoints of its members.

National Cattlemen's Association

The National Cattlemen's Association supports the concept of patenting, but their present policy calls for a beef cattle exemption on patent royalties. They state that: "because of the many potential economic and humanitarian benefits plus our industry's increased potential competitiveness worldwide, we support the principle of patenting the techniques and processes." They go on to express concern for patenting breeds or individual cattle "because of the potential of monopoly, liability, legal involvement, and federal regulations." They conclude by urging Congress to exempt domestic beef animals from patent rights.

Other Livestock Commodity Groups

The commodity groups for pork, dairy, and poultry, unlike the National Cattlemen's Association, have not taken an official position.

National Farmers Union

The National Farmers Union has expressed support for a moratorium on animal patents. They were joined by the National Farmers Organization, the American Agriculture Movement, the Coalition to Save the Family Farm, and the League of Rural Voters. These groups feel that more time is needed to investigate and review several areas of concern. Among these are the potential effects of animal patents on the gene pool; whether patents will lead to a greater economic concentration in breeding stock production; and whether costs will be passed on to the consumer if producers are forced to pay royalties to the patent owners.

They suggest that US farmers might be placed at a competitive disadvantage if forced to pay royalties on transgenic livestock, while their European competitors remain exempt from payments. Currently, most European countries do not grant animal patents. They also point to a long history of advances within both the research community and the livestock industry without the incentive of animal patents.[1]

---

[1]   See Appendix 6 for a synopsis of these views. (Ed.)

These groups feel strongly that the issues surrounding animal patents are of such magnitude that they should not be left to Patent Office employees, but should be more appropriately addressed by the elected representatives of the US public.

National Farmers Organization

The National Farmers Organization testified on behalf of themselves, the American Agriculture Movement, the International Alliance for Sustainable Agriculture, the League of Rural Voters, the National Farmers Union, the United Farmers Union, and the United Farmers Organization. They supported a moratorium to provide time to examine the economic, social, and ethical effects of animal patents.

They highlighted four areas of concern for further examination: the effects of patents on traditional breeding practices; the possibility that patents may shrink the gene pool; the possibility that patents may increase the concentration of those producing breeding stock; and the impact on consumers if farmers have to pay royalties for their livestock.

Echoing the previous testimony given by the National Farmers Union, they claim that patents will be a disadvantage to US farmers because European farmers do not have to pay patent royalties. They also cite the accelerated acquisition of seed companies by major corporations after patent protection was granted to plant varieties as a harbinger of things to come.

Wisconsin Farmers Union

The Wisconsin Farmers Union supported a moratorium on animal patents to allow a more careful examination of the economic, moral, ethical, health, and environmental concerns posed by patents. They argue that public funds have been the basis for biotechnology research, even for the multinational companies. If this is the case, then granting a monopoly market position to these corporations is not fair and patents are not necessary to promote scientific progress.

They feel that patented animals will cost more than if competition were allowed. They also point out collection of royalties would be nearly impossible given the large volume of animal sales. A "farmer exemption" was accepted as a partial solution.

For the dairy industry, they argue that the problem of overproduction will be exacerbated by patents. In addition, many farmers have improved milk yields through classical genetic breeding, and these breeds are not eligible under the current policy of the Patent and Trademark Office. This inequity might speed the vertical integration of family farms.

Texas Department of Agriculture

The Texas Department of Agriculture (TDA) sent out a questionnaire to Texas livestock producers concerning the animal patent issue in December 1987. Of those who responded, 96 percent said they opposed the patenting of farm animals. In a letter to the Texas representatives in Washington, TDA called for a temporary moratorium on animal patents.

The TDA letter made several predictions based on trends in the seed industry and on recent patent cases involving microorganisms. These included the following concerns:

(1) In many cases, livestock producers would not be able to own their animals outright.

(2) Patented animals were likely to increase the input costs of farming.

(3) Farmers and ranchers, even those with very large operations, would not be able to obtain animal patents.

(4) Once a trait was patented, it would not be possible for a producer to use or breed animals with that trait even if it could be produced by conventional breeding methods.

(5) Certain labels such as "lite beef" could be preempted and restricted as a trademark for cattle with a patented trait even if low-fat cattle could be produced by other means.

(6) Animal patents would likely accelerate the trend towards increasing concentration in agriculture.

It should be pointed out that this particular letter was highly controversial among Texas producers. The original survey (with an accompanying letter that many considered inflammatory and suggestive) was sent to 1740 Texas livestock producers. The actual number of livestock producers in Texas in 1987 was as follows: cattle—146,000; dairy—6900; sheep and goats—8500; hogs—13,000; poultry, no figures but less than 5000 (Texas Farm Bureau, personal communication). Thus, there are roughly 179,000 livestock producers in Texas. The TDA of Agriculture received 488 replies representing 0.3 percent of the producers. This survey has been questioned as to how representative it really is of Texas livestock producers. The Texas Farm Bureau, which represents the majority of livestock producers in Texas, supports the patenting of animals.

Common Concerns

Perhaps the most frequently mentioned concern by all of the commodity groups has been how excess offspring will be treated. Many farmers will sell excess offspring (e.g. young dairy calves) to their neighbors. They have no idea whether or not their neighbors will sell these calves for veal, rear them as milking cows, or sell them as breeding stock. If animals sold for breeding stock are not exempt from royalties, how can all of these small farm transactions be policed? It is a tough question to answer.

The other reoccurring concern has been that patents will essentially prevent small farmers from purchasing transgenic animals because of their high prices. In this scenario, only a broad farmers' exemption will open up the market to all farmers. But another conflicting scenario has recently been

128

revealed by some of the companies. They claim that a broad farmers' exemption will force companies to sell only to the very large farms, and small farmers will no longer have access to transgenic animals. In this scenario, the companies, in order to get a return on their investment, will enter into bailment contracts with commercial farms. A bailment contract allows companies to "lend" their animals out. The commercial farms rear the animals, but the offspring still belong to the company. Profits are shared according to the contract. A good analogy is taking a car to a garage to be fixed. The car is placed in the protection of the garage, which must return the car in an agreed-upon condition. The advantage to the company, obviously, is that the animals do not change ownership. Obviously, the biotechnology companies are not going to be willing to enter into 10,000 bailment contracts with small farmers. Instead, they will choose to "lend" their animals to the large corporate farms who can produce thousands of offspring. If this really does happen, the small farmer will be cut out entirely.

The Farmers' Exemption

Currently, the solution that has been proposed to circumvent many of the problems involved in collecting royalties on livestock is a broad farmers' exemption. This legislation was stalled in the Senate after passing the House in September 1988. It will probably be considered during the next session of Congress.[2] The legislation exempts farmers who buy transgenic livestock from the normal provisions of patent law. They will be free to use or sell offspring of genetically modified animals for any purpose without infringing on the patent of the company that engineered the animal in the first place. The legislation was supported in the House by all of the farm organizations that had spoken out on animal patents. However, some of these groups supported the farmers' exemption legislation solely as a means to block competing legislation to enact a moratorium. Most of the farm and commodity groups acknowledge that companies will have to have some return on their research investments to make transgenic animal research worthwhile. The issue that remains to be resolved is exactly how to do this in a commodity business where significant markups to cover millions of dollars of laboratory work have never been done before.

As this paper goes to press, several agricultural organizations, commodity groups, and representatives from industry and the Congress are meeting to develop a more equitable solution. They hope to develop a means whereby both those who carry out transgenic animal research and those who will raise transgenic animals will benefit. If a solution can be agreed upon, it will be presented to the next session of Congress to be considered.

Acknowledgements

I would like to thank the following people for supplying me with information and insights on a very complex issue: Lisa J. Raines, Industrial Biotechnology

---

[2]   See discussion in O'Connor's paper and Appendix 3. (Ed.)

Association; David Beier, House Subcommittee on Courts, Civil Liberties, and Administration of Justice; Kevin W. O'Connor, Biological Application Program, Office of Technology Assessment; Don E. Rawlins, Director, NER Division, American Farm Bureau Federation; Al Keating, Director, Livestock Department, American Farm Bureau Federation; Larry McKenzie, Assistant Director, National Affairs, American Farm Bureau Federation.

References

Callow, E. H. (1961) Comparative Studies of Meat. VII. A Comparison between Hereford, Dairy Shorthorn, and Friesian Steers on Four Levels of Nutrition. *J. Agric. Sci.*, **56**: 265.

Cartwright, T. C., G. F. Ellis, Jr., W. E. Kruse, and E. K. Crouch (1964) Hybrid Vigor in Brahman Hereford Crosses. *Texas Agric. Exp. Sta. Tech. Monogr.*, no. 1.

Council for Agricultural Science and Technology (1979) *Impact of Government Regulations on the Beef Industry.* Report no. 79.

—— (1980) *Food from Animals: Quantity, Quality and Safety.* Report no. 82.

—— (1982) *The US Sheep and Goat Industry: Products, Opportunities, and Limitations.* Report no. 94.

Dickerson, G. (1970) Efficiency of Animal Production—Molding the Biological Component. *J. Anim. Sci.*, **30**: 849–859.

Dikeman, M. E. (1983) Animal Production Systems to Meet Consumer Demands—US and Canada. In: *Meat Science and Technology International Symposium Proceedings.* Chicago: National Livestock and Meat Board.

Lasley, J. F. (1978) *Genetics of Livestock Improvement.* Englewood Cliffs, NJ: Prentice-Hall.

—— (1981) *Beef Cattle Production.* Englewood Cliffs, NJ: Prentice-Hall.

National Commission on Dairy Policy (1988) *Report and Recommendations.* Washington, DC.

Notter, D.R., J. O. Saunders, G. E. Dickerson, G. M. Smith, and T. C. Cartwright (1979) Simulated Efficiency of Beef Production for a Midwestern Cow–Calf–Feedlot Management System. II. Mature Body Size. *J. Anim. Sci.*, **49**: 83.

Oltjen, R. R. (1982) Breeding, Feeding and Management of Bulls for Meat Production. Paper presented at the US Beef Symposium, *Beef from Young, Intact Males*, Kansas State University, Manhattan, Kansas.

Reimund, D. A., N. L. Brooks, and P. D. Velde (1986) *The US Farm Sector in the Mid-1980's.* ARED/ERS/USDA. Agricultural Economic Report no. 548. Washington, DC.

Rogers, G. B., L. A. Voss, W. L. Hensen, and H. B. Jones (1977) Marketing and Integration in the Poultry and Egg Industries. *US Department of Agriculture, Poultry and Egg Situation*, PES 294, p. 39.

Schwulst, F. J. (1982) Production by Crossbred Ewes (Finn–Dorset × Rambouillet) in Northwestern Kansas. *Kansas Agric. Exp. Sta. Res. Bull.*, no. 64.

US Congress, Office of Technology Assessment (1982) *Impacts of Applied Genetics: Micro-Organisms, Plants, and Animals.* Washington, DC.

US Department of Agriculture (1982) *Agricultural Statistics 1982.* Washington, DC: US Government Printing Office.

ADDITIONAL READING

McAnelly, L. (1988)   Ownership of Genes—Who Will Control the Raw Materials of Agriculture? *Grassroots* (spring): 3, 4, 20.

Raines, L. J. (1988)   The Mouse That Roared. *Iss. Sci. Technol.*, **70** (summer): 64–70.

Sorensen, A. A. (1987)   *Animal Patents: Agriculture's Perspective.* Park Ridge, Illinois: American Farm Bureau Federation.

US Congress, Office of Technology Assessment (1989)   *New Developments in Biotechnology: Patenting Life.* Washington, DC.

Addendum

Background

Currently, each breed of beef cattle has its own registry association (similar breed associations have been established for goats, sheep, swine, poultry, and horses). Purebred breeders are the seed stock producers for the livestock industry. The associations receive and approve applications for registration according to certain requirements and issue registration certificates. These certificates can range from $35.00 up to $1000.00 or more depending on the animal (horses tend to be in the higher price category). Following the first introduction of an exotic breed, prices for individuals are high because of a small supply. As the number of animals from these breeds increases, prices tend to become much lower. The major source of income for most breed associations is from registration fees. Many purebred associations have strict regulations on the use of artificial insemination for breeding. Blood typing of bulls is required by most purebred beef cattle associations, and only limited ownership is permitted. Other bulls may be owned by a cooperative and sire as many as 200,000 offspring. Most associations allow the use of frozen semen after the death of the bull, but in some cases there is a time limit after which it can no longer be used for insemination purposes. The proven benefits of good quality breeding stock insure that these guidelines are followed.

Proposal

Farmers who purchase transgenic livestock will be required by contract to register any offspring sold for breeding purposes. Animals that are used solely for food or fiber will be exempt from registry fees. In order to obtain registry papers, both parents must be registered as transgenic for the particular trait in question. The registry fee will be paid to the appropriate Registry Association and passed on to the patent holder. Registered animals will receive an official registry tag (e.g. a small diode chip attached to the ear) which will identify that animal as transgenic. Farmers selling either semen or embryos from transgenic animals will also be required to register so that the resulting offspring can be tagged. Since most transgenic animals will be purebred because of the expense involved (e.g. offspring of a registered Angus bull genetically modified for disease resistance), they could be referred to as "purebred plus" strains. Although it is not logistically possible to police a registry system, there will be ample incentives to participate. Farmers who purchase non-registered transgenic animals would have no guarantee that the trait they are paying for had been passed on to the offspring. In the case of disease resistance, this would mean they would have to take their chances on an unreliable breeding source and a possible outbreak of disease. Only registered purebred plus animals would receive top dollars from livestock producers. Since the current US purebred associations have been very successful without policing, and registration fees are accepted by livestock producers, fees for purebred plus strains should also be readily accepted. For example, it has been estimated that about 15 percent of US farmers now register Purebred cattle.

In the few large vertically integrated livestock operations, the incentive to purchase additional transgenic animals would be to prevent lines from becoming too inbred. Inbreeding is usually accompanied by a decline in vigor (e.g. decreased fertility, mothering ability, viability, and growth rate).

Currently the purebred associations mostly rely on peer pressure for results. Prestige, mystique, and improved net income are all a part of owning a purebred animal. Advantages to using the purebred associations to collect what are, in essence, royalties include:

(1) The purebred associations are already in place and doing well. They are an accepted and respected part of the livestock industry.

(2) The purebred associations are going to want to keep a sharp eye on transgenics anyway. If involved from the start, they are less apt to view them as "threats" to their purebred lines.

(3) The collection of registration fees for transgenics will also let the purebred associations make a little bit of money on the side. This too will encourage their active participation. They do, after all, already have a list of customers and potential customers.

Companies might want to consider "diagnostic kits" to easily identify their purebred plus animals from regular strains. These tests could either be made available with the registration fee or sold separately (that way, those farmers who decide to take their chances on unpapered animals would still have to pay to find out if their gamble paid off). Of course, if the companies can engineer transgenic livestock that produce sterile F2s (grandchildren), royalty collection systems may very well become obsolete.

Perspective of Agribusiness: What Do Packers and Processors Want in Livestock and Poultry?

Patrick Luby

INTRODUCTION

There may be as many perspectives on what processors want in livestock and poultry as there are agribusiness firms in the industry. Therefore, these remarks may or they may not represent industry thinking. However, I believe there is much common ground on some of the core thoughts.

Consumer demand for meat continues to evolve. This evolution affects what packers and processors want in livestock and poultry. Packers once sold mostly fresh meat—beef in carcasses or halves or quarters, poultry as fresh whole chickens or turkeys. Retailers prepared and cut meat into smaller package sizes in the store. Households were larger. The number of women in the commercial work force was small and the cooking or preparation of meat for serving was commonly done in the home.

CURRENT SITUATION FOR MEAT PROCESSORS

The situation is now considerably changed. Households are smaller. The proportion of adults in the work force is at a record high. Time available for home preparation of food is scarce. People are very mobile and "eat around the clock" and "around the town" at many kinds of locations.

The relative cost of slicing and packaging of meat in the retail store continues to rise. The technology to process and prepare meat and meals featuring meat at the packer and processor level continues to advance. There are many economies of performing processing and packaging functions at the processor level. The use of large and high speed slicing and packaging machinery favors the processor over the retailer or home preparer. Economies of large scale in the use of management and labor also favor food and meat preparation by large processors. Technological advances in the preparation, preservation, and packaging of meat adds to the trend towards large-scale commercial plants instead of home preparation.

With these trends, packers and processors view fresh meat more as a raw material to be used in food processing and less as a commodity to sell. The commercial chicken industry was originally developed by feed companies and cooperatives as a way of selling surplus feed and utilizing assets in feed

134

production. They produced and sold fresh, iced whole chickens. It was supply-driven. Contrast that with today. The chicken industry is increasingly demand-driven. It is powered by consumer and marketing firms who process and merchandise chicken pieces and meals featuring chicken pieces. In many cases, these products are processor-branded. The end consumer is the focus. The retailer remains very important, but performs different functions. As a result, the chicken industry today produces a lower percentage of whole chickens.

Similarly, the beef packer produces far fewer carcasses, halves or quarters. Most beef is now cut up at the packer level into primal and sub-primal cuts, and boxed for retailer display and merchandising with relatively little further effort.

Likewise, the turkey industry produces a smaller proportion of whole turkeys. However, it produces many times more turkey parts and breast meat portions for today's smaller households and foodservice and deli use.

Thus, the industry's needs are, as always, shaped by consumer demand and demographics, and the technological and scientific advances in production, processing, preservation, transportation, marketing, and other areas.

CONSUMER DEMAND

The consumer increasingly knows and demands quality. Consumers are more knowledgeable about and demand better nutrition. They want more leanness and less fat in their meat, particularly less visible fat. However, they want their meat to taste good. They want it to be tender and satisfying. They demand consistency of quality. They get it in other food and non-food products and don't understand why it shouldn't be possible in meat.

Consumers want safe products. Of course, packers, processors, and farm producers and feeders do too. Modern measurement capabilities increasingly permit us to detect unsafe characteristics of products. Today's communication methods allow any product safety problem to reach the attention of most consumers almost immediately.

The demand for meat can change much faster than formerly. In an earlier generation, most meat was prepared for use in our homes, typically by the mother of the family. She typically cycled a fixed number of menus past her family. They were menus in which she had confidence in preparing and serving, menus that met with satisfaction from her family. These menus often used meats produced on the farm. In others, they used meats from local butchers in stores where she shopped. She had confidence in the butcher's meat selection. Under these conditions, demand for meat changed very slowly. The supply of meat might change considerably, causing prices to gyrate. But demand was fairly constant.

Contrast that with today. Demand for meat can change easily. In fact, in the last decade or so, we have seen the demand for meat change much more than in previous times. More people eat meals away from home. They can change demand by merely pointing to a different line on a menu or making a different selection at a fast food establishment. They can easily select different prepared meats from a deli or a frozen food case. More people eat meat prepared for them outside the home.

We have seen how much and how fast demand for meat can change by observing the rapid decline in meat demand during the harsh recession from 1979 to 1982. Or by observing the continued decline in the demand for beef and to a lesser extent, pork, from 1982 to 1985. Or by noting the rapid increase in the demand for poultry during that time period. The issue of safety and its potential effect on demand was vividly exemplified from the feature concerning the potential of salmonella in chicken on a popular television program in March 1987. As we have witnessed during the 1980s, these demand swings have huge financial implications for livestock and poultry producers, processors, and packers, as well as allied industries and grain producers. For example, the gross income from the production of cattle and calves fell from $35.7 billion in 1979 to $29.4 billion by 1986. In real, deflated dollars the decline was even more severe. Consumers want safe food and safe meats, and so do farmers and all of agribusiness.

In addition to quality, consistency, nutrition, meatiness, low fat, taste, safety, and convenience, consumers want efficiency, low costs, and moderate prices. Indeed, meat is in a fiercely competitive market today. Its competitors are not only other food products, but all goods and services in society. There are many things we can spend our incomes for today that were unknown a decade ago. Health care increasingly takes a large proportion of our income. Meat is in a very competitive marketplace. For years, spending for meat at retail accounted for about 4 percent of consumers' disposable personal income. From 1980 to 1987, spending for beef, pork, and poultry declined from 3.80 percent of disposable income to only 2.67 percent. For beef and pork, the decline was even more severe, from 3.28 percent to 2.20 percent. The producers, processors, and marketers of meat products are forced to be extremely efficient to keep their product competitive.

PROCESSOR REQUIREMENTS

What do packers and processors want in animals and poultry? It mirrors what consumers want from packers and processors. To satisfy consumer demand, processors want consistent, high-quality animals and birds. They want meatiness and low fat. Processors want animals with meat that will be tasty, tender, and have positive eating characteristics which will result in general consumer satisfaction and warrant further future purchases. For beef, this is probably meat with characteristics of the Choice grade, but with minimal wastiness and low external fat covering. For pork, it means hogs with a high percentage of lean cuts, high carcass yields, and low fat cover.

Processors also want consistency of quality, again reflecting consumers' expectations and demand for consistent visual and eating characteristics.

136

Processors want animals and birds which will produce safe meat. This and many production issues may loom larger to processors of red meat than of poultry because, for the most part, processors of red meat do not own or feed animals and have little knowledge of the rations or additives that may be used or their withdrawal times. Pork processors, in recent years, have been pressing for a better and mandatory animal identification system, partly to trace any problems of safety in animals and meat.

Processors are very concerned with efficiencies, low cost, and prices. Since the meat processing industry is very competitive and since it serves production industries which are somewhat cyclical and seasonal, it often has excess processing capacity. Since more meat will be consumed at lower prices than at higher prices, and since, everything else being equal, processing and marketing costs will be lower per unit or per pound with greater throughput, the processing industry is interested in animals and birds that are relatively efficient and low in cost to produce. Since feed costs make up a majority of animal and bird production costs, this means the production of animal units with a favorable feed conversion rate and other characteristics that result in low production costs per unit.

Since animal and poultry carcasses are used more and more as raw material by processors to produce small consumer-sized products, processors prefer large animals of consistent size and conformation yielding large, lean, consistent size, and quality of cuts. With the trend toward boneless cuts with minimal external fat covering, large muscles in cuts such as the pork loin allow for better presentation in the marketplace. In addition, large animals and large cuts are more efficient to slaughter, cut, bone, and handle thus allowing lower costs per pound processed. Consistent, large-sized cuts with minimal bone and fat usually result in better boning yields. Uniform conformation of animals and cuts along with consistent size enhance the possibilities for further mechanization and automation of slaughtering, cutting, boning, and processing functions, thus further lowering costs.

INCENTIVE AND COORDINATION SYSTEMS

How can these changed traits in animals be achieved? How can the processing industry encourage increased production of these traits? How can processors encourage the rapid adaptation of production methods to achieve the desired traits? What changes, if any, are needed in the pricing or payment methods?

The livestock red meat industry has historically been made up of hundreds of thousands of independent producers, breeders, and feeders, and several thousands of packers, processors, and purveyors, with ownership of animals and meat changing hands several to many times in the lengthy process of getting meat from the breeder to the consumer. Almost full reliance on the price system and open markets has marked the industry. Relatively little integration of ownership or decision making at the various levels has occurred. Relatively few long-term contractual relationships have existed. Yet, considerable change has occurred in the traits of commercial hogs and cattle over the last several decades. These changes have generally been in the direction outlined in this paper toward traits desired by processors and consumers. Change has occurred fairly rapidly at times, such as in the case of hogs in the late 1950s and 1960s.

The red meat industry has generally relied on a pricing system based on live weights and estimated quality and yield characteristics for "finished" animals, that is, carcass characteristics. Some purchasing, based directly on carcass weights and carcass quality, has occurred, but it has never achieved "majority status." However, since the introduction of machinery and computing technology in the 1950s and early 1960s to weigh, grade, and assess easily, quickly, and cheaply the quality characteristics of individual carcasses, the live payment system has reflected this carcass information. This has greatly enhanced the "quality" or reflectiveness of the bidding and payment based as it is on the estimated quality and commercial value of the animals.

The commercial poultry industry is relatively much younger. From its origins in the 1930s, and particularly following World War II, it has been organized in a much more integrated fashion. Led early by large feed firms, and more recently by consumer-branded processing firms, production and marketing decisions have historically been made by fewer people. Decisions involving quality traits and size of birds have been coordinated within fewer firms and people.

Although proof is difficult to establish, the more integrated poultry industry has probably achieved greater consistency of quality characteristics in their products, a faster rate of change in achieving goals, and greater production efficiencies than has the more loosely organized livestock industry. Of course, the shorter reproduction times of poultry contributes to more rapid change and progress.

Will the independent organization of the far-flung red meat industry slow its ability to respond to future change in quality traits of animals or meat, which may be achieved by animal patents or other means? Will the system of payment encourage the adaptation of new methods to achieve more desirable product traits and characteristics?

There are several trends which seem to point in the direction of the red meat industry being able to adapt to new technologies in genetics or other fields. The number of producers and feeders of cattle and hogs continues to decline, a trend that has been taking place for four or five decades. The quality of managers involved in feeding livestock continues to improve. Three large participants in the fresh beef packing industry now account for about two-thirds of the fed beef slaughter and an increasing, but still much smaller, proportion of hog slaughter. Much more advanced technologies for accurately, automatically, cheaply, and quickly measuring the fat, bone, and muscle content of animals, carcasses, and cuts may be available soon. Longer-term contracts between slaughterers and further processors should be possible, utilizing quality and size information. In short, the declining number of participants in the feeding and packing industry, combined with advancing technology, should provide for enhanced measurement of quality characteristics and concomitant improvements in the reflectiveness of payment systems based on these characteristics.

The processing industry's fundamental needs are responding to changing consumer demand and utilizing processing efficiencies essential to competing in today's competitive marketplace. Processors want quality animals and birds of large and consistent size and conformation that will provide lean, tasty, and safe meat products of consistent quality. They want these products designed and produced efficiently to lower the price to consumers and to increase the amount of meat produced and marketed. Pricing systems, whether they operate under the more integrated poultry industry or the less coordinated red meat industry, must provide incentives for farmers to achieve desired quality traits and equitable payments for those quality characteristics. These requirements apply whether the desired change is achieved through animal patenting or by other means.

CONCLUSIONS

If the impacts of biotechnology on livestock and poultry are as great as some suggest, agribusiness will be affected in a significant manner. The quality of the meat produced will be more attractive to consumers, thus potentially raising the demand for meat. The cost of producing meat would be reduced, thus lowering the price to consumers. Together they would cause the production and consumption of meat to increase.

Coordination of supply and demand in beef and pork is presently accomplished almost exclusively through the price system. In the past, the red meat industries, particularly pork, have made significant progress toward larger, leaner animals by using the pricing system to establish the appropriate economic rewards for the desired carcass characteristics. With fewer, larger participants in this competitive industry, and with likely technological improvements in methods of animal identification and carcass quality measurements, most of the value improvements made possible by animal patenting should be achievable in a fairly efficient manner through a judicious use of the pricing system. However, the largely integrated poultry industry will probably maintain an advantage in its ability to adopt accurately and quickly any significant changes brought about by patenting.

The agribusiness sector has traditionally invested very little in livestock production operations. There are several reasons for this. The amount of capital employed in the feeding of livestock is very large compared with that involved in packing and processing. Returns are extremely volatile. In most cases, packers are not certain they could achieve lower costs than current producers. Packers have also been reluctant to compete with farmer feeders, particularly in hogs, from whom they purchase their animals. It is more likely that some form of contracting, rather than packer ownership, will evolve slowly as a means to achieve results not readily available through a complete reliance on the price system. There have already been some small tendencies for more contracting between packers and farmer-feeders, and between slaughterers and further processors.

The livestock sector is very large and dispersed, geographically and by ownership. Change is likely to proceed slowly. Within the livestock sector, change is likely to come most quickly from participants who have the most to gain relative to the investment and degree of risk. Change could begin with producers or processors. Consumers are likely to be the principal ultimate beneficiary receiving higher-quality meat at a lower real cost.

The collection of royalties is one issue for patented livestock. It could be collected by the holder of the patent at the original transaction for the patented livestock. Another possibility for collection is at the packing plant, with the packer acting as agent for the patent holder. However, in the widely dispersed livestock industry where ownership may change several times, this would require an extensive and accurate paper trail and animal identification system, making it a costly approach. Other technology than record-keeping for carcass quality classification and valuation at the packing house should be available in the near future and may be employed by meat packers, or alternatively by US Department of Agriculture inspection personnel working within these plants if an attractive payment system is set up by the patent holder.

An Evaluation of the Ethical Arguments Commonly Raised against the Patenting of Transgenic Animals

Baruch A. Brody

INTRODUCTION

On April 7, 1987, Donald J. Quigg, Commissioner cf Patents and Trademarks, announced that:

> The Patent and Trademark Office now considers non-naturally occurring non-human multicellular living organisms, including animals, to be patentable subject matter within the scope of 35 USC 101. (Committee on the Judiciary, 1988: p. 22)[1]

Slightly more than one year later, on April 13, 1988, patent no. 4,736,866 was issued to Harvard University.[2] It covers a new breed of genetically altered mice that can serve as a more effective model for studying how genes contribute to the development of cancer and for testing new anticancer drugs because the genetic altering results in half the females of the breed developing cancer (*Wall Street J.*, 1988: p. 26).

In response to the earlier announcement, a number cf bills were introduced in Congress. One (HR 3119, introduced on August 5, 1987 by Congressman Rose and others) mandated a two-year moratorium on patenting new animals while Congress studied the issues. It explicitly argued that the decision to allow such patents raises such fundamental economic, environmental, and ethical questions that it should be made by Congress, and not by the Patent and Trademark Office. Another (S 2111, introduced on February 29, 1988 by Senator Hatfield) simply banned such patents, presumably because its author judged that these questions clearly indicated that patenting is inappropriate. A series of hearings were held in the second half of 1987, but no bill actually passed both houses of Congress and became law.[3]

The debate surrounding both the announcement of the Patent Office and the subsequent proposed legislation raised many ethical issues. Indeed, a perusal of the testimony presented by opponents of patenting in the four 1987 hearings (Committee on the Judiciary, 1988) and in other writings produced

---

[1] See Appendix 4 for a synopsis of these hearings.   [2] See Appendix 2.
[3] See also O'Connor's paper above.

141

by these opponents reveals that the language of ethics was essential to much of that opposition. This paper critically evaluates the arguments the opponents presented. It concludes that the opponents failed to make their case, and that the proponents of the patenting of transgenic animals can offer a strong moral defense of their position.

MORAL ARGUMENTS RESTING UPON METAPHYSICAL AND/OR
THEOLOGICAL ASSUMPTIONS

The most fundamental moral arguments opposing patenting employ metaphysical and theological claims as their point of departure. They raise questions about the relation between the living and the non-living, and about the relation between human beings and the world which they inhabit. Moral conclusions are drawn at the end of these arguments, but they begin with non-moral philosophical and theological claims.

There is one feature of these arguments that needs to be noted. The proponents themselves recognize that they need to do a lot more work to articulate the inchoate concerns they feel. This is why the recent statement of the religious leaders against animal patenting called for a moratorium on patenting while a process of "thoughtful reflection and judgment on these matters by churches and religious institutions, as well as by other concerned groups in our society" is carried out. All that we can do is examine the articulations of concern that have already been developed. We need to be sensitive, however, to the possibility that further articulations of reasons for opposing patenting may be forthcoming.

Shortly after the *Diamond v. Chakrabarty* decision in which the Supreme Court ruled that a living microorganism was patentable, Leon Kass published an important essay in which he raised a number of fundamental questions about the patenting of living organisms of any size or complexity. Here, we focus on one argument which he stated as follows:

> Consider first the implicit teaching of our wise men, that a living organism is no more than a composition of matter, no different from the latest perfume or insecticide. What about other living organisms—goldfish, bald eagles, horses? What about human beings? Just compositions of matter? Here are deep philosophical questions to which the Court has given little thought, but in its eagerness to serve innovation, it has, perhaps unwittingly, become the teacher of philosophical materialism. (Kass, 1985: pp. 149–50)

Reinforcing Kass's point was the fact that the majority in *Diamond v. Chakrabarty* was required to find that the organism was a composition of matter, because the statute authorizing patents refers to "any new and useful process, machine, manufacture, or composition of matter" as a patentable object, and the relevant microorganism only fell under the last phrase. This aspect of the decision was also the basis of criticism of it by a working party of the World Council of Churches (1982):

> The U.S. Supreme Court decision on patenting of life forms rested upon a specific, highly reductive conception of life, which sought to remove any distinction between living and non-living matter that could serve as an obstacle to the patenting of living but unnatural organisms. (p.47)

This is obviously not the place to examine the great philosophical debate between materialists, who see living objects as nothing more than complexly organized matter, and non-materialists, who insist that living objects are more than that. Let us leave that question unresolved. Let us go further and agree with Kass that it would be inappropriate for society to adopt a social policy that committed us as a society to a materialistic conception of life. Still, there is nothing in the decision to patent living things—even under the current language of the patenting statute—that commits us to a materialistic conception of life. Even those who believe that living beings are more than compositions of matter believe that they are at least compositions of matter, and it is only as compositions of matter that we patent them.

A second argument, that some of the genetic engineering being patented confuses what must be kept distinct, is found in a passage in the recent statement of religious leaders against animal patenting (*Statement*, n.d.). They make the following claim:

> The combining of human genetic traits with animals, with the results to be patented and owned, raises unique moral, ethical, and theological questions, such as the sanctity of human worth, which must be examined.

A good example of what they have in mind is, of course, the introduction of genes for the human growth hormone into farm animals to produce greater growth.

The sanctity of human worth is, of course, a fundamental moral principle of our society, standing behind our belief that humans cannot be killed or mistreated, are entitled to freedom from enslavement, and so forth. Since we allow animals to be killed for food and to be owned, we do not subscribe to a similar sanctity of animal worth principle. After all, a sanctity of worth principle would seem to imply at least the following two elements: (1) the life of the entity in question is of sufficient value that it can be taken only in the most extreme circumstances (e.g. self-defense); (2) the individual is free to act as it desires, for it should not be treated as a mere means for others to attain their ends. By killing animals for use as food, we show that we do not ascribe such significance to their lives. By allowing them to be owned by those who would raise them for use as food, as a source of various byproducts (e.g. wool), as objects to be entered into competitions, or even as pets, we show

143

that we are willing to treat animals as mere means to human ends. All of this is, of course, perfectly compatible with insisting that unnecessary animal suffering should be eliminated. So our moral life, as currently constituted, rests upon the distinction between humans and animals. It would seem, then, that the religious leaders see such genetic experiments as imperiling the belief in the sanctity of human worth by breaking down the barrier between humans and other animals.

Do they? If it were possible (and it is not possible either now or in the foreseeable future) to alter genetically animals so that they had more of those capacities and features (e.g. the capacity to form moral judgments or the capacity to experience the beautiful and the sublime) which we see as distinctive to humans, then we would face difficult moral questions as to how such creatures should be treated and as to whether we can continue to maintain a sharp divide between humans and other animals. But, of course, none of these issues is raised by farm animals who grow more because they have a gene that leads them to produce human growth hormone. Nor would they be raised by any of the genetic alterations of animals that will be produced in the foreseeable future. So in what ways do these experiments raise questions about the sanctity of human worth? And in what way does the patenting of their results imperil that belief?

We turn finally to an interconnected series of arguments about man's control over nature, man's responsibility toward nature, and the need to preserve species and protect their integrity which are probably the leading cause of metaphysical and theological disquiet about the patenting of transgenic animals and about the genetic engineering it will promote. A powerful statement of this set of issues is contained in the following testimony of the Rev. Wesley Granberg-Michaelson, appearing on behalf of the National Council of Churches, on November 5, 1987:

> When the National Council of Churches has issued this statement of concern, it comes from the background of Judeo-Christian thinking about how we relate to the natural environment. In a nutshell that background says that we have a responsibility for preserving the integrity of the creation, and for working with it in order to preserve its intrinsic values . . . the doctrine of trust in legal parlance is synonymous to what we are talking about theologically or religiously when we think about the relationship of the creation to humanity. The Judeo-Christian view says that the creation is, in essence, held in trust; there are limitations on what we can do. We have a responsibility to see that its integrity is preserved. This background has led to legislation such as endangered species laws, animal welfare laws, laws regarding environmental quality. (Committee on the Judiciary, 1988)

There are several points which I want to make about this argument:

(1) The presentation of the Judeo-Christian tradition is somewhat misleading. As John Passmore showed in his ground-breaking study, *Man's
Responsibility for Nature* (1974), the traditional Judeo-Christian image
was that of man's dominion over nature. To give but one example,
Calvin repeatedly talked about the fact that God created all things for
man's sake. It is only in recent years that the theme of man's stewardship
over nature has become more predominant.

(2) The traditional idea of a steward or of a trustee is the idea of a person
who manages property for the benefit of other persons (present and
future) who are its owner. There is nothing in the traditional conception
of stewardship or trusteeship which even suggests that the property is to
be managed to preserve its integrity for its own sake. Property held in
trust can be radically transformed by trustees if it serves the best interest
of its human owners, present and future. One religious notion of
stewardship is the notion that man must treat the property he owns as a
trust for those human beings who will follow in future generations and
cannot over-exploit it so as to maximize his current benefit. This notion
of stewardship is analogous to the legal notion of trusteeship, but it is
not the notion that Granberg-Michaelson is employing. He is using the
different notion of the steward who protects the integrity of the property
for the property's sake.

(3) This radically new notion may be morally desirable, but its claims
demand considerable justification, and only those who are prepared to
accept its many radical implications are entitled to use it as the basis for
arguing against transgenic animals and the patenting of them. This
argument is analogous to some of the arguments used by some animal
rights advocates, an argument which we will examine in the next section,
in that it is based upon a radical revision in our metaphysical conception
of the relation of human beings to non-human nature, and not merely on
the adoption of the traditional notion of stewardship.

MORAL ARGUMENTS INVOLVING CLAIMS ABOUT ANIMAL RIGHTS

In the current debate surrounding the patenting of transgenic animals, the
animal rights movement has taken a leadership role in opposing such
patenting. Particularly prominent has been the opposition of the Humane
Society of the United States. Its president, John Hoyt, presented a number of
major arguments in his testimony before Congress. For our purposes, we will
focus on three of his arguments.

(1) The development of transgenic animals, encouraged by patenting, will
lead to far more animal suffering than changes produced through selective breeding and crossbreeding:

Genetic engineering is of a wholly different order of magnitude, in that in traditional breeding practices, genes cannot be exchanged between unrelated species. Furthermore, genetic changes can be wrought very rapidly through genetic engineering . . . If the patenting of animals is permitted, there will surely be a dramatic increase in the suffering of animals . . . This for the reason that the outcome of many genetic experiments cannot be predicted in relation to the animals' health and welfare . . . (Committee on the Judiciary, 1988: pp. 62–3)

An example often used by Michael Fox, the Society's Scientific Director, is the health problems (arthritis, lethargy, defective vision) of the US Department of Agriculture's transgenic pigs carrying the human growth gene.
(2)   Patenting reflects an inappropriate sense of human control over animal life and an underestimation of the value of non-human life:

From an ethical perspective, the patenting of animals reflects a human arrogance towards other living creatures that is contrary to the concept of the inherent sanctity of every unique being and the recognition of the ecological and spiritual interconnectedness of all life. (Committee on the Judiciary, 1988: pp. 64–5)

(3)   The patenting of animal life is the first step towards a decline in the belief in the sanctity and dignity of life:

To permit the patenting of just one animal will effectively eliminate all constraints . . . against genetically altering all other animals including human beings. (Committee on the Judiciary, 1988: p. 65)

There is a crucial difference between these three arguments. The first appeals only to the moral claim that animal suffering is wrong and should be avoided, a claim that is consonant with most moral views about animals. The second and third appeals go beyond that and depend upon far more controversial claims which will be identified below. This difference will be essential to our analysis of the arguments.

Let us first examine argument (1). The history of western moral thought shows a tremendous diversity in attitudes towards animal suffering (US Congress, Office of Technology Assessment, 1986b: chapter 4). Cartesians have been least sympathetic to any concern about such suffering. Aquinas and Kant saw the moral significance of humaneness towards animals as due to the way in which it encourages humans not to be cruel to each other. It is only in the Benthamite tradition that animal suffering and human suffering began to be seen as morally similar to each other, although even contemporary Benthamites such as Peter Singer allow for some significant differences in degree. Finally, contemporary thinkers such as Tom Regan have advanced the idea that animals have a presumptive right not to be harmed. Obviously, this is not the place to attempt to resolve this dispute. How then shall we assess argument (1)? I suggest the following: recent federal legislation (including the Animal Welfare Act of 1985) and regulations (including the 1985 PHS policy) covering animal research clearly indicate that our society now accepts the idea that animal suffering has moral significance and should be avoided. The fact that it mandates costly improvements in animal care clearly indicates that our society also accepts the idea that human interests do not always outweigh animal interests. The fact that the conducting of the research is not regulated—except for the rules covering the anesthetizing of animals—clearly indicates that we still see human interests as taking precedence over those of animals. All of that being the case, we should, I suggest, evaluate argument (1) in light of the current socially adopted attitudes towards animal suffering, keeping in mind that the more one ascribes moral significance to animal suffering, the more one will be troubled by argument (1).

It might be suggested that the current regulatory mechanisms will protect animals against unnecessary harm in the research that patenting will encourage. This seems not to be true. The Animal Welfare Act does not apply to rodents, birds, and farm animals intended for use as food or livestock (US Congress, Office of Technology Assessment, 1986b: chapter 13). The PHS regulations apply only to federally funded research. It appears then that there are no regulations in place to protect many animals used in research in industrial laboratories.

Leroy Walters of the Kennedy Center for Bioethics has pointed out in his congressional testimony that:

> The ethical issues related to interspecies gene transfers or the patenting of animals will probably be clarified if they are distinguished analytically from the animal-welfare question . . . Further, the goal of securing more humane treatment can be, and is being, approached directly through such means as legislation and regulations . . . (Committee on the Judiciary, 1988: p. 388)

This point is correct. Argument (1) really cannot show that the encouragement of the development of transgenic animals by patenting is wrong because it will lead to inappropriate animal suffering. Regulations appropriately governing such research are an alternative way of dealing with that problem. We can have the benefits of biotechnology while protecting animals from inappropriate suffering. But we need to remember that a failure to strengthen the regulatory scheme to protect against unnecessary suffering of farm animals, birds, and rodents in industrial research will pose a moral problem for the whole system of research encouraged by the issuing of patents. That, I believe, is the appropriate conclusion to be drawn by those who are committed to the understanding of the moral significance of animal suffering embodied in current legislation and regulation. Naturally, the greater the moral significance one ascribes to animal suffering, the stronger the regulations one will require to meet this problem.

Arguments (2) and (3) are very different, as we have suggested above. They appeal to stronger moral claims than the claim that animal suffering should be avoided. However, it is unclear as to what claims are being presupposed. Argument (2) talks about "the inherent sanctity of every unique being." Those who talk about the sanctity of something are usually ascribing great value to its continued existence and flourishing. As pointed out in the last section, it is hard to see how a society that is willing to slaughter animals for food can be viewed as committed to a belief in the inherent sanctity of every unique being. So argument (2) is appealing to premises about animals not acceptable by most, and should be advocated only by those who are prepared to accept all of its radical implications.

A similar type of premise must be presupposed by those who advocate argument (3). Why can we not differentiate between patenting genetically altered animals and patenting genetically altered humans? Most people would, I submit, have no difficulty doing so, and one need not lead to the other. One will lead to the other only if we treat the distinction between animals and humans as insignificant, and that claim of the insignificance of the human/animal distinction must be the presupposition of those who offer argument (3).

I conclude about arguments (2) and (3) that Leroy Walters was right when he claimed that:

> The proposal to patent non-human animals should be viewed in the context of other ways in which we relate to the animal kingdom . . . When compared with the ethical issues involved in our breeding, buying, selling, confining, eating, and performing research on animals, the ethical questions surrounding animal patents seem relatively less important . . . (Committee on the Judiciary, 1988: pp. 388–9)

What conclusion can be drawn from this analysis of the arguments offered by the animal rights movement? We should, I believe, conclude that our regulations governing research on animals to minimize suffering should be strengthened to protect farm animals, birds, and rodents used in privately funded research. However, unless we are prepared to alter radically the entire way in which we relate to the animal kingdom, none of the currently articulated arguments offered by this group should lead us to oppose the patenting of transgenic animals.

TWO OTHER MORAL ARGUMENTS

In this section, I will evaluate two additional moral arguments, the claim that allowing the patenting of transgenic animals would promote international injustice and the claim that allowing the patenting of transgenic animals would be harmful to the environment.

148

The first of these arguments is the claim that the patenting of transgenic animals is inappropriate because of its dire economic implications for the third world. Typical of such claims is the following argument offered by Jack Doyle:

> One [issue] is applying high technologies like agricultural biotechnology to countries that might not be able to afford them—or the social and economic consequences they spawn. The genes of high-tech agriculture lodged in every new crop variety or livestock breed can carry with them high capital and extensive infrastructure costs . . . Secondly, there are questions of access. If, for reasons of competitiveness, we begin to hoard scientific advances for commercial and/or political reasons, and only make such discoveries and developments available for a price, that can only breed mistrust and anger and invite charges of technological imperialism from other nations. (Doyle, n.d.: pp. 7–8)

The argument has both a consequentialist component (patenting and the biotechnology that it encourages will lead to bad results for underdeveloped countries) and an equity component (it is unfair for more developed countries to imperialistically exploit less developed countries through biotechnology and its patenting).

There are extraordinarily important but difficult moral and factual issues raised by such claims. In truth, we lack a theory of justice for the international context, a theory that will enable us to evaluate the moral aspects of the relations between the developed and developing worlds. But we don't need such a fundamental theory to recognize the fallacy committed in the argument: let us grant for now the factual claim that paying both for the patents and for the infrastructure required to use transgenic animals (or plants) would pose great burdens on developing countries, ones they would have difficulty assuming. Let us also grant for now the moral claim that requiring them to assume those costs would be unfair and/or unjust. Why not see helping these countries take advantage of the gains from biotechnology as an obligation to be met by the developed countries through appropriate economic aid, the cost of which is fairly distributed among all of the citizens of the developed country? Why put the whole burden of that aid on one industry? In other words, the patent office is not the place to structure a morally appropriate program for the international economic order.

The second of these arguments has been raised by the National Wildlife Federation. It is not opposed either to the development of transgenic animals or even to their release into the wild. It is concerned, however, with the environmental impact of releasing transgenic animals into the wild, and it believes that the encouragement offered by patenting should be withheld at least until better environmental protection laws are passed. To quote from the testimony of Margaret Mellon, the Manager of its Biotechnology Project, on November 5, 1987:

The current biotechnology framework covers only two narrow categories of animals—invertebrate plant pests and animals used as pesticides. It is wholly inadequate to address the environmental issues raised by engineered animals. Since animals will be engineered, albeit at a slower rate, even in the absence of animal patenting, new control programs will be needed regardless of whether the patent law is extended. But in the case that Congress sees fit to extend patent protection to animals, it is imperative that it link that decision to the enactment of new legislation. (Committee on the Judiciary, 1988: p. 431)

The tone of this presentation of the argument is radically different from the presentation of similar concerns by the Foundation on Economic Trends, which strongly suggests that no system of regulation is likely to be able to do the job (undated). Little argumentation is provided by the Foundation to support that suggestion.

The question of the adequacy of the current regulatory scheme lies beyond the scope of this paper, for it can only be resolved after many technical issues raised about the details of the current scheme are clarified. Of particular concern, however, is the apparent reluctance of the Environment Protection Agency (EPA) to regulate higher forms of life under the Toxic Substances Control Act and of the Fish and Wildlife Service to regulate the use of transgenic animals under its regulatory policies (US Congress, Office of Technology Assessment, 1988). But the general consequentialist argument that we must be careful to regulate the release of new entities into the environment to protect against unintended and unexpected damage certainly seems sound. Moreover, there seems to be no reason not to apply it here by insisting that any system of patenting must be accompanied by a careful review of the current regulatory scheme and by such revisions as are necessary to make it adequate to cover the release of transgenic animals into the wild. Carrying out such a review and making such revisions would enable us to obtain the consequentialist benefits of a system of patenting without having to pay environmental prices.

CONCLUSIONS

Where then do we stand? We have seen that the moral arguments normally raised against the patenting of transgenic animals fail. At most, they suggest the real need to strengthen our regulatory schemes governing research on animals and the release of transgenic animals into the wild, and the need to reconsider in a general fashion the problem of justice between countries. None of them provide us with moral reasons to oppose the patenting of transgenic animals, unless we also are prepared to adopt radically new approaches to fundamental metaphysical issues surrounding the relation of humanity to the environment and to the world of animals.

There are, moreover, strong moral arguments for allowing the patenting of transgenic animals. The most important of these is the consequentialist claim already alluded to—the claim that such a patenting system promotes beneficial consequences by providing an incentive to create useful inventions. There is no doubt that this is the most widely used argument by proponents of patenting transgenic animals. Thus, in testifying before Congress on June 11, 1987, Assistant Commissioner for Patents, Rene Tegtmeyer, asserted:

> By granting the right to exclude others, the law provides an incentive for those who create and develop new technology . . . The grant of patent rights has in fact encouraged research and provided useful new products including research into solutions of problems such as those associated with genetic disorders and increasing food yields. (Committee on the Judiciary, 1988: p. 21)

Similar claims were advanced by many others who testified on behalf of the biotechnology industry, on behalf of some segments of the agricultural community, or on behalf of communities of research scientists (Committee on the Judiciary, 1988: pp. 140–9, 118–121, 211–4).

By their very nature, consequentialist arguments provide greater or lesser support for a social policy, depending upon the probability of the outcome (the higher the probability, the stronger the support) and upon the desirability of the outcome (the more desirable the outcome, the stronger the support). This fundamental feature of consequentialist arguments makes their support difficult to assess in particular cases, for it is often hard to tell how desirable will the outcomes be and how likely are they to occur. This holds in our case as well. How much benefit will accrue from the development of new animal breeds by a biotechnology encouraged by patents? How likely is it that these benefits will actually be produced? These are not easy questions to answer. What can be said, however, is that the tremendous growth of the biotechnology industry, both nationally and internationally (US Congress, Office of Technology Assessment, 1986a), based upon the tremendous growth of the scientific community's efforts in this area, suggests that a large number of knowledgeable observers are prepared to invest their time and energy and/or their money on the assumption that biotechnology, in general, and the development of transgenic animals, in particular, holds out tremendous possibilities for useful—and marketable—advances. Given that fact, and given the general experience of the USA with the ways in which patents do encourage inventions, it seems reasonable to conclude that there is substantial consequentialist moral support for the patenting of transgenic animals.

A second, less often explored argument is suggested in the following very important remark made by Leroy Walters in his testimony of November 5, 1987:

> The moral justification for legal practices like patenting and copyright have received scant attention in the literature of ethics. The general

rationale for both the copyright and patent systems is that they encourage the investment of time and energy in the act of creating . . . Unless and until these revered systems produce serious harm to human or animal welfare, they should be preserved intact as an ethically appropriate way of acknowledging the initiative and creativity of authors and inventors. (Committee on the Judiciary, 1988: p. 389)

There are actually two very different moral justifications for patenting contained in Dr Walters's remarks. The first, that the system of patents encourages inventions, has just been discussed. The second, suggested at the very end of his remarks, is a very different argument. This argument is that inventors are entitled to patents as an acknowledgment of their efforts. This important argument deserves further elaboration.

There are several different moral bases for any system of property rights, and each of them can be applied to intellectual property rights as well. In an important recent discussion Alan Goldman has divided them into forward-looking arguments (the appeals to consequences which we discussed above) and backward-looking arguments (Goldman, 1987). The latter justify property rights as entitlements to the fruits of our labor, drawing upon themes deriving from John Locke's seminal discussion of property rights (Locke, 1960). Applied to the area of patenting transgenic animals that result from biotechnological research, this argument concludes that inventors are entitled to patent rights as a way of giving them the fruits of their labor when their labor is more intellectual than physical.

Given, then, that the moral arguments against patenting have failed and that the moral arguments for the patenting of transgenic animals seem appropriate, I conclude that those who would oppose the patenting of transgenic animals must either shift the basis of their opposition to other non-moral considerations or must give us some reason to support (and accept the radical implications of) their rethinking of the entire relation between humanity and the natural order.

References

Committee on the Judiciary (1988) *Patents and the Constitution: Transgenic Animals*. Washington, DC: Government Printing Office.

Doyle, J. (n.d.) *Ethical Aspects of Biotechnology*.

Foundation on Economic Trends (n.d.) *Talking Points on Animal Patenting*.

Goldman, A.H. (1987) Ethical Issues in Proprietary Restrictions on Research Results. *Science, Technology and Human Values*, **12** (winter): 22–30.

Kass, L. (1985) Patenting Life. In: *Toward a More Natural Science*. New York: Free Press.

Locke, J. (1960) *Second Treatise on Government*, ed. P. Laslett. Cambridge: Cambridge University Press.

Passmore, J. (1974) *Man's Responsibility for Nature*. London: Duckworth.

Statement of Religious Leaders Against Animal Patenting (n.d.).

US Congress, Office of Technology Assessment (1986a) *Commercial Biotechnology: An International Analysis*. New York: Pergamon Press.

—— (1986b) *Alternatives to Animal Use in Research, Testing and Education*. Washington, DC: Government Printing Office.

—— (1988) *Federal Regulation and Animal Patents*. Washington, DC: Government Printing Office.

Wall Street Journal (1988) Patents for Genetically Altered Mouse Opens Era for Research. April 13: 26.

World Council of Churches, Working Group Sub-Unit on Church and Society (1982) Manipulating Life. *Church and Society*, **73** (Sept./Oct.): 29–51.

PART TWO
APPENDIXES

Contents of Part Two

Animals - Patentability

A decision by the Board of Patent Appeals and Interferences in *Ex parte Allen*, ___ USPQ ___ (Bd. App. & Int. April 3, 1987), held that claimed polyploid oysters are nonnaturally occurring manufactures or compositions of matter within the meaning of 35 U.S.C. 101. The Board relied upon the opinion of the Supreme Court in *Diamond v. Chakrabarty*, 447 U.S. 303, 206 USPQ 193 (1980) as it had done in *Ex parte Hibberd*, 227 USPQ 443 (Bd. App. & Int., 1985), as controlling authority that Congress intended statutory subject matter to "include anything under the sun that is made by man." The Patent and Trademark Office now considers nonnaturally occurring non-human multicellular living organisms, including animals, to be patentable subject matter within the scope of 35 U.S.C. 101.

The Board's decision does not affect the principle and practice that products found in nature will not be considered to be patentable subject matter under 35 U.S.C. 101 and/or 102. An article of manufacture or composition of matter occurring in nature will not be considered patentable unless given a new form, quality, properties or combination not present in the original article existing in nature in accordance with existing law. See e.g. *Funk Bros. Seed Co. v. Kalo Inoculant Co.*, 333 U.S. 127, 76 USPQ 280 (1948); *American Fruit Growers v. Brogdex*, 283 U.S. 1, 8 USPQ 131 (1931); *Ex parte Grayson*, 51 USPQ 413 (Bd. App. 1941).

A claim directed to or including within its scope a human being will not be considered to be patentable subject matter under 35 U.S.C. 101. The grant of a limited, but exclusive property right in a human being is prohibited by the Constitution. Accordingly, it is suggested that any claim directed to a non-plant multicellular organism which would include a human being within its scope include the limitation "non-human" to avoid this ground of rejection. The use of a negative limitation to define the metes and bounds of the claimed subject matter is a permissible form of expression. *In re Wakefield*, 422 F.2d 897, 164 USPQ 636 (CCPA 1970).

Accordingly, the Patent and Trademark Office is now examining claims directed to multicellular living organisms, including animals. To the extent that the claimed subject matter is directed to a non-human "nonnaturally occurring manufacture or composition of matter - a product of human ingenuity" (*Diamond v. Chakrabarty*), such claims will not be rejected under 35 U.S.C. 101 as being directed to nonstatutory subjected matter.

4-7-87
_____
Date

_____
Donald J. Quigg
Assistant Secretary and Commissioner
of Patents and Trademarks

159

United States Patent [19]

Leder et al.

[11] Patent Number: 4,736,866
[45] Date of Patent: Apr. 12, 1988

[54] **TRANSGENIC NON-HUMAN MAMMALS**

[75] Inventors: **Philip Leder,** Chestnut Hill, Mass.; **Timothy A. Stewart,** San Francisco, Calif.

[73] Assignee: **President and Fellows of Harvard College,** Cambridge, Mass.

[21] Appl. No.: **623,774**

[22] Filed: **Jun. 22, 1984**

[51] **Int. Cl.^{4}** **C12N 1/00; C12Q 1/68; C12N 15/00; C12N 5/00**

[52] **U.S. Cl.** **800/1;** 435/6; 435/172.3; 435/240.1; 435/240.2; 435/320; 435/317.1; 935/32; 935/59; 935/70; 935/76; 935/111

[58] **Field of Search** 435/6, 172.3, 240, 317, 435/320, 240.1, 240.2; 935/70, 76, 59, 111, 32; 800/1

[56] **References Cited**

U.S. PATENT DOCUMENTS

4,535,058 8/1985 Weinberg et al. 435/91
4,579,821 4/1986 Palmiter et al. 435/240

OTHER PUBLICATIONS

Ucker et al, Cell 27:257–266, Dec. 1981.
Ellis et al, Nature 292:506–511, Aug. 1981.
Goldfarb et al, Nature 296: 404–409, Apr. 1981. Huang et al, Cell 27:245–255, Dec. 1981.
Blair et al, Science 212:941–943, 1981.
Der et al, Proc. Natl. Acad. Sci. USA 79:3637–3640, Jun. 1982.
Shih et al, Cell 29:161–169, 1982.
Gorman et al, Proc. Natl. Acad. Sci. USA 79:6777–6781, Nov. 1982.
Schwab et al, EPA–600/9–82–013, Sym: Carcinogen, Polynucl. Aromat. Hydrocarbons Mar. Environ., 212–32 (1982).
Wagner et al. (1981) Proc. Natl. Acad. Sci USA 78, 5016–5020.
Stewart et al. (1982) Science 217, 1046–8.
Costantini et al. (1981) Nature 294, 92–94.
Lacy et al. (1983) Cell 34, 343–358.
McKnight et al. (1983) Cell 34, 335.
Binster et al. (1983) Nature 306, 332–336.
Palmiter et al. (1982) Nature 300, 611–615.
Palmiter et al. (1983) Science 222, 814.
Palmiter et al. (1982) Cell 29, 701–710.

Primary Examiner—Alvin E. Tanenholtz
Attorney, Agent, or Firm—Paul T. Clark

[57] **ABSTRACT**

A transgenic non-human eukaryotic animal whose germ cells and somatic cells contain an activated oncogene sequence introduced into the animal, or an ancestor of the animal, at an embryonic stage.

12 Claims, 2 Drawing Sheets

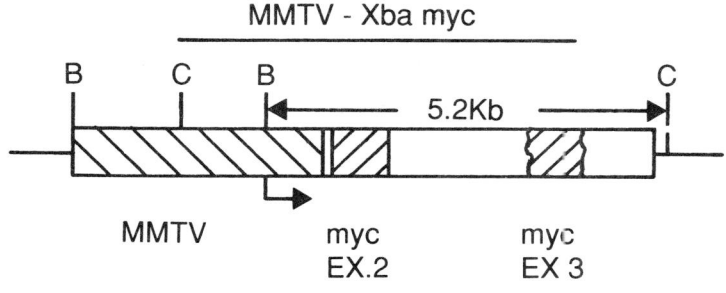

MMTV - Xba myc

B   C   B   C

5.2Kb

MMTV   myc   myc
            EX.2   EX 3

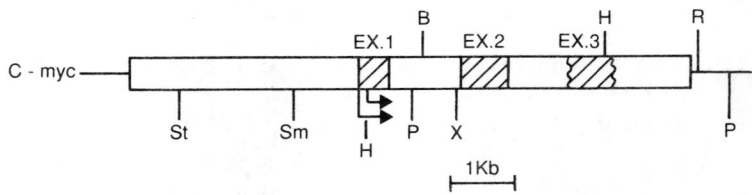

FIG 1

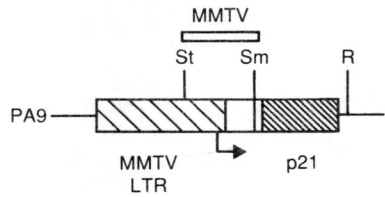

FIG 2

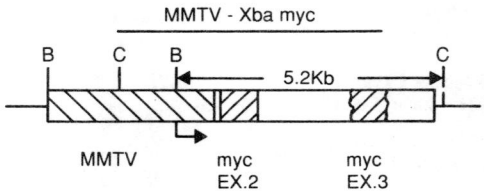

FIG 3

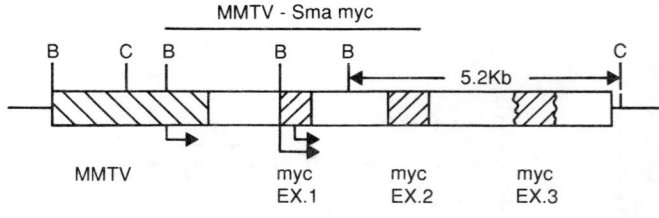

FIG 4

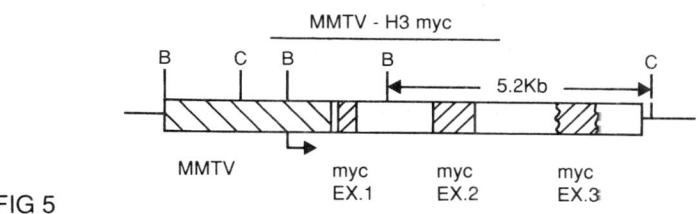

FIG 5

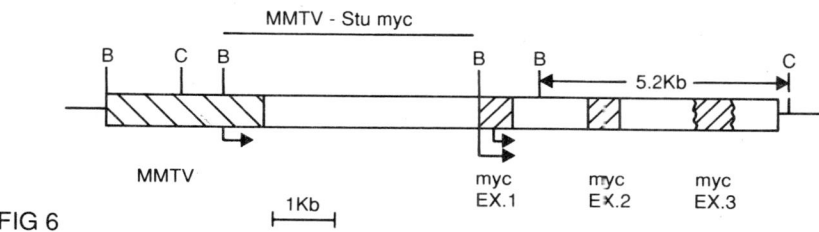

FIG 6

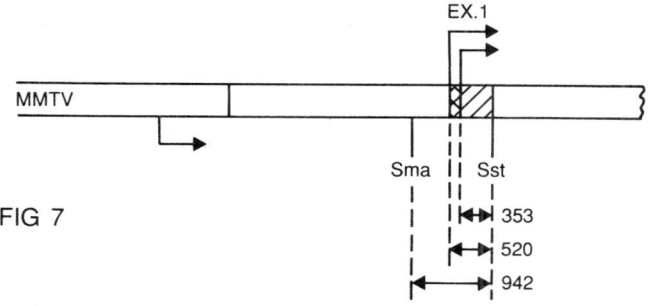

FIG 7

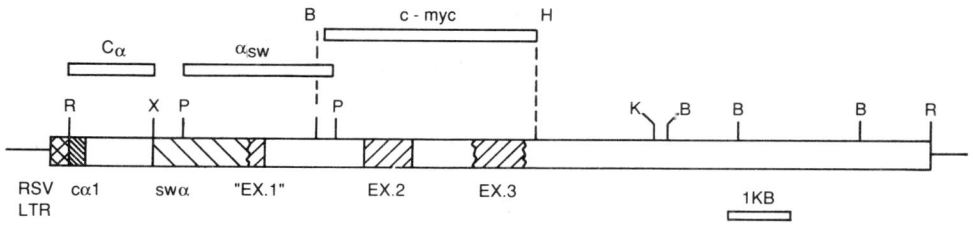

FIG 8

163

TRANSGENIC NON-HUMAN MAMMALS

BACKGROUND OF THE INVENTION

This invention relates to transgenic animals.

Transgenic animals carry a gene which has been introduced into the germline of the animal, or an ancestor of the animal, at an early (usually one-cell) developmental stage. Wagner et al. (1981) *P.N.A.S. U.S.A.* 78, 5016; and Stewart et al. (1982) *Science* 217, 1046 describe transgenic mice containing human globin genes. Constantini et al. (1981) *Nature* 294, 92; and Lacy et al. (1983) *Cell* 34, 343 describe transgenic mice containing rabbit globin genes. McKnight et al. (1983) *Cell* 34, 335 describes transgenic mice containing the chicken transferrin gene. Brinster et al. (1983) *Nature* 306, 332 describes transgenic mice containing a functionally rearranged immunoglobin gene. Palmiter et al. (1982) *Nature* 300, 611 describes transgenic mice containing the rat growth hormone gene fused to a heavy metal-inducible metalo-thionein promoter sequence. Palmiter et al. (1982) *Cell* 29, 701 describes transgenic mice containing a thymidine kinase gene fused to a metalothionein promoter sequence. Palmiter et al. (1983) *Science* 222, 809 describes transgenic mice containing the human growth hormone gene fused to a metalothionein promoter sequence.

SUMMARY OF THE INVENTION

In general, the invention features a transgenic non-human eukaryotic animal (preferably a rodent such as a mouse) whose germ cells and somatic cells contain an activated oncogene sequence introduced into the animal, or an ancestor of the animal, at an embryonic stage (preferably the one-cell, or fertilized oocyte, stage and generally not later than about the 8-cell stage). An activated oncogene sequence, as the term is used herein, means an oncogene which, when incorporated into the genome of the animal, increases the probability of the development of neoplasms (particularly malignant tumors) in the animal. There are several means by which an oncogene can be introduced into an animal embryo so as to be chromosomally incorporated in an activated state. One method is to transfect the embryo with the gene as it occurs naturally, and select transgenic animals in which the gene has integrated into the chromosome at a locus which results in activation. Other activation methods involve modifying the oncogene or its control sequences prior to introduction into the embryo. One such method is to transfect the embryo using a vector containing an already translocated oncogene. Other methods are to use an oncogene whose transcription is under the control of a synthetic or viral activating promoter, or to use an oncogene activated by one or more base pair substitutions, deletions, or additions.

In a preferred embodiment, the chromosome of the transgenic animal includes an endogenous coding sequence (most preferably the c-myc gene, hereinafter the myc gene), which is substantially the same as the oncogene sequence, and transcription of the oncogene sequence is under the control of a promoter sequence different from the promoter sequence controlling transcription of the endogenous coding sequence. The oncogene sequence can also be under the control of a synthetic promoter sequence. Preferably, the promoter sequence controlling transcription of the oncogene sequence is inducible.

Introduction of the oncogene sequence at the fertilized oocyte stage ensures that the oncogene sequence will be present in all of the germ cells and somatic cells of the transgenic animal. The presence of the oncogene sequence in the germ cells of the transgenic "founder" animal in turn means that all of the founder animal's descendants will carry the activated oncogene sequence in all of their germ cells and somatic cells. Introduction of the oncogene sequence at a later embryonic stage might result in the oncogene's absence from some somatic cells of the founder animal, but the descendants of such an animal that inherit the gene will carry the activated oncogene in all of their germ cells and somatic cells.

Any oncogene or effective sequence thereof can be used to produce the transgenic mice of the invention. Table 1, below, lists some known viral and cellular oncogenes, many of which are homologous to DNA sequences endogenous to mice and/or humans, as indicated. The term "oncogene" encompasses both the viral sequences and the homologous endogenous sequences.

TABLE 1

Abbreviation	Virus	Abbreviation	Virus
src	Rous Sarcoma Virus (Chicken)	ski	Avian SKV T10 Virus (Chicken)
yes	Y73 Sarcoma Virus (Chicken)	rel	Reticuloendotheliosis Virus (Turkey)
fps	Fujinami (St Feline) Sarcoma Virus (Chicken, Cat)	sis	Simian Sarcoma Virus (Woolly Monkey)
abl	Abelson Marine Leukemia Virus (Mouse)	N-myc	Neuroblastomas (Human)
ros	Rochester-2 Sarcoma Virus (Chicken)	N-ras	Neuroblastoma, Leukemia Sarcoma Virus (Human)
fgr	Gardner-Rasheed Feline Sarcoma Virus (Cat)	Blym	Bursal Lymphomas (Chicken)
erbB	Avian Erythroblastosis Virus (Chicken)	mam	Mammary Carcionoma (Human)
fms	McDonough Feline Sarcoma Virus (Cat)	neu	Neuro, Glioblastoma (Rat)
mos	Moloney Murine Sarcoma Virus (Mouse)	ertAl	Chicken AEV (Chicken)
raf	3611 Murine Sarcoma$^+$ Virus (Mouse)	ra-ras	Rasheed Sarcoma Virus (Rat)
Ha-ras-1	Harvey Murine Sarcoma Virus (Rat) (Balb/c mouse; 2 loci)	mnt-myc	Carcinoma Virus MH2 (Chicken)
Ki-ras 2	Kirsten Murine Sarcoma Virus (Rat)	myc	Myelocytomatosis OK10 (Chicken)
Ki-ras 1	Kirsten Murine Sarcoma Virus (Rat)	myb-ets	Avian myeloblastosis/ erythroblastosis Virus E26 (Chicken)
myc	Avian MC29 Myelocytomatosis Virus (Chicken)	raf-2	3611-MSV (Mouse)
		raf-1	3611-MSV (Mouse)
		Ha-ras-2	Ki-MSV (Rat)
myt	Avian Myelo Blastomas (Chicken)	erbB	Erythroblastosis Virus (Chicken)
fos	FBJ Osteosarcoma Virus (Mouse)		

The animals of the invention can be used to test a material suspected of being a carcinogen, by exposing the animal to the material and determining neoplastic growth as an indicator of carcinogenicity. This test can be extremely sensitive because of the propensity of the transgenic animals to develop tumors. This sensitivity will permit suspect materials to be tested in much smaller amounts than the amounts used in current animal carcinogenicity studies, and thus will minimize one source of criticism of current methods, that their validity is questionable because the amounts of the tested material used is greatly in excess of amounts to which humans are likely to be exposed. Furthermore, the animals will be expected to develop tumors much sooner because they already contain an activated oncogene. The animals are also preferable, as a test system, to bacteria (used, e.g. in the Ames test) because they, like humans, are vertebrates, and because carcinogenicity, rather than mutogenicity, is measured.

The animals of the invention can also be used as tester animals for materials, e.g. antioxidants such as beta-carotine or Vitamin E, thought to confer protection against the development of neoplasms. An animal is treated with the material, and a reduced incidence of neoplasm development, compared to untreated animals, is detected as an indication of protection. The method can further include exposing treated and un-treated animals to a carcinogen prior to, after, or simultaneously with treatment with the protective material.

The animals of the invention can also be used as a source of cells for cell culture. Cells from the animals may advantageously exhibit desirable properties of both normal and transformed cultured cells; i.e., they will be normal or nearly normal morphologically and physiologically, but can, like cells such as NIH 3T3 cells, be cultured for long, and perhaps indefinite, periods of time. Further, where the pro-moter sequence controlling transcription of the oncogene sequence is inducible, cell growth rate and other culture characteristics can be controlled by adding or elimi-nating the inducing factor.

Other features and advantages of the invention will be apparent from the descrip-tion of the preferred embodiments, and from the claims.

DESCRIPTION OF THE PREFERRED EMBODIMENTS

The drawings will first briefly be described.

DRAWINGS

FIG. 1 is a diagrammatic representation of a region of a plasmid bearing the mouse myc gene and flanking regions.

FIG. 2 is a diagrammatic representation of a region of a plasmid, pA9, bearing the mouse mammary tumor virus long terminal repeat (MMTV LTR) sequences.

FIGS. 3–6 and 8 are diagrammatic representations of activated oncogene fusions.

FIG. 7 is a diagrammatic representation of a probe useful for detecting activated myc fusions.

MMTV-MYC FUSED GENES

Gene fusions were made using the mouse myc gene and the MMTV LTR. The myc gene is known to be an activatable oncogene. (For example, Leder et al. (1983) *Science* 222, 765 explains how chromosomal translocations that characterize Burkitt's Lymphoma and mouse plasmacytomas result in a juxtaposition of the myc gene and one of the immunoglobulin constant regions; amplification of the myc gene has also been observed in transformed cell lines.) FIG. 1 illustrates the subclone of the mouse myc gene which provided the myc regions.

The required MMTV functions were provided by the pA9 plasmid (FIG. 2) that demonstrated hormone inducibility of the p21 protein; this plasmid is described in Huang et al. (1981) *Cell* 27, 245. The MMTV functions on pA9 include the region required for glucocorticoid control, the MMTV promoter, and the cap site.

The above plasmids were used to construct the four fusion gene constructions illustrated in FIGS. 3–6. The constructions were made by deleting from pA9 the Sma-EcoRI region that included the p21 protein coding sequences, and replacing it with the four myc regions shown in the Figures. Procedures were the conventional techniques described in Maniatis et al. (1982) *Molecular Cloning: A Laboratory Manual* (Cold Spring Harbor Laboratory). The restriction sites shown in FIG. 1 are StuI (St), SmaI (Sm), EcorRI (R), HindIII (H), PvuI (P), BamHI (B), XbaI (X), and ClaI (C). The solid arrows below the constructions represents the promoter in the

MMTV LTR and in the myc gene. The size (in Kb) of the major fragment, produced by digestion with BamHI and ClaI, that will hybridize to the myc probe, is shown for each construction.

MMTV-H3 myc (FIG. 5) was constructed in two steps: Firstly, the 4.7 Kb Hind III myc fragment which contains most of the myc sequences was made blunt with Klenow polymerase and ligated to the pA9 SmaI-EcoRI vector that had been similarly treated. This construction is missing the normal 3' end of the myc gene. In order to introduce the 3' end of the myc gene, the PvuI-PvuI fragment extending from the middle of the first myc intron to the pBR322 PvuI site in the truncated MMTV-H3 myc was replaced by the related PvuI-PvuI fragment from the mouse myc subclone.

The MMTV-Xba myc construction (FIG. 3) was produced by first digesting the MMTV-Sma myc plasmid with SmaI and XbaI. The XbaI end was then made blunt with Klenow polymerase and the linear molecule recircularized with T4 DNA ligase. The MMTV-Stu myc (FIG. 6) and the MMTV-Sma myc (FIG. 4) constructions were formed by replacing the p21 protein coding sequences with, respectively, the StuI-EcoRI or SmaI-EcoRI myc fragments (the EcoRI site is within the pBR322 sequences of the myc subclone). As shown in FIG. 1, there is only one StuI site within the myc gene. As there is more than one SmaI site within the myc gene (FIG. 4), a partial SmaI digestion was carried out to generate a number of MMTV-Sma myc plasmids; the plasmid illustrated in FIG. 4 was selected as not showing rearrangements and also including a sufficiently long region 5' of the myc promoter (approximately 1 Kb) to include myc proximal controlling regions.

The constructions of FIGS. 4 and 6 contain the two promoters naturally preceding the unactivated myc gene. The construction of FIG. 5 has lost both myc promoters but retains the cap site of the shorter transcript. The construction of FIG. 3 does not include the first myc exon but does include the entire protein coding sequence. The 3' end of the myc sequence in all of the illustrated constructions is located at the HindIII site approximately 1 Kb 3' to the myc polyA addition site.

These constructions were all checked by multiple restriction enzyme digestions and were free of detectable rearrangements.

PRODUCTION OF TRANSGENIC MICE
CONTAINING MMTV-MYC FUSIONS

The above MMTV-myc plasmids were digested with SalI and EcoRI (each of which cleaves once within the pBR322 sequence) and separately injected into the male pronuclei of fertilized one-cell mouse eggs; this resulted in about 500 copies of linearized plasmid per pronucleus. The injected eggs were then transferred to pseudo-pregnant foster females as described in Wagner et al. (1981) *P.N.A.S. U.S.A.* 78, 5016. The eggs were derived from a CD-1 X C57B1/6J mating. Mice were obtained from the Charles River Laboratories (CD^R-1-Ha/Icr (CD-1), an albino outbred mouse) and Jackson Laboratories (C57B1/6J), and were housed in an environmentally controlled facility maintained on a 10 hour dark : 14 hour light cycle. The eggs in the foster females were allowed to develop to term.

ANALYSIS OF TRANSGENIC MICE

At four weeks of age, each pup born was analyzed using DNA taken from the tail of a Southern hybridization, using a ^{32}P DNA probe (labelled by nick-translation). In each case, DNA from the tail was digested with BamHI and ClaI and probed with the ^{32}P-labeled BamHI/HindIII probe from the normal myc gene (FIG. 1).

The DNA for analysis was extracted from 0.1–1.5 cm sections of tail, by the method described in Davis et al. (1980) in Methods in Enzymology, Grossman et al., eds. 65, 404, except that one chloroform extraction was performed prior to ethanol precipitation. The resulting nucleic acid pellet was washed once in 80% ethanol, dried, and resuspended in 300 µl of 1.0 mM Tris, pH 7.4, 0.1 mM EDTA.

Ten µl of the tail DNA preparation (approximately 10 µg DNA) were digested to completion, electrophoresed through 0.8% agarose gels, and transferred to nitrocellulose, as described in Southern (1975) *J. Mol. Biol.* 98, 503. Filters were hybridized overnight to probes in the presence of 10% dexxtran sulfate and washed twice in 2 X SSC, 0.1% SDS at room temperature and four times in 0.1 X SSC, 0.1% SDS at 64° C.

The Southern hybridizations indicated that ten founder mice had retained an injected MMTV-myc fusion. Two founder animals had integrated the myc gene at two different loci, yielding two genetically distinct lines of transgenic mice. Another mouse yielded two polymorphic forms of the integrated myc gene and thus yielded two genetically distinct offspring, each of which carried a different polymorphic form of the gene. Thus, the 10 founder animals yielded 13 lines of transgenic offspring.

The founder animals were mated to uninjected animals and DNA of the resulting thirteen lines of transgenic off spring analyzed; this analysis indicated that in every case the injected genes were transmitted through the germline. Eleven of the thirteen lines also expressed the newly acquired MMTV-myc genes in at least one somatic tissue; the tissue in which expression was most prevalent was salivary gland.

Transcription of the newly acquired genes in tissues was determined by extracting RNA from the tissues and assaying the RNA in an Sl nuclease protection procedure, as follows. The excised tissue was rinsed in 5.0 ml cold Hank's buffered saline and total RNA was isolated by the method of Chrigwin et al. (1979) *Biochemistry* 18, 5294, using the CsCl gradient modification. RNA pellets were washed twice by reprecipitation in ethanol and quantitated by absorbance at 260 nm. An appropriate single stranded, uniformly labeled DNA probe was prepared as described by Ley et al. (1982) *PNAS USA* 79, 4775. To test for transcription of the MMTV-Stu myc fusion of FIG. 6, for example, the probe illustrated in FIG. 7 was used. This probe extends from a Smal site 5′ to the first myc exon to an Sstl site at the 3′ end of the first myc exon. Transcription from the endogenous myc promoters will produce RNA that will protect fragments of the probe 353 and 520 base pairs long; transcription from the MMTV promoter will completely protect the probe and be revealed as a band 942 base pairs long, in the following hybridization procedure.

Labelled, single-stranded probe fragments were isolated on 8M urea 5% acrylamide gels, electroeluted, and hybridized to total RNA in a modification of the procedure of Berk et al. (1977) *Cell* 12, 721. The hybridization mixture contained 50,000 cpm to 100,000 cpm of probe (SA = 10^8 cpm/µg), 10 µg total cellular RNA, 75% formamide, 500 mM NaCl, 20 mM Tris pH 7.5, 1 mM EDTA, as described in Battey et al. (1983) *Cell* 34, 779. Hybridization temperatures were varied according to the GC content in the region of the probe expected to hybridize to mRNA. The hybridizations were terminated by the addition of 1500 units of Sl nuclease (Boehringer Mannheim). Sl nuclease digestions were carried out at 37° C. for 1 hour. The samples were then ethanol-precipitated and electrophoresed on thin 8M urea 5% acrylamide gels.

Northern hybridization analysis was also carried out, as follows. Total RNA was electrophoresed through 1% formaldehyde 0.8% agarose gels, blotted to nitrocellulose filters (Lehrach et al. (1979) *Biochemistry* 16, 4743), and hybridized to nick-translated probes as described in Taub et al. (1982) *PNAS USA* 79, 7837. The tissues analyzed were thymus, pancreas, spleen, kidney, testes, liver, heart, lung, skeletal muscle, brain, salivary gland, and preputial gland.

Both lines of mice which had integrated and were transmitting to the next generation the MMTV-Stu myc fusion (FIG. 6) exhibited transcription of the fusion in salivary gland, but in no other tissue.

One of two lines of mice found to carry the MMTV-Sma myc fusion (FIG. 4) expressed the gene fusion in all tissues examined, with the level of expression being particularly high in salivary gland. The other line expressed the gene fusion only in salivary gland, spleen, testes, lung, brain, and preputial gland.

Four lines of mice carried the MMTV-H3 myc fusion (FIG. 5). In one, the fusion was transcribed in testes, lung, salivary gland, and brain; in a second, the fusion was transcribed only in salivary gland; in a third, the fusion was transcribed in none of the somatic tissues tested; and in a fourth, the fusion was transcribed in salivary gland and intestinal tissue.

In two mouses lines found to carry the MMTV-Xba myc fusion, the fusion was transcribed in testes and salivary gland.

RSV-MYC FUSED GENES

Referring to FIG. 8, the plasmid designated RSV-S107 was generated by inserting the EcoRI fragment of the S107 plasmacytoma myc gene, (Kirsch et al. (1981) *Nature* 293, 585) into a derivative of the Rous Sarcoma Virus (RSV) enhancer-containing plasmid (pRSV cat) described in Gorman et al. (1982) *PNAS USA* 79, 6777, at the EcoRI site 3' to the RSV enhancer sequence, using standard recombinant DNA techniques. All chloramphenicol acetyl transferase SV40 sequences are replaced in this vector by the myc gene; the RSV promoter sequence is deleted when the EcoRI fragments are replaced, leaving the RSV enhancer otherwise intact. The original translocation of the myc gene in the S107 plasmacytoma deleted the two normal myc promoters as well as a major portion of the untranslated first myc exon, and juxtaposed, 5' to 5', the truncated myc gene next to the α immunoglobulin heavy chain switch sequence.

The illustrated (FIG. 8) regions of plasmid RSV-S107 are: crosshatched, RSV sequences; fine-hatched, alpha 1 coding sequences; left-hatched, immunoglobulin alpha switch sequences; right-hatched, myc exons. The thin lines flanking the RSV-S107 myc exon represent pBR322 sequences. The marked restriction enzyme sites are: R, EcoRI; X, Xbal; P, Pst 1; K, Kpn 1; H, HindIII; B, BamHI. The sequences used for three probes used in assays described herein (C-α, α-sw and c-myc) are marked.

PRODUCTION OF TRANSGENIC MICE

Approximately 500 copies of the RSV-S107 myc plasmid (linearized at the unique Kpn-1 site 3' to the myc gene) were injected into the male pronucleus of eggs derived from a C57BL/6J x CD-1 mating. Mice were obtained from Charles River Laboratories (CD-1, an albino outbred mouse) and from Jackson Laboratories (C57BL/6J). These injected eggs were transferred into pseudopregnant foster females, allowed to develop to term, and at four weeks of age the animals born were tested for retention of the injected sequences by Southern blot analysis of DNA extracted from the tail, as described above. Of 28 mice analyzed, two males were found to have retained the new genes and both subsequently transmitted these sequences through the germline in a ratio consistent with Mendelian inheritance of single locus.

First generation transgenic offspring of each of these founder males were analyzed for expression of the rearranged myc genes by assaying RNA extracted from the major internal tissues and organs in an Sl nuclease protection assay, as described above. The hearts of the offspring of one line showed aberrant myc expression; the other 13 tissues did not.

Backcrossing (to C57B1/6J) and in-breeding matings produced some transgenic mice which did not demonstrate the same restriction site patterns on Southern blot analysis as either their transgenic siblings or their parents. In the first generation progeny derived from a mating between the founder male and C57BL/6J females, 34 F1 animals were analyzed and of these, 19 inherited the newly introduced gene, a result consistent with the founder being a heterozygote at one locus. However, of the 19 transgenic mice analyzed, there were three qualitatively different patterns with respect to the more minor myc hybridizing fragments.

In order to test the possibility that these heterogenous genotypes arose as a consequence of multiple insertions and/or germline mosaicism in the founder, two F1 mice (one carrying the 7.8 and 12 Kb BamHI bands, and the other carrying only the 7.8 Kb

169

BamHI band) were mated and the F2 animals analyzed. One male born to the mating of these two appeared to have sufficient copies of the RSV-S107 myc gene to be considered as a candidate for having inherited the two alleles; this male was back-crossed with a wild-type female. All 23 of 23 backcross offspring analyzed inherited the RSV-S107 myc genes, strongly suggesting that the F2 male mouse had inherited two alleles at one locus. Further, as expected, the high molecular weight fragment (12 Kb) segregated as a single allele.

To determine whether, in addition to the polymorphisms arising at the DNA level, the level of aberrant myc expression was also altered, heart mRNA was analyzed in eight animals derived from the mating of the above double heterozygote to a wild-type female. All eight exhibited elevated myc mRNA, with the amount appearing to vary between animals; the lower levels of expression segregated with the presence of the 12 Kb myc hybridizing band. The level of myc mRNA in the hearts of transgenic mice in a second backcross generation also varied. An F1 female was backcrossed to a C57B1/6J male to produce a litter of seven pups, six of which inherited the RSV-S107 myc genes. All seven of these mice were analyzed for expression. Three of the six transgenic mice had elevated levels of myc mRNA in the hearts whereas in the other three the level of myc mRNA in the hearts was indistinguishable from the one mouse that did not carry the RSV-S107 myc gene. This result suggests that in addition to the one polymorphic RSV-S107 myc locus from which high levels of heart-restricted myc mRNA were transcribed, there may have been another segregating RSV-S107 myc locus that was transcriptionally silent.

CARCINOGENICITY TESTING

The animals of the invention can be used to test a material suspected of being a carcinogen, as follows. If the animals are to be used to test materials thought to be only weakly carcinogenic, the transgenic mice most susceptible of developing tumors are selected, by exposing the mice to a low dosage of a known carcinogen and selecting those which first develop tumors. The selected animals and their descendants are used as test animals by exposing them to the material suspected of being a carcinogen and determining neoplastic growth as an indicator of carcinogenicity. Less sensitive animals are used to test more strongly carcinogenic materials. Animals of the desired sensitivity can be selected by varying the type and concentration of known carcinogen used in the selection process. When extreme sensitivity is desired, the selected test mice can consist of those which spontaneously develop tumors.

TESTING FOR CANCER PROTECTION

The animals of the invention can be used to test materials for the ability to confer protection against the development of neoplasms. An animal is treated with the material, in parallel with an untreated control transgenic animal. A comparatively lower incidence of neoplasm development in the treated animal is detected as an indication of protection.

TISSUE CULTURE

The transgenic animals of the invention can be used as a source of cells for cell culture. Tissues of transgenic mice are analyzed for the presence of the activated oncogene, either by directly analyzing DNA or RNA, or by assaying the tissue for the protein expressed by the gene. Cells of tissues carrying the gene can be cultured, using standard tissue culture techniques, and used, e.g., to study the functioning of cells from normally difficult to culture tissues such as heart tissue.

DEPOSITS

Plasmids bearing the fusion genes shown in FIGS. 3, 4, 5, 6, and 8 have been deposited in the American Type Culture Collection, Rockville, Md., and given,

170

respectively, ATCC Accession Nos. 39745, 39746, 39747, 39748, and 39749.

OTHER EMBODIMENTS

Other embodiments are within the following claims. For example, any species of transgenic animal can be employed. In some circumstances for instance, it may be desirable to use a species, e.g., a primate such as the rhesus monkey, which is evolutionarily closer to humans than mice.

We claim:

1. A transgenic non-human mammal all of whose germ cells and somatic cells contain a recombinant activated oncogene sequence introduced into said mammal, or an ancestor of said mammal, at an embryonic stage.

2. The mammal of claim 1, a chromosome of said mammal including an endogenous coding sequence substantially the same as a coding sequence of said oncogene sequence.

3. The mammal of claim 2, said oncogene sequence being integrated into a chromosome of said mammal at a site different from the location of said endogenous coding sequence.

4. The mammal of claim 2 wherein transcription of said oncogene sequence is under the control of a promoter sequence different from the promoter sequence controlling the transcription of said endogenous coding sequence.

5. The mammal of claim 4 wherein said promoter sequence controlling transcription of said oncogene sequence is inducible.

6. The mammal of claim 1 wherein said oncogene sequence comprises a coding sequence of a c-myc gene.

7. The mammal of claim 1 wherein transcription of said oncogene sequence is under the control of a viral promoter sequence.

8. The mammal of claim 7 wherein said viral promoter sequence comprises a sequence of an MMTV promoter.

9. The mammal of claim 7 wherein said viral promoter sequence comprises a sequence of an RSV promoter.

10. The mammal of claim 1 wherein transcription of said oncogene sequence is under the control of a synthetic promoter sequence.

11. The mammal of claim 1, said mammal being a rodent.

12. The mammal of claim 11, said rodent being a mouse.

*   *   *   *   *

HOUSE PASSAGE OF ANIMAL PATENT BILL (HR 4970)*

Cong. Rec. 9/13/88, p. H7436

TRANSGENIC ANIMAL PATENT REFORM ACT

Mr. KASTENMEIER. Mr. Speaker, I move to suspend the rules and pass the bill (H.R. 4970) to amend title 35 of the United States Code relating to animal patents, as amended.

The Clerk read as follows:

H.R. 4970

Be it enacted by the Senate and House of Representatives of the United States of America Congress assembled.

SECTION 1. SHORT TITLE.

This Act may be cited as the "Transgenic Animal Patent Reform Act".

SEC. 2. INFRINGEMENT OF PATENT.

Section 271 of the title 35, United States Code, is amended by adding at the end the following new subsection:

"(g)(1) It shall not be an act of infringement for a person whose occupation is farming to reproduce a patented transgenic farm animal through breeding, use such animal in the farming operation, or sell such animal or the offspring of such animal.

"(2) Notwithstanding the provisions of paragraph (1), it shall be an act of infringement for a person to sell the germ cells, semen, or embryos of a patented transgenic farm animal.

"(3) For purposes of paragraphs (1) and (2)—

"(A) the term 'transgenic farm animal' means a farm animal whose germ cells contain genetic material originally derived from another animal other than the parent of the farm animal; and

"(B) the term 'farm animal' means any animal used or intended for use as food or fiber.".

SEC. 3. SPECIFICATION FOR PATENT APPLICATION.

Section 112 of title 35, United States Code, is amended by adding at the end the following new paragraph:

"With respect to an invention involving biological material, the Commissioner may accept a deposit of biological material to satisfy any requirement of this section if made accessible under such conditions as the Commissioner may require.".

SEC. 4. PATENTABILITY OF HUMAN BEINGS.

Section 101 of title 35, United States Code, is amended by adding before the period at the end a comma and the following: "except that human beings are not patentable subject matter".

The SPEAKER pro tempore. Pursuant to the rule, a second is not required on this motion.

The gentleman from Wisconsin [Mr. KASTENMEIER] will be recognized for 20 minutes and the gentleman from California [Mr. MOORHEAD] will be recognized for 20 minutes.

The Chair recognizes the gentleman from Wisconsin [Mr. KASTENMEIER].

Mr. KASTENMEIER. Mr. Speaker, I yield myself such time as I may consume.

(Mr. KASTENMEIER asked and was given permission to revise and extend his remarks.)

Mr. KASTENMEIER. Mr. Speaker, today I am pleased to offer a bill, Transgenic Animal Patent Reform Act, aimed at responding to availability of patent protection for transgenic animals. As my colleagues know, as of April 1, 1988, because of a decision of the Patent Office it is possible to obtain patent protection for genetically altered animals.

Consideration of this bill represents the

* This article first appeared in BNA's Patent, Trademark & Copyright Journal Vol. 36

conclusion of the hearings held by the committee, and other factual inquiries undertaken by the Office of Technology Assessment and the Library of Congress. The subcommittee conducted 4 days of hearings on this subject over the last 14 months. The subcommittee heard testimony from over 30 witnesses and the hearing record is over 930 pages.

As my colleagues know, the gist of the controversy about patenting animals is the result of a decision of the Patent and Trademark Office last April 1987 to assert that genetically altered animals—other than human beings—are patentable subject matter. In April of this year the PTO granted the first patent for a genetically altered animal useful in cancer research. The Patent Office considered that it was legally sound to permit the patenting of animals that have been substantially altered through human intervention. The result reached by the Patent Office was based on the Supreme Court decision in the 1980 Chakrabarty case.

The Chakrabarty case ruled that living matter is patentable.

The Committee on the Judiciary concluded that the current patent law should be amended, however, in three important respects. The bill H.R. 4970 does just that.

First, the patent law should be amended to provide for an exemption from liability for farmers who reproduce patented animals. In addition, we should amend title 35 in two other respects: First, to clarify the Patent Commissioner authority to require deposits of biological materials; second, to statutorily exclude human beings from "patentable subject matter." I hope that after full and fair consideration of the matter that my colleagues will support this bill.

BACKGROUND

PATENTING ANIMALS

Three months ago the Patent Office made headlines by issuing a patent for a genetically altered mouse. Harvard researchers—with funding by DuPont—had succeeded in altering the genetic makeup of a mouse so that it could be used in medical research on breast cancer. That simple act has produced hundreds of news articles around the world and storms of protest.

Pending before the Congress have been two proposals dealing with the patentability of genetically altered animals. Congressman Rose proposed that there be a 2-year moratorium on the issuance of any patents on genetically altered animals. That measure was defeated in committee by a 2-to-1 vote. The measure before us today is a bill that

H7437

would exempt from patent liability farmers for the international reproduction of patented animals.

The controversy about this issue has been extensive. Opponents of patenting animals have raised questions about the morality of patents on animals. They have also claimed that patent protection will produce economic concentration, despoil the environment, increase animal suffering and stifle research. Proponents of patent protection argue that the grant of a limited right to exclude others from copying your research is a necessary incentive for the research community. The business community and many in the medical and academic community favor extending patent protection to this area of science. Opponents have included religious leaders, some environmentalists and some farm organizations.

Sorting out the facts of this controversy has been the business of the subcommittee I chair. Over the past year we have held 4 days of hearings on this subject, hearing from over 30 witnesses and compiling over 900 pages of testimony. In addition, the committee commissioned research papers by the science advisers to the Congress and legal experts. Evaluation of competing claims produces the following answers:

WHAT IS A TRANSGENIC ANIMAL?

It is now possible to transfer from one animal to another a single gene. Using a variety of techniques scientists can now alter animals to produce certain types of desired results. For example, transgenic animals include a mouse that has been

174

modified to make it useful in the treatment of breast cancer. Other research as resulting the production of human medical drugs by animals through their mammary glands. Finally, researchers hope to alter certain animals to produce leaner, healthier meat.

WHAT IS A PATENT?

A patent is a Government granted right to exclude others from making, using, or selling your invention. To obtain a patent the inventor must prove that the invention is useful and not an obvious extension of the existing technology. A patent exists only for 17 years, after which the technology is available to everyone in the public domain.

WHY DID THE PATENT OFFICE DECIDE TO PATENT ANIMALS?

The Supreme Court of the United States decided in 1980 that living matter (a micro-organism that ate oil spills) was protectible under the patent law. The Court reasoned that there was no legal reason to differentiate between machines and arrangements of proteins. Thus, they concluded that any invention under the Sun that was the product of significant human intervention was patentable.

WHAT ARE THE LIMITS OF PATENT PROTECTION FOR ANIMALS?

The Patent Office will not grant patents on human beings, but will evaluate all other claims for other animals using traditional patent criteria. Some question remains about whether farmers who reproduce patented animals would be committing an act of patent infringement. The Kastenmeier bill answers that question by exempting reproduction by farmers from liability.

IS OWNERSHIP OF ANIMALS ETHICAL?

Mere ownership of animals has not traditionally been considered immoral. Nor has the breeding of animals. Proponents of biotechnology argue that the use of this technology to alter animals is just a more precise—albeit scientifically more difficult—method of achieving changes through breeding. Opponents of this type of research argue that animal suffering will inevitably increase.

Researchers claim that the opposite is true because with better animal models fewer test animals will be required. They also assert that genetic engineering can make animals more disease resistant.

WILL PATENTED ANIMALS PRODUCE UNDESIRABLE CONSEQUENCES FOR FARMERS?

Even without patented animals the average family farmer in the United States faces an uncertain future. One congressional study has already predicted a loss of 1 million farms as a result of factors largely separate from biotechnology. The availability of more efficient livestock poses a difficult challenge for the agricultural community. We all know of the existing dairy surpluses and must question how much more we need. There are two important steps we can take to help farmers.

First, we can avoid the intrusion of the patent law enforcement process by passing a farmer's exemption.

Second, we should adopt a regulatory process similar to that I recently offered (H.R. 4971) that calls on the U.S. Department of Agriculture to issue permits before this research hits the agricultural economy. Similar regulatory authority should also be given to the Environmental Protection Agency to regulate the release of genetically altered animals into the wild.

WHY SHOULDN'T THERE BE A MORATORIUM ON PATENTS FOR ANIMALS?

We have already had a moratorium for the last year. In April 1987 the Patent Office announced that they would accept applications for patent protection for genetically altered animals. Through my intervention no such patent issued for the last year. During that time we have endeavored to study the serious issues presented by this controversy. It is my sense that a moratorium bill can not pass the Congress. Moreover, a moratorium bill begs the important questions. A moratorium does not answer the fundamental questions. In my view a more responsive approach is to resolve the conflicting views in a permanent legislative bill.

1. The granting of patents for transgenic animals by the Patent Office is left unaffected, but the rights patent owners obtain are more limited than those applicable to other types of inventions. The bill adopts a number of limitations similar to those applicable to patented plants in the Plant Variety Protection Act. The bill creates an exemption to protect farmers from the intrusion of Federal patent law into the reproduction or use activities that occur on a family farm. Under current patent law, a farmer who obtains a patented animal would likely also obtain the right to use the animal for the intended use such as milking or slaughter. It is uncertain, however, whether the farmer would be liable for an act of patent infringement if the farmer reproduced the patented animal. Therefore, the legislation proposes that on-farm reproduction is not an act of patent infringement. In addition, the bill makes two other policy decisions affecting farmers. First, it prevents direct competition by the farmer against the patentholder by making the sale of embryo, germ cells, or semen of a patented animal an act of patent infringement. Second, the bill recognizes the reality of agricultural practice by providing that the sale of a patented animal or its offspring is not an act of infringement. In many instances farmers as a routine but incidental part of their business sell the offspring of their animals. This type of activity should not become a part of the patent law infringement process.

PROPONENTS OF GRANTED PATENTS FOR
GENETICALLY ALTERED ANIMALS

Reagan administration.—

Medical organizations: National Coalition for Cancer Research, American Medical Association, and the American Society for Microbiology, Infectious Diseases Society of America.

Business Organizations: Industrial Biotechnology Association, Association of Biotechnology Companies, Pharmaceutical Manufacturers Association, Chemical Manufacturers Association, and the Animal Health Institute.

Legal organizations: American Bar Association, Intellectual Property Owners, and the American Intellectual Property Law Association.

Universities: University of Wisconsin, and the University of Ohio.

CONCLUSION

This bill is a fair balance between the needs of the industry and the farm community. It has the support of the Committee on the Judiciary and the entire agricultural community. I urge my colleagues to support this measure.

□ 1245

Mr. Speaker, I reserve the balance of my time.

H7438

Mr. MOORHEAD. Mr. Speaker, I yield myself such time as I may consume.

Mr. Speaker, I rise in support of H.R. 4970. The subcommittee chairman, the gentleman from Wisconsin [Mr. KASTENMEIER] worked long and hard on the drafting of this complicated legislation. I want to commend him again for his leadership. The only part of this bill which I am concerned about is that we may have gone too far in drafting the "farmers exemption." I can support in principle a limited exemption for farmers, but I believe the provision contained in H.R. 4970 is too broad. It is important to preserve the economic incentive for the biotech industry to develop genetically improved animals for farmers. If a farmer can purchase a single transgenic animal and then reproduce and sell that animal in perpetuity then we may well have diminished the value of patents for farm animals and established a precedent for weakening other parts of our patent law.

Aside from the broad farmers exemption, H.R. 4970 is a good bill. I would like to ask the gentleman from Wisconsin, the chairman of the subcommittee, as this bill moves down the legislative road will we be able to modify this exemption either in the other body or in conference?

Mr. KASTENMEIER. Mr. Speaker, will the gentleman yield?

Mr. MOORHEAD. Mr. Speaker, I am happy to yield to the gentleman from Wisconsin [Mr. KASTENMEIER].

Mr. KASTENMEIER. Mr. Speaker, I am pleased to reply.

As the gentleman from California, with his own considerable efforts in this connection, and he was at every hearing on the matter, knows, this formulation was arrived at after consultation with many people. I believe that the bill in its present form is supportable. It certainly is urgently needed, because patenting will go forward, and the whole agricultural community will find they will not have in place the exemption that they would have every right to expect. The overwhelming burden of testimony was to that effect.

We have included provisions making it infringement to sell semen and other generative materials. The farmer exemption also, as the gentleman knows, is to farm animals which are used with respect to food and fiber alone, so there are substantial limitations in this act.

Having said that, and I say, the bill in its present form is, I think, eminently supportable. I do realize that the industry may not in the final analysis want this version. They have been consulted, and I think the gentleman from California knows that last Friday, for example, earlier last week, they declined to continue our discussions, so that we are left, frankly, with no further alternative at this point but to proceed in this fashion. I think it is quite supportable that we do.

The gentleman from California and I have dealt with the Senate on many occasions with respect to patents, copyrights and other matters, and we, of course, will need to entertain their views on this question, and so long as the basic legislative purposes of this bill remain, we would certainly consider obviously whatever modifications the Senate might care to make.

Mr. MOORHEAD. Mr. Speaker, reclaiming my time, I thank the gentleman.

Mr. Speaker, our technology is such that we can create things never before thought possible. In so doing we are advancing through unchartered waters. I understand why animal rights groups are concerned, they do not want to see more abuse and misuse directed toward animals. Although there is no indication that there will be any more abuse toward animals, however, we can't guarantee that. I also understand the concern of our church groups. They too are concerned with where this type of research may lead. But even the church groups are hard pressed to give reasons for their opposition. We are tinkering with the very concept of creation. And to be honest, that makes me a little nervous, too. However, if we were to ban this research, if we were to declare a moratorium, I don't believe it would stop it because this research is worldwide. All we would accomplish is to make such development more difficult in this country and hurt our industry and put them at a serious disadvantage.

Our hearings and research have not produced any information that would indicate that this type of research and experimentation is dangerous, or that it's unethical or evil. That's not to say that some day it might take a turn in the wrong direction. Congress has the ability to monitor research and development in this area and as soon as we detect abuse we can move in and remedy the situation—what we are talking about here is genetically improved farm animals for food and genetically altered laboratory animals for research and treatment of human diseases. In the area of human medicine, the goal is the development of model animals for pharmaceuticals and medical research. For example, a Japanese company has genetically engineered silkworms to produce a hepatitis vaccine. American scientists are presently engineering strains of laboratory mice that can be affected with the AIDS virus, so that cures for the disease can be tested in mice, instead of primates because chimps and humans are the only known species that are susceptible to AIDS.

On April 12, 1988, the U.S. Patent Office awarded Harvard University a patent for a genetically engineered mouse, the first patent ever for an animal. This special mouse would involve inserting a gene from another animal into the mouse embryo in order to give the mouse characteristics that mice don't

177

naturally have. These mice are extremely sensitive to cancer causing chemicals and will develop tumors quickly if exposed to even small amounts. This research is thought to be extremely helpful in early detection of breast cancer in women. In the food area, research is directed at producing leaner meat, more productive cows, and disease resistant animals. The same type of gains that breeders have been working on for 10,000 years.

Improved source of food and medical research to combat the human hunger and disease in the world are so important. If we are ever to find the cure for cancer and other dreaded diseases we must support this type of research.

I urge my colleagues to vote favorably for H.R. 4970.

Mr. Speaker, I yield such time as he may consume to the gentleman from New York [Mr. FISH], ranking member on the full Committee on the Judiciary.

(Mr. FISH asked and was given permission to revise and extend his remarks.)

Mr. FISH. Mr. Speaker, I rise in support of H.R. 4970. I also would like to commend the gentleman from Wisconsin [Mr. KASTENMEIER] and the gentleman from California [Mr. MOORHEAD] for the hard work and leadership they devoted to this legislation. The incentives provided by our patent system are an important inducement to our inventors and to companies investing in research and development. H.R. 4970 would permit the present practice of issuing patents for the development of new transgenic animals but it would also provide an exemption from infringement for farmers. This bill is particularly important to the biotechnology industry. Mr. Speaker, biotechnology is not a product you can patent, but rather it's a group of processes that have in common the use of genetically altered living organisms to produce new medical, agricultural, chemical, energy and waste cleanup products that will enhance our future. Biotechnology was invented in America. The U.S. industry's 1986 revenues exceeded $600 million. Their 1988 revenues are projected to be at least $900 million. Thousands of new,

high-paying jobs are being produced as a result. Because so many of the biotech inventions are protected by patents, the future of that industry depends greatly on what Congress does to protect U.S. patents from unfair foreign competition.

Research in the biotechnology area has the potential of providing great benefits to the human race. The world's population of almost 5 billion people is projected by the World Bank to double within the next 50 years. The National Academy of Sciences estimates currently that some 20 million people in the developing world starve to death each year and that over 500 million more suffer from severe malnutrition.

H7439

In view of these sobering realities, it is an ethical imperative, to provide every reasonable incentive to those entities which conduct agricultural research and development and that is the primary purpose of H.R. 4970. A Public Perception Survey on Science, Biotechnology, and Genetic Engineering, conducted by the Congressional Office of Technology Assessment ending last year showed strong public support for such research. For instance, 83 percent favor using genetically engineered organisms on a small scale for medical research, 42 percent favored use on a large scale basis; 86 percent would be willing to have their child undergo human gene therapy if the child had a disease that was usually fatal; and 82 percent favored continued research in genetic engineering and biotechnology.

This is important legislation and I urge a favorable vote.

Mr. KASTENMEIER. Mr. Speaker, I yield myself such time as I may consume.

Mr. Speaker, I would just like to say in conclusion that I would like to thank members of the subcommittee, particularly the gentleman from California [Mr. MOORHEAD], for their contribution to this bill, and the gentleman from Oklahoma [Mr. SYNAR], who offered an important amendment, as well as others whom we have consulted with, including members of other committees with important jurisdiction in this field.

Mr. ROSE. Mr. Speaker, I rise in support of this legislation, and I commend you for the hard work that you have put into drafting legislation that exempts farmers from patent liability for breeding genetically altered farm animals, using them in farming operations or selling the animals or their offspring. This exemption answers one of my major concerns about the patentability of life and should adequately insulate family farms from many of the negative economic impacts that are anticipated as large chemical and pharmaceutical corporations play a more dominant role in our Nation's agricultural industry.

Mr. Speaker, as you know, I have voiced several other concerns about the direction that animal patenting can and may take. I still have very strong feelings about the need to provide legislation that will provide patent liability exemptions that will allow badly needed medical and scientific research to proceed with a minimal amount of litigation and impediment. The current patent law makes little or no concessions between the difficulty of protecting a slight, and often barely detectable, change in a patented research animal's genetic code for 17 years and the need for all researchers to have all of the best tools, whether animal, vegetable or mineral, to pursue cures for AIDS, cancer, and many other diseases that plague our society.

In turn, I think Congress must have a better definition of how much genetic material constitutes the legal definition of what constitutes a human being. Should an animal that contains one-half of a human code be considered human? How about one-quarter human genetic material? Should genetically altered fetuses be considered patentable subject matter under current patent law? Although such animals are not currently being patented, I am certain that such technology will exist in the near future.

On a separate but related issue, somewhere down the line, hopefully in the near future, some efforts must be taken to properly regulate the release of genetically engineered animals into the work environment, into the home environment and, perhaps, into the wild.

Mr. Speaker, I understand that you too have been drafting a more comprehensive animal patenting and generic engineering bill that addresses many of the concerns that I have mentioned and many other issues. I encourage you to continue your work with this issue, and I hope that you will continue to give myself, our colleagues, and the American public adequate opportunity to address their concerns about these issues and to reach a consensus on what amendments are, or might be, necessary to our Nation's present patent law and genetic engineering policies to properly introduce this new era in science to the American public.

Mr. SYNAR. Mr. Speaker, Chairman KASTENMEIER has done a tremendous job handling a very emotional and controversial issue in a thorough and thoughtful way.

I am convinced that fears of turning the animal kingdom upside down or handing the ownership of future breeding rights to corporate America are unfounded.

When the bill came before the committee, I was concerned about its effect on America's farmers, many of whom are barely surviving. New royalty requirements for use of patented animals could dramatically increase their costs.

The bill includes an amendment I offered in the Judiciary Committee that exempts farmers from any requirement that royalties be paid for the use of patented animals

The farmers exemption is supported by all of the major farm groups. It will reduce the recordkeeping burdens on American farmers, and will eliminate any uncertainty about whether farmers who intentionally reproduce a patented animal would be committing an act of patent infringement.

Animal patents offer great hope for advancement in medicine and agriculture. This bill ensures patent protection for researchers in this new field, while also protecting farmers from the burdens of royalty payments for farm animals.

Mr. Speaker, I have no further

requests for time, and I yield back the balance of my time.

Mr. MOORHEAD. Mr. Speaker, I have no further requests for time, and I yield back the balance of my time.

The SPEAKER pro tempore (Mr. GRAY of Illinois). The question is on the motion offered by the gentleman from Wisconsin [Mr. KASTENMEIER] that the House suspend the rules and pass the bill, H.R. 4970, as amended.

The question was taken; and (two thirds having voted in favor thereof) the rules were suspended and the bill as amended, was passed.

A motion to reconsider was laid on the table.

GENERAL LEAVE

Mr. KASTENMEIER. Mr. Speaker, I ask unanimous consent that all Members may have 5 legislative days in which to revise and extend their remarks on H.R. 4970, the bill just passed.

The SPEAKER pro tempore. Is there objection to the request of the gentleman from Wisconsin?

There was no objection.

101ST CONGRESS
1ST SESSION
H. R. 1556

To amend title 35, United States Code, relating to animal patents.

IN THE HOUSE OF REPRESENTATIVES

MARCH 22, 1989

Mr. KASTENMEIER introduced the following bill; which was referred to the Committee on the Judiciary

---

A BILL

To amend title 35, United States Code, relating to animal patents.

1   *Be it enacted by the Senate and House of Representa-*

2   *tives of the United States of America in Congress assembled,*

3   **SECTION 1. SHORT TITLE.**

4   This Act may be cited as the "Transgenic Animal

5   Patent Reform Act".

6   **SEC. 2. INFRINGEMENT OF PATENT.**

7   Section 271 of title 35, United States Code, is amended

8   by adding at the end the following new subsection:

9   "(h)(1) It shall not be an act of infringement for a person

10   whose occupation is farming to reproduce a patented trans-

11   genic farm animal through breeding, use such animal in the

2

1 farming operation, or sell such animal or the offspring of such

2 animal.

3   "(2) Notwithstanding the provisions of paragraph (1), it

4 shall be an act of infringement for a person to sell the germ

5 cells, semen, or embryos of a patented transgenic farm

6 animal.

7   "(3) For purposes of paragraphs (1) and (2)—

8   "(A) the term 'transgenic farm animal' means a

9   farm animal whose germ cells contain genetic material

10   originally derived from another animal other than the

11   parent of the farm animal; and

12   "(B) the term 'farm animal' means any animal

13   used or intended for use as food or fiber.".

14 **SEC. 3. SPECIFICATION FOR PATENT APPLICATION.**

15   Section 112 of title 35, United States Code, is amended

16 by adding at the end the following new paragraph:

17   "With respect to an invention involving biological mate-

18 rial, the Commissioner may accept a deposit of biological ma-

19 terial to satisfy any requirement of this section if made acces-

20 sible under such conditions as the Commissioner may

21 require.".

22 **SEC. 4. PATENTABILITY OF HUMAN BEINGS.**

23   Section 101 of title 35, United States Code, is amended

24 by adding before the period at the end a comma and the

3

1 following: "except that human beings are not patentable sub-

2 ject matter".

O

100TH CONGRESS		REPORT
2d Session	HOUSE OF REPRESENTATIVES	100–888

TRANSGENIC ANIMAL PATENT REFORM ACT

AUGUST 26, 1988.—Committed to the Committee of the Whole House on the State of the Union and ordered to be printed

Mr. KASTENMEIER, from the Committee on the Judiciary, submitted the following

REPORT

together with

ADDITIONAL VIEWS

[To accompany H.R. 4970]

[Including cost estimate of the Congressional Budget Office]

The Committee on the Judiciary, to whom was referred the bill (H.R. 4970) to amend title 35 of the United States Code relating to animal patents, having considered the same, report favorably thereon with an amendment and recommend that the bill as amended do pass.

CONTENTS

The amendment is as follows:

Strike out all after the enacting clause and insert in lieu thereof the following:

SECTION 1. SHORT TITLE.

This Act may be cited as the "Transgenic Animal Patent Reform Act".

SEC. 2. INFRINGEMENT OF PATENT.

Section 271 of title 35, United States Code, is amended by adding at the end the following new subsection:

"(g)(1) It shall not be an act of infringement for a person whose occupation is farming to reproduce a patented transgenic farm animal through breeding, use such animal in the farming operation, or sell such animal or the offspring of such animal.

"(2) Notwithstanding the provisions of paragraph (1), it shall be an act of infringement for a person to sell the germ cells, semen, or embryos of a patented transgenic farm animal.

"(3) For purposes of paragraphs (1) and (2)—

"(A) the term 'transgenic farm animal' means a farm animal whose germ cells contain genetic material originally derived from another animal other than the parent of the farm animal; and

"(B) the term 'farm animal' means any animal used or intended for use as food or fiber.".

SEC. 3. SPECIFICATION FOR PATENT APPLICATION.

Section 112 of title 35, United States Code, is amended by adding at the end the following new paragraph:

"With respect to an invention involving biological material, the Commissioner may accept a deposit of biological material to satisfy any requirement of this section if made accessible under such conditions as the Commissioner may require.".

SEC. 4. PATENTABILITY OF HUMAN BEINGS.

Section 101 of title 35, United States Code, is amended by adding before the period at the end a comma and the following: "except that human beings are not patentable subject matter".

I. PURPOSE

The Transgenic Animal Patent Reform Act of 1988 amends title 35, United States Code, to make changes to the United States patent law relative to the patenting of genetically altered animals. The legislation creates an exemption from patent liability for farm-

ers who intentionally reproduce patented animals. The legislation 3
also authorizes the development of a deposit requirement involving
biological materials, if found necessary by the Commissioner. Finally, the legislation clarifies that human beings are not patentable
subject matter.

II. LEGISLATIVE HISTORY

The Subcommittee on Courts, Civil Liberties and the Administration of Justice conducted four days of hearings on the subject of
patentability of genetically altered life forms (other than human
beings).[1] Legislation relating to this issue was introduced by Congressman Robert W. Kastenmeier on June 30, 1988. The bill, H.R.
4970, was favorably reported by the Subcommittee on July 13, 1988.
The Subcommittee rejected a two year moratorium bill, H.R. 3119,
that had been introduced by Congressman Rose (North Carolina).
The Committee on the Judiciary, with a quorum present, by voice
vote approved the bill on August 2, 1988. The Committee adopted
two amendments and rejected one amendment.

The Committee adopted an amendment that deleted a statutory
research exception. It was argued that such a statutory exception
was unnecessary in light of the existing judicially fashioned doctrine.

Second, the Committee adopted an amendment, offered by Mr.
Synar (Oklahoma) that clarified the farmers' exemption. The
amendment removed from judicial consideration the size limitations (with respect to size of farm) found in the bill reported by the
Subcommittee.

Finally, the Committee rejected by a vote of 22-10 an amendment offered by, Mr. Morrison (Connecticut) that would have
placed a two year moratorium on the issuance of patented for genetically altered animals, or a shorter period in the event that the
commercialization of such animals was subject to a "federal regulatory review and approval process which includes environmental,
health and safety, and biomedical ethical standards." Various arguments were offered against the amendment, including: (1) the negative impact of a patent moratorium on research in areas relevant
to biomedical research; (2) the negative repercussions a moratorium
would have on United States competitiveness in light of the availability of patent protection in many other countries; (3) a moratorium would set a bad precedent for the patent law to deny protection
for only one set of inventions based on moral, ethical or regulatory
concerns. It was also argued that an adequate regulatory framework existed for the commercialization of patented transgenic animals. Finally, it was argued that the amendment would have left
too much discretion in interpreting its terms in the Commissioner
of the Patent and Trademark Office.

---

[1] *Patents and the Constitution: Transgenic Animals Hearings before the Subcommittee on
Courts, Civil Liberties and the Administration of Justice of the House Committee on the Judiciary,* 100th Cong., 1st Sess. (1987). These hearings are completely summarized later in this report.

4

III. Introduction and Summary

On April 12, 1988 the United States Patent and Trademark Office granted the first United States patent for a genetically altered animal.[2] The patent was granted to a Harvard University researchers, Dr. Philip Leder and Timothy Stewart, who had developed a genetically altered mouse that was useful in cancer research. The Patent Office decision was a logical and legally appropriate extension of existing judicial interpretations of the patent statute. The Supreme Court has previously upheld the granting of patents to microorganisms, thus the extension of the law to animals was predictable. The application of a broad reading of the patent law by the Patent Office was not unanticipated. As the Supreme Court said in *Diamond* v. *Chakrabarty*:

> This Court has frequently observed that a statute is not confined to the "particular application[s] * * * contemplated by the legislators". This is especially true in the field of patent law. A rule that unanticipated inventions are without protection would conflict with the core concept of the patent law that anticipation undermines patentability * * * inventions most benefiting mankind are those that "push back the frontiers of chemistry, physics, and the like * * * legislative or judicial fiat as to patentability will not deter the scientific mind from probing into the unknown no more than Canute could command the tides. Whether * * * claims are patentable may determine whether research efforts are accelerated by the hope of reward or slowed by want of incentives, but that is all."[3]

The granting of a patent on a genetically altered animal was, however, not without controversy.[4] Support for patenting genetically altered animals (in addition to the Administration) has come from the biomedical community (American Medical Association, National Coalition for Cancer Research, Infectious Diseases Society of America, American Society for Microbiology), industrial or business groups (Industrial Biotechnology Association, Association of Biotechnology Companies, Pharmaceutical Manufacturers Association, Chemical Manufacturers Association, Intellectual Property Owners, Inc. and the Animal Health Institute), legal professional organizations (American Bar Association, American Intellectual Property Law Association), farm Groups (American Farm Bureau Federation), universities (University of Wisconsin) and individual companies (Dupont, Monsanto, Pioneer HiBred Intl., Upjohn, Embryogen, and Integrated Genetics). Editorial support for patented animals came from the New York Times, The Chicago Tribune, and the New Republic. Opposition to patenting animals emerged

---

[2] Patent Number 4,736,866 covers a transqenic non-human animal whose germ cells and somatic cells contain an activated oncogene sequence introduced into the animal, or an ancestor or the animal, at an embryonic stage.

[3] 447 U.S. 303, 315–17 (1980).

[4] Davis and Stipp, *Patent for Genetically Altered Mouse Opens Era for Research, Spurs Protests,* Wall Street Journal, April 14, 1988 at 32; Gladwell, *Mouse Patent May Bolster Research Efforts: New Genetic Techniques Could Reduce Drug Costs,* Washington Post, April 13, 1988 at F 1; Schneider, *Mouse Patent Is Issued to Harvard, World's First Higher Life Form,* N.Y. Times, April 13, 1988 at 1.

from religious organizations, animal rights groups and some environmentalists. 5

Prior to the issuance of the first patent on a genetically altered animal the Subcommittee on Court, Civil Liberties and the Administration of Justice had conducted a set of hearings on the subject of patents on higher life forms. The text of the report that follows is a summary of the hearings conducted by the Subcommittee as well as a reflection of other work undertaken for the Subcommittee by the Office of Technology Assessment and the Library of Congress.[5]

IV. OVERVIEW

During the past 14 months the Subcommittee on Courts, Civil Liberties and the Administration of Justice of the Committee on the Judiciary has conducted an inquiry into the nature of the United States patent system and its application to transgenic animals. This report presents the findings and recommendations of that inquiry.

This report is divided into five parts. Part One consists of background information. Included in Part One are chapters which outline the nature of the hearing process and provide a summary of the statements of the witnesses.[6] The concluding chapters of Part One are papers prepared by the Office of Technology Assessment and the Library of Congress on the scientific issues presented by research in the area of transgenic animals.

Part Two of the report consists of six chapters. Chapter 6 contains an overview of the patent system and sets forth the constitutional basis for American patent law. Chapter 7 describes the evolution of patent law and its application to living organisms including transgenic animals. Chapter 8 provides a discussion of how other countries' patent laws address the question of patenting higher life forms. Chapter 9 analyzes the current caselaw on the subject of a research exception to the general rules on patent infringement. Chapter 10 assesses the legal doctrines of implied use and exhaustion of patent remedies. Chapter 11 gives a description of trade secret protection and compared that form of intellectual property protection to patent protection.

Part Three consists of one chapter (12) and provides an overview of the Federal regulatory apparatus with respect to the development of transgenic animals.

Part Four, which consists of three chapters, provides the major arguments against patenting animals and offers a response to each

---

[5] For additional treatment of the subject reference should be made to the following articles: Merges, *Intellectual Property in Higher Life Forms: The Patent System and Controversial Technologies*—Maryland L. Rev.—(1988); Adler, *Controlling the Applications of Biotechnology: A Critical Analysis of the Proposed Moratorium on Animal Patenting*, 1 Harv. J. of Law and Tech. 1 (1988); *What Price Mighty Mouse*, New Republic, May 23, 1988; Raines, The Mouse That Roared, Issues in Science and Technology, Summer 1988 at 64 (1988); R. Dresser, Ethical and Legal Issues in Patenting New Animal Life, (1988); American Farm Bureau Federation, Animal Patents; Agriculture's Perspective, August 25, 1988.

[6] *Patents and the Constitution: Transgenic Animals: Hearings before the Subcommittee on Courts, Civil Liberties and the Administration of Justice of the House Comm. on the Judiciary*, 100th Cong., 1st Sess. (1987) [hereinafter citations to witness statements are cited as *Testimony of——*].

The summary of witness statements was prepared at the request of the Committee by the Library of Congress, Science Policy Research Division.

6 of the claims. Chapter 13 relates to the moral arguments that have been used to oppose the patenting of animals. Chapter 14 assesses the impact of biotechnology on agriculture. Chapter 15 summarizes the economic arguments concerning the relationship between patent protection and economic concentration.

Part Five sets forth the findings and recommendations of the report.

PART ONE

CHAPTER 1.—COMMITTEE HEARINGS AND INVESTIGATIONS

In April 1987, a part of the Department of Commerce, the Patent and Trademark Office's the Board of Patent Appeals and Interferences, decided in the case of *In re Allen* that altered animals can be patentable subject matter.[7]

Immediately after the decision by the Patent and Trademark Office in the *Allen* case the Chairman of the Subcommittee on Courts, Civil Liberties and the Administration of Justice announced that the Subcommittee would conduct a series of hearings on the implications of patenting animal life. The *Allen* decision generated great public controversy and support for the Chairman's decision became apparent.[8]

The Subcommittee conducted 4 days of hearings, with 30 witnesses, on July 11, 1987, July 22, 1987, August 21, 1987 (in Madison, Wisconsin), and November 5, 1987. The witnesses represented the Administration, various business and farm organizations, patent lawyers, animal rights activists, ethicists environmentalists, academics, researchers and religious organizations. The witnesses were evenly divided between persons who supported the Patent Office decision to permit the patenting of animal life forms and those who had questions about the decision.

Among the witnesses with concerns about decision, two positions emerged. Some witnesses—such as Jeremy Rifkin on behalf of the Foundation for Economic Trends—were basically opposed to any patentability of animals under any circumstances. The second group of witnesses in this category—largely representing the views of various family farm organizations—urged a moratorium on patentability until certain questions could be resolved. Support for the decision of the Administration to permit the patenting of animals came from biotechnology companies and trade associations, the largest farm organization, patent lawyers and intellectual property owners, scientists and researchers. Proponents of patenting genetically altered animals argued that the general patent statute required this result. These witnesses saw the patent law as an important incentive for the development of innovations. Most of these witnesses concluded that the Patent and Trademark Office is an inappropriate place to make moral judgments or to exercise regula-

---

[7] *In re Allen,* 2 U.S.P.Q.2d 1545 (1987).

[8] *Manbeast: Patent Pending,* U.S. NEWS AND WORLD REPORT, April 27, 1987 at 18; *Animal Patent Debate Heats Up,* SCIENCE NEWS, Aug. 1, 1987 at 69; Jones, *In Search of a More Perfect Pig,* L.A. TIMES, July 12, 1987 at 1; Spotts, *U.S. Stands at crossroad on genetic alternation,* CHRISTIAN SCIENCE MONITOR, April 27, 1987 at 1; *Religious Groups Join Animal Patent Battle,* 237 SCIENCE 480 (1987). Weis, *How Do You Patent a New Elephant,* WASH. POST, Sept. 20, 1987, at C.3.

tory authority based on health and safety concerns. Finally, many 7
of these witnesses concluded that the existing regulatory process is
adequate for transgenic animals.

The requests for a moratorium or a ban on patenting animals
were a primary focus of the hearings. The requests were founded
on moral objections, environmental and regulatory concerns, fears
about economic concentration, alarm over the implications for
animal rights, and the potentially disruptive impact the patenting
of animals could have on the farm community. Some of these concerns were more capable of objective and factual analysis. Questions about the adequacy of the regulatory framework for biotechnology in general, and the protection of the environment and
animal rights, fell into this category. The other concerns were
more difficult to subject to such analysis, since they were highly
subjective in nature.

The Office of Technology Assessment (OTA) was instrumental in
the Subcommittee's analysis of the factual issues. It provided the
Subcommittee with background materials and a copy of its earlier
report on animal rights, which placed the issue of patenting animals in context.[9] In addition, OTA conducted a workshop on the
federal regulatory framework for animal biotechnology, designed
solely to obtain factual information from the various federal agencies about their role in the regulation of transgenic animals.[10]

The Subcommittee also greatly benefited from work done in earlier Congresses by the House Committee on Science and Technology. Over a period of years, that Committee has carefully monitored
the science and regulatory framework for biotechnology. The excellent work done by that Committee has materially assisted the Subcommittee in its understanding of the issue of patenting animals.

CHAPTER TWO.—SUMMARY OF TESTIMONY BY JILL T. SWERDLOFF,
TECHNICAL INFORMATION SPECIALIST, AND SARAH E. TAYLOR, ANA-
LYST IN LIFE SCIENCES, SCIENCE POLICY RESEARCH DIVISION

The following statements are summaries of the testimony printed in: U.S. Congress, House Committee on the Judiciary, Subcommittee on Courts, Civil Liberties, and the Administration of Justice,
"Patents and the Constitution: Transgenic Animals," hearings
June 11, July 22, August 21 and November 5, 1987, Serial No. 100-
23 (Washington, DC: U.S. Government Printing Office, 1988).

The bracketed page numbers to the right of each summary indicate the corresponding page of full text in the printed hearings.

JUNE 11, 1987

1. Dr. Rene Tegtmeyer, Assistant Commissioner for Patents, U.S.
Patent and Trademark Office, (p. 4).

Dr. Tegtmeyer, the Assistant Commissioner for Patents, testified
on the evolution of the patent law which formed the foundation of

---

[9] As early as November 1985, the Subcommittee had requested that the OTA study questions
relating to intellectual property protection and biotechnology. For a more thorough review of
the issues presented by the use of animals in research *See* OFFICE OF TECHNOLOGY ASSESSMENT,
ALTERNATIVES TO ANIMAL USE IN RESEARCH, TESTING, AND EDUCATION (1986) [hereinafter cited
as ALTERNATIVES].
[10] OFFICE OF TECHNOLOGY ASSESSMENT, FEDERAL REGULATION AND TRANSGENIC ANIMALS
(1988).

8   the PTO decision in April 1987 to permit the granting of patents
for genetically engineered animals and plants. He began by explaining that patent rights are protected by the Constitution. In
1790 Congress enacted the first Federal Patent and Copyright statutes. Section 1 of the 1790 Patent Act (Patent Act) defines the
standards for obtaining a patent. Dr. Tegtmeyer highlighted key
cases that define these statutory standards and he noted that
under these standards naturally occurring objects, including living
organisms, traditionally were not considered patentable subject
matter. As a result of genetic engineering, the questions arose
whether or not "man made" living organisms were patentable subject matter.

Dr. Tegtmeyer described the case of *Diamond v. Chakrabarty,*
447 U.S. 303, 206 USPQ 193 (1980) in which the Supreme Court
considered the patentability of a genetically engineered bacterium.
The Court determined that Congress intended the patent standards
of the Patent Act to be construed broadly. The Court ruled that the
distinction to be made in determining patentability was not between living and inanimate things, but rather between products of
nature and human-made inventions. After *Chakrabarty,* Dr. Tegtmeyer explained, microorganisms were considered to be patentable,
but there were still questions concerning the patentability of
higher life forms, i.e., animals and plants.

Dr. Tegtmeyer described key cases decided by the Board of
Patent Appeals after the *Chakrabarty* decision that addressed the
patentability of biological matter. *Ex parte Hibbard,* 227 USPQ 443
(Bd. App. & Inf. 1985) involved a patent claim on a maize seed,
plant and tissue culture. The Board rules that the two laws enacted by Congress to provide patent-like protection of plant materials (i.e., the Plant Protection Act and Plant Variety Protection Act)
did not preclude patentability under the Patent Act.

The case of *Ex parte Allen,* 2 USPQad 1425 (Bd. App. & Int. April
3, 1987) involved a patent claim for a method of inducing polypoidy
(sterility) in oysters, and the sterile oyster made by the process.
While the Board refused to grant a patent for the oyster on other
grounds, it reasoned that the *Chakrabarty* decision required only
that patentable subject matter be made by man, and the fact that a
method of making the invention was controlled by nature was irrelevant.

Dr. Tegtmeyer discussed the PTO's April 7, 1987 decision to "consider nonnaturally occurring non-human multi-cellular living organisms, including animals to be patentable subject matter," in accordance with the PTO's interpretation of the *Ex parte Allen* decision. The relevant case law involving the interpretation of standards of patentability were not public policy determinations. "It was
the Board's [of Patent Appeals] responsibility to determine the
intent of Congress" in enacting the statutory standards, relying on
the past body of case law as a foundation. Additionally, he stated
that the "Supreme Court decision and rationale in *Chakrabarty* did
not leave much room to refuse to consider living things as patentable subject matter if they were a product of human intervention.
The Court and the Board did not, and should not impose their
views on what the law should be based on their concept of public
policy."

Dr. Tegtmeyer concluded, that the granting of a patent provides   9
an incentive to those who develop new technology. However, the
patent does not grant the holder the right to make, use or sell their
inventions. He contended that "safety, efficacy, environmental or
similar concerns" are to be controlled by law other than the patent
law.

2. Dr. Thomas Wagner Edison Animal Biotechnology Center,
Ohio University, Athens, Ohio, (p. 34).

The term transgenic animal was introduced and defined by Dr.
Wagner as an animal "genetically distinct from other animals of
its species or breed." He explained that at present and in the near
future, the technology of genetic engineering is capable only of producing minor changes in the animal and cannot change the basic
identity of the animal or create a truly "new" type of animal. It is
Dr. Wagner's opinion that genetic engineering is appropriate only
for "agricultural livestock in synthetic agricultural ecosystems"
and not for wild animals or humans.

He contended that this technology will benefit agricultural economics through improvements in animal production efficiency and
animal health. Medical and pharmaceutical research will also benefit from genetic engineering through the development of animal
models with traits desirable for studying human diseases. Mr.
Wagner stated that he considers genetically engineered animals a
safe method of experimentation because the only way a transgenic
animal may pass on the transferred genes is by mating with their
own species.

3. Mr. John A. Hoyt, President Humane Society of the United
States, (p. 55).

Mr. Hoyt called for legislation to prohibit the issuance of animal
patents. It is the position of the Humane Society that the issue of
classifying animals as patentable subjects is more than a question
of the legal authority to do so, but rather a question of ethics, morality, and a proper regard for the essence of life.

Mr. Hoyt classified the argument made in support of genetic engineering that man has already been changing domesticated animals for thousands of years as invalid because he views genetic engineering as a faster and a completely different technique than traditional breeding methods. He stated that animal patents, by encouraging gentic engineering of animals, will increase animal suffering, create new man-made animal health problems, and cause a
loss of genetic diversity in the gene pool. He also argued that
animal patents are unnecessary and will increase competitiveness
and decrease collaboration among industry, government and university, which will result in costly duplication of studies.

Finally, Mr. Hoyt suggested that to uphold the principles of de-
mocracy in the context of genetic engineering, it is necessary to respect the rights of all beings who are part of the same ecological
community, and to allow patenting of one animal will eliminate
the constraints against altering all other animals, including
humans.

4. Mr. Jack Doyle, Director, Agricultural Resources Project, Environmental Policy Institute, (p. 67).

Mr. Doyle expressed support for an amendment placing a moratorium on animal patents to give Congress and the public time to

10   consider the ramifications of the PTO policy. He argued that the animal patent would be a source of economic power enabling a few companies to "get rich quick" through monopoly-like practices, while passing along higher costs to farmers and consumers. Mr. Doyle questioned the need for an animal patent to achieve advances in livestock productivity because we already have seen advances in agriculture without the incentive of a patent.

Mr. Doyle stated that the PTO decision inadvertently may favor the commercialization of genetically-engineering products over more traditional products with similar qualities. Mr. Doyle questioned the equity of denying a patent to livestock breeders who have altered animal characteristics through traditonal breeding practices, while granting patents to genetic engineers. He stated also, that products that are not genetically engineered are "less complicated, safer in the environment, and cheaper to use."

JULY 22, 1987

5. Congressman Charlie Rose, North Carolina, 7th District, (p. 107).

Congressman Charlie Rose informed the Subcommittee that he planned to introduce legislation establishing a moratorium on the issuance of animal patents, to provide Congress with time to investigate the problems he sees arising from this policy. He expressed concern about possible economic and ethical implications of animal patents. Representative Rose suggested that the new PTO patent policy may place major chemical, biotechnological, and pharmaceutical companies in a position of economic power that would allow them to virtually take over animal husbandry in America. Also, he argued that Congress has not yet had the opportunity to study the ethical implications of transferring human genes into the genetic code of other animals to create a patentable life form. Representative Rose urged that Congress also address the issues surrounding the deliberate release of genetically altered animals into the environment, which he stated is unregulated.

Representative Rose argued that establishing patent policy has traditionally been the duty of Congress, and that "Congress cannot allow an issue of such magnitude as animal patenting to be decided by the Appeals Board at the U.S. Patent and Trademark Office."

6. Dr. A. Ann Sorenson, Assistant Director, Natural and Environmental Resource Division, American Farm Bureau Division, (p. 116).

Dr. Sorenson lent support for the granting of animal patents because they act as an incentive for the commercialization of genetically improved animal breeds.

She addressed some of the issues surrounding animal patent rights including the beneficial role genetic engineering could play in animal production. She asserted that genetic engineering will allow for more rapid and targeted changes in breeding, the development of totally new agricultural products, and the potential ability to produce non-food products from livestock, such as protein-based pharmaceutical.

Dr. Sorenson contended that the trend toward vertical integration in food production and the decline of family farming are not issues to be addressed by the patent law, and should be handled by some other means.

She addressed some of the environmental and moral implications of genetically modified animals, stating that "it is in the best interest of biotechnology companies to maintain as complete as gene pool as possible for future use." Similarly, she stated that "there is no reason to believe that a scientist or company will deliberately create transgenic animals with traits that will subject them to stress."

In order to bridge the gap between initial research in biotechnology and the utilization and commercialization of its discoveries, Dr. Sorenson offered two possible solutions: "the granting of patent rights which confer a monopoly for an extended period but allow access to the process itself, or trade secret protection which allows access to the product but not the process." She described science as "working in a building block fashion—one discovery building on another," and for this reason she preferred the patent rights to trade secret protection.

Dr. Sorenson called for a set of guidelines for the Patent Office to follow concerning issues such as determining if animals meet patent requirements, defining the scope of the patent coverage, and detailing enforcement procedures of animal patent law.

7. Mr. Cy Carpenter, President, National Farmers Union (NFU), testifying also on behalf of National Farmer Organization (NFO), American Agriculture Movement (AAM), Coalition to Save the Family Farm, and League of Rural, Voters, (p. 114).

Mr. Carpenter expressed support for a moratorium on the issuance of animal patents, on behalf of the several groups he represented. He explained that a moratorium is needed to give Congress adequate time to investigate and review several areas of concern, including: what effects animal patents will have on the gene pool, whether animal patents will result in greater economic concentration in breeding stock production, and what will be the impact on consumers if producers are forced to pay royalties to the owners of animal patents?

On an international level, Mr. Carpenter suggested that the American farmers will be at a competitive disadvantage if they are forced to pay patent royalties while their European competitors are exempted from these payments, because most European countries do not now grant animal patents.

Mr. Carpenter noted that advances in research and industry have been achieved in the past without the incentive of animal patents. He urged that animal patents not be granted except as under specific legislation, and argued that Congress should not allow the resolution of this policy "to be handled by the Patent Office employees when the American people elected Congress for just such a purpose."

8. Mr. William H. Duffy, General Patent Counsel, Monsanto, on behalf of, Industrial Biotechnology Association, and the Intellectual Property Owners, Inc., (p. 135).

Mr. Duffey expressed strong support for the PTO policy to issue animal patents. He said he had recently attended a conference in Geneva on the subject of biotechnology patents and, in his opinion, America is the world leader in patent policy, and suggested, "lag-

12   ging European countries will soon catch up with our modern bio-tech patent practices."

From an industrial and economic perspective, Mr. Duffey argued that biotechnology should be a top government priority, if OTA is correct in estimating that it will be a $100 billion industry by the end of this century. To maintain America's competitiveness in the field of biotechnology, Mr. Duffey argued Congress should not consider limiting protection for biotech inventions.

He also stated that the act of issuing patents is morally neutral, and cautioned that the patent system is the wrong place to regulate matters of ethical or moral concern.

9. Professor Robert Merges, Columbia University School of Law, Julius Silver Program in Law Science and Technology, (p. 173).

Mr. Merges argued that animals should not be excluded from patent protection for ethical or economic reasons; "both animal treatment and farm policy are, and should be, outside the purview of the patent system." He does, however, believe that Congress should consider legislation to provide two limited exemptions from patent infringement liability: a Farmer's Livestock Exemption and a Research Exemption. The first would allow farmers to breed and sell animals who are the offspring of patented animals without having to pay royalties a second time (to the patentee). The second would not allow a patentee to prevent research experimentation using patented products or processes for bona fide research activities designed to further scientific knowledge. Both of these limited liability exemptions are paralleled in legislation Congress passed under the Plant Variety Protection Act (7 U.S.C. Section 2543.4).

Mr. Merges argued that these exemptions are a way for Congress to provide "Farm Aid" to those who will bear some of the cost of the new era of animal research, while still recognizing the importance of intellectual property rights in encouraging agricultural innovation.

10. Mr. Reid Adler, Finnegan, Henderson, Farabow, Garrett, & Dunner, Washington, D.C., (p. 151).

Mr. Adler testified that "the policy choice to patent animals is not only reasonable, legal and authorized by statute, but is imperative." He contended that the patent is necessary to provide an incentive for the agricultural research and development needed to alleviate predicted world-wide food shortages.

His testimony reviewed "the evolutionary application of intellectual property law to living organisms" by explaining the significance of the *Chakrabarty Hibberd* and *Allen* cases [see testimony of Dr. Tegtmeyer], and how they relate to the PTO policy decision to issue animal patents. He stated that criticisms of this policy are, in part, due to a fundamental misunderstanding of patent law. He described the law as granting the right to exclude others from making, using or selling a creation, but that it does not grant an unconditional right to produce the creation.

He reviewed the "requirements for patentability: utility, novelty, and statutory subject matters," and stated that the Supreme Court confirmed that Congress intended for these requirements to be broadly interpreted.

He discussed existing legal limitations on a patentee's rights to exclude others from making or using an invention. He compared the protection provided plant inventions under the Plant Variety 13 Protection Act which expressly excuses from infringement the use and reproduction of a protected variety for plant breeding or other bona fide research purposes. He contrasted the judicially-created "experimental use doctrine", and explained that the key criterion of the doctrine is that "there must be no intended commercial use of the patented article . . . if the exception is to be recognized at all." But he noted that the boundary between permissible research uses and impermissible infringement is not totally clear. He explained that the experimental use doctrine does not protect the experimental breeding (i.e. making) of a patented animal in order to add improved traits (i.e. using) with long-range commercial interests (i.e. selling) in mind. He stated that a concern for Congress should be whether the Courts will recognize as an "experimental use" the research needed to improve a patented living organism when no practical way to avoid infringing breeding exists and no direct commercial benefit is attained at the patentee's expense.

Mr. Adler then went on to analyze the concept of a farmers' use exception. He explained that under the Plant Variety Protection Act, farmers are entitled to save seeds of cash crops and to plant the seed for self use or to sell to other farmers, but that similar actions with patented plants would constitute infringement. He responded to advocates of a farmers' use exception for patented plants and animals by emphasizing that the relevant policy issue is not whether farmers are more important to society than inventors but rather, how to make the patent incentive system work for both. He asserted that in whatever mode the acquisition of improved, patented varieties may occur, the cost of an invention will find a market equilibrium point where both the patentee and purchaser are satisfied, or the transaction will not occur. "The terms set cannot be odious to either party, or again the transaction will not occur . . . it is quite reasonable to believe that necessary business transactions will continue to occur with the assistance of appropriate contracting and licensing practices." He implied that a legislatively created farmers' use exception would interfere with the natural market equilibrium and deprive the agricultural community of the patent system's benefits.

He concluded by stating that the "patent system can be a powerful mechanism for maintaining public access to both raw and refined genetic materials of biotechnology research" and recommended that the United States create a National Library of Germplasm Resources "to facilitate germplasm collection and conservation."

AUGUST 21, 1987

11. Dean Leo Walsh, College of Agriculture, University of Wisconsin, Madison, Wisconsin, (p. 208).

Mr. Walsh addressed four possible effects of animal patents that he is most concerned about: will patenting distract the research results? Will animal patenting lead to loss of genetic diversity? And, will animal patents lead to increased market concentration? Dean Walsh emphasized the positive aspects of animal patenting in his assessment of these concerns, but stated that "despite the benefits which U.W.-Madison and the college derive from patenting, we re-

14   alize that a balance must be struck between patent holders and patent users." He offered several recommendations for action which he feels would "ensure that patent users, particularly farmers, are not gouged by the patenting of animals." These recommendations include: a university research exemption, compulsory licensing of the patent, public research focusing efforts on helping the smaller firms stay competitive in the market place, public institutions cooperating in establishing and maintaining a gene bank to preserve genetic diversity, public research focusing on discoveries which reduce purchased inputs in agriculture, and "university researchers should continue to assess economic and sociologists effects of technology introduced into farming."

Dean Walsh "urged Members not to take action which would unduly restrict development of biotechnology and use of recombinant based technology in agriculture."

12. Dr. Winston Brill, Vice President, Agricetus, Middleton, Wisconsin, (p. 218).

Dr. Brill emphasized that mankind will experience a tremendous increase in the need for production over the next forty years, and our government must play a role in keeping U.S. agriculture competitive in this challenge. Patents and regulatory policies are important to U.S. competitiveness, according to Dr. Brill, because companies such as Agricetus depend on patent protection to justify major investments in biotechnology.

Dr. Brill also explained the current capabilities and limitations of genetic engineering so as to dispel any fears and/or myths concerning the creation of "monster animals". He explained that genetic engineering can only add one or, at most, a few genes to the tens of thousands of genes in the recipient organism, which produces more specific and predictable results than traditional breeding methods.

13. Mr. Richard D. Godown, President, Industrial Biotechnology Association, (p. 259).

Mr. Godown focused on dispelling what he considers to be "myths" surrounding the patenting of genetically engineered animals and on the Federal Government's regulation of transgenic animals (i.e., animals in which the germ line has been modified through recombinant DNA techniques). The "myths" that Mr. Godown addressed included: that genetic engineering will be used to create half-man, half-beast creatures, that it will increase animal suffering, and that breeds improved through genetic engineering will hurt the small farmer economically. Mr. Godown stated also that it would be a myth to assume that the United States holds an unquestioned lead in animal biotechnology. He countered the first so-called myth by stating that the "addition of a single human gene to an animal that possesses tens of thousands of genes will not produce human traits or characteristics." He cited the potential of genetic engineering to increase diseases resistance as a means of reducing animal suffering. He also stated that increased production resulting from genetic engineering "will help the small farmer stay competitive by reducing farm costs." He listed several examples of foreign research initiatives that threaten America's lead in the biotechnology industry.

Mr. Godown addressed regulatory issues associated with assuring 15
the safety of meat of transgenic animals, animal welfare protection, and the containment of transgenic animals. He concluded by
stating that already existing regulatory mechanisms in these areas,
together ensure that there is adequate protection of the public and
experimental animals.

14. Mr. Michael Ostrach, Senior Vice President and General
Counsel, Cetus Corporation, (p. 295).

Mr. Ostrach asserted "that a revision of existing statutory policy
concerning the patenting of animals is both unnecessary and
unwise." Mr. Ostrach offered three main points in support of his
position against a moratorium on animal patents. First he claimed
"there is no valid reason to upset the existing statutory basis for
issuance of patents that involve animals." Congress should address
public policy considerations directly, rather than through changes
in the patent system. Second, he argued that animal patents will
not increase animal suffering, will not alter economic realities, and
do not present unique environmental hazards; therefore the existence of patent involving animals, does not raise any novel policy
issues that require congressional action. Third, "a stable patent
and regulatory process for agricultural biotechnology will foster
continued American dominance as it has with pharmaceuticals."

In addition to these three points. Mr. Ostrach contended that the
livestock farmer's exemption, proposed by some advocates of
animal patents to reduce the farmers recordkeeping duties associated with licensing patented animals, is not "necessary." He contended that "the commercial reality of the marketplace will cause
the cost of a patented animal to reflect the rights of the farmer to
use the animal. If opportunities exist to avoid rewarding the inno-
vator appropriately for its contribution, the original purchase price
will reflect that and be higher. Thus, the exemption will cause the
prices of patented animals to be abnormally high to reflect the lost
sales caused by the exemption."

15. Mr. Nicholas J. Seay, Patent Attorney, Isaksen, Lathrop,
Esch, Hart & Clark, Madison, Wisconsin, (p. 352).

Mr. Seay urged that the appropriate "action" for Congress at
this point is "not to take action" regarding animal patents. He,
therefore, recommended against the enactment of a moratorium on
animal patents. He explained that the Nation's patent policy has a
strong influence on the biotechnology industry because it is critical
to ensuring that businessmen will make long-term investments in
developing products which might not be ready for sale until the following decade.

Mr. Seay argued that the PTO decision was merely an "incremental step forward in an area where the law and the science are
working together," and does not represent any departure from
prior precedent.

He addressed the concern that animal patents would create a
monopoly in agriculture by explaining that a patentee can take
nothing away from general use in our society; he may only protect
that which he adds. The existence of these patented products,
whether plant or animal, merely offers the farmer an alternative
means toward increased productivity.

16   Mr. Seay argued that the patent system ought to be morally and ethically neutral. From an international perspective, he explained that the reason the United States is in a minority permitting the issuance of animal patents is because the United States is a leader in the area of intellectual property laws and not a follower.

16. Mr. Stuart Huber, President, Wisconsin Farmers Union, Farmers Union Milk Marketing Cooperative (FUMMC), Madison, Wisconsin, (p. 306).

Mr. Huber stated that Congress should impose a moratorium on animal patents to allow itself and the public time to examine the economic, moral, ethical, health, and environmental concerns posed by animal patents. He argued that public funds have been the basis for biotechnology research, even for the multinational corporations. Therefore, he questioned both the fairness in granting a monopoly market position to these corporations through a patent, and the necessity of patents to promote scientific progress.

Mr. Huber suggested that a patented animal would most likely cost more than if competition were allowed, and that it would be hard to enforce an animal patent given the large volume of animal sales that occur among farmers and others. He admitted that the "farmer exemption" suggested by some animal patent advocates, might be a partial solution but argued that it almost makes the whole process nonsensical.

For the dairy industry, Mr. Huber argued that the problem of overproduction would certainly be made worse with the patenting of animals. Additionally, he pointed out that many farmers have dramatically improved livestock yields through classical genetic breeding. These breeds would not be eligible to receive patents under the PTO policy. Mr. Huber contended that this would have a chilling effect on family farm breeding and speed the vertical integration of family farms.

17. Mr. Dennis Jelle, President, National Farmers Organization, on behalf of the National Farmers Organization, American Agriculture Movement, International Alliance for Sustainable Agriculture, League of Rural Voters, National Farmers Union, United Farmers Union, United Farmers Organization, (p. 316).

Mr. Jelle testified in support of a moratorium on the issuance of animal patents, to provide time to examine the economic, social, and ethical effects of the animal patent. Four areas were cited in the testimony as concerns that need to be addressed, including: the animal patent's effect on traditional breeding procedures, the effect on the shrinkage of the gene pool, the effect on increasing the concentration of those producing breeding stock, and the impact on consumers if farmers have to pay royalties for their livestock.

Mr. Jelle interpreted the reaction of the seed industry since the enactment of the statutes providing patent-like protection for plant breeds as an accelerated acquisition of the independent seed companies by major corporations. He stated that this reaction illustrates what may happen if animal patenting is allowed to proceed. He claimed that the animal patent will be a disadvantage to the American farmer in international competition because European farmers do not have to pay patent royalties (because animal breeds are not patentable in Europe).

18. Mr. Tom Saunders, Wisconsin Farm Unity Alliance, (p. 321).

Mr. Saunders, a dairy farmer, testified that it is very important   17
for Congress to enact a moratorium on the issuance of animal patents.

Mr. Saunders argued that patenting genetically altered or "non-naturally occurring" organisms will have the opposite effect of the original patent law. Instead of providing economic protection for small firms and individuals, the PTO policy will result in a less diverse productive base, providing no protection for small and independent production units. Therefore, he stated that the patenting of animals will lead to increased concentration in livestock breeding and production.

Mr. Saunders further testified that bio-genetic research is proceeding without the benefit of patents, with much of the research being done with public funds at publicly supported unversities. He argued that this is the correct manner in which controversial research should occur because it allows for both open and democratic discussion and evaluation of research.

19. Ms. Debra Schwarze, Attorney, Wisconsin Family Farm Defense Fund, (p. 329).

Ms. Debra Schwarze advocated a moratorium cn the issuance of animal patents based on several concerns regarding such patents, including overproduction and food safety. She cited the case of bovine growth hormone (BGH), a drug produced by biotechnology, which increases the productivity of dairy cows. She questioned the use of a technology that increases production in a surplus market which she feels will inevitably lead to an increase in corporate owned farms and a reduction in the number of family farms. She asserted that consumers perceive potential food safety problems related to new uses of biotechnology, and questioned the Food and Drug Administration (FDA) and the United States Department of Argiculture's (USDA's) knowledge and skill in their ability to test genetically altered foods for safety to humans.

Additionally, she commented that environmentalists support a moratorium on animal patents so that risks to the environment maybe assessed before the introduction of new technology.

In conclusion Ms. Schwarze arrested that public university research has failed to create the necessary infrastructure to assess the risks posed by animal patients because they receive funding from large corporations. Ms. Schwarze called for Government, not profit-seeking corporations and universities, to set the pace of acceptance of animal patents by enacting a moratorium on the issuance of such patents to allow time for public debate and the development of specific legislation.

NOVEMBER 5, 1987

20. Reverend Wesley Granberg-Michaelson on behalf of the National Council of Churches, (p. 393).

Reverend Granberg-Michaelson testified that "the development and patenting of transgenic animals is an unprecedented shift in humanity's relationship to the God given natural environment," and therefore, asked Congress to adopt measures halting the implementation of the PTO policy. He contended that this request is not founded on a basic opposition to genetic engineering or biotechnol-

18   ogy, but rather a concern that the rapid pace of this technology will leave society unable to consider its moral consequences.

From a biblical standpoint, Reverend Granberg-Michaelson stated that man is entrusted with the responsibility "to preserve the integrity of the creation" of life. He argues that animal patenting may result in the erosion of this societies sense of this responsibility because of "subtle economic pressure to view animal life as if it were an industrial product invented and manufactured by humans."

He warned that all innovation does not result in "progress" and may instead result in unforseen environmental consequences, as in the case of the gypsy moth. Reverend Granberg-Michaelson also expressed concerns that the animal patent "could further concentrate the economic power of corporate forces in agriculture." He stated that life forms created by genetic engineering cannot be developed through natural classical breeding methods and, therefore, the two "breeding" methods cannot be considered alike.

He questioned that the public interest would be best served by a process motivated by economic gains, and stressed the need for a clearer understanding of what genetic engineering will be used for, and who will be using it.

21. Rabbi Michael Berenbanm, Scholar-in-Residence, Religious Action, Center of Reform Judaism, (p. 403).

Rabbi Berenbanm classified the questions concerning the issuance of animal patents to be ethical rather than technical. He posed several questions that he believes must be answered in order to understand what must be done regarding this issue: what constitutes life and what is merely an inert manufactured commodity; what are the limits and frontiers of scientific knowledge; should there by constraints on scientific experimentation and/or industrial exploitation of these experiments? He also questioned "who shall regulate, who shall decide?"

Rabbi Berenbanm asserted that animal patents raise important concerns and therefore decisions in this area should not be made by Patent Office employees, but should be the responsibility of our elected officials. He supported the call for a two year moratorium on the issuance of animal patents in order to allow the religious community time to study the issues and their implications. He expressed concern that genetically engineered animals "may transgress a boundary of nature" and that if we proceed too quickly "we may lose our reverence for life and diminish our own humanity."

22. Dr. Leroy Walters, Kennedy Institute of Ethics, Georgetown University, (p. 371).

Dr. Walters testimony addressed the ethical issues in the patenting of non-human animals. He reviewed the issues surrounding a 1984 debate, over whether the deliberate transfer of genes across species lines and into the germlines of new species should be prohibited under the National Institutes of Health (NIH) research guidelines (the Recombinant DNA Advisory Committee-RAC Guidelines). Jeremy Rifkin led the effort to ban interspecies germline transfer. Dr. Walters explained that the NIH committee rejected the proposed prohibition on the grounds that the research was important to the treatment of disease and the development of more efficient food sources, making it a moral imperative that they oppose the prohibition. He noted that the NIH received substantial public support for its position.

Dr. Walters stated that since 1984, there has been "a vertiable explosion of scientific research" in the field of interspecies germ-line transfers. He highlighted the current goals of such research, and its potential benefits.

The review of the 1984 debate was used by Dr. Walters to show the "parallels between an earlier public-policy debate and the patent question currently confronting the U.S. Congress." Some of the parallels cited included the issues of gene-transfer between species, the importance of the distinction between "human" and "non-human" organisms, the likelihood of increased animal suffering and the loss of benefits that could result from overly restrictive regulation.

Dr. Walters suggested several conclusions from his narrative statement. First be cautioned that "some ethical objections to both transgenic animal research and the patenting of non-human animals can probably be ignored as misguided and/or irrelevant." Second, ethical issues of animal patenting need to be "distinguished analytically from the animal-welfare question." Third, he advised to view the animal patent proposal in the same context as we view other animal practices such as selling, breeding, and eating. Fourth, the patent system serves as an encouragement for creativity by assuring the creator control over the product, which should be preserved unless the system produces serious harm to human or animal welfare. Fifth, Dr. Walters contended that we should continue to attempt to define appropriate boundaries between human and non-human organisms as biomedical research and technology advances, to reach a "social consensus on reasonable ethical limits to human curiosity and ingenuity."

23. Ms. Margaret Mellon, Manager, Biotechnology Project of the National Wildlife Federation (p. 419).

Ms. Mellon's testimony called for a two-year delay in the issuance of animal patents so that the consequences of the PTO policy might be considered. She stated that the animal patent "challenges the basic policy assumption that drives the patent law—that the inventions encouraged, on balance, will benefit society." Ms. Mellon argued that the patenting of animals will encourage the use of "genetic engineering techniques, even where classical techniques would otherwise suffice." She also considered the patent a stimulus to the development of new and controversial technologies that would develop more slowly, and with greater understanding, if a patent were not involved. She was especially concerned about the possibility of genetically-engineered animals being released into the wild, such as fish and oysters. She explained that while the Federation does not necessarily oppose genetic engineering, it believes more attention should be paid to the broad environmental impact of the patent policy. Ms. Mellon pointed out that there may be long-term ramifications in the engineering of wild organisms, and asked if there is "a point at which the manipulated populations of animals would cease to be wild?"

Theoretically, she considered, concerns about wildlife could be addressed by "patent law" or "regulating legislation," but she pointed out that there is no regulating legislation currently apply-

20 ing to genetically engineered animals. In her conclusion, she stated that if Congress decides to extend patent law to include animals, then legislation is needed to "charge a Federal agency with the evaluation and control of the deliberate and inadvertent release of engineering organisms into the environment."

24. Mr. Geoffrey Karny, Principal Dickstein, Shapiro and Morin, (p. 433).

Mr. Karny testified that there is "absolutely no reason to prohibit or delay patents on transgenic animals." He reinforced his position, noting, that patenting and regulation of transgenic animals are entirely separate issues, with different goals. The Government seeks to stimulate invention through the patent, an idea recognized in the Constitution, while regulation focuses on risks and mandating restrictions of a product.

Mr. Karny stated that according to a scientific consensus, that risk posed by transgenic animals is no greater than the risk from classical breeding techniques. However, he acknowledged that historical concerns will require Federal oversight for genetic engineering technology. He explained that "biotechnology will be regulated by various Federal agencies under their existing statutory authority over the same products made by conventional techniques." Mr. Karny explained in detail the jurisdiction of the agencies most involved in animal biotechnology oversight, which are NIH and USDA. Although he contended that there is adequate Federal oversight of transgenic animals, he recognized the concern for oversight of planned release of transgenic animals into the environment. If more oversight were called for, he stated that USDA has the statutory authority to exercise such oversight without the need for new legislation.

Mr. Karny contended that prohibiting or delaying patents on transgenic animals could seriously delay new life-saving medicines and major agricultural breakthroughs because the patent provides the incentive for a company to invest its resources in developing new technologies. Additionally, he proposed that a delay or prohibition will also effect America's competitive position, while other countries are trying to commercialize their products of biotechnology in the international market.

25. Dr. Alan Smith, Vice President, Integrated Genetics, Framingham, Massachusetts, (p. 462).

Dr. Smith testified in opposition to the proposed moratorium on animal patents, asserting that it will hinder the development of transgenic animals. He cited two general commercial applications of transgenic research: developing animal models for studying human disease, and developing improved breeds of farm animals. Dr. Smith explained that transgenic animals may also be used for pharmaceutical protein production.

Pharmaceutical proteins, such as TPA, a protein that dissolves blood clots, can be produced in the milk of transgenic animals, and will be a much less costly means of production than the alternative methods, according to Dr. Smith.

He stated that inexpensive production of pharmaceutical proteins will have a beneficial impact on health care, but a moratorium on animal patents will delay further research in the United States. Dr. Smith contended that in order for the United States to

remain competitive, patents are necessary to stimulate further research, to protect disclosure of information and to encourage investment in the industry.

Dr. Smith stated that in his opinion, transgenic animals are patentable because they are man-made, and therefore consistent with
the Supreme Court ruling in *Chakrabarty*. Dr. Smith asserted that
the Patent system is not the proper place to address issues of ethical, moral or social concern. He stated that such issues are the
same as those reviewed in the past in regard to "farming and sanctity of life, animal breeding programs, laboratory animal experimentation and safety and efficacy of drugs."

The environmental impact of transgenic animals producing pharmaceutical proteins will be negligible, according to Dr. Smith, because it requires few animals that are kept under closely monitored conditions.

26. Mr. Jeremy Rifkin, President, The Foundation on Economic
Trends, (p. 484).

Mr. Rifkin interpreted the Patent and Trademark Office decision
to issue animal patents to mean that "all life can now be regarded
as a manufacture or composition of matter" and a genetically altered animal will be considered like any other inanimate human
invention. He stated that the patent decision signals the beginning
of a "transition from the age of fossil fuels and petrochemicals into
the age of biological resources" which could lead to the exploitation
of all living things by corporations for commercial gain.

Mr. Rifkin asserted that the immediate impact of this patent
policy will be felt "in agriculture," as it provides the incentive to
chemical, pharmaceutical and biotechnology companies to "complete their takeover of American agriculture." He described the development of a new era in tenant farming, where farmers will
lease their plants and animals as well as their land.

Mr. Rifkin explained that there are two issues in the debate over
genetic engineering that are in direct conflict with each other: the
rapid commercialization of biotechnology products and the ethical
and social concerns related to biotechnology. He contended that the
resolution of this conflict will determine how future generations
will define life. Mr. Rifkin asserted that ethical concerns should
override commercial pressures, "leading Congress to prohibit the
patenting of animals."

27. Dr. John F. Barnes, Alliance for Animals, Federated Humane
Societies of Wisconsin, (p. 348).

Dr. Barnes testified that "animal patenting is not acceptable
from either a moral, ethical, biological or economic standpoint." He
asserted that if animal patenting were allowed, it would compro-
mise the integrity of animal species and ultimately lead to the control of life forms by a few multinational corporations. Dr. Barnes
contended that by making no distinction between living things and
inanimate objects, the "new patent regime" redefined the entire
animal kingdom in "technological terms to suit the commercial
needs of the market place." He stated that "privatizing and exploiting animals in the development and implementation of subjects to
be patented would be a vast enterprise."

Dr. Barnes concluded by posing several questions concerning ac-
countability in the following serious issues: the release of genetic

22   aberrants into the environment, the creation of a "Frankenstein Monster" resulting from breeding of genetically altered animals, and the possibility that an "Andromeda Factor could mistakenly be created or inadvertently escape from a laboratory isolation unit and threaten life on earth."

28. Mr. Russ Weisensel, Wisconsin Agribusiness Council, (p. 350).

Mr. Weisensel testified that "new technologies and new techniques are going to be absolutely necessary if we are going to feed this human population and, at the same time, protect our delicate environmental balance."

Mr. Weisensel stated that he does not believe that corporate involvement in agriculture is a threat to the family farm, as animal patent critics have suggested. He noted that the corporate farms of the 1930's were responsible for giving family farms access to the "top bloodlines for livestock." In addition, he explained "today the top patent lines for livestock are available to everyone in agriculture because of the cooperative and corporate structure of artificial insemination groups." Mr. Weisensel views the patenting of animals as part of this continuing process.

Mr. Weisensel then described several areas in medical research that have benefited or could benefit from genetic engineering. He stated that although we think big companies will benefit from this process, educational opportunities have been helped through products these companies have patented. He concluded by stating that "every action of our society has a social and moral and economic implication but so does every roadblock have the same moral, social and economic impact, and we should not use fear to avoid making progress.

29. Bishop Schumacher, (p. 351).

Bishop Schumacher testified in favor of the proposed mortorium on animal patents, stating that more time is needed to discuss and debate the issue, and to gain more information about animal patenting and its consequences.

The General Secretary of the National Council of Churches prepared a statement from which Bishop Schumacher quoted the following: "The gift of life from God in all of its forms, and species, should not be regarded solely as if it were a chemical product, subject to genetic alteration and patents for economic benefits." He stated that at this time, most churches have not prepared statements on this issue, but he contended that there is debate going on and that they need the time required to get these statements together.

CHAPTER 2.—BACKGROUND

Humans have bred animals for thousands of years. Until the end of the last century, however, selection was the only method for improving animal varieties. Since 1938, artificial insemination has been used in animal breeding. Other techniques involving sperm storage, estrous synchronization, superovulation, embryo recovery, transfer and storage, sex selection and twining have also been

used.[11] As the World Intellectual Property Organization has noted, 23
"by continuing two [or more of these techniques, total control of
the reproductive process can be achieved." [12] It is in this context
that the issue of transgenic animals has arisen.

CHAPTER 3.—TRANSGENIC ANIMALS

Recent scientific advances have allowed researchers to modify
life forms. In the last 7 years researchers have genetically altered
mice,[13] hamsters and rats,[14] hogs,[15] poultry [16] [17] cattle,[18]
sheep, [19] and fish.[20] Set forth below is an edited excerpt from a
staff paper prepared by OTA which describes the relevant scientific
techniques.[21]

CHAPTER 4.—MODERN TECHNIQUES FOR PRODUCING TRANSGENIC ANIMALS

Laboratories around the world are conducting research that involves inserting genes from vertebrates (including humans and
other mammals) into bacteria, yeast, or mammalian cells in culture. This research is aimed primarily at increasing understanding
of the organization and function of the hereditary material DNA:
deoxyribonucleic acid.

DNA, packaged in genes, encodes the information that directs
the construction and function of all higher organisms. It does so by

[11] *Subcomm. on Investigations and Oversight of the House, Comm. on Science and Technology,*
98th Cong., 1st Sess., ANIMAL SCIENCE: ADVANCES IN REPRODUCTIVE AND HEALTH TECHNOLOGIES,
COMM. PRINT (1983).

[12] WORLD INTELLECTUAL PROPERTY ORGANIZATION, COMMITTEE OF EXPERTS ON BIOTECHNOLOGI-
CAL INVENTIONS AND INDUSTRIAL PROPERTY, INDUSTRIAL PROPERTY PROTECTION OF BIOTECHNO-
LOGICAL INVENTIONS, BioT/CE/II/2, at para. 42, p. 19 (1985).

[13] Thompson, *From Mice, Anticlotting Drug,* WASH. POST, A1, Oct. 27 1987 (genetically altered
mouse produces tissue-type plasminogen activator, TPA, that can dissolve blood clots); Schmeck,
Gene Altered Mice Make Human Protein in their Milk, N.Y. TIMES, B1. Oct. 27, 1987; Gordon et.
al., *Production of Human Tissue Plasminogen Activator in Transgenic Mouse Milk,* 5 BIOTECH-
NOLOGY 1183 (1987); Maugh, *Caltech Genetic Engineers Cure an Inherited Disorder in Mice,* section 1, pg. 3, L.A. TIMES, April 27, 1987 (curing "shiverer mutation"); Nerenbeng et. al. *The tat
Gene of Human T- Lymphotoropic Virus Type 1 Induces Mesenchymal Tumors in Transgenic
Mice,* 237 SCIENCE 1324 (1987); Hirrichs, *A Transgenic Mouse Model for Human NeuroFibromato-
sis,* 237 SCIENCE 1340 (1987) (mouse model for research on human diseases such as multiple scle-
rosis).

[14] ABSTRACTS IN BIOCOMMERCE 5 (August 1987) (a Japanese company to start production of
alpha interferon by hamsters).

[15] Please supply footnote.

[16] Bylinsky, *supra,* at note 7; Newark, *Protein Production in Transgenic Animals,* 5 BIOTECH-
NOLOGY 874 (September, 1987).

[17] Bylinsky, *Here Comes the Bionic Piglets,* FORTUNE 74 (Oct. 26, 1987); Hadington, *Transgenic
Sow,* 328 NATURE 6 (1987); Hammer, *et.al. Productions of Transgenic Rabbits, sheep and pigs by
microinjection,* 315 *Nature* 680 (June 1985); Greenberg, *Animal Biotechnology Cambridge Focuses
on Advanced Breeding Methods,* 7 GENETIC ENGINEERING NEWS 8 (1987).

[18] Wimeke, *Calves Colored Successfully in U.W. Experiment,* STATE JOURNAL, Sept. 9, 1987 at
1; *Compare* Rohter, *Mexican Rancher Breeds Minature Cows,* C1, N.Y. TIMES, Dec. 29, 1987
(small cattle produced by traditional breeding).

[19] *Protein Production in Transgenic Animals,* 5 BIOTECHNOLOGY 874 (September 1987); Simons
et al., *Alteration of the quality of milk by expression of sheep beta—lactoglobulin in transgenic
mice,* 328 NATURE 530 (1987).

[20] Work on transgenic fish has been conducted in Canada, Japan, France, Norway and the
United Kingdom, on such fish as rainbow trout, salmon, and medaka. Maclean *et al. Introduction of Novel Genes into Fish,* 5 BIOTECHNOLOGY 275 (March 1987). The goal of this research is to
improve growth rate. The authors note that: ". . . work on transgenic fish should be conducted
distant from rivers and lakes with secure containment facilities from the fish, to ensure that
genetically modified fish do not find their way into natural ecosystems." *Ibid.*
See also Moffat, *Fish Incorporate Rat Growth Hormone Genes,* 7 GENETIC ENGINEERING NEWS
1 (September 1987).

[21] OTA, TRANSGENIC ANIMALS, Feb. 2, 1988. The references found in the text of the staff paper
have been deleted.

24   regulating the enormous variety of biochemical activities in living
cells. Understanding has advanced to the level that some bacteria,
yeast, or cell cultures can now be used as factories for the production of high quality pharmaceuticals such as human insulin, interferon, and growth hormones, for use in the treatment of human
disease. As compared to other areas of scientific research, the
needs for equipment and training of personnel in this area are
modest.

A variety of techniques, mostly developed from early bacterial
research, can now be used to insert genes from one animal into another. These techniques are known by a number of exotic names,
such as microinjection, cell fusion, electroporation, and transformation. This report focuses largely on microinjection, because it is
now the method most likely to lead to practical applications in
mammals. The future may see other methods of gene insertion
become more widely used as techniques are refined and improved.
If protocols for human gene therapy now being developed in
animal models and laboratory cultures of mammalian cells prove
successful and broadly adaptable to other mammals, other gene insertion techniques may well supplant microinjection. The costs of
such techniques are not prohibitive. In the early 1980's, researchers
refined techniques for producing transgenic animals so that they
could be applied successfully with properly trained and skilled staff
and about $50,000 worth of equipment. Rearing and maintenance
facilities for the most commonly used research organism, the
mouse, cost between $10,000 and $100,000 on an annual basis.

Although the number of laboratories working with transgenic
animals remains small (fewer than 100 worldwide), and researchers
with the required skill and experience are not common, the
number of research programs using these techniques has grown
steadily in recent years. For reasons of convenience, most research
involving transgenic mammals continues to be done using mice, although some research programs on larger mammals have begun. It
appears that within the next 5 or 10 years, some animals of research utility or substantial economic importance will be subjects
of transgenic modifications. Besides mice, the principal candidates
for transgenic modifications include cattle, swine, sheep, poultry,
and some fish.

GENE INSERTION INTO BACTERIA

Procedures to produce transgenic organisms (those that have integrated DNA from foreign sources) were first developed in bacteria. The techniques for introducing a foreign gene into a bacterium
and achieving normal expression and function are fairly simple.
Certain bacterial enzymes, known as restriction enzymes, have the
ability to recognize specific, short sequences of DNA (between 4
and 12 nucleotide base pairs in length) and cut the DNA molecule
where these sites occur. Over 400 restriction enzymes are known,
and are capable of cutting DNA molecules at over 100 different recognition sequences. Using these enzymes, it is possible to extract
an entire gene that has been identified in the hereditary material
of an organism. This gene can be linked with a DNA carrier molecule called vector, which is then inserted into a bacterium. The

vector can exist in the bacterial cell, carrying along with it the in- 25
serted gene. It is by this method, for example, that the gene for
human insulin can be inserted into the bacterium *Escherichia coli,*
which then produces quantities of human insulin that can be extracted and administered to human diabetics.

GENE INSERTION INTO ANIMALS: MICROINJECTION [22]

Inserting a gene from one animal into another animal is more
complicated than insertion into bacteria and, at present, less precise. The cells of animals generally do not carry plasmids, or DNA
molecules, which can be used to transport genetic material between
different cells. To compensate for this lack of a convenient delivery
vehicle, researchers inject highly purified copies of the gene of interest directly into the fertilized animal's egg. Shortly thereafter
the fertilized egg is surgically implanted in the female's reproductive tract. This injection process is quite delicate, and only a small
fraction of the injected eggs survive. Even fewer express the inserted gene.

In experiments with mice, the fertilized eggs are placed under a
special microscope, and positioned and held in place by a special
glass tube that can be moved with a sensitive set of mechanical
manipulators, called a micromanipulator. Another tube with a
smaller point (about one-twenty four millionth of an inch in diame-
ter) is then used to penetrate the egg membrane into the cellular
subunit that will develop into the nucleus, known at this stage as
the pronucleus. The penetrating tube carries a small amount of a
buffer solution that delivers numerous highly purified copies of the
gene of interest into the pronucleus of the recipient egg. The injected eggs are then placed back into the appropriate location in the
reproductive tract of a hormonally receptive female mouse, who
brings them to term.

Overall, this process is tedious, labor intensive, and inefficient. In
an experienced laboratory, only approximately 85 of every 100 eggs
that are collected prove suitable for injection; of these injected
eggs, about 60 eggs survive the injection procedure; 6 of the injected eggs that were returned to the host mother result in live births,
and 1 or 2 will produce transgenic mice. By this method, the gene
for human growth hormone was introduced into mice, making
them larger than normal in size. This method has also been used to
produce mice that secrete the anti-clotting agent tissue-plasmino-
gen activator (TPA) in their milk.

As crude and tedious as this process is, it compares favorably in
at least three respects with older techniques for producing commercially bred transgenic animals, such as selective breeding.

—The precision with which a specific gene can be inserted into a
desired host greatly reduces the time needed to establish a line
of animals carrying the desired trait. Through this process, it
is possible to produce a line carrying the desired trait after as
little as one generation. In contrast, selective breeding requires
many generations to establish a desired trait (usually a poly-

---

[22] For a discussion of other techniques of genetic alteration, *see* Chapter 5, Transgenic Animals, at 29–30 (e.g. viral vectors).

26 genic one) in a line, while at the same time minimizing additional, unwanted characteristics. In the past, this minimization was not always possible.

—The process permits the specific gene of interest to be transferred with great confidence, if not efficiency, and without any accompanying, unwanted genetic material. Often, the breeding procedures traditionally used by animal breeders have caused the transfer of the desired gene to be accompanied by the simultaneous transfer of large amounts of additional genetic material, often complicating or confounding the objective of the breeding programs.

—With the proper preparation, the process enables genes from almost any organism to be inserted into the desired host, whether a mouse or another animal. Historically, genetic material could only be transferred between closely related species, or different strains within a species.

WHERE THESE TECHNIQUES ARE LIKELY TO LEAD

The traditional methods of gene transfer have been used for thousands of years to alter animals, plants and microbes to serve human purposes. To many interested parties, the new techniques involve no radical departure from historical practices. Instead they simply enable plant and animal breeders to accomplish the same goals more quickly, easily, and surely. If there is a fundamental difference between the traditional and new techniques, it is that breeders now have a greatly augmented ability to move genes between organisms that are not close genetic relatives. Students of species and species formation are in general agreement that nothing in transgenic animal research or its potential commercial applications threatens any species; such threats are more likely to occur through patterns of land use planning and habitat destruction resulting from other human activities.

It is reasonable to expect that the use of transgenic techniques will be substantially similar to that historical techniques, and to similar ends. Economic incentives are likely to dictate the order in which different transgenic animals are produced. It is likely that transgenic agricultural animals such as livestock and poultry will be produced first. The view most widely held among researchers is that it may be at least 10 years before commercial herds or flocks of transgenic livestock are produced. An optimistic, but clearly minority, view sees production within 3 or 4 years.

The near future will most likely see the majority of transgenic animal research focus on traits involving a single gene. Single genes have already been introduced into animals, allowing them to produces t-PA and a human growth hormone gene introduced into mice and pigs has produced larger, leaner animals. The potential exists for genes to be introduced into an animal to enable it to resist disease and parasites. By contrast, manipulation of complex traits influenced by more than one gene is technically more difficult and will develop more slowly (perhaps within 10 to 30 years). Examples of the objectives of such manipulation include changes in the amount of growth possible on a limited food regime, and the alteration of behavioral characteristics.

Much transgenic animal research will involve the insertion of genes from humans into other organisms. The principle reason for this is one of convenience: because of the growing amount of research aimed at identifying, extracting, and characterizing human genes, those genes will become more common and available. Because of the range of genetic variation within any species, and the fundamental similarity in genetic structure and organization in all mammals, a simple examination on an isolated gene will not reveal the species from which it was derived. If there is no identifying link between a gene and the organism that carries it, using the most readily availabale genetic material will probably be the most convenient option and thus the deciding factor in selecting genes for insertion into other organisms.

It is unlikely that genes from animals will be introduced into humans in the near future. Biological considerations as well as ethical, psychological, and aesthetic reasons dictate such a result. Somatic cell human gene therapy, even with human genes, is being approached with considerable caution. If animal genes are inserted into humans, the potential human immune responses will cloud the interpretation and understanding of the experiment's results. Advances in DNA chemistry may ultimately simplify some of the ethical, psychological, and aesthetic questions as the capability advances to synthesize genes entirely of human manufacture.

CHAPTER 5.—TRANSGENIC ANIMALS

(Prepared by Congressional Research Service, The Library of Congress)

ABSTRACT

In April 1987, the U.S. Patent and Trademark Office (PTO) announced, for the first time, that patents could be issued for animals developed through genetic engineering. The PTO decision has heightened debate about the benefits and risks of genetically engineering animals. In this context, some critics have raised concerns about whether the technology could be used to produce "monster-like" animals or "humanoid" creatures. This report considers the scientific validity of these concerns by discussing the strengths and limitations of available techniques, and the scientific impediments to creating such animals.

SUMMARY

In April 1987, the U.S. Patent and Trademark Office (PTO) announced, for the first time, that patents could be issued for animals developed through genetic engineering technology In this context, some critics have raised concerns about whether the technology could be used to produce "monster-like" animals or "humanoid" creatures. Because transgenic research is in its infancy, scientists are reluctant to predict what will be possible in 20, 50 or 100 years.

Genetically engineered animals, i.e., "transgenic animals" are made using so-called "gene transfer methods," to insert foreign genes into a recipient species. Currently available gene transfer methods include "microinjection," "viral vectors," and "chimera"

28   methods. Although the strengths and limitations of these methods differ, they are generally inefficient, capable of transferring only one or two genes, and the effects cannot generally be predicted.

So far, these techniques have been used to produce a variety of relatively simple transgenic animals, including a hog with unusually lean meat (and with some skeletal defects), and a mouse that synthesizes a human drug in its milk. The chimera method appears to have potential in the nearer term to produce significantly changed animals through interspecies manipulation. A simple chimera technique has been used to merge the early embryos of a goat and sheep to produce an animal known as the "geep".

Several significant scientific hurdles stand in the way of rapid advances in perfecting these methods, absent some unforeseen and revolutionary discoveries. Therefore, many scientists believe advances will be achieved slowly and incrementally, providing an opportunity to contemplate the implications as they develop.

The Federal Government has no uniform policy specifically addressing transgenic research, although a variety of research and regulatory policies, on an ad hoc basis, influence the progress of transgenics. Should Congress decide that additional policies are needed, it may wish to explore such avenues as the possible roles of voluntary research guidelines, the Recombinant DNA Advisory Committee Guidelines, and the Congressional Ethics Board.

INTRODUCTION

In April 1987, the U.S. Patent and Trademark Office (PTO) announced for the first time, that genetically-engineered animals could be patented.[23] The PTO decision has heightened debate about the benefits and risks of general engineering. Some critics have raised concerns that the technology may be used to fashion "monster-like" animals or "humanoid" creatures. This report considers the scientific validity of these concerns by discussing the strengths and limitations of available technology, and the scientific impediments to creating such animals.

RECOMBINANT DNA TECHNOLOGY

In 1953, Doctors Watson and Crick discovered the structure of deoxyribonucleic acid (DNA). DNA is a helical molecule contained in the cells of all organisms. It is responsible for passing on hereditary characteristics to subsequent generations and for directing the manufacture of proteins that make-up the entire organism. The chemical and structural language of the DNA code of inheritance is the same throughout the known plant and animal kingdoms. However, the unique message contained in the DNA of a particular organism is a composite of the message of all genes making-up the DNA molecule. A gene is a unit of the DNA molecule that controls the expression of a single inherited characteristic.

Since Watson and Crick's early discovery, advances in many fields of science, including genetics and molecular biology, have enabled scientists to isolate single genes, analyze their structures,

---

[23] Discussed in: U.S. Library of Congress. Congressional Research Service. Patenting Life, Issue Brief IB87-222, by Sarah E. Taylor (numbers from the original.)

make copies of genes, and to manipulate the entire DNA molecule by inserting genes or deleting or disabling them. Humans have long manipulated the genetic make-up of plants and animals indirectly through traditional practices of selective breeding. However, only the recent scientific advances have provided the capability to manipulate the genetic code of organisms directly. This direct manipulation of genetic material is referred to as recombinant DNA (rDNA) technology, or "genetic engineering". Through genetic engineering, an organism can be endowed with characteristics that would be difficult to achieve through traditional breeding.

The first commercial applications of genetic engineering focused on one-celled organisms, such as bacteria. For example, a human gene responsible for the synthesis of human insulin was spliced into the DNA of the *Escherichia coli* bacteria. The engineered bacteria was then used to produce insulin for use as a human pharmaceutical for treatment of diabetes. More recently rDNA technology has been applied to multi-cellular plants and animals.

The term, "transgenic animal," is used to refer to a multi-celled animal that results when rDNA techniques are used to introduce genes from one species into the DNA of another. In a multi-cellular animal, all body cells, except the reproductive cells (eggs and sperm), have an identical DNA composition. To incorporate a rDNA change uniformly into the DNA of all body cells, and to enable the animal to pass on the characteristic to future generations, genetic manipulations must be applied to the "germ line" (reproductive cells) of an animal, after the egg has been fertilized by the sperm cell, during the earliest stages of development of the embryo (before it becomes a "blastocyst", i.e., an embryo of 8 cells).

Because germ line cells are used to engineer transgenic animals, the progress of the development of transgenic animals is highly dependent on scientific advances regarding the harvesting, handling and storage of reproductive materials. Key developments in these areas include: superovulatory drugs, which cause a female animal to produce several "ripe" egg cells for harvesting at one time; cryopreservation, which has enabled reproductive materials, including sperm, eggs and embryos, to be stored for prolonged periods; and embryo transfer—permitting embryos to be collected from one female animal (or from an in vitro fertilization procedure), and then transferred to a foster mother. In fact, the advanced technology of the United Kingdom in these areas has been a key reason for that country's prominent position in transgenic research.[24]

TECHNIQUES USED TO MAKE TRANSGENIC ANIMALS

Some observers of transgenic research have raised questions about "how far" scientists can go in recombining genetic material from different animal species. Some observers have become concerned that transgenic research could lead to the development of "monster" animals or "humanoid" creatures. Clearly, transgenics have not yet produced such animals. However, because transgenics

---

[24] See Moffatt, Anne Simon, U.K. Scientists Succeed in Transformation of Animals into Factories for Protein Production. Genetic Engineering News, v. 7, Oct. 1987, p. 1, 9; Greenberg, Susan. Animal Biotechnology Cambridge Focuses on Advanced Animal Breeding Methods, GEN, v. 7, Oct. 1987, p. 8, 9.

30   is such an infant science, and because such significant scientific hurdles must be overcome before capabilities are much improved, it is difficult to predict what will be the capabilities of transgenics in 20, 50, or 100 years. However, many emphasize that the rate of progress is likely to be so slow and resource—intensive as to provide a safeguard against unchecked development of transgenic creatures of the kind some observers seem to fear. These concerns may be evaluated by examining the gap between what kind of scientific information is considered necessary to develop a transgenic animal and what scientists are able to do now.

GENETIC CHARACTERIZATION

Before an effective gene transfer can be made to produce a transgenic animal with a desirable characteristic, the genes that control the characteristic of interest in the gene donor species must be identified and characterized. This is not a simple matter.

Relatively few genetic characteristics considered to have commerical potential have been identified. For istance, the characteristics most often mentioned as being goals of transgenic research in agricultural animals are increased growth, changes in body composition (e.g., lower percent body fat), disease resistance, and the production of chemicals that would make useful pharmaceutical products (e.g., Tissue Plasminogen Activator, a drug being experimentally produced in the milk of transgenic mice). However, relatively little is known about the genes that must be manipulated to achieve desired effects in these areas.

Much transgenic research in agricultural animals has focused on growth hormone genes. This is, in part, because growth hormone genes are relatively well understood, and because increased growth of agricultural animals is a goal of transgenic research. However, animal growth is controlled by a variety of genes, most of which are unknown. Transfers of growth hormone genes are considered to be relatively simple and are only scratching the surface of what is needed to influence animal growth in a commercially valuable manner.[25]

Another problem scientists face is the inability to predict the characteristics that will result from a particular gene transfer (predictive genetics). Gene transfer effects are currently learned through a "trial and error" method. Therefore, the effects obtained sometimes take scientists by surprise. For example, when a human growth hormone gene was transferred into the DNA of a mouse, the mouse grew to approximately twice its normal size.[26] However, when a similar experiment was done with a hog, the hog developed leaner meat, but the size of the animal was not influenced.[27]

The information regarding gene characterization and predicting gene effects is very limited. Developing a more complete foundation of information would represent a significant scientific challenge

---

[25] Personal communication, Dr. Vern Pursel, U.S. Dept. of Agriculture (USDA), Animal Science Institute (ASI), Agricultural Research Service (ARS) Reproduction Laboratory. Nov. 6, 1987, 344–2814.

[26] Palmiter, R. D., G. Norstedt, et al. Metaallothionein-human GH fusion Genes Stimulate Growth of Mice. Science v. 222, 1983. p. 809–14.

[27] Personal communication. Dr. Vern Pursel, USDA, ARS, ASI, Reproduction Laboratory. Nov. 6, 1987, 344–2814.

were it needed for only one species of commercial importance. 31
However, such information is desired for several species, and frequently principles that govern in one species are inapplicable in
another.[28]

GENE TRANSFER METHODS

Once genes of interest are identified in a donor species, they
must be isolated, copied and transferred to the DNA of the recipient species. Chemicals known as "restriction enzymes" are available for cutting away the gene of interest from the surrounding
DNA. Techniques have been developed that are effective for a wide
range of organisms. However, once a gene is isolated, the process of
transferring a gene to the DNA of the recipient species is a more
challenging matter, and one that must be tailored for each species.[29]

There are several factors that influence the effectiveness of a
gene transfer method. An "ideal" gene transfer method would have
several characteristics. First, a molecular marker should be fas-
tened to the gene so that its ultimate incorporation into the DNA
of the recipient species can be detected. Next, for the method to be
practical for commercial purposes, it should provide reasonable efficiency in the number of recipient cells inoculated with donor
genes that actually incorporate the gene into the DNA, and express
the donor characteristic. In addition, the method should allow scientists to exert control over the number of copies of a gene that are
incorporated into the recipient DNA, and over the location of gene
insertion. Without such control, a gene may insert in such a way as
to interfere with normal DNA function, or so that the donated
gene is expressed unpredictably. The method should be capable of
transferring a large enough piece of genetic material so that the
genes necessary for the expression of a desired characteristic can
be transferred. Genes typically range in size from 1,000 to 50,000
"base pairs". Most gene transfer methods currently available can
handle only genes at the lower end of this range.[30]

Although there are a variety of gene transfer techniques, only
three techniques are in use for making transgenic animals.[31] [32]
None of the methods conforms to the criteria of an "idea" method,
and the relative advantages and limitations of each method differs.
As noted above, gene transfer techniques designed to result in a
transgenic animal must be applied to germ line cells. The three
methods target the gene transfer at different stages of early embryonic development.

---

[28] See Moffatt, Ann Simon. U.K. Scientists Succeed in Transformation of Animals into Facto-
ries for Protein Production. Genetic Engineering News, v. 7, Oct. 1987, p. 1, 9. Greenberg, Susan.
Animal Biotechnology Cambridge Focuses on Advanced Animal Breeding Methods, GEN, v. 7,
Oct. 1987, p. 8, 9.

[29] Moses, Phyllis B APPENDIX: Gene Transfer Methods Applicable to Agricultural Organisms. In, National Research Council. Committee on a National Strategy for Biotechnology in
Agriculture. Agricultural Biotechnology: Strategies for National Competitiveness. 1987. p. 151.

[30] Moses, Phyllis. p. 152–53.

[31] What do you get if you cross . . .? The Economist, Aug. 15, 1987, p. 68.

[32] Personal Communication, Dr. R. D. Palmiter, University of Washington—Seattle. Nov. 23,
1987, (206) 543–2100.

32   *Microinjection*

The gene transfer method that is most commonly used to produce transgenic animals is termed, "microinjection". For a short period after an egg cell has been fertilized by a sperm cell, the "pronucleus" contributed by each, the egg and sperm, coexist together inside the new one-celled embryo. Each pronucleus contains strands of DNA which accounts for half the genetic make-up of the embryo. The egg and sperm pronuclei soon merge, endowing the developing embryo with a full genetic complement. The pronucleus contributed by the sperm cell has been found to be particularly receptive to absorbing stray pieces of DNA and incorporating it into its preexisting DNA structures. Microinjection capitalizes on this receptivity.

Microinjection involves injecting into the sperm pronucleus through a tiny needle, strands of DNA containing the gene(s) to be transferred. Through a yet unknown mechanism, the DNA is sometimes incorporated into the preexisting DNA structures inside the sperm pronucleus. The foreign genes are introduced into the embryo so early, that they are incorporated into the chromosomes of the embryo, and as the embryonic cell divides, became part of the genetic make-up of every cell of the organism.[33]

The major advantage of gene transfer using microinjection is the fact that the gene insertion occurs so early in the development of the organism, it has an opportunity to become a uniform part of all cells of the organism, just as the genes contributed naturally by the egg and sperm are. When a gene is not so uniformly incorporated, scientists cannot control in what body tissue a gene will be expressed. The offspring of a gene transfer by microinjection is considered a "pure" transgenic animal, in contrast to a "mosaic" animal whose body cells lack genetic uniformity, discussed below. However, there are significant limitations to microinjection.

The primary limitation is that microinjection is a laborious and inefficient procedure. To perform microinjection, a fertilized egg cell must be injected during the window of time when the two pronuclei exist. Only one cell can be injected at one time, the cell must be handled carefully so that the needle may be inserted into the microscopic pronucleus without destroying the cell. In short, it is a tedious, labor-intensive process requiring highly skilled scientists.

A second limitation is that microinjection is relatively inefficient. Results so far indicate that of the egg cells injected, less than 8 percent of mouse cells and between .5 and 1 percent of agricultural animal cells (hogs and sheep) develop to produce transgenic embryos. Up to 65 percent of the transgenic animals born demonstrate characteristics that indicate the transferred gene is functional (i.e., the gene is being "expressed"). Some cells never incorporate the foreign DNA into the preexisting DNA structure, and other cells seem to incorporate the DNA in a way that is lethal to the cell.[34] The particular gene being transferred appears to influence

---

[33] Moses, p. 157-158.
[34] Personal communication. Dr. Harold Hawk, USDA, ARS, ASI, Reproduction Laboratory. Nov. 6, 1987, 344–2836.

the success rate. The inefficiency and labor intensity of the mi-   33
croinjection procedure make it costly and of limited value in
"scaled-up" commercial applications.

Viral Vectors

A second technique that has been used to transfer genes into the
DNA of early embryos, has been to attach the gene of interest onto
a virus which serves as a "vector" (carrier). The virus transports
the passenger gene into the embryonic cell where it facilitates the
incorporation of the gene(s) into the cellular DNA. A virus is a tiny
infective particle composed of protein and nucleic acids (the same
kind of material that DNA is made of). In fact, some viruses are
little more than a strand of DNA covered by a protein coat. Other
viruses (retroviruses) are made of another type of nucleic acid,
known as ribonucleic acid (RNA).

Different viruses are able to infect different species of animals
and possess varied mechanisms of infection and reproduction. However, a characteristic common to viruses, and one that helps to
make them effective vectors of foreign genes is their dependence on
a host cell to reproduce. Viruses invade a host cell and convert the
cell's metabolic machinery to its own use. This conversion occurs
through different mechanisms of interaction with the DNA of the
host cell.[35] Retroviruses and some other viruses achieve the conversion by integrating their own genetic material into that of the
host cell. Other viruses remain an independent but functional
strand of genetic material. The use of viruses as vectors of foreign
genes makes use of these processes to incorporate foreign genes
into host embryonic cells so that the genes are functional.[36] Ideally, the viral vector has been disabled to silence its disease-causing
properties.

Viral vectors have been used to produce transgenic animals to
only a limited extent. Viruses are generally a more efficient means
of incorporating foreign DNA into a host cell than microinjection.
Some retroviruses have produced an incorporation rate of 70 to 80
percent in certain agricultural species (chickens), but only 1 to 2
percent of the animals were able to pass the characteristic on to
their offspring.[37] However, there are relatively few identified viruses that have appropriate characteristics for making transgenic
agricultural species. This is a key reason that microinjection remains the dominant method of gene transfer in these species.

In addition, viral vectors are used when an embryo has developed to a 4 to 8 cell stage. Typically, an embryo inoculated with a
viral vector will not become infected uniformly. Some cells take up
the vector and passenger gene(s) and some do not. Therefore, the
transgenic offspring is typically a "mosaic," i.e., some cells are
transgenic, and some are not. As noted above, it is difficult for scientists to control gene expression in a mosaic animal because they
cannot control in what tissues the transgenic cells appear. Selective breeding can be used to "breed out" much of the undesirable

---

[35] Arms, Karen and Pamel S. Camp. Biology, 2nd ed. Saunders College Publishing, Philadel-
phia. p. 321–27.
[36] Moses, p. 163–69.
[37] Personal communication. Dr. Lyman Crittenden, USDA, ARS, Regional Poultry Research
Laboratory, Lansing, MI. Dec. 3, 1987, (517) 317–6828.

34   mosaic characteristic to achieve a nearly uniform transgenic
animal.

Another disadvantage of viral vectors is that they can carry passenger DNA of limited size. The size of the virus appears to influence the size of the passenger DNA strand it carries. This limitation puts a cap on the number of genes a particular virus is capable of transferring. In addition, the DNA of the virus itself can
sometimes interfere with the incorporation and expression of passenger genes.[38]

Chimera

A third way that foreign genes can be transferred to a developing embryo to produce a transgenic animal is through a "chimera."
This technique is just beginning to be explored as a way to produce
transgenic animals.

The last stage of embryonic development before an embryo im-
plants in the wall of the mother's uterus is termed the "blastocyst." A blastocyst possess the unique characteristic of being able
to compensate for cells lost without it affecting the normal development of the organism. For example, in a procedure known as
"twinning" a bovine (cow) blastocyst has been divided into two (or
more) cell masses, each transferred to a different foster mother.
Each cell mass compensates for the half that was lost, and develops
into a normal cow. The cows resulting from this procedure are genetically identical "twins."[39]

The procedure used to make a chimera also makes use of the
compensatory characteristic of a blastocyst. A chimera is made by
substituting embryonic cells of one organism for some of the cells
of the blastocyst of another. Depending on the cell lines mixed by
this process, the blastocyst sometimes continues to develop. This
technique has been used successfully to transfer the embryonic
cells of one variety of mouse into the blastocyst of another variety
of mouse to produce a mouse/mouse chimera.[40] The technique has
also been used to mix two closely related species, the goat and
sheep, to produce the so-called "geep." [41] These animals are simple
chimeras, as opposed to "transgenic chimeras" (described below).
Simple chimeras have been developed because they enable scientists to study such reproductive processes as "cell differentiation,"
i.e., trying to determine how uniform embryonic cells eventually
develop into different kinds of body cells—such as brain, skin, and
bone cells.

Simple chimeras are mosaic animals, with each body cell being
entirely one variety or species (goat/sheep) of animal, but the
entire organism being composed of cells of two or more varieties/
species of animal. For example, the geep has two lines of sperm
cells: goat and sheep. Thus, if a geep mates with a goat, the offspring will be entirely goat, but if it mates with a sheep, the offspring will be sheep. As one can see, chimeras are able to repro-

---

[38] Personal communication, Dr. R. D. Palmiter, University of Washington—Seattle. Nov. 23,
1987, (206) 543-2100.
[39] What do you get if you cross . . . ? The Economist, Aug. 15, 1987, p. 68.
[40] Personal communication, Dr. R. D. Palmiter, University of Washington—Seattle. Nov. 23,
1987, (206) 543-2100.
[41] What do you get if you cross . . .? The Economist, Aug. 15, 1987, p. 68.

duce, unlike a hybrid animal like a mule (horse/donkey hybrid), 35
which is sterile. Although the development of chimeras are a relatively new phenomenon, it is evident that they can be made from
cell lines of different varieties of the same species, or of closely related species.

Transgenic chimeras are made the same way as simple chimeras,
except that before the embryonic cells are added to the blastocyst,
foreign genes are transferred to the embryonic cells using a gene
transfer method such as a viral vector. The transgenic embryonic
cells are then added to the blastocyst, which then develops into a
mosaic organism composed of transgenic cells and nontransgenic
cells. Although this technique has only recently undergone experimentation, it appears possible that the embryonic cells that serve
as carriers of the foreign genes might be of the same or a different
species than the recipient blastocyst. For example, one might envision a transgenic geep whose transgenic sheep cells contain a gene
for bovine growth hormone.

The primary advantage of using embryonic cells to transfer foreign genes is the ability to use relatively efficient methods of gene
transfer into the embryo, like viral vectors, together with the ability to screen the cells for proper gene incorporation before transferring the cells to the blastocyst. The technique, in some cases, circumvents the need to grow up an animal to maturity to observe
whether a desirable gene incorporation has taken place. A key limitation of the technique is that it produces a mosaic animal, and
selective breeding techniques must be applied to increase the uniformity of the transgenic body cell type.

SCIENTIFIC HURDLES INFLUENCING FURTHER PROGRESS

The above description only highlights the techniques that are
being employed to produce transgenic animals, and some strengths
and limitations of each.[42] The techniques are in their infancy and
it is very difficult to achieve desired effects. The information that
is needed to perfect gene transfer techniques represent such significant scientific hurdles that most scientists are reluctant to predict
what eventually can be achieved. Absent some unforeseen and revolutionary discoveries, progress is expected to be incremental. It
appears that some of the most important hurdles lie in the following areas:

(1) Learning what genes must be manipulated to achieve desirable characteristics (animal growth, disease resistance, body composition, animal models);

(2) Learning how to improve the efficiency of gene transfer so
that a higher percentage of embryos develop into transgenic offspring;

(3) Learning how to insert genes into the DNA of the recipient
cell at a target site so that the gene will be expressed predictably
and without interfering with other essential functions of the DNA;

---

[42] See Moses, p. 149–192, for a more detailed discussion, including citations for original research.

36   (4) Learning how to regulate genes, i.e., turn them on and off in appropriate tissues at appropriate periods in the animals life cycle.[43]

WILL SCIENTISTS BECOME FRANKENSTEINS?

While the above discussion of gene transfer methods provides some indication of current scientific capabilities, it does not answer directly the question of whether scientists can use these techniques to make "monster" animals. As noted above, transgenic work is at an experimental stage and effects cannot be reliably predicted. Therefore, sometimes undesirable effects are obtained by chance. For instance, the hog that developed lean meat from the transfer of a human growth hormone gene, described above, also developed a type of arthritis. Some scientists observe however, that undesirable effects may result from traditional selective breeding. For example, some commercial turkeys have been bred so large as to have such large breasts they are unable to mate. Likewise, some untoward effects might be obtained from the crossing of a St. Bernard dog with a Chihuahua.

A second fact scientists often cite, is that gene transfers generally involve the addition of genes. Thus, transferred genetic characteristics are generally cumulative of those already present. Because the most serious genetic diseases known are the result of one or more gene "deletions," (e.g., Lesch-Nyhan, a serious neurological disease that causes death during childhood) removal of a gene is considered more likely to cause serious effects than gene additions. Radiation can, in effect, delete genes, and transgenic researchers argue that research in radiation biology has been permitted for decades.[44]

Finally, gene transfer techniques are currently able to transfer only up to two genes at a time. However, unlike natural breeding which involves the transfer of thousands of genes, genetic engineering circumvents the biological "controls" that influence what genetic combinations will be accepted and rejected. Therefore, some people might object to the effects of the transfer of one or two genes. Because characteristics of interest to researchers in transgenics are controlled by many genes, some scientists believe it will be many years before significant changes in genetic characteristics of animals can be obtained through genetic engineering.

Chimera research appears to have greater potential to produce offspring possessing dramatic characteristics in the near term than genetic engineering.[45] Because relatively few simple or transgenic chimeras have been developed, and those that have been developed involved the same or closely related species, it is unclear whether different enough species can be combined to produce "monster" animals. However, some critics of the technology find the geep to

---

[43] Personal communication. Dr. Vern Pursel, USDA, ARS, ASI, Reproduction Laboratory. Nov. 6, 1987, 344-2814.
  What do you get if you cross. . .? The Economist, Aug. 15, 1987, p. 68.
  Personal communication. Dr. Harold Hawk, USDA, ARS, ASI, Reproduction Laboratory. Nov. 6, 1987, 344-2836.
[44] Personal Communication, Dr. R. D. Palmiter, University of Washington—Seattle. Nov. 23, 1987, (206) 543-2100.
[45] Personal communication. Dr. Bob Wall, USDA, ARS, ASI, Reproductive Laboratory. Nov. 25, 1987, 344-2836.

be an objectionable development. In addition, some chimeras that   37
might be scientifically possible to develop, e.g., a human/human
chimera, would clearly raise ethical issues. Please note: there is no
known evidence anyone has tried to produce a human chimera, or
that it would be possible. Also, currently, research on human embryos is not being funded by the Federal Government. Human
embryo research can be undertaken if only private funds are used,
as is done with the human in vitro fertilization centers in the
United States.

The cost and human effort involved in research seems to provide
a disincentive for researchers to undertake frivolous projects. In
addition, the systems by which government funds are appropriated
to researchers (e.g., competitive grants) is designed to allocate
funds to projects having scientific merit. However, "ethical
review," is not part of that system.

POINTS FOR FURTHER CONSIDERATION

There is no national policy that specifically addresses transgenic
research. A variety of Federal policies embodied in the rules that
govern the biomedical and agricultural research that is funded,
and the kinds of products that require prior approval (e.g., drugs)
influence the direction of transgenic research, however.

Should the Congress determine that something more than these
ad hoc policies are needed to guide the direction of scientific research regarding transgenic animals, other avenues that might be
considered include:

(1) encourage scientists to develop voluntary transgenic research
guidelines applicable to privately and publicly funded research;

(2) encourage the National Institutes of Health to expand the Recombinant DNA Advisory Committee guidelines to address the appropriate use of transgenic methods; and

(3) consider whether ethical implications of the research should
be put before the Congressional Ethics Board (legislative body created by P.L. 99-158).

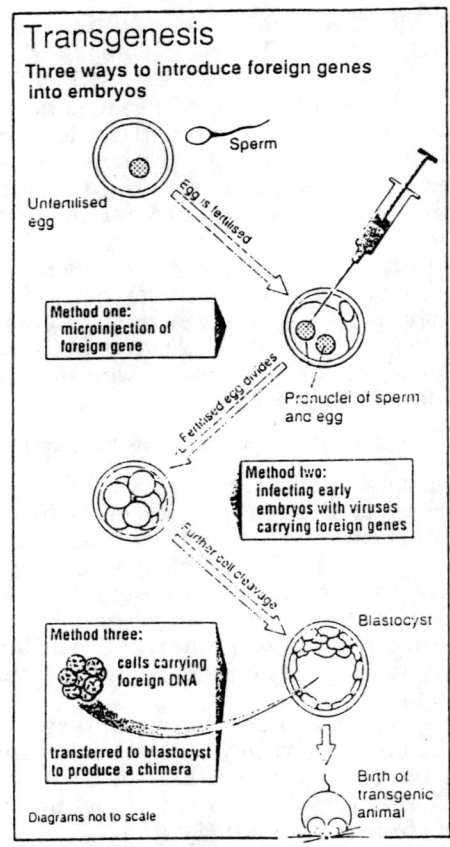

Transgenesis

Three ways to introduce foreign genes into embryos

Sperm

Unfertilised egg

Egg is fertilised

Method one: microinjection of foreign gene

Fertilised egg divides

Pronuclei of sperm and egg

Method two: infecting early embryos with viruses carrying foreign genes

Further cell cleavage

Blastocyst

Method three: cells carrying foreign DNA transferred to blastocyst to produce a chimera

Birth of transgenic animal

Diagrams not to scale

Source: Adapted from Annual Review of Genetics

Source: The Economist, Aug. 15, 1987, p. 68.

PART TWO

CHAPTER 6.—LEGAL BACKGROUND

Microorganisms *per se* have been patentable under United States law since 1980, when the United States Supreme Court held that living organisms are a patentable subject matter within the meaning of section 101 of the Patent Act.[46] In *Diamond* v. *Chakrabarty*,[47] the Court opened wide the door for intellectual property

---

[46] *Diamond* v. *Chakrabarty,* 447 U.S. 303 (1980).
[47] 447 U.S. 303 (1980).

protection of biotechnology. A $4 billion industry has arisen in the wake of that decision.[48]

Cases decided since *Chakrabarty* now include both plants [49] and animals [50] in the range of patentable inventions. In April 1987, the Patent and Trademark Office relied on *Chakrabarty* and allowed the patenting of animals made through human interventions. It was this decision that generated the recent controversy. To properly assess the impact of the Office's decision, some background about patent law is helpful.

OBTAINING A PATENT/ATTRIBUTES OF A PATENT

A grant of a patent is authorized by statute, 35 U.S.C. section 101, *et. seq.* This enabling statute is, in turn, authorized by a grant of legislative authority in the United States Constitution, Article I, section 8, clause 8. The founders were unanimous in deciding to continue the precedents found in common law and state statutes. They authorized limited terms of protection from use by others when certain conditions were met. The constitutional grant is:

> The Congress shall have the power . . . to promote the progress of Science and the Useful Arts by securing for limited times to Authors and Inventors the exclusive right to their respective writings and discoveries.[51]

This authorization does not require that a patent law be created. Nonetheless, every Congress from the First to the 100th has recognized the importance of enacting a patent law, and in doing so, the Congress is bound and guided by two separate constitutional mandates. First, the term of protection must be limited. At first, patent laws provided for a term of 14 years; in 1861, the length of term was increased to seventeen years.[52] Second, the Congress must take into account the incentive the term of protection provides for the creation of new inventions, as well as consider the public interest, which in some situations would seem to dictate an end to the monopoly granted. It is not the case, however, that each invention must be judged solely by the public interest. Other considerations are also important. For example, if Congress were to eliminate the required public disclosure of the manner of practicing the invention or to increase the term of exclusive rights disproportionately to 50 years, the public interest would be disserved.

The Supreme Court has described the purposes of the patent system. It should:

> promote . . . progress by offering a right of exclusion for a limited period as an incentive to inventors to risk the often enormous cost . . . in return of the right of exclusion

---

[48] Schneider, *States Spurring Outlays In Biotechnology Field,* NEW YORK TIMES, Feb. 20, 1988 at A-7; OFFICE OF TECHNOLOGY ASSESSMENT, OWNERSHIP OF HUMAN TISSUES AND CELLS, 56 (1986) (350 biotech companies).

[49] *In re Hibberd,* 227 U.S.P.Q. 443 (PTO Bd. App. + Int. 1985).

[50] *In re Allen,* 2 U.S.P.Q. 2d 1425 (PTO Bd. App. + Int. 1987); *See also* PTO Policy, 1077 OFF. GAZ. PAT. OFF. 24 (April 1987).

[51] U.S. Const. Art I, § 8, cl. 8.

[52] *Compare,* Act of April 10, 1790, sect. 1 Stat. 109, 110 (1790), *with* Act of July 8, 1870, sect. 22, 16 Stat. 198, 201 (1870).

40   . . . the patent laws impose upon the inventor and requirement of disclosure.[53]

Our patent system establishes a patent as a property right, and
thereby provides at least three benefits to the development of technology.[54] First it provides an incentive to invent by offering a potential reward to the inventor. It further provides an incentive to
competitors to produce a different but competitive product. Second,
it can serve to stimulate the investment of risk capital in the invention by granting certain exclusive rights to the inventor. Third,
the patent system requires early public disclosure of technological
information, thereby reducing the likelihood of duplicative research efforts.

The term of patent protection is 17 years from the date the
patent issues. To obtain a patent, an applicant must create an invention. The invention must be *useful, novel*, and *nonobvious*.[55] In
other words, it must be the first of a kind, it must be useful, and it
must constitute something more than a trivial extension of what
was previously known.[56] The concept of utility is a minimal requirement. It means that the invention must be capable of performing some beneficial function.[57] Nonobviousness, on the other
hand, is of overriding importance.[58] These guidelines have traditionally excluded some kinds of inventions from patentability, including those that are products of nature,[59] mathematical formu-
las,[60] and those that preexist in the public domain.[61] There is only
one subject that is statutorily excluded from patentability those inventions which relate to nuclear materials.[62]

---

[53] *Kewanee Oil Co.* v. *Bicron Corp.*, 416 U.S. 470, 480 (1974). *See also Dawson Chemical Co.* v.
Rohm and Haas Co., 448 U.S. 176, 215 (1980); ("[T]he essence of a patent grant is the right to
exclude others from profiting by the patented invention."); *Kendall* v. *Winsor, 62 U.S.* (21 How.)
322, 329 (1859) (". . . Rights and welfare of the community must be fairly dealt with an effectu-
ally guarded." [in the patent system]); *Sinclair and Carrol Co., Inc.* v. *InterChemical* Corp., 325
U.S. 327, 331 n. 1 (1945); *United States* v. *Masonite Corp.* 316 U.S. 265, 278 (1942); (. . . "Reward
of inventors is secondary and merely a measure to [promote the progress of science and the
useful arts].""); *see also Griffith Rubber Mills* v. *Hoffar*, 313 F.2d 1, 3 (9th Cir. 1963) (patents
issued for the public good).
[54] PRESIDENT'S COMMISSION ON THE PATENT SYSTEM, TO SECURE THESE RIGHTS * * *, (1966).
[55] 35 U.S.C. 101, 102, and 103.
[56] *Graham* v. *John Deere Co.*, 383 U.S. 1 (1966).
[57] *Hildreth* v. *Mastoras*, 257 U.S. 27, 34 (1921); *E.I. DuPont de Nemours & Co.* v. *Berkley & Co.,
Inc.*, 620 F.2d 1247, 1260 n. 17 (8th Cir. 1980).
[58] *See, e.g., Curtiss-Wright Corp.* v. *Link Aviation, Inc.*, 182 F. Supp. 106, 124 U.S.P.Q. 222
(N.D.N.Y. 1959); *Graham* v. *John Deere, Co.*, supra, note ———; Merges, *Commercial Innovation
and Patent Standards, Economic Perspectives on Innovation*, CAL. L. REV. ——— (1988) (forthcoming) (criticizing the commercial success and other secondary tests used by the Courts of Appeals for the Federal Circuit to determine obviousness).
[59] *Funk Bros. Seed Co.* v. *Kalo Inoculant Co.* 333 U.S. 127 (1948); Bozicevic, *Distinguishing
"Products of Nature" from Products Derived from Nature*, 69 J. PAT. OFF. SOC'Y., 415, 416–17
(1987).
[60] *Parker* v. *Flook*, 437 U.S. 584 (1978), *Gottschalk* v. *Benson*, 409 U.S. 63 (1972).
[61] *See generally* 1 P. ROSENBERG, PATENT LAW FUNDAMENTALS (1986); *see generally* Note Ethical Considerations in the Patenting of Medical Processes, 65 Tex. L. Rev. 1139 (1987).
[62] The Atomic Energy Act of 1954 provides that: "No patent shall hereafter be granted for
any invention or discovery which is useful solely in the utilization of special nuclear material or
atomic energy in an atomic weapon." 68 Stat. 919 (1954), 42 U.S.C. 2181(a).
Through this exclusion, Congress extended the government monopoly over fissionable materials and atomic weapons established in other sections of the *Atomic Energy Act. Boskey, Inventions and the Atom*, 32 J. PAT. OFF. SOC'Y. 563 (1950). Because of the destructive potential of
fissionable material and the grave dangers to the public health and safety attending its production, the proponents of the explicit exclusion argued that government ownership of such material was necessary and that private patents were inappropriate in an area reserved exclusively to
the Government. *See* S. Rep. No. 1211, 79th Cong., 2d Sess. 14–15, and 26 (1946). Proponents also
contended that private development should not be permitted in an area which future interna-
Continued

An Inventor must apply to the patent office for a grant of a patent. This document gives the inventor the right to exclude others from making, using, and selling the invention. It includes a "specification," describing the invention. By statute, the specification must provide:

(1) a written description of the invention;

(2) a disclosure of how to make and use the invention, thus providing an enabling disclosure; and

(3) the best mode contemplated by the inventor of executing the invention.[63]

Thus, the application must include sufficient information to "enable" a person skilled in the relevant area of technology to make and use the invention defined in the claims of the patent.[64] In some extraordinarily complex areas, however, it might be difficult for the inventor to meet the enablement requirements, including reduction to practice without undue experimentation. The person skilled in the art to which the specification is addressed draws on a common body of knowledge familar to those working in the field of endeavor to which the invention relates. The patent specificiation is not a blueprint for the execution of a process, rather it is a general description of a process which would allow a person skilled in the art to both practice the invention and to learn what activity would constitute infringement of the patent claims.[65] In these areas, which often include biotechnology, a procedure in addition to the written enablement option is available. For example, an applicant who wishes to patent microorganisms or transgenic animals may deposit a sample of the organism in a certified depository.[66] The organism is then stored, catalogued, and made available as a publicly available stock reagent.

The Patent and Trademark Office has indicated in proposed ruling-making that deposits of animal inventions might not be required.[67] Current understanding of the subject of transgenic ani-

---

tional agreements might subject to Government control, that an area so closely related to the Government's national defense interest should not come under private control, and that a patent monopoly by a private individual is inappropriate in such a novel and important field. Valimont, *Atomic Energy Patent Provisions and the American Economy*, 31 J. PAT. OFF. SOC'Y. 743 (1949).

In 1974, the Court of Customs and Patent Appeals in *Piper* v. *Atomic Energy Commission*, 502 F.2d 1393, 183 U.S.P.Q. 235 (C.C.P.A. 1974); found that the purpose of the Act's exclusion of special nuclear material or atomic energy was to expand the private sector's participation in the development of atomic energy, yet to avoid the disclosure of information that could be militarily useful to foreign interests.

As a result of this concern, Congress passed 35 U.S.C. 181, which gives the Commissioner of Patents the authority to withhold the grant of a patent whenever the attendant publication or disclosure of an invention might be detrimental to the national security. Thus, both the statutory exclusion of private patents relating to special nuclear material and atomic energy and the Commissioner's ability to withhold the grant of a patent on national security grounds promotes the preservation and maintenance of the national security.

[63] 35 U.S.C. 112, first paragraph. The original Patent Act of 1790 set forth the first two of these requirements.

[64] *In re Moore*, 439 F. 1232, 169 U.S.P.Q. 236 (C.C.P.A., 1971).

[65] *Kaiser Industrial Corp.* v. *Jones and Laughlin Steel Corp.*, 181 U.S.P.Q. 193, 211 (W.D. Pa. 1974).

[66] *See generally In re Lundak*, 773 F. 2d 1216 (Fed. Cir. 1985); *see also* 52 FED. REG. 34080 (Sept. 9, 1987) (Notice of Proposed Rulemaking).

[67] 52 FED. REG. at 34081, (because there is no available depository and because transgenic animals will be derived from known and readily available animals and developed using known reproducible processes.)

Continued

42 mals, however, casts doubt on this preliminary decision. The complexity of some transgenic animals makes it likely that there will be difficulties in describing the invention in sufficient detail to meet the "enablement requirements."

The grant of a patent is not *per se* a grant of monopoly power. Rather, a patent entitles its owner to an intangible property right that is enforceable as if it were real property. While it permits the patentee to exclude others from making, using and selling a patented invention, it grants neither the right to make, use or sell (i.e., market) the invention nor the right to occupy an entire field of technology. Rather, it is designed to encourage others to "invent around" the patent. The grant of a patent does not obviate the numerous other legal restrictions and premarket regulatory approvals required for the sale of products in commerce. In fact, it is possible to patent an item that cannot be sold. The following are examples:

(1) a weapon, such as a gun, is prohibited from sale in interstate commerce under some circumstances;

(2) the Food and Drug Administration must approve any sale or a drug to be used to treat human beings;

(3) the Department of Agriculture must approve a meat product before it may be sold in interstate commerce;

(4) the Department of Agriculture must approve a patented seed before it may be sold as a certified seed; and

(5) some common law doctrines, such as nuisance and tort law, may bar inventions for sale.[68]

The right to exclude others from profiting from the invention is enforceable in the federal courts, which may grant injunctions or award damages for such an infringement.[69]

A patent owner must also give up an important right when applying for a patent. Because the patent specification must describe the manner and process of making and using the invention[70] and

---

The deposit option or requirement is also relevant to the question of diversity of germplasm. Critics of plant patenting (and more recently animals patents) have asserted that this form of intellectual property protection will rapidly decrease the available gene pool. *Testimony of Doyle.* One possible solution to this concern is to establish a National Germphasm Library for generically altered plants and animals. *See Testimony of Adler.* It is likely that the existing depository institutions, that meet the requirements of the Budapest Convention will be able to perform such a function.

It is important to acknowledge both the concern over genetic diversity and the multiple factors at work to produce this result. The United States Congress has recognized that the ". . . extinction of plant and animal species is an irreparable loss with potentially serious environmental and economic consequences for developing and developed countries alike." Foreign Assistance of 1961, § 119, added by Pub. L. 98–164, 97 Stat. 1045, 22 U.S.C. 2151q. *See also,* OFFICE OF TECHNOLOGY ASSESSMENT, TECHNOLOGIES TO MAINTAIN BIOLOGICAL DIVERSITY (March 1987). The concern of critics of plant variety patent protection does not appear substantiated in the context of plants. The House Committee on Agriculture in fact found an increase in genetic diversity in the wake of enactment of the Plant Variety Protection Act. H.R. Rep. No. 1115, 96th Cong., 2d Sess. at 4 (1980).

On the other hand, the risk to the United States posed by potential depletion of germplasm is significant because of the relative paucity and narrowness of our own gene pool. OFFICE OF TECHNOLOGY ASSESSMENT, COMMERCIAL BIOTECHNOLOGY: AN INTERNATIONAL ANALYSIS, 172 (1984); OFFICE OF TECHNOLOGY ASSESSMENT, IMPACTS OF APPLIED GENETICS 154–57 (1981). The narrowing of the genetic base in agriculture, however, predates both the creation of patent protection for plant varieties and the evolution of biotechnology. Factors such as market integration and processing of livestock and mechanization of harvesting and processing of food crops may ultimately have already done more damage to genetic diversity than any other development.

[68] 18 U.S.C. 922; Federal Food Drug and Cosmetic Act, sect. 510, Federal Meat Inspection Act, 21 U.S.C. 360; 21 U.S.C. sections 610, and 134a–134h; Federal Seed Act, sect. 201, 7 U.S.C. 1571; and *see, e.g., Patterson* v. *Kentucky,* 97 U.S. 501 (1879).

[69] 35 U.S.C. 283 and 284 and 271.

[70] 35 U.S.C. 112, first paragraph.

the best mode for creating the invention must be disclosed, and be- 43
comes public information upon issuance of the patent, trade secret
protection is unavailable.[71]

CHAPTER 7.—APPLICATION OF PATENT LAW TO LIVING ORGANISMS

As previously noted, current law makes living organisms, including genetically engineered plants, animals, and microorganisms,
are eligible for patent protection.

Historically, a living organism was considered ineligible for protection because it was a product of nature or because the inventor
was unable to describe or achieve "perfect" replication.[72]

In 1930, Congress for the first time enacted explicit patent protection for plants, the Plant Patent Act of 1930,[73] heeding years of
advocacy by Thomas Edison, Luther Burbank and other equally
prominent scientists.[74] The Plant Patent Act recognizes that not
all plants are products of nature and that new varieties are capable of development. The application of the Plant Patent Act extended only to asexually reproduced varieties, which had originally
been excluded from patent protection in the belief that they could
not consistently be replicated.[75] The Act allowed the patentability
of products of nature that were produced through the use of
human intervention (i.e. plant breeding) but otherwise followed the
general outline of the general patent law, except that it contained
a more liberal description requirement.[76]

Over the next 40 years, changes in plant breeding technology
and United States entrance into international conventions calling
for the protection of plants, led Congress to review the status of
patent protection for sexually reproduced plants.[77] In 1970, Congress passed the Plant Variety Protection Act (PVPA), which
grants patent-like protection to sexually reproduced plants such as
vegetables and grains.[78] PVPA authorizes the Department of Agri-

---

[71] See discussion of trade secret protection, infra. Because a patented invention was, by definition, not in the public domain before issuance, the grant of a patent does not deprive the public
of the invention.

[72] Ex parte Latimer, 1889 DEC. COMM'R. OF PAT. 123 (1889); see generally Rossman, Plant Patents, 13 J. PAT. OFF. SOC'Y. 7 (1931); Magnuson, A Short Discussion on Various Aspects of Plant
Patents, 30 J. PAT. OFF. SOC'Y. 493 (1948); Memorandum of Patent Commissioner Thomas E. Rob-
ertson Printed in Plant Patent Hearings Before the House Comm. on Patents on H.R. 11372, 71st
Cong., 2d Sess. 4, 7 (1930).

In 1873 the United States Patent Office granted a patent to Louis Pasteur for "Yeast, free
from organic germs of disease, as an article of manufacturer." Patents were also granted on
both bacterial and viral vaccines since 1877. I. COOPER, BIOTECHNOLOGY AND THE LAW, Section
2.02 (1987).

[73] 35 U.S.C. 161–164.

[74] R. ALLYN, THE FIRST PLANT PATENTS 61–83 (1934).

[75] S.Rep. No. 315, 71st Cong., 2d Sess. 5 (1930); H.R. Rep. No. 1129, 71st Cong., 2d Sess. 6
(1930).

[76] 35 U.S.C. 162.

[77] Beier, Patents in a Time of Rapid Scientific and Technological Change, in BIOTECHNOLOGY
AND PATENT PROTECTION: AN INTERNATIONAL REVIEW (OECD, 1985); Bryne, The Agritechnical
Criteria in Plant Breeder's Rights Law, 22 IND. PROP. 293 (1983); WORLD INTELLECTUAL PROPERTY
ORGANIZATION, COMMITTEE OF EXPERTS ON BIOTECHNOLOGICAL INVENTION AND INDUSTRY PROPER-
TY, INDUSTRIAL PROPERTY PROTECTION OF BIOLOGICAL INVENTION, WIPO (BIOT/CE/II/2/1985).

Plants are protected in a multilateral agreement called the International Convention for the
Protection of New Varieties of Plants (UPOV) entered in force, Nov. 8, 1971, T.I.A.S. 10199. The
United States is a member of UPOV. The Plant Variety Protection Act provisions conform to
the requirements of UPOV.

[78] 7 U.S.C. 2321–2582; Pub. L. 91–577; 84 Stat. 1542. Excluded from protection are fungi, bacteria and first generation hybrids. There was no need to include hybrids because they have a

Continued

44   culture to grant patent-like protection for a period of 18 years to sexually reproduced plants. The standard for "certificate" issuance is similar to that used for patent protection, but there are some differences. The description requirements are less onerous, and protected varieties need only be novel, distinct and uniform, rather than novel and nonobvious, as required by the general patent law.[79] In addition, as discussed below, the PVPA contains a research and experimentation exception,[80] a compulsory license that allows others to use the invention without permission when the Secretary of Agriculture determines that there is a risk of an inadequate food supply as a result of the patent owner's failure to practice the invention,[81] and an exemption from liability for farmers.[82]

DEVELOPMENT OF PATENT LAW ON THE PATENTABILITY ON ANIMALS

In April 1969, a patent application defined the claimed invention as a chicken produced by a unique breeding process. The Patent and Trademark Office examiner found that the chicken did not constitute a patentable subject matter. The Board of Patent Appeals (within the Patent and Trademark Office) agreed, and the patent was denied, although on other grounds.[83]

In 1972 and 1974, two applications challenged this position. In 1974, inventors Bergy et. al. applied for protection for an invention defined as a biologically pure culture of a specified microorganism capable of producing the antibiotic lincomycin in a recoverable quantity upon fermentation. The PTO opined that this subject matter was not patentable under the general patent law, which, strictly construed, precluded the patenting of living organisms. According to the PTO, Congress knew how to provide protection for living subject matter, because it had done so in the plant patent statutes. The absence of similar legislation protecting patents of living organisms led the PTO to conclude that Congress did not intend to extend such protection. On appeal, the Court of Customs and Patent Appeals concluded that the subject matter was not excluded from the category of patentable inventions simply because it was alive.[84] The court found that the claimed biologically pure culture was an industrial product useful in an industrial process, and that biologically pure cultures of microorganisms are more similar in nature and commercial use to inanimate chemical compositions such as reactants, reagents, and catalysts, than they are to horses and honeybees, or raspberries and roses. Finally, the court rejected as "farfetched" the PTO's concern that such a decision would necessarily make patentable all new, useful, and unobvious species of plants, animals and insects.[85]

The Supreme Court's seminal decision in *Diamond* v. *Chakrabarty*[86] followed. In that case, the Court was called upon to decide

---

built-in protection through breeder control of inbred parental stock. The 1970 act originally excluded soup vegetables, but those plants were subsequently incorporated by Congress within the PVPA in 1980. P.L. 96–574 (1980).
[79] 7 U.S.C. 2401(a), 2422.
[80] 7 U.S.C. 2544.
[81] 7 U.S.C. 2404.
[82] 7 U.S.C. 2543 (relating to the right to save seed and crop exemptions).
[83] *In re Merat*, 519 F.2d 1390, 186 U.S.P.Q. 471 (C.C.P.A. 1975).
[84] *In re Bergy*, 563 F.2d 1031, 195 U.S.P.Q. 344 (C.C.P.A. 1977).
[85] *Id.* at 1038.
[86] 447 U.S. 303 (1980).

whether a new microorganism—in the form of a bacterium [87]—constituted a manufacture or composition of matter within the meaning of the general patent statute. IKn a 5–4 decision, the Supreme Court decided that the human-made living microorganism defined in the patent application was patentable subject matter. The Court concluded that by its use of such expansive terms as "any manufacture" and "any composition" of matter, Congress plainly intended that the patent laws be broadly interpreted.[88] In determining the scope of 35 U.S.C. (101, the relevant distinction was not between living and inanimate things, but between products of nature, whether living or not, and human-made inventions.[89]

The *Chakrabarty* Court said that:

> A rule that unanticipated inventions are without protection would conflict with the core concept of the patent law that anticipation undermines patentability. The inventions most benefiting mankind are those "push back the frontiers of chemistry, physics, and the like". . . . We are told that genetic research and related technological developments may spread pollution and disease, that it may result in a loss of genetic diversity, and that its practice may tend to depreciate the value of human life. . . .
>
> It is argued that this court should weigh these potential hazards . . . [W]e disagree. The grant or denial of patents on micro-organisms is not likely to put an end to genetic research or to its attendant risks. The large amount of research that has already occurred when no researcher had sure knowledge that patent protection would be available suggests that legislative or judicial fiat as to patentability will not deter the scientific mind from probing into the unknown any more than Canute could command the tides. Whether respondent's claims are patentable may determine whether research efforts are accelerated by the hope of reward or slowed by want of incentives, but that is all.[90]

Following the *Chakrabarty* decision, the Commissioner of Patents and Trademarks announced that the PTO would examine patent applications directed to microorganisms and that if the products involved were the result of human intervention (*i.e.*, not products of nature) such products would be considered to be patentable subject matter.[91]

---

[87] Claim 7 in the Chakrabarty patent application read as follows: A bacterium from the genus Psuedomonas containing therein at least two stable energy-generating plasmid, each of said plasmid providing a separate hydrocarbon degradative pathway. *Appendix A to Petitioner's Brief for writ of certiorari* 90, *Diamond* v. *Chakrabarty*, 447 U.S. 303 (1980). The utility of the invention was a human-made bacterium capable of breaking down crude oil.

[88] 447 U.S. at 308.

[89] *Diamond* v. *Chakrabarty*, 447 U.S.C. 303, 309, 311–12 (1980). *See also*, Kass, *Patenting Life*, 63 J. OF PAT. OFF. SOC'Y. 571 (1981); Maggs, *New Life for Patents*, 1980 S. CT. REV. 57 (1981); Schlosser, *Patenting Biological Inventions 12* TOLEDO L.REV. 925 (1981); Biggart, *Patentability in the United States of Microorganisms, Processes Utilizing Microorganism Products Produced by Microorganism Mutation and Genetic Modification Techniques*, 22 IDEA 113 (1981).

[90] 447 U.S. 303, 316–7 (1980).

[91] 997 OFF. GAZ. PAT. OFF. 24 (1987). The PTO has been criticized for its failure to extend the rationale of *Chakrabarty* to plants immediately. Adler, *Biotechnology Development and Transfer: Recommendation for an Integrated Policy*, 11 RUTGERS COMPUTER & TECH. L.J. 469, 478, 481 (1985); OFFICE OF TECHNOLOGY ASSESSMENT, IMPACTS OF APPLIED GENETICS, at 241 (1981) (*Chakrabarty*) could be read as applying to any nonhuman genetically altered organism).

46   *Ex Parte Hibberd,*[92] was the next important decision to consider the question of statutory construction of the Patent Act as it related to the patenting of a living subject matter. The invention in Hibbard's application was directed to a process and to products where maize plants, seeds, any tissue cultures were caused to have an elevated tryptophan[93] content. The level of tryptophan was greater than that obtainable without using Hibbert's invention. Although the PTO examiner acknowledged that the invention met the criteria for patentability, it took the position that the general patent law did not protect these specific plant materials because the subject matter could have been protected under one of the laws specifically relating to plants. In rejecting this contention, the Board of Patent Appeals relied on the Supreme Court analysis in *Diamond* v. *Chakrabarty,* concluding Congress did not intend the plant specific acts to be the exclusive forms of protection for plant life. Following this decision, the Commissioner of Patents and Trademarks announced[94] that, in the future, the PTO would examine applications on inventions relating to plant life.

On April 11, 1987, the Patent and Trademark Office Board of Patent Appeals and Interferences decided *Ex Parte Allen,*[95] relating to an application to patent a polyploid Pacific oyster. The oyster was created not by biotechnology but a mechanical process involving the application of hydrostatic pressure to an oyster. The Board rejected the application, deciding that it did not satisfy the "nonobviousness" test for patentability because the oyster was not significantly different from those that were produced by other known processes. Nonetheless, it did answer the threshold legal question of the patentability of higher life forms under the general patent law, and it answered it affirmatively. The Board relied heavily on the Supreme Court's analysis in *Chakrabarty* in concluding that the polyploid oysters were non-naturally occurring manufactuers or compositions of matter within the scope of a patentable subject matter.

After *Allen* decision, the Commissioner of Patents and Trademarks issued a notice[96] stating that the Patent and Trademark Office would examine applications directed to non-naturally occurring nonhuman multicellular living organisms, including animals, and would consider them a patentable subject matter.

This notice, like the other notices that followed significant decisions pertaining to the patentability of living subject matter, defined future PTO practice in examining applications to patent similar subject matter. It indicated that the *Allen* decision would not affect the principle that products found in nature will not be considered a patentable subject matter, on the grounds that they do not constitute patentable subject matter.

In addition, it stated that an invention defined to include a human being within its scope will not be considered a patentable

---

[92] 227 U.S.P.Q. 443 (P.T.O. Bd. App. & Int. 1985).
[93] An amino acid present in maize plants which is one of the limiting nutrients in animal feed.
[94] 1060 OFF. GAZ. PAT. OFF. 4 (1985).
[95] 2 U.S.P.Q. 2d 1425 (P.T.O. Bd. Pat App & Int. 1987).
[96] 1077 OFF. GAZ. PAT. OFF. 24 (1987)

subject matter, noting that the Constitution prohibits the grant of 47 any property rights in a human being.[97]

On April 12, 1988 the Commissioner issued a patent for genetically-altered animal.[98] The patent covers animals whose gene sequence has been modified to be useful in cancer research.

CHAPTER 8.—PATENT PROTECTION

INTERNATIONAL PERSPECTIVE

According to various news stories about the PTO's April 1987 decision on patenting animals, the United States is the only country in the world to grant such patents. This is not true, since genetically altered animals are already patentable in a number of other countries. A recent survey of international patent laws shows that 53 countries have *not* affirmatively excluded animals from patent protection.[99] In several countries, animals are patentable either in practice or in theory. In those countries, including Japan, Australia, Argentina, the Netherlands, New Zealand, Turkey, Brazil, Greece, Hungary and Canada,[100] animals are entitled to patent protection either generally or through the use of engineered human intervention in an organism.[101]

It is more difficult to categorize those countries adhering to the European Patent Convention (EPC). Under the EPC, "essentially biological processes" for the production of plants or animals" and "plant or animal varieties" are excluded from patent protection.[102] Until recently, most commentators assumed that this provision precludes the patenting of animals.[103] However, the EPC does not necessarily dictate a general exclusion of the patenting of animals. While "animal varieties" are excluded *per se*, the answer is less clear for animals individually. By analogy to the plant contest, the European Patent Office (EPO) has permitted the patenting of prop-

---

[97] U.S. CONST. Amend. XIII (prohibition on involuntary servitude); *see Clyatt* v. *United States*, 197 U.S. 207 (1905).

[98] *See* chapter *Legislative History, supra* note 2.

[99] WORLD INTELLECTUAL PROPERTY ORGANIZATION, EXCLUSIONS FROM PATENT PROTECTION; HL/CE/IV/INF/1 (Sept. 7, 1987) (hereinafter WIPO EXCLUSIONS).

[100] *See generally* WIPO INDUSTRIAL PROPERTY PROTECTION OF BIOTECHNOLOGICAL INVENTIONS, Biot/CE/III/2 at 23–26 (Apr. 8, 1987) (uncertainty is described on the question of animal patents) (hereinafter *WIPO Apr. 8, 1987*).

The situation in some countries is unclear. For example, in Canada, the Patent Appeal Board In re Abitibi, 62 C.P.R. 2d 81, 90 (1982) stated that "[i]f an inventor creates a new and unobvious insect which did not exist before and thus is not a product of nature, and can recreate it uniformly and at will, and it is useful . . . then it will be every bit as much of a tool of man as a microorganism." This decision was impacted by the Canadian Federal Court of Appeal's decision in Pioneer Hi-Breed Limited v. Commissioner of Patents (Mar. 11, 1987) which is currently pending before the Canadian Supreme Court. The *Pioneer* case upheld the rejection of claims directed at soybeans by cross-breeding techniques. The opinion, however, implies merely that living subject matter is not *per se* excluded from patentability. Commentators read the Canadian cases as permitting animals to be patentable. In Germany the Supreme Court of the Federal Republic of Germany in "Rote Taube" (Red Dove) (1970), 1 IIC 136 (1970) affirmed that animal breeding methods were inventions, but rejected the process patent claim because of insufficient disclosure. A subsequent decision by the Court modified the disclosure requirement. *Toll wutvirus*, S. Ct. Fed. Rep. Germ (Feb. 12, 1987). The Court held that while repeatability is required, the enablement requirements can be satisfied by deposit of an organism which demonstrates the claimed characteristics.

[101] R. Schwabs, D. Conlin, D. Jeffrey [hereinafter Bent] *Intellectual Property Rights in Biotechnology Worldwide* (1987) at 539–549. The Japanese Patent Office recently announced a decision to grant patent applications for genetically altered non-human animals. IP ASIS, May 27, 1988 at 11.

[102] E.P.C. ARTICLES 52 and 53.

[103] *See* WIPO EXCLUSIONS, at 3, BENT at 154.

48 agating material, treated with chemical agents, for certain cultivated plants.[104] Recently the EPO has granted a patent for a genetically altered plant. [105] Animals that have been treated and altered by human intervention (often described as somatic gene therapy) are arguably equally patentable. The same analogy applied to the "biological processes" exclusion supports the argument that that exclusion also does not preclude the patenting of animals.[106] The European Patent Office has recognized that the process for treating a plant or *animal* to improve its properties or to alter yield or growth is a technical invention, and is thus *not* excluded from patentability.[107] In sum, it is at least arguable that the European Patent Convention will be construed to permit the patenting of animals.[108]

There are other foreign laws that appear, directly or indirectly, to limit the patentability of animals. The European Patent Convention exclusions described above were derived from consultations in the early 1960's. The EPC's exclusion relating to plants (i.e., either "plant varieties or "biological processes") came about a multilateral intellectual property convention (UPOV), which extended patent-like protection to plants, was pending. According to one commentator, the EPC's exclusion of animal varieties was based on:

(1) [the impossibility of providing] an enabling disclosure for animal breeding methods . . .;
(2) the absence of any established depository institutions; and
(3) the fact that animal reproduction techniques (*e.g., cloning*) until very recently had not permitted the uniform propagation of varietal characteristics.[109]

The exclusions in the laws of other countries may also have been based on the general rule in internationally accepted patent law dening patentability to products of nature.[110] While such an exclusion might justify the exclusion of traditional animal breeding, it is not a sufficient basis to bar multicellular organisms that have been altered significantly through recombinant DNA technology. When many of these foreign patent laws were developed, the science associated with modern biotechnology was not well developed or understood, so that the issue of patenting animals produced through human intervention was not even debated.

The absence of comparable foreign laws does not support the opposition to the patenting animals. First, there is no international consensus on this issue. Second, other nations, at least in theory,

---

[104] EPO, Ciba/Geigy, T 49/83, OJ 1984, 112.
[105] European Patent Office, Pat. No. 122,791 (1988) *See generally,* Teschemacher, *The practice of the European Patent Office regarding the grant of patents for Biological Inventions* 19 IIC 18 (1988).
[106] STRAUS, INDUSTRIAL PROPERTY PROTECTION OF BIOTECHNOLOGICAL INVENTION (WIPO/BIG/281) at 77–79 (July 1985) (discusses why the EPC exclusion of "essentially biological process" occurred and why it is outmoded relative to RDNA).
[107] Guidelines For Examination, European Patent Office (Part C, Chapter IV, 3.4).
[108] Teschemacher and Remond (DPO), Symposium on the Protection of Biotechnological Invention (WIPO/Cornell Univ. June 4, 5, 1987) at 6–7. J. CURRY, THE PATENTABILITY OF GENETICALLY ENGINEERED PLANTS AND ANIMALS IN THE U.S. AND EUROPE (1987) at 80; 4 BIOTECHNOLOGY LAW REP. 307 (item BLR 434) (1985); WIPO/Apr. 8, 1987 at 67.
[109] *Bent supra* note 74 at 155.
[110] As early as 1862 American law excluded products of nature, but included discoveries wherein the new principle brought to light is embodied and set to work. *Morton* v. *New York Eye Infirmary,* 17 F. Cas 879 (C.S.D.N.Y., 1862) (No. 9865).

make animals patentable. Third, the evolution of science and hu- 49
mankind's abilities to "technically" intervene in microorganisms
and multicellular organism differentiates genetically altered plants
and animals from those produced by traditional breeding techniques. It is fair to say that an international consensus has not yet
been reached on whether the differences between the creative
genius of various biotechnologies and those used to create other
products justify a denial of patentability.

CHAPTER 9.—RESEARCH OR EXPERIMENTAL USE EXCEPTION

As noted earlier, the United States patent system is based on the
grant of authority contained in Article I, Section 3, clause 8 of the
Constitution "to promote the progress of science and useful arts."
President Johnson's Commission on the Patent System described
one of the objectives of the patent law:

> [B]y affording protection, a patent system encourages
> early public disclosure of technological information, some
> of which would otherwise be kept secret. Early disclosure
> reduces the likelihood of duplication of effort by others
> and provides a basis for further advances in the technolo-
> gy involved.[111]

Additionally, "one of the benefits of a patent system is its so-
called "negative incentive" to "design around" a competitor's products, even when they are patented, thus bringing a steady flow of
innovations to the marketplace." [112]

From as early 1813, American courts have fashioned an exception to the constitutional and statutory right to exclude others
from "using" a patented invention. In general terms, the exception
extends to research and experimentation with a patented invention, and is of immediate importance to biotechnology for at least
two reasons. First, biotechnology, almost by definition, requires extensive laboratory experimentation. Second, flexibility in this area
prevents the monopolization of an entire field of research. One
commentator has gone so far as to suggest that a broadly construed
research exception is vital for continued technology advancement
in the United States.[113]

The court in the first American case to recognize an experimental use exception concluded that one should be able to construct an
invention "for the purpose of ascertaining the sufficiency of the invention to produce the desired effects." [114] There have been only a
few subsequent cases that have relied on this doctrine. At a minimum they stand for the proposition that "a defendant who makes
and uses a patented product or process does not infringe if the use
is for purposes of research or experimentation and not for
profit." [115] As the Court of Appeals for the Federal Circuit has con-

---

[111] PRESIDENT'S COMMISSION ON THE PATENT SYSTEM, TO SECURE THESE RIGHTS, —— (1965).
[112] *State Industries* v. *A.O. Smith Corp.*, 751 F.2d 1226, 1236 (Fed. Cir. 1985).
[113] Hantman, *Experimental Use as an Exception to Patent Infringement*, 67 J. PAT. OFF. SOC'Y.
617 (1985) [hereinafter HANTMAN].
[114] *Whittemore* v. *Cutter*, 29 F. Cas., 1220, 1121 (C.C.D. Mass. 1813) (No. 17,600) (Justice Story
acting as a Circuit Court Judge).
[115] D. CHISUM, PATENTS, § 16.03 [1] (1987).

50   strued the law, the "research" exception does not apply if the experimental use [is] coupled with commercial use".[116] It is also possible to argue that the law of experimental use is broader and applies to testing a patented invention for adaption to the experimenter's business provided that such use is not for profit.[117]

In assessing the question of experimental use it is also important to review the actions of Congress on this issue. In at least two instances Congress has been forced to directly confront the issue.

In 1970 when Congress was importuned to expand America's intellectual property protection to encompass plant varieties, it did so but specifically included a statutory research exception. The Congress specifically excepted "bona fide" research from the exclusive rights Congress granted to persons who developed new and unique plant varieties.[118]

The second instance in which Congress squarely faced the question of experimental or research exception was in the wake of the *Roche* decision. The Court in *Roche* held it to be an act of patent infringement for a generic drug company to use a patented drug for FDA tests. The *Roche* Court, in *dicta*, read the research exception very narrowly. Within months of a decision by the Court of Appeals for the Federal Circuit, Congress acted to directly overturn the narrow result reached by the court. In the Drug Price Competition and Patent Term Restoration Act of 1984 Congress declared that the use of a patented invention in preparation for the submission of data to the Food and Drug Administration in connection with approval for marketing a drug was not an act of patent infringement.[119]

Thus, in two cases Congress has recognized the need to fashion a more expansive research exception while at the same time preserving the essence of patent law protection. The interface and possible conflict between these statutes and the case law under the general patent law has never been comprehensively addressed by Congress.

In order to offer guidance to policy makers on the question of experimental or research exceptions, it is also relevant to measure and assess the treatment of this issue in the laws of other developed countries. As a general proposition in Western Europe, "acts done for experimentation purposes relating to the subject-matter of the patented invention" do not constitute infringement.[120] Similarly the working of a patented invention "for purposes of experimentation or research" is expressly exempted from infringement by the Japanese patent law.[121]

---

[116] *Roche Products, Inc.* v. *Bolar Phamaceutical Co., Inc.* 733 F.2d 858, 221 U.S.P.Q. 937 (Fed. Cir. 1984), cert. denied, 469 U.S. 856 (1984), *see also Pfizer Inc.* v. *International Rectifier Corp.*, 217 U.S.P.Q. 157 (C.D. Ca. 1982).

[117] HANTMAN, supra, at 644; Eisenberg, *Proprietary Rights and the Norms of Science in Biotechnology Research*, 97 YALE L.J. 177, 220–22 (1987) [hereinafter, *Biotech Research*].

[118] 7 U.S.C. 2544. This amendment was made, in part, because of the involvement of publicly funded research on plants.

[119] Public Law 98–417, 202, 98 Stat. 1585, 1603 (1984); 35 U.S.C. 271(e)(1).

[120] [European] Community Patent Convention Art 31 (b). While this Convention is not in force, legislation to this effect is either in place or proposed in West Germany, France, the United Kingdom, Italy, Denmark, Norway, Sweden, the Netherlands, Belgium, Luxembourg, Ireland, Greece and Spain. R. SCHWAAB, D. JEFFERY, D. CONLIN, S. BENT, INTELLECTUAL PROPERTY RIGHTS IN BIOTECHNOLOGY WORLDWIDE at (1987).

[121] Japanese Patent Law of 1978, Article 68(1).

Despite the relative uncertainty in the American caselaw and 51
the possible conflict between the two specific federal statutes and
existing case law a legislatively crafted consensus seems possible.
To borrow an analysis from a European commentator, the easiest
method of limiting and describing the "experimental use or research exception" is to differentiate between experimentation *on* a
patented invention and experimentation *using* a patented invention in order to accomplish another purpose. With the former type
of experimentation constituting the scope of the exception. Under
this approach the following acts would not constitute patent
infringement:

(1) testing an invention to determine its sufficiency or to
compare it to prior art;

(2) tests to determine how the patented invention works;

(3) experimentation on a patented invention for the purpose
of improving on it or developing a further patentable invention;

(4) experimentation for the purpose of "designing around" a
patented invention; and

(5) testing to determine whether the invention meets the
tester's purposes in anticipation of requesting a license.[122]

These exceptions, coupled with the relatively rare, genuine academic experiment,[123] give some meaning to the phrase experimental or research exception. In light of the relative ambiguity of the
current law, however, it would appear desirable to codify a coherent set of principles to guide conduct in this area. Because Western
Europe and Japan already have a set of statutory rules in this area
it cannot be strenuously argued that legislation in this area, is
likely to cause any serious trade distorting effect. Thus, the Congress should consider in other legislation adopting a statutory research exception modeled after those laws. The clearest statement
on this question appears to be the Japanese law. Therefore, Congress should, at some future point, amend title 35 to provide that
use of a patented invention or process is not an act of infringement
if done for the purpose of experimentation or research.[124] This requirement should not apply only to biotechnology but should
extend to all patented inventions.

CHAPTER 10.—DOCTRINE OF EXHAUSTION OF REMEDIES/IMPLIED LICENSES

As described earlier in this report, substantial concern has been
raised about the potential liabilities of family farmers for the use
and intentional reproduction of genetically altered animals.[125] A

---

[122] P. CHROCZIEL, DIE BENUTZING PATENTIERER ERFINDUNGEN ZU VERSUCHS—UND FOR-
SCHUNGSZWECKEN, 174 *et. seq.* (1986) (cited in BENT, supra).

[123] *Ruth v Stearns-Roger Mfg. Co.* 13 F. Supp. 697, 29 U.S.P.Q. 400 (D. Colo. 1935), *rev'd on
other grounds,* 87 F. 2d 35, 32 U.S.P.Q. 227 (10th Cir. 1936) (Colorado School for Mines not liable
for experimentation.)

[124] An alternative formulation would be to state that: the use of the patented product that
comprises, or consists of, genetic information for the development of another such product shall
not be regarded as permitted experimental use if the progeny of the developed product obtained
from such a use is used in identical or differentiated form for use other than private or experimental purposes. *WIPO Apr. 8, 1987* at 71.

[125] *See Testimony of R. Merges* (drawing a distinction between intentional reproduction designed to produce a desired trait and natural mating).

52 possible response to these concerns was the suggestion from the Patent and Trademark Office that the exhaustion of patent rights doctrine or "implied us" doctrine might answer these concerns.[126] Upon closer examination, however, these legal doctrines seem helpful only in allowing a farmer to milk or slaughter a cow, but do not address reproduction liability under the laws for patented animals.

Since at least 1873 the first authorized sale of a patented product exhausts the rights of the patent holder as to that product. As the Supreme Court said in *Adams* v. *Burke*:

> . . . When the patentee, or the person having his rights, sells a machine or instrument whose sole value is in its use, he received the consideration for its use and he parts with the right to restrict that use. The article passes without the limit of the monopoly . . .[127]

Similarly the Supreme Court has extended the exhaustion doctrine to preclude imposition of restrictions on the right to resell the patented product.[128] Thus, the person who purchases a product from a patent owner may use or resell the product free of control or conditions imposed on the person by the patent owner.[129] These cases, however, appear to sound in patent misuse. As a matter of equity, the courts have since the 19th century declined to permit patent holders to engage in resale price maintenance and some types of territorial restrictions on the sale of patented products.[130] This doctrine standing alone does not appear to address the concerns of farmers. It would appear to merely insulate the subsequent sales of a genetically altered animal from the imposition of anticompetitive conditions by the patent holder but does not reach the use of a patented animal to produce further offsprings.

The closely related doctrine of "implied licenses"—also mentioned by the Patent and Trademark Office [131]—seems to be an incomplete answer to the concerns of farmers. Under this legal doctrine when a person purchases a patented product which is useful in the practice of a patented process there is an implied license to use the product, provided that the product so purchased has no practical uses outside of such patented process or composition. The doctrine of implied also includes repair or the use of replacement parts on the invention.[132] This doctrine, however, does not appear to extend very far because "repair" is limited so as to preclude "reconstruction."[133] Thus, it would seem that the intentional reproduction of a transgenic animal would not be free from patent liability because of the doctrine of "implied license." The act of reproduction is clearly not a patented process so the contemplated use does not fit within this legal principle. More importantly, the in-

---

[126] *Testimony of Tegtmeyer.*
[127] 84 U.S. (17 Wall) 453, 456–57 (1873).
[128] *Keeler* v. *Standard Folding Bed Co.*, 57 U.S. 659 (1895).
[129] D. CHISUM, PATENTS, § 16.03(2) (1987).
[130] D. CHISUM, PATENTS, § 19.04 (1987).
[131] *See Testimony of Tegtmeyer.*
[132] *See, e.g., Met-Coil Systems Corp.* v. *Korners Unlimited, Inc.*, 803 F.2d 684, 231 U.S. P.Q. 474 (Fed. Cir. 1986); *See, e.g., Bloomer* v. *Millinger*, 68 U.S. (1 Wall.) 340 (1863); *Cotton Tie Co.* v. *Simmons*, 106 U.S. 89 (1882); *Ar Mfg.* v. *Convertible Top Replacement Co.*, 365 U.S. 336, 346 (1961).
[133] Farley, *Infringement Questions Stemming from the Repair or Reconstruction of Patented Combination*, 68 J. PAT. OFF. SOC'Y. 149 (1986).

tentional reproduction of a transgenic animal may have the effect 53
of recreating or reconstructing the patented invention, therefore,
there can be no implied license.

If farmers expect relief from patent law liability for reproduction
of transgenic animals they must look outside the caselaw of "exhaustion of patent rights" and "implied licenses" suggested by the
Patent and Trademark Office.

CHAPTER 11.—TRADE SECRET PROTECTION

Opponents of patenting animals have tended to avoid any detailed discussion of the alternative legal regimes that could be used
to displace or supplement the patent law. On the other hand, proponents of patent protection for genetically altered animals have
asserted, without much analysis, that if patents are not available
trade secret protection would supplant it, and that this legal
format would be less desirable. Because of the paucity of material
in the record on this subject, it is appropriate to discuss trade
secret protection in some detail.

The most widely used definition of a "trade secret" is found in
the American Law Institute's first Restatement of Torts, section
757 comment b (1939):

> A trade secret may consist of any formula, pattern,
> device or compilation of information which is used in one's
> business, and which gives him an opportunity to obtain an
> advantage over competitors who do not know or use it.
> . . . Some factors to be considered in determining
> whether given information is one's trade secret are: (1) the
> extent to which the information is known outside of this
> business; (2) the extent to which it is known by employees;
> (3) the extent of security measures; (4) the value of the in-
> formation to the business and its competitors; (5) the
> amount of money expended . . . in developing the informa-
> tion; and (5) the ease or difficulty with which the informa-
> tion could be properly acquired or duplicated by others.

A trade secret differs substantially from a patent. A patent is a
statutory creation of the Congress pursuant to a grant of authority
from the Constitution, whereas trade secrets are a product of state
law—both statutory and common law.[134] While a patent requires
novelty, unobviousness and utility, a trade secret must only meet a
lower threshold of commercial value. A patent is protected against
reverse engineering and independent discoveries whereas a trade
secret is not. The term of protection of a patent is 17 years, whereas a trade secret continues to exist until public disclosure. But the
most important difference between a patent and a trade secret is in
the treatment which must be given to the information. A central
purpose of the patent law is the disclosure of scientific information
once the patent has been issued. The public at large benefits from
this type of disclosure system. Moreover, the patent owner need not
take steps to prevent dissemination of that information by employ-

---

[134] I. COOPER, BIOTECHNOLOGY AND THE LAW, section 11.01 (1985); *Biotech Research, supra* chapter 10 note 7, at 190–95.

54 ees or licensees. In contrast, a trade secret must be maintained as confidential in order to secure status as protected property.

While some products within biotechnology can be, and indeed are, protected by trade secrets, such protection is less desirable than patent protection for most proprietors.[135] There are several reasons why trade secret protection may also be less than an adequate solution in the context of genetically altered animals.

First, as with many other biotechnology products, genetically altered animals have incorporated into the "new" animal a "new" genetic map. Thus, in some instances a skilled researcher may be able to "reverse engineer" the product and, thereby deny the creator any effective trade secret protection.[136] This type of "reverse engineering" would appear to require locating where a particular set of genetic materials has been added to the genome and exactly what type of genetic material has been added. It is possible, however, that certain types of manipulation involving non-recombinant DNA techniques would not be discernible from a mere examination of the product.[137]

The second potential problem with trade secrecy protection in biotechnology may be the lack of economic certainty. For a company that has invested a large sum of money in the research product, the risk that someone else may independently invent the same product and then patent it could present too great a risk. The risk is further exacerbated by the prospect of *reverse engineering*. The third problem with trade secrecy, in those States which have adopted the Restatement definition of trade secrets, is that the protected information must be used in a business to be categorized as a trade secret. In some instances utility in a business context may be difficult to establish when there is no existing market for the research.[138] This requirement may impede, or prevent, the protection of information generated in a research context.[139] Trade secret protection can also be jeopardized by inadequate security measures relative to employees and former employees. A final problem presented by trade secret protection in the biotechnology area is the prevalence of public funding and, university-based research. For many researchers in the academic community, public disclosure is either an attitudinal or institutional imperative. Thus, in many collaborative projects the disclosure of research results acts to bar trade secret protection.[140]

---

[135] *See* I. COOPER, BIOTECHNOLOGY AND THE LAW, ch. 11 (1985).

[136] *Biotech Research,* supra *chapter 10* note 7, at 193,

[137] *See, e.g., In re Allen,* 2 U.S.P.Q. 2d 1425 (P.T.O.Bd. App. & Int. 1987) (use of heat and pressure to produce a polyploidy oyster). It is also possible for researchers to mask genetic changes to limit the chances of "reverse engineering." The use of such techniques, however, may make the cost associated with trade secret protection prohibitive.

[138] For a more complete description of the relationship between university research and the commercial marketplace, see Blumenthal, Epstein, Maxwell, *Commercializing University Research; Lessons from the Experience of the Wisconsin Alumni Research Foundation,* 314 NEW ENGLAND J. MED. 1621 (1986).

[139] *Biotech Research, supra chapter 10* note 7, at 192; The Uniform Trade Secrets Act which has been adopted by 10 states, does not include this requirement. Id.

[140] *Biotech Research, supra chapter 10* note 7, at 194. According to one biotechnology attorney, disclosure to the government may be a limitation on trade secret protection. I. COOPER, BIOTECHNOLOGY AND THE LAW, § 1101 at 11–14 (1985); OFFICE OF TECHNOLOGY ASSESSMENT, COMMERCIAL BIOTECHNOLOGY: AN INTERNATIONAL ANALYSIS 385 (1984) (trade secrets in biotech maybe short in duration).

In sum, while trade secret protection may present an alternative   55
form of intellectual property protection, it is not an effective alternative to patent protection. On the other hand, a statutory denial of patent protection would drive innovators into trade secrets and, thereby, deny public disclosure, limit the information in the public domain and provide a monopoly with an unlimited term. The benefits of shared information and open research can be harvested only so long as the patent system offers a viable alternative to secrecy.

PART THREE

CHAPTER 12.—REGULATION OF TRANSGENIC ANIMALS

One of the issues continually raised by some of the witnesses (opposed to animal patents) before the Subcommittee was the alleged inadequacy of the existing federal regulation of biotechnology.[141] The Subcommittee also received extensive documentation about the nature and the extent of the regulatory process.[142]

This report is not the place to rehash in intricate detail the entire regulatory process for biotechnology:[143] suffice to say that the Office of Science and Technology Policy has issued a Coordinated Framework for the Regulation of Biotechnology.[144] Under the framework a Biotechnology Science Coordinating Committee (BSCC) has been created. The BSCC includes representatives from the relevant federal agencies. The BSCC's task is to serve as a coordinator; to promote consistency; and to facilitate cooperation and identify gaps in scientific knowledge. Under the framework a "lead agency" is designated for each biotechnology project based on the intended product. Once assigned, the "lead agency" regulates the product or process under the existing statutes and regulations applicable to the work of that agency. If necessary, other agencies may also be involved depending on the product involved.

The aforementioned testimony and materials outline, in detail, statutes which apply to each relevant federal agency. Perhaps a useful heuristic device for illustrating the application of these laws and regulations is to take two hypothetical product developments and trace the likely regulatory path each would take. The examples chosen are similar to research activities already undertaken.

Hypothetical No. 1

Professor Smith at the University of Wisconsin undertakes a series of experiments with the goal of altering the genetic makeup of a mouse to obtain an animal which would express tissue-type

---

[141] Biotechnology has been broadly defined to mean a technique that uses living organisms (or parts of organisms) to make or modify products, to improve plants or animals, or to develop microorganisms for specific uses. OFFICE OF TECHNOLOGY ASSESSMENT, COMMERICAL BIOTECHNOLOGY: AN INTERNATIONAL ANALYSIS 3 (1984). Biotechnology has also been defined as "the application of biological systems in organisms to technical and industrial processes." Office of Science and Technology Policy, Proposal for a Coordinated Framework of Regulation of Biotechnology; Notices, 49 FED. REG. 50,856–50,906 (Dec. 31, 1984).

[142] *See Testimony of Godown* (Appendix); *Testimony of Karny,* and OFFICE OF TECHNOLOGY ASSESSMENT, FEDERAL REGULATION OF TRANSGENIC ANIMALS, (1988). *See generally* Karny, REGULATION OF THE ENVIRONMENTAL APPLICATIONS OF BIOTECHNOLOGY, May 6–7, 1988 (presented at Am. Bar. Ass'n. Comm. on Env. Law Conf.)

[143] *See Testimony of Godown, Karny, Mellon. See also* OFFICE OF TECHNOLOGY ASSESSMENT, FEDERAL REGULATION OF TRANSGENIC ANIMALS (1988).

[144] 51 FED. REG. 23,303 (June 26, 1986) (hereinafter "Framework").

56   plasminogen activator (TPA) from its mammary glands. The TPA, once expressed, would be used for the treatment of both humans and animals. The initial research is partially financed by a grant from the National Science Foundation (NSF) and the National Institutes of Health (NIH). The researcher uses a process of microinjection to accomplish the gene transfer.[145]

Under hypothetical No. 1, the initial experiments would be governed by guidelines issued by the National Institutes of Health.[146] These Guidelines are applicable to all grantees of Federal funds from NIH and NSF involved in this type of research. The NIH has a sanctioning authority the ability to terminate current and future funding to the researcher or sponsoring organization who violates the Guidelines. In this case the whole university could be barred from receiving NIH or NSF research funds if a violation occurred.[147]

The Guidelines themselves do not regulate the product of the research—in this case the TPA—rather they address proper methods of use of the tools of the researcher. These tools include recombinant DNA molecules and organisms and viruses containing recombinant DNA molecules. These Guidelines address the proper techniques for the construction and handling of these biotechnology tools. These Guidelines which were first developed, in a large part, voluntarily by the research community, were originally more stringent and have gradually been relaxed as scientific knowledge has advanced and as researchers have obtained more experience.[148] The Guidelines would not be applicable directly to some other possible methods of altering the genes of animals (such as cell fusion, electroporation, transformation, or the microinjection of unaltered DNA).[149] Such techniques would be regulated, however, to the extent that such research involved the use of a recombinant DNA molecule in the process. It should be noted that based on current scientific understanding that the most likely technique to be used for creation of a transgenic animal microinjection of DNA—altered molecules which is covered directly by the Guidelines.[150]

The NIH Guidelines cover DNA experiments with whole animals of the transgenic type. Under the Guidelines in this case the researcher would be required to notify the Institutional Biosafety Committee (IBC) before initiation of the experiment. The IBC is supposed to assure implementation of the NIH Guidelines and approve the experiment. The NIH has also proposed guidelines which specify containment levels for the animals involved in the experiments.[151] Under the proposed guidelines most transgenic animals

---

[145] Under the Patent and Trademark Act Amendments of 1980, Public Law 96–517, 94 Stat. 3015, non-profit organizations and universities retain title to patentable inventions made in the course of government sponsored research, 35 U.S.C. ch. 38; *See generally* M. KENNEY, BIOTECHNOLOGY: THE UNIVERSITY INDUSTRIAL COMPLEX 278–9 (1986).

[146] Guidelines for Research Involving Recombinant DNA Molecules. 51 FED. REG. 16,958 (May 7, 1986).

[147] NIH has imposed sanctions on 2 scientists. *See, e.g.* 1294 NATURE 391 (1981); *Genetic Scientist is Punished for Test Violations,* WASH. POST, Mar. 23, 1981, at A1.

[148] Korwek and de la Cruz, *Federal Regulation of Environmental Releases of Genetically Manipulated Microorganisms;* 11 RUTGERS COMPUTER & TECH. L.J. 301, 303–305 (1985).

[149] Unless the technique used also involved the use of recombinant DNA. OFFICE OF TECHNOLOGY ASSESSMENT, FEDERAL REGULATION OF TRANSGENIC ANIMALS (1988).

[150] *Id.*

[151] Notice of Proposed Actions under NIH Guidelines, Notice, 52 Fed. Reg. 29,800 (Aug. 11, 1987).

must be kept under Level 1 containment conditions throughout the 57 course of research.[152] Transgenic animals would be subject to a higher level of containment if the inserted genetic material was derived from a pathogen. For example, if a mouse was genetically engineered to be susceptible to the AIDS virus by inserting the human gene responsible for making human cells susceptible, this experiment would be subject to Level 1 containment. If the transgenic mouse was then injected with AIDS virus, it would then be subject to a higher level of containment, based on the greater risk.[153]

The NIH Guidelines also set forth review processes for the deliberate release of organisms into the environment. This review could involve persons outside the IBC, including the Recombinant DNA Advisory Committee (RAC) of the NIH and the Director of the NIH, and in some instances could require publication of the proposed release in the Federal Register.[154]

The welfare of the animals involved in these experiments is also federally regulated.[155] It should be noted that some states or localities also may have animal cruelty or other statutes which regulate the use of research animals.[156]

---

[152] There are four containment levels for DNA research; Level 1 is the lowest. Level 1 containment establishes conventional primary laboratory containment procedures for small laboratory animals and equivalent techniques for animals that are too large for laboratory containment. These procedures include the following:

1. When a transgenic animals dies or is euthanized, the carcass must be disposed of to avoid its use as food for human beings or animals unless for use is specifically authorized by an appropriate federal agency. A record must be maintained for the experimental use and disposal of each animal or group of animals for three years.

2. Access to the containment areas shall be limited or restricted when experimental animals are being held.

3. All transgenic newborns will be permanently market within 72 hours after birth if their size permits. If their size does not permit marking, their containers should be marked. In addition, transgenic animals should contain marker genes that allow for identification of transgenic animals from among non-transgenic animals by means of genetic testing.

4. Animals that are too large to confine in laboratories must be confined in securely fenced areas or otherwise confined to miminize the possibility of escape or theft. Containment areas must be locked an patrolled or monitored at frequent intervals.

5. A double barrier must be provided to separate males from females, unless reproductive studies are part of the experiment or other measures are undertaken to avoid reproduction. Reproductive incapacitation may be undertaken if necessary.

6. Animal containment areas must be in accordance with federal law and animal care requirements under the Animal Welfare Act.

[153] See also Leary Why No Mouse Should Ever Escape an AIDS Experiment, N.Y. TIMES, Feb. 2, 1988 at C1; Booth, Of Mice, Oncogenies and Rifkin, 239 SCIENCE 341 (1988).

[154] See Testimony of Karny.

[155] The researcher, as a recipient of NIH and NSF funds, is bound by the NIH Guide for the Care and Use of Laboratory Animals. The NIH guide for the Care and Use of Laboratory Animals addresses institutional policies, laboratory animals, husbandry, veterinary care, and physical plant requirements. It lists procedures for anumal research involving hazardous agents. These standards are also followed voluntarily by nearly 500 other institutions that use animals for experimental purposes. These institutions are certified as being in compliance by a private, non-profit organization called the American Association for Accreditation for Laboratory Animal Care. See OFFICE OF TECHNOLOGY ASSESSMENT, ALTERNATIVE TO ANIMALS USE IN RESEARCH, TESTING, AND EDUCATION (1986), [hereinafter OTA, Alternatives] at 344–345. The Animal Welfare Act does not apply to rats and mice the most commonly used (i.e. 75%) type of lab animals. The Animal Welfare Act would, however, apply to dogs, cats, rabbits, guinea pigs, hamsters and non-human primates.

[156] Office of Technology Assessment, Alternatives to Animal Use in Research, Testing and Education, Ch. 14, but these statutes frequently exclude most laboratory animals. It is beyond the scope of this report to provide an extensive discussion of the need for alternatives to animal use in research and testing. Our sister committee on Science and Technology has recently conducted hearings on this subject, ALTERNATIVES TO ANIMAL USE IN RESEARCH AND TESTING: HEARING BEFORE THE SUBCOMM ON SCIENCE, RESEARCH AND TECHNOLOGY OF HOUSE COMM. ON SCIENCE AND TECHNOLOGY, 99th Cong. 2d Sess.(1986); and the Office of Technology Assessment has issued a report to address this topic. More importantly, the Congress in 1985 enacted several measures to directly address this question, the most important of which was the Food Security Act (which included amendments to the Animal Welfare Act.) See Pub. L. 99–198, 99 Stat. 1645 (1985).

58   Assuming for the sake of argument that these experiments produced a potentially viable commercial product in the form of an animal drug or a pharmaceutical product suitable for humans, further regulation of the TPA expressions of the mice would be required. In this hypothetical, expression of TPA from the mammary glands of mice for use in humans and animals would require the approval of the Food and Drug Administration.[157] The FDA regulates human food, veterinary drugs, the use of those drugs in food-producing animals, human drugs and biologicals, as well as food and drug labeling.[158] In addition, to the extent that the animals treated by this drug are to be consumed by humans, the product would be further regulated by the U.S. Department of Agriculture.[159]

Hypothetical No. 2

Dr. Jones, a researcher with the Hog Wild Company, a private company which received no federal funds, undertakes research to produce a transgenic pig for interstate sale. If Jones' research succeeds, the pig will be reproduced and marketed on the basis of its disease resistance and leaner meat.[160]

Under the facts of the hypothetical listed above the initial research could be undertaken without direct federal regulations. Most biotechnology companies, however, have voluntarily chosen to adopt and comply with the NIH Guidelines. In fact, according to the General Accounting Office, the degree and nature of compliance by private concerns is greater than that found in the public sector.[161]

Under the facts of this hypothetical the research conducted by this company would not be governed by the provisions of the Animal Welfare Act relating to the care of the animals is because farm animals are involved. The meat products produced by the pigs would be governed by provisions of Federal law administered by the USDA.[162]

---

[157] Food, Drug and Cosmetic Act and the Public Health Service Act, 21 U.S.C. 301 *et seq.*, and the Public Health Service Act, 42 U.S.C. 201 *et seq.*

[158] JAFFE, *Inadequacies in the Federal Regulation of Biotechnology*, 11 HARV. ENVTL. L. REV. 491, 517-18 (1987) [hereinafter JAFFE]; Comment, *Regulation of Genetically Engineered Foods Under the Federal Food, Drug, and Cosmetic Act*, 33 AM. U. L. REV. 899 (1984).

[159] *Jaffe. supra* note ____, at 501-509.

[160] This example is, in effect, a combination of the Agricultural Research Service, U.S. Department of Agriculture's work on swine and poultry. [cite]; FEDERAL REGULATION AND ANIMAL PATENTS SUPRA note ____ at 6. These experiments used microinjection and have an efficiency rate of 1.0%. *Id* Commercialization of these experiments is more than 10 years away.

[161] U.S. General Accounting Office, Role of Institutional Biosafety Committees, GAO/RCED, 88-64BR (1987).

[162] This regulation would be under the Federal Meat Inspection act, and is mandatory, OFFICE OF TECHNOLOGY ASSESSMENT; FEDERAL REGULATION OF TRANSGENIC ANIMALS at 7-8. The Federal Meat Inspection Act and the Poultry and Poultry Products Inspection Act governs the inspection of such products. Unfortunately, in some cases whether a meat product is regulated—including those which are the product of genetic engineering—depends on the appearance of the animal. This method of classification for regulatory purposes is difficult to justify. For example, both "cattalo" and "beefalo" should be subjected to inspection without stretching the law. *See* generally Jones, *Legal and Regulatory Aspects of Genetically Engineered Animals.* J. Evans, Genetic Engineering of Animals (1986).

It should be noted that once the product (the pig) has been sold 59
to a farmer the provisions of the Animal Welfare Act also do not
apply.[163]

The Environmental Protection Agency (EPA) has two statutory
authorities which can come into play with transgenic animals.
Under the Federal Insecticide, Fungicide Rodenticide Act (FIFRA)
EPA can regulate "pesticides." This authority has been used to regulate microorganisms. The second statute is the Toxic Substances
Control Act (TSCA) which arguably includes both microorganisms
and transgenic animals within its preview as "chemical substances." To date, however, the EPA has only chosen to include the
former.

Some critics of the regulation of transgenic animals have criticized the absence of a single, centralized environmental agency to
review work done in connection with transgenic animals. Aside
from EPA's involvement in environmental impact statements
(when required) there is no single federal regulatory agency for
transgenic animals. The absence of a central regulatory agency is
apparently based on an assessment of the risks involved in the use
of this technology.

The operative assumption made by Congress in creating a regulatory apparatus has been that environmental assessment should be
conducted in the context in which the work is being done or the
product produced.[164]

This report concludes that the assessment of the risks of introducing DNA-engineered animals into the environment and into
commerce should be based on the nature of the organism and the
environment into which it is introduced, not on the method by
which it was produced.[165]

This is not to say that the regulatory scheme reviewed here
should not be altered. Experimentation and production of transgenic animals has only partially adequate federal regulation. There
are no doubt some deficiencies in these regulations. Therefore, legitimate health and safety concerns should be addressed in the context of proposed legislation without attempting to engraft such
changes on the patent system.[166]

---

[163] Farmers are exempt from the duty of care requirements which apply to laboratory researchers and farm groups wish to keep it this way. As the American Farm Bureau Federation
told the Committee the application of federal regulation in this area would be:

(1) prohibitively expensive (requiring an increase in the budget of the USDA from $4 million/
year to at least $100 million);

(2) unwise because there is not scientifically documented evidence of farm animal abuse by
farmers; and

(3) unjustified because animal welfare activists would be attempting to impose care and treatment standards for companion animals on farm animals (anthropomorphism).

(4) unnecessary because abused animals produce products which leave their owners at a competitive disadvantage.

Letter from Dr. A. Ann Sorensen, Assistant Director, Natural and Environmental Resources
Division, AFBF, to the Honorable Robert W. Kastenmeier, Feb. 2, 1988.

While groups like the Farm Bureau recognize the need for further research in this area generally, they question the assumption that transgenic animals will be mistreated. In fact they
suggest that genetically altered animals may be treated better or derive benefits as a result of
such alterations. For example, genetic engineering may rapidly permit the development of disease resistant animals. *See also Testimony of Wagner, Brill, and Walter.*

[164] National Academy of Sciences, Introduction of DNA-engineered Organisms into the Environment: Key Issues (1987).

[165] *Id.* at 22.

[166] See, *Recommendations, infra.*

60   PART FOUR

CHAPTER 13.—MORAL ARGUMENTS AGAINST PATENTING ANIMALS

Several witnesses—most notably the National Council of Church-es—urged the Congress to adopt a temporary prohibition of the patenting of animals.[167] Some of these objections appear to be aimed at barring research on transgenic animals, others address what appear to be economic issues associated with the arguments used and an examination of the factual basis of the claims or their relevance to the debate.

Several witnesses appear to echo and rely upon an argument by Jerry Rifkin that transgenic animals and patents associated with them violate "species integrity." Rev. Granberg-Michaelson uses the phrase "creation's inherent structures and boundaries." This claim is, as Dr. Leroy Walters, Professor of Bioethics at Georgetown University, put it:

> * * * based on an implausible philosophy of nature, one that ignores evolutionary theory and the findings of 20th century biology.[168]

As the Office of Technology Assessment points out:

> . . . There is no consistent or absolute rule that species are discretely bounded in any generally applicable manner.[169]

In 1980 the National Council of Churches, the Synagogue Council of America and the United States Catholic Conference wrote to President Carter calling for an examination of patent law in light of *Chakrabarty* and a review of the moral and ethical issues. In turn the President subsequently appointed a Commission for the Study of Ethic Problems in Medicine and Biomedical and Behavioral Research. This Commission issued its report in 1982.

The report of the President's Commission speaks to the issue:

> In the absence of specific religious prohibitions, either revealed or derived by rational argument from religious premises, it is difficult to see why "breaching species barriers" as such is irreligious or other-wise objectionable. In fact, the very notion that these are barriers that must be breached prejudges the issue. The question is simply whether there is something intrinsically wrong with intentionally crossing species lines. Once the question is posed in this way the answer must be negative—unless one is willing to condemn the production of tangelos by hybridizing tangerines and grapefruits or the production of mules by the mating of asses with horses.[170]

---

[167] *See Testimony of Granberg-Michaelson, Hoyt, and Rifkin.*

[168] *Testimony of Walters.*

[169] OFFICE OF TECHNOLOGY ASSESSMENT, TRANSGENIC ANIMALS 8–9 (1988); *see also Testimony of L. Walters*; 50 FED. REG. 9761, 9763, 9765 (Mar. 11, 1985) (comments of Dr. Singer and Dr. Joklik).

[170] PRESIDENT'S COMMISSION FOR THE STUDY OF ETHICAL PROBLEMS IN MEDICAL AND BEHAVIORAL RESEARCH, SPLICING LIFE: THE SOCIAL AND ETHICAL ISSUES OF GENETIC ENGINEERING WITH HUMAN BEINGS 57 (1982).

Moreover, using current techniques the insertion of one gene into an animal with 50,000 to 100,000 or more genes would not disrupt something fundamental in the animal's architecture. Finally, the Rifkin concept that species of animals have the right "to exist as a separate identifiable creature" has no known foundation in biology. This is so because the animals being genetically altered have "already been far more altered by human intervention . . . (through traditional breeding) . . . than transgenic manipulations are likely to lead to, even within the next several decades."[171]

As the representative of one farm organization put it:

> . . . when someone suggests that animals should have their own gene make up, they should recall that most [domesticated] animals are the offspring of planned mating.[172]

Thus, the first moral argument used against this research activity appears to ignore the findings of modern science.

The second moral argument appears directed at the "concentration of economic power of corporate forces in agriculture."[173] This argument appears not to be directly based on a commonly held religious view, rather it appears to be based on a political or economic world view.[174] To the extent that it expresses concern about *existing* economic concentration in agriculture it is based on widely recognized facts. American agriculture is already very economically concentrated.[175] Increased economic concentration in agriculture is based on a large number of factors including market forces, economics of scale, public policy factors (e.g. commodity support programs, agricultural credits, and tax policy) and international trade and competition. What is unclear—and certainly unproven—is the connection between patent protection and economic concentration.

The vast majority of products sold by farmers are not currently the subject of patent protection. In these market sectors, economic concentration exists to varying degrees for reasons outside of intellectual property protection. For example, the poultry industry appears to be highly concentrated without patents. In the area of plants (sexually and nonsexually reproduced) the existing research does not establish the existence of a casual connection between plant patent protection and social disadvantages.[176]

To the extent that these economic arguments appear directed against the patent system in general, they are contradicted by 200 years of political support for the patent system and the concensus it represents. Moreover, the existing economic literature about the impact of patents does *not* substantiate any claims of harm to human welfare.

The third moral argument made against patenting animals is that it will inevitably and necessarily lead to increased animal suf-

---

[171] Office of Technology Assessment, Transgenic Animals, 10 (1988) (parenthetical added).
[172] C. Swank, Exec. V.P. Ohio Farm Bureau Federation, Letter to Dr. W. Garland, N.I.H., Oct. 1, 1984 at 2."
[173] *Testimony of Granberg-Michaelson.*
[174] Rifkin.
[175] See pages — to —, *infra.*
[176] See Chapter — on the Impact of Biotechnology on Agriculture, *infra.*

62   fering. This argument appears to ignore the nature and purpose of transgenic animal research. Transgenic animal research is currently focused on developing improved models for human disease research; second, for breed improvement for farm animals; and third, the use of transgenic animals to produce drugs for human diseases.[177]

Each of these research goals is legitimate and traditional in our culture. Animal breeding to improve human productivity and nutrition has occurred for millenia. The use of animals to assist in the development of human therapies also has been long recognized.[178] The mere fact that such work involves confinement of, or experimentation with, animals necessarily means that appropriate statutes and regulations should come into play. As this report explains in detail in an earlier section, these regulations already cover must of the work done with transgenic animals.

Complaints by animal welfare advocates about the treatment of animals in labs or on farms *in general,* are better directed at those laws whose purpose is the protection of animal welfare.[179] Even here, however, advocates such as the Humane Society have not demonstrated a factual basis for their assertion that animal patenting will inevitably lead to increased animal suffering. In fact, the evidence is to the contrary. Witnesses in the field pointed to improvements in animal welfare that have occurred as a result of transgenic animal research.

The *potential* use of patented products or techniques in a way that causes animal suffering is not reason to deny patent protection. If we were to accept this logic, then any product or process, that offends moral views a groups within society would not be patentable.[180]

We have not asked—nor should we ask the Patent Office—to act as a health and safety regulatory agency. Concerns about animal welfare can be—and are—addressed in a separate regulatory framework.[181]

The fourth moral argument offered by critics of patenting animals suggests that producing new life forms simply for the sake of profit "strikes many as morally offensive." [182] Apparently, as the

---

[177] Dr. Leroy Walters's testimony, two examples of transgenic animal experiments which cured mice afflicted with human-like diseases by introducing new genes into their germlines. *Testimony of Walters* at 10.

[178] Food Security Act of 1985, Pub. L. 99–198, 99 Stat. 1354,1645, section 1751(1)(1985).

[179] Feder, *Beyond White Rats and Rabbits,* N.Y TIMES, Feb. 28, 1988, at C1 (describes reductions in the use of animals in research). Possible amendments to the Animals Welfare Act include: (1) greater encouragement of alternatives to the use of animals in research and testing; (2) restriction on the use of certain animals; (3) restrictions on the use of certain research protocals; (4) federal regulation of animals users; or (5) enhanced enforcement. OFFICE OF TECHNOLOGY ASSESSMENT, ALTERNATIVES, *supra,* note ——, 26-9 Whether these suggestions are meritorious will, of course, be determined by the respective Agriculture Committees.

[180] Immediate examples of such products or processes would include:
  (1) Tobacco related products or processes;
  (2) firearms or weapons;
  (3) abortion related instruments;
  (4) birth control devices; and
  (5) cattle prods, cattle branding instruments, animal cages, etc.

[181] *See* pages — to —, *infra.* The arguments about animal suffering were also made by Jeremy Rifkin and Dr. Michael Fox of the Humane Society in 1984 to the NIH. The NIH Recombinant DNA Advisory Committee responded that Recombinant DNA techniques, in fact, involved more precise, and therefore, more humane change in animals. The RAC also argued that to the extent that there is pain imposed on lab animals, it is outweighted by the potential benefits for both animals and humans. 50 Fed. Reg. 9761, 9764-65 (Mar. 11, 1985).

[182] *Testimony of Granbery-Michaelson.*

argument goes, this possibility will change the way we relate to 63 animals. The trust of this argument ignores millennia of animal domestication and traditional animal breeding. We already own, buy and sell animals as property. Moreover, within generally agreed upon norms of animal welfare, we already confine, eat and perform research upon animals. Thus, as Dr. Walters of Georgetown University puts it: ". . . [in comparison] patenting animals . . . seems relatively benign".[183]

The final moral argument against animal patents suggests that transgenic animal research (and patents) are inappropriate when a human gene is used. While it is true that much transgenic animals research involves a transfer of genes from humans to other organisms. This fact alone should not be cause for concern. Human genes have been successfully transferred to microorganisms that in turn have produced valuable medical advances, such as human growth hormone. The use of human genes is based on the convenience of using a better known substance.[184] Moreover, the transfer of a single human gene to another animals does not give that animal human characteristics. Rather the recipient animals only express a single function dictated by the inserted gene.

The use of human genes in animals can also enhance animal welfare. Research in this area has included transfer of a human gene into an animal to *prevent* the animal from contracting a disease. Finally, it must be noted that the use of human genes is *scientifically necessary* when the transgenic animal is being developed to create a model for the study of human disease. This type of research clearly does not endanger animal welfare or produce monsters.[185] Rather it produces more precise breeding results for a social beneficial purpose.[186]

One glaring and inexplicable omission from most of the submissions by persons using moral arguments against patenting animals is the lack of an explicit recognition of the benefits of research in this area. An important ethical question is the proper balance between potential suffering of some animals in exchange for a potential benefit to the well being of other animals, including human beings.[187] This report is not the place to resolve that debate. We do, however, need to keep in mind that persons (or, more accurately, classes of persons and animals) stand to benefit from transgenic animal research and those benefits must be weighed against the

---

[183] *Testimony of Walters.*

[184] Palmiter and Brinster, letter to Dr. W. Garland, NIH Sept. 27, 1984 at 5.

[185] The argument concerning the insertion of animal genes into humans has raised more serious debate. *See* OFFICE OF TECHNOLOGY ASSESSMENT, TRANSGENIC ANIMALS; OFFICE OF TECHNOLOGY ASSESSMENT, HUMAN GENE THERAPY, (198—); *Testimony of Walters* at 16. This possibility does not appear to be implicated in any way by the decision of the Patent and Trademark Office, because patent claims involving human beings will be rejected.

[186] National Research Council, Board on Agriculture, AGRICULTURAL BIOTECHNOLOGY at 33 (1987) ("genetic engineering will give breeders unparalleled precision in manipulating desired traits . . . [and] up the process.").

[187] Animal use in research, testing, and education creates a conflict of interest between the liberty that humans have to use animals for human ends (knowledge, health, safety) and the need that animals have to be free of suffering. When the suffering inflicted on animals is not necessary to satisfy a desirable human objective, the animal interest will prevail. And when the suffering is unavoidable, the human interest will be controlling. Animals are morally entitled to be treated humanely; whether they are entitled to more than that is unclear. OFFICE OF TECHNOLOGY ASSESSMENT, ALTERNATIVES TO ANIMAL USE IN RESEARCH, TESTING AND EDUCATION 82-83 (1986) Holtzman, *Patenting Certain Forms of Life: A Moral Justification*, HASTING CENTER REP. 9 (June, 1979).

claimed harm.[188] The development of improved human disease models assists the creation and development of new drug therapies. Research in this area can reduce animal suffering. Transgenic animal research also involves development of animals that can produce pharmaceutical proteins useful in treating humans. These potential benefits can not occur if this research is stopped.[189] One Federal agency (the NIH/RAC) concluded that the benefits of transgenic animal research made it a *moral imperative* to oppose a ban on such work.[190] The denial of sufficient patent-based, economic incentive would slow the possible advances in this area. Thus, the alleged drawbacks from animal patents should be evaluated in comparison to the possible benefits. If we had accepted these arguments made by Rifkin in 1980 in connection with the *Chakrabarty* decision, we would not have a $4 billion biotechnology industry.[191] If the NIH had adopted these arguments in 1984, much valuable research would have been lost.[192] The arguments used by opponents of biotechnology in this debate are similar to those they made earlier—and that were rejected—in different fora. Before we accept the claim that patenting animals is immoral more careful scrutiny is required. As the President's Commission for the Study of Ethical Problems in Medicine and Biomedical and Behavioral Research concluded the morality of the technique being used is not wrong, rather moral questions can occur when man is not careful to properly regulate the consequences of this research.[193] As addressed elsewhere in this report, the patent law is *not* the appropriate focus for such regulations.

CHAPTER 14.—IMPACT OF BIOTECHNOLOGY ON AGRICULTURE

Many witnesses who appeared before the Committee stressed the potentially negative impact of biotechnology on the family farm.[194] These cries for understanding and assistance should not go unheard. A truly sympathetic response to these concerns must be based, however, on a firm understanding on the existing realities of modern American agriculture.[195] A candid assessment of

---

[188] S. Olson, Biotechnology: An Industry Comes of Age at 6 (1986) (biotechnology can be used to make animals more productive, more resistant to disease or environmental stress or more nutritious . . . and have a dramatic effect on food production and hunger).

[189] As the Dean of the University of Wisconsin Graduate School put it:

. . . Rifkin could sentence humans to continued suffering . . . even after future understanding shows safe ways to prevent such suffering and loss of life. R. Bock, letter to Dr. W. Garland, NIH Sept. 24, 1984, *Board on Agriculture*, NATIONAL RESEARCH COUNCIL, AGRICULTURE IN TRANSITION at 5 (1988).

("Biotechnology offers tremendous potential for . . . animal production . . . [it] can increase the efficiency of producing animals products that are leaner and more nutritious").

[190] 50 Fed. Reg. 9761 (March 3, 1985).

[191] Schneider, *Science Debates Using Tools to Redesign Life*, N.Y. TIMES, June 8, 1987 A 17.

[192] Rifkin and his Foundation on Economic Trends also sued to halt research on transgenic animals, but lost in Federal court. *Foundation on Economic Trends* v. *Block* (D.D.C., Civ. 84-3045).

[193] President's Commission for the Study of Ethical Problems in Medicine and Biomedical and Behavioral Research, SPLICING LIFE: THE SOCIAL AND ETHICAL ISSUES OF GENETIC ENGINEERING WITH HUMAN BEINGS 77-9 (1982).

[194] *Testimony of Carpenter, Huber, Hefner, Saunders, and Schwarze.*

[195] Robbins, *Down on the Superfarm: Bigger Share of Profits*, N.Y. TIMES, Aug. 4, 1987 at A14 (discussing existing economic concentration in agriculture; *e.g.* in 1985 the top 1.2% of farmers produced ⅓ of the total output and 55% of the profits of all 2.2 million farms). *Preexisting* concerns about the diminished role of the family farm or fears of economic concentration predate patents for animals. These concerns must be separated from the claims that patenting animals will adversely change the projected future of agriculture.

the interrelationship between biotechnology and agriculture must 65 also include a recognition of the potential benefits of this new technology.

A recent survey of agriculture by the United States Congress, Office of Technology Assessment is a useful starting point.[196] The OTA projects a decline in the number of farms from 2.2 million in 1982 to approximately 1.2 million in 2000.[197] Moreover, by the year 2000, the 50,000 largest farms will produce 75 percent of all farm products sold. Thus, even without the emergency of transgenic animals, American agriculture is undergoing a dramatic change. The factors influencing this change include: technology, associated economies of scale, specialization, and capital factors.[198]

In the context of such dramatic changes it is hazardous to speculate about the consequences of any single variable. This makes assessing the alleged adverse impact of patent protection for animals speculative at best. There are some available agricultural experiences which are relevant. First, have some segments of the livestock market become more economically concentrated despite the absence of patent protection? Clearly the experience of farmers in the poultry sector (turkey and chicken) is instructive. In both areas the industry has become more technology dependent (e.g. artificial insemination) and vertically integrated.[199] These developments have occurred without recombinant DNA technology or patent protection. Similarly, projected consolidation into larger dairy farms is already underway. These changes will likely occur regardless of how the patent question is resolved.

Second, has the extension of patent protection to plants and plant varieties produced demonstrably bad results? The available evidence suggests a cautious no. The limited assessments of the Plant Variety Protection Act (PVPA) have concluded that: (1) "increases in prices, market concentration . . . and declines in in information exchange . . . have been nil or modest in nature";[200] (2) " . . . current genetic uniformity is a market phenomenon and . . . largely unrelated to the [PVPA];"[201] and (3) "[p]atents were found to be important in providing for investment in new products and processes."[202]

The available evidence suggests that patenting transgenic animals will have only a marginal effect on the overall agriculture picture in the United States. Even this projected response is incomplete. What many of the critics of biotechnology in agriculture fail to mention, or choose to ignore, are the benefits of such technological changes. As discussed earlier in this report, this new area of re-

---

[196] Office of Technology Assessment, Technology, Public Policy, and the Changing Structure of American Agriculture, (1985).

[197] *Id.* at 19–20.

[198] *Id.* at 21–22.

[199] Office of Technology Assessment, Impacts of Applied Genetics, (1981).

[200] L.J. Butler, B.W. Marion, The Impacts of Patent Protection on the U.S. Seed Industry and Public Plant Breeding, at 79 (1985).

[201] W. Lesser, R. Masson, An Economic Analysis of the PVPA, at 3 (1983).

[202] *Id.* at 1, D. Plucknett et al., Gene Banks and the World's Food at 38–39 (1987) (plant breeder's rights have stimulated private investment in crop breeding research and has *not* meant the demise of public institutions involvement in plant breeding and there is no evidence that plant breeding rights impedes the conservation, exchange and utilization of crop germ plasm.)

66   search is aimed at producing *better* agricultural products.[203] For example, the creation of disease-resistant farm animals can hardly be said to be motivated by an antipathy to farmer's interests.[204] Similarly the development of more nutritious poultry or leaner meat is intended to enhance the markets of farmers. Finally, as the OTA recognized, these new technologies have the potential of allowing future demand to be met by "fewer aminals, less land . . . and less demand on natural resources. . . ."[205] Thus, a final benefit of this new technology may be to permit greater product output per farm.

Unfortunately, however, the bitter reality of modern agriculture may be that the development of new technologies will also serve to enhance the position of the large farmer.[206] Without a concerted public sector investment in this area of research, development and dissemination of information about the benefits of this technology will be of little value to the small and moderate sized farmers.[207] It is for this reason that a strong commitment must be made to the entire agricultural community concerning the continuity of public sector technology generation and transfer.[208] This treatment of biotechnology and agriculture, however, does not lead to the conclusion that the patent-based incentives for research in the area should be muted by denial of patent protection. To the contrary, the potential benefits of this technology require both public and private sector involvement. Patent protection is a modest incentive to achieve the goal of stimulating work in agriculture of a socially beneficial nature.

CHAPTER 15.—PATENTS AND ECONOMIC INCENTIVES

Much of the sound and fury about the patentability of life forms has been over whether a patent system is a necessary form of incentive for innovation, or instead a source of monopoly power.

The existence of competing views about the economic impact of patents is not new. Since the 18th century, economists have debated the impact of the patent system. In 1776, Adam Smith found that patents are a good way of rewarding the risk and expense of inventing.[209] Nine years later, Jeremy Bentham praised the patent system concluding it had "an infinite effect and costs nothing."[210] John Stuart Mill opined that to deny patent protection would be a "gross immorality."[211] On the other hand, modern economists have argued that the market distortions caused by the patent system are potentially very large.[212]

---

[203] National Academy of Science, National Research Council, Board on Agriculture, Designing Foods, 1988; Sun, *Designing Food by Engineering Animals,* 240 Science 136 (April 8, 1988).

[204] *Testimony of Brill* (foreign governments are targeting this area of research).

[205] TECHNOLOGY/AMERICAN AGRICULTURE, at 206.

[206] TECHNOLOGY/AMERICAN AGRICULTURE at 216.

[207] *Id.* As former University of Wisconsin researchers described the nature of the impact of the PVPA as dependent on the continued availability of continued public sector research. L.J. Butler and B.W. Marion, The Impact of Patent Protection on the U.S. Seed Industry and Public Plant Breeding (1985).

[208] BIOTECHNOLOGY AND AGRICULTURE: HEARINGS BEFORE THE SUBCOMM. ON INVESTIGATIONS AND OVERSIGHT OF THE HOUSE COMM. ON SCIENCE AND TECHNOLOGY, 99th Cong., 2d Sess, 106 (1985) (statement of Dr. Ronald D. Kuntson); *see also Testimony of Walsh.*

[209] A. Smith, THE WEALTH OF NATIONS, Book IV, ch. VII, pt. III (1776).

[210] J. Bentham, A MANUAL OF POLITICAL ECONOMY, vol. III, p. 71, (1785).

[211] J. S. Mill, PRINCIPLES OF POLITICAL ECONOMY, book V, ch. X (1848).

[212] F. Scherer, INDUSTRIAL MARKET STRUCTURE AND ECONOMIC PERFORMANCE (1980).

It would be tempting to summarize the disputes between the economists about the patent system by quoting Professor Machlup, who 30 years ago surveyed the literature in this area for the Senate Judiciary Committee.[213] Machlup concluded:

No economist, on the basis of present knowledge, could possibly state with certainty that the patent system, as it now operates, confers a net benefit or a net loss on society.[214]

This assessment would, however, leave an incomplete picture. The more recent literature strongly suggests that the patent system serves as a strong incentive for innovation in some industrial sectors. The available evidence does not ratify the fears of those who oppose patents on the basis of monopoly power.

While a complete discussion of the relationship of the economics of the patent system is beyond the scope of this report some observations are in order. First, the patent laws are based on some economic assumptions that appear reasonable based on our current economic system. Patent laws are thought to produce an important incentive for individual and organizational innovators.[215] Proof of this incentive is frequently alleged by recitation of the negative, that is, if inventions become public when made then why would a firm assume the costs and risks of experimenting with a new product?[216] Without a patent system another firm could sit on the sidelines, take no risks, and duplicate the product once it succeeds. Innovators themselves certainly support the patent system. Corporate innovators (and investors) make investment decisions, in part, on the basis of the strength of the patent system. In turn this understanding makes patent protection a central feature of innovation.[217]

The another argument made in favor of patent protection is the favorable comparison to trade secret protection.[218] Under trade secret protection, knowledge is not disseminated as quickly or as widely. Thus, in the view of some commentators the patent system is justified by a comparison to the existing trade secret alternative.[219]

It should also be noted that the economic consequences of patent protection varies substantially from industry to industry. Professor Mansfield has reviewed studies in the patent area and concluded that pharmaceutical, and to a lesser extent chemical, companies are dependent on patent protection. Even within the pharmaceutical industry there is a high degree of limitation. Nonetheless, phar-

---

[213] Machlup, An Economic Review of the Patent System, Study No. 15, Subcomm. on Patents, Trademarks, and Copyrights, of the Senate Comm. on the Judiciary, 85th Cong. 2d Sess. (1958).
[214] Id. at 79; see also Priest, What Economists Can Tell Lawyers about Intellectual Property, 8 RES. IN L. AND ECON. 19 (1986).
[215] Machlup, supra note 179, at 21.
[216] See Mansfield, Intellectual Property Rights, Technological Change and Economic Growth, 1988 (a paper presented to the Conference on Intellectual Property Rights and Capital Formation in the Next Decade) at 10.
[217] Oppenlander, The Influence of the Patent System on the Readiness to Invest: An Empirical Analysis, INDUSTRIAL PROPERTY 494 (Dec. 1986). PRESIDENT'S COMMISSION ON THE PATENT SYSTEM, "TO PROMOTE THE PROGRESS OF THE USEFUL ARTS." (1966).
[218] Machlup supra note 179.
[219] See generally BOWMAN, PATENT AND ANTITRUST LAW: A LEGAL AND ECONOMIC APPRAISAL 2 (1973) (Patents increase efficiencies); POSNER, ECONOMIC ANALYSIS OF LAW, 2d Ed. at 55 (1977) (resources can be wasted when strenuous efforts are made to penetrate commercial secrecy); ADLER, BIOTECHNOLOGY AS AN INTELLECTUAL PROPERTY, 224 SCIENCE 357, 61 (1984); Machlup, supra note 179.

68   maceutical firms patent 80 percent of their inventions and such protection is believed to be essential for 30 percent of their innovations.[220] The cost of imitation for ethical drugs is 30 percent, or about three times higher than the imitation costs for chemicals. Thus, it appears that the central role patent protection plays appears largely dependent on the particular industrial sector involved.

It is logical to assume that the importance of patent protection for transgenic animals would be similar to that in the pharmaceutical industry. Some transgenic animals (human drugs and research animals) are similar in some ways to products the ethical drug market. The existing literature on pharmaceutical industry research suggests that the absence of patent protection may produce economic concentration, as innovators vertically intergrate to forestall piracy.[221] To the extent that the market for transgenic animals is analogous to that for patented plants, positive findings about patent protection have been made by agricultural economists.[222]

In conclusion it seems safe to reiterate that the political justification for the patent system (i.e. an incentive to create) has support in the economic literature. It is also safe to conclude that the parade of horribles offered by opponents of patenting animals remain largely unproven. Finally, it appears likely that the availability of patent protection for genetically altered animals will have a positive effect on the stimulation of investment in this area of research.

PART FIVE

FINDINGS AND RECOMMENDATIONS

PATENT SYSTEM

Finding

The United States patent law is derived from the United States Constitution, Article 1, section 8, clause 8. The patent law is designed to further the public interest by providing for public disclosure, providing an incentive for creators, by adding to the base of knowledge by limiting the term of exclusive rights, and by adding knowledge to the public domain.

Finding

The availability of patent protection is not the exclusive motivation for scientific research. The absence of patent protection would not serve to prevent research on transgenic animals, but it would

---

[220] *See Mansfield, supra* note 182.

[221] A. Kirim, *Reconsidering Patents and Economic Development: A Case Study of the Turkish Pharmaceutical Industry*, 13 WORLD DEV. 2198 (1985) (concentration of pharmaceutical industry higher partially due lack of patent protection for pharmaceuticals); Lunn, The Roles of Property Rights and Market Power in Appropriating Innovative Output, 19 J. Leg. Stud. 423 (1985).

[222] *Lesser supra*, note 167; *Bulter supra*, note 168; Evenson, *Intellectual Property Rights and Agribusiness Research and Development. Implications for Public Agricultural Research system*, 65 Amer. J. Agr. Econ. 967 (1983) (increase in plant breeding after PVPA). PERRIN ET AL., SOME EFFECTS OF THE U.S. PLANT VARIETY PROTECTION ACT OF 1970 (1983). (a three fold increase in the number of soybean varieties since the PVPA); also the PVPA contributed to the objective of increased agricultural productivity).

likely serve to discourage investment in this area of research by   69
the private sector.

Finding

The current patent law is designed to be expansive in terms of
the types of inventions which are patentable. The flexibility of
United States patent law has fostered the growth and development
of United States innovation, especially in the area of biotechnology.
United States patent law is generally viewed as the best in the
world in the area of biotechnology.

Finding

The availability of patent protection for biologically derived inventions has been the catalyst for the current biotechnology industry. Prior to the *Chakrabarty* decision in 1980, life science research
was centered in academia, with little effort to secure societal benefits through the development of commercial products. No capability
existed to aggregate the capital necessary to conduct development
and obtain regulatory approval for food, drug or diagnostic products. Industrial activity was generally focused on microorganisms
for fermentation and antibiotic production which were protected as
trade secrets. Eight years of R&D by the new biotechnology industry has demonstrated that life sustaining, critical products can be
produced through recombinant DNA techniques and systems—
these are now entering the marketplace. The technology is now
poised to use mammalian systems (cells and animals) to produce
complex, highly specific products for human use. It is clear that the
cost of bringing such products to the public is very large, and
meaningful patent protection for animals is the major factor in obtaining venture and development capital.

Finding

The single most important Congressional issue concerning biotechnology and transgenic animals is whether to ratify the existing
judicial and administrative practice with respect to the patentability of higher life forms. In general, the patent law is carefully
crafted to provide an incentive to creators and to further the public
interest. The existing laws are written in general terms to protect
virtually all forms of significant and unique human innovations.
The Supreme Court decision in *Chakrabarty* affirmed the basic
principle of patent law that an act of human intervention distinguishes a patentable invention from a product of nature. The subsequent decision of the Patent and Trademark Office with respect
to animals modified by human intervention is both logical and a
legally valid extension of existing patent law.

The proposal pendings before the Congress to impose a moratorium or a prohibition on the issuance of any patents for genetically
altered animals [223] are unwise and unnecessary. The prohibition
proposed by pending legislation would serve to stifle important innovations. The existing research on transgenic animals is designed

---

[223] H.R. 3119 (Rose, N.C.); see S. 2111 (Hatfield); 100th Cong. 2d Sess. 134 CONG. RECORD S
1620, (daily ed. Feb. 29, 1988 Feb. 29, 1988) The Hatfield bill would prohibit the patenting of
genetically altered or modified animals.

253

70   to benefit both humans and animals. One type of research is directed at developing animal models for the development of new human therapies. Another type of research is aimed at creation of anim.. ?ls whose end products (such as meat or milk) are more nutritious to humans. Finally, transgenic animals offer a potential source of new human drugs. These tangible benefits must be weighed against the claimed harm of patenting animals. A thorough examination of the asserted harms from transgenic animal research does not substantiate many of the alleged problems. Many of the arguments against patenting animals are, in reality, arguments against the existence of the research in the first place. The patent law is not the place to exercise moral judgments about scientific activities. As the *Los Angeles Times* put it:

> Genetic engineering is just the latest example of humanity's effort to control its environment and thereby improve its life. The more food that can be produced for a hungry world, the better off people will be. This is a wholly worthwhile goal, and the Patent Office is right to encourage it by offering commercial protection to those who develop these techniques. Enlightened discussion and debate over these issues are worthwhile, and remind us to remain vigilant over the use of these powerful new tools. But discussion should not be allowed to halt progress.

On the other hand, some of the critics of patenting life forms, have raised valid concerns about the regulatory apparatus for transgenic animals. This report concludes that some marginal changes can be made in the way in which transgenic animals are regulated. These changes are recommended, not as a precondition to the issuance of a patent, but rather independently as a part of a more coherent and sound public policy.

Changes in the Patent Law

The Committee concludes that three amendments would be desirable in the general patent law. One of the proposed changes (a research exemption) would apply across the board to all patentable inventions; whereas the other two proposals are limited to patents on higher life forms. Enactment of these reforms does not need to precede the issuance of a patent for a transgenic animal. The Congress has the authority to modify the nature and extent of a patent once issued, if such a change is necessary to meet an important regulatory purpose.[224]

More importantly, consideration of legislation in this area will be possible before any commercially viable products enter the marketplace. According to the Office of Technology Assessment it will be at least 5 years before genetically altered livestock will be seen on the family farm.

---

[224] In 1984 the Court of Appeals for the Federal Circuit decided the case of *Roche Products, Inc.*, v. *Bolar Pharmaceutical Co., Inc.* 733 F.2d 858 (Fed. Cir.), *cert. denied*, 469 U.S. 856 (1984). In response the Congress amended the patent law to permit conduct which would have been an act of patent infringement under the pre-existing law. Pub. L. 98–417. The constitutionality of this type of legislative initiative is discussed at length in the Report of the Committee on the Judiciary. H.R. Rept.No. 857, 98th Cong., 2d Sess. 27–30 (1984).

Deposit

The first proposed change in the patent law is to authorize the creation or designation of a certified depository for the placement of gemplasm for transgenic animals. This depository can serve two significant functions: first it can assist a patent applicant in meeting the "enablement" requirement of the patent law; second, it can facilitate legitimate research and experimentation. Creation of a government depository, or a government certified institution, can also contribute to maintaining genetic diversity through the creation of a national germplasm bank. Deposits made into such a center should be carefully regulated. Access to the depository should be guaranteed so as to meet the disclosure requirements of the patent law. Access should not be granted, however, until the patent has been issued. Once the patent has been issued the nature of the access must be carefully circumscribed. The accessors must undertake not to provide access to unauthorized third parties, agree not to export the deposited materials; agree not to use the deposited materials for infringing purposes (that is, to only engage in research and experimentation as authorized by law), and agree to meet any regulatory requirements concerning containment of the organism.

Farmers Exemption

The third and most important area of reform in our patent law is to clarify the rules of the road with respect to liability for reproduction of an animal from patented transgenic animals. As discussed earlier in this report in greater detail, the law on this subject is somewhat murky. The existing precedents are not terribly helpful.[225] Thus, it will be useful for Congress to anticipate this issue and attempt to address it before uncertainty produces unnecessary transaction or enforcement costs.

Before addressing the question from a patent law perspective it should be kept in mind that the vast majority of the transactions involving transgenic animals will probably be dealt with through the use of contracts. Marketplace solutions are likely to be the most efficient method of allocating the costs of enforcement. Thus, it is likely that the patent owner will allocate the costs of enforcement into the initial costs of the product. For example, a genetically altered cow that cost one million dollars to develop could be sold for a thousand dollars if the patent owner claims no residual rights to fees based on the reproduction of the animal. On the other hand the developer of the cow may choose to sell the animals for one hundred dollars if the purchaser agrees to make small payments for the offspring produced by the cow. This type of pricing policy and enforcement mechanism is already prevalent in some segments of the livestock market and is likely to be repeated for patented animals.[226]

[225] A possible approach to liability for reproduction of a living matter is to make it an act of infringement unless the replication is an unavoidable part of another act. WIPO APRIL 8, 1987 at 69.
[226] Lesser, Applying Animal Patents in Agriculture: Lessons for Farmers and the Patent Office for Self-Reproducible Animals, WIPO Conference, Cornell Univ., June 4–5, 1987.

There are, however, some lingering questions about the appropriate role the patent law should play in the enforcement of rights in the area of reproduction. The only time that Congress has faced this question with respect to life forms was in the context of the Plant Variety Protection Act. In the PVPA a policy decision was made to exempt farmers from liability for reproduction when the farmer used the seeds for his/her own domestic purposes. It would appear that a similar small farmer exemption makes sense in the area of animals. Higher life forms like plants and animals differ from other patented technologies insofar as they are "self reproducing."

As the American Farm Bureau Federation put it "farmers hate paperwork". It is unrealistic to expect farmers to become involved in patent enforcement unless it is in their own self interest. For the foreseeable future most of the transgenic animals produced will be useful in the context of a laboratory, thus, the creation of a limited farm-based exemption will not immediately serve to encumber the financial rewards available to transgenic animal innovators. On the other hand we are not exactly certain about how the marketplace will respond to the existence of transgenic livestock. The type of exemption anticipated here is limited to the ability of a farmer to reproduce without liability a genetically altered animal for his/her own purposes. This approach, however, does have the advantage of being the least socially disruptive approach. Farmers would not have to concern themselves about "patent royalties". A "small farmer exemption" also neatly avoids problems which occur with respect to unintentional reproduction by transgenic animals. More importantly, adoption of this approach enables Congress to subsequantly expand the coverage of a patent on a transgenic animal if the market place response to the farmers exemption is not conducive to the stimulation of innovation. Finally, as with plants in the PVPA farmers exemption, genetic drift will serve to reduce the likelihood that a "copy" of the patented transgenic animals contains the desired trait. After a generation or two even the farmer who had purchased a transgenic animal will be back in the market to obtain a pure "breed." The financial impact of a farmers exemption may be slight, but the potential social benefits large. The presence of a "small farmer exemption" will remove farmers as involuntary patent enforcers. Finally, it will help balance the negotiations on patent licensing, thereby leaving enforcement questions more of ten to the market place.

V. SECTION-BY-SECTION ANALYSIS OF H.R. 4970

Section 1 is the short title, "Transgenic Animal Patent Reform Act".

Section 2 contains an amendment to section 271 of title 35 to provide an exemption from patent liability for farmers.

Proposed section 271(g)(1) provides that it shall not be an act of infringement for a person whose occupation is farming to reproduce a patented transgenic farm animal through breeding, to use such an animal in the farming operation or to sell such an animal or the offspring of such an animal. The terms "transgenic farm animal" and "farm animal" are defined in proposed section

271(g)(3). The exemption for the use of a farm animal that is covered by a patent is a clarification of current law. Under current patent law there is an implied use exception to the scope of the patent. The purchaser of a patent is expected to use the patented invention for the purpose intended. Thus, this part of the exemption merely ratifies the current law. The other portions of the exemption do, however, go beyond current law.

The exemption for farmers who intentionally reproduce patented farm animals is necessary, because it is likely that without this amendment, courts would find such activity an act of patent infringement.[227] By the very nature of their occupation farmers will use patented animals on their own farms for reproductive purposes. Because this is an area in which contractual solutions are unlikely to be effective a statutory exemption is necessary. A similar exemption exists for patented plants in the Plant Variety Protection Act,[228] the only other American intellectual property law that regulates rights in self-reproducing subject matter. The existence of a farmers exemption has a number of beneficial results: (1) it reduces burdensome recordkeeping, (2) it avoids placing farmers in the role of patent enforcers; (3) it reduces uncertainly about the law; and (4) it will not destroy the market for patented transgenic farm animals. The market for patented farm animals will continue because of genetic drift.[229] In addition, it is likely that farmers and patent owners will reach contractual understandings with respect to liability rather than relying on the patent law.[230] These contractual solutions will let the marketplace determine the fair value of the patented animal and the nature of payments, if any, for the sale of such animals or their offsprings. The existence of a farmers exemption will prevent patent holders from using the threat of patent infringement litigation to extract concessions from farmers when the parties are negotiating licensing agreements.

The third element of the farmers exemption authorizes the sale of a patented animal or its offspring by a farmer without patent infringement liability. The approach taken in the bill is somewhat similar to the "first sale" doctrine in the copyright law, wherein the rights of the property holder over activity after the first sale are limited.[231] The ability of a farmer to compete with the patent owner in the commercial context is limited by the provisions of proposed section 271(g)(2).

Proposed section 271(g)(2) provides that it shall be an act of patent infringement for a person to sell the germ cells, semen or embryos of a patented transgenic farm animal.

Proposed section 271(g)(3) contains definitions for the terms "transgenic farm animals" and "farm animals" as used in this section of title 35.

---

[227] Merges, *Intellectual Property in Higher Life Forms: The Patent System and Controversial Technologies,* —Maryland L. Rev.—(1988).

[228] 7 U.S.C. 2321, 2324 (1980).

[229] Merges, *supra* note 2.

[230] *See* W. Lesser, *Applying Animal Patents in Agriculture,* at 9 (unpublished paper presented at the Symposium on the Protection of Biotechnological Inventions, June 4, and 5 1987, Ithaca New York, sponsored by the World Intellectual Property Organization and Cornell University).

[231] 17 U.S.C. 109(a); *see generally* M. Nimmer, Nimmer on Copyright section 8.12[B].

74   *Section 3* provides that section 112 of title 35, United States Code is amended to authorize the Commissioner of the Patent and Trademark Office to accept a deposit of biological materials to satisfy the requirements of the section. Once such a deposit is made it shall be made accessible only to the extent, and under such conditions, required by the Commissioner. This section is largely a restatement and clarification of existing law and practice.

Section 4 provides that human beings are not patentible subject matter. This section codifies existing Patent Office practice.

The amendments made by this bill are to become effective on the date of enactment.

VI. Oversight Findings

The Committee makes no oversight findings with respect to this legislation.

VII. Statement of the Committtee on Government Operations

Pursuant to clause 2(l)(3)(D) of rule XI of the Rules of the House of Representatives, no oversight findings have been submitted to the Committee by the Committee on Government Operations.

VIII. New Budget Authority

Pursuant to clause 2(l)(3)(B) of Rule XI of the Rules of the House of Representatives, the bill creates no new budget authority or increased tax expenditures for the Federal government.

IX. Inflation Impact Statement

Pursuant to clause 2(l)(4) of rule XI of the Rules of the House of Representatives, the Committee believes that the bill will not have a foreseeable inflationary impact on the prices or costs in the operation of the national economy.

X. Federal Advisory Committee Act of 1972

The Committee finds that this legislation does not create any new advisory committee within the meaning of the Federal Advisory Committee Act of 1972, 5 U.S.C. Appendix.

XI. Cost Estimate

Pursuant to clause 7 of rule XIII of the rules of the House of Representatives, the Committee agrees with the cost estimate submitted by the Congressional Budget Office.

XII. Committee Vote

On August 2, 1988 the Committee—with a quorum of members present—favorably reported by voice vote H.R. 4970.

XIII. Congressional Budget Office Cost Estimate   75

U.S. Congress,
Congressional Budget Office,
Washington, DC, August 25, 1988.

Hon. Peter W. Rodino, Jr.,
Chairman, Committee on the Judiciary, House of Representatives, Washington, DC.

Dear Mr. Chairman: The Congressional Budget Office has reviewed H.R. 4970, the Transgenic Animal Patent Reform Act, as ordered reported by the House Committee on the Judiciary, August 2, 1988.

Based on information provided by the Patent and Trademark Office (PTO), we expect that no additional costs to the federal government or to state or local governments would be incurred as a result of enactment of this legislation. H.R. 4970 would amend current law to establish that it is not an act of infringement for a farmer to reproduce a patented transgenic farm animal through breeding, use such animal in the farming operation, or sell such animal or its offspring. However, the bill would provide that it is an act of infringement for a person to sell the germ cells, semen, or embryos of a patented transgenic farm animal. A final provision of the bill would prohibit the patenting of human beings.

If you wish further details on this estimate, we will be pleased to provide them. The CBO staff contact is Douglas Criscitello, who can be reached on 226–2850.

Sincerely,

C.G. Nuckols
(For James L. Blum, Acting Director).

XIV. Changes in Existing Law Made by the Bill, as Reported

In compliance with clause 3 of Rule XIII of the Rules of the House of Representatives, changes in existing law made by the bill, as reported, are shown as follows (existing law proposed to be omitted is enclosed in black brackets, new matter is printed in italic, existing law in which no change is proposed is shown in roman):

TITLE 35, UNITED STATES CODE

*   *   *   *   *   *   *

PART II—PATENTABILITY OF INVENTIONS AND GRANT OF PATENTS

*   *   *   *   *   *   *

CHAPTER 10—PATENTABILITY OF INVENTIONS

*   *   *   *   *   *   *

§ 101. Inventions patentable

Whoever invents or discovers any new and useful process, machine, manufacture, or composition of matter, or any new and

76　useful improvement thereof, may obtain a patent therefor, subject to the conditions and requirements of this title, *except that human beings are not patentable subject matter.*

*　　*　　*　　*　　*　　*　　*

CHAPTER 11—APPLICATION FOR PATENT

*　　*　　*　　*　　*　　*　　*

§ 112. Specification

The specification shall contain a written description of the invention, and of the manner and process of making and using it, in such full, clear, concise, and exact terms as to enable any person skilled in the art to which it pertains, or with which it is most nearly connected, to make and use the same, and shall set forth the best mode contemplated by the inventor of carrying out his invention.

The specification shall conclude with one or more claims particularly pointing out and distinctly claiming the subject matter which the applicant regards as his invention.

A claim may be written in independent or, if the nature of the case admits, in dependent or multiple dependent form.

Subject to the following paragraph, a claim in dependent form shall contain a reference to a claim previously set forth and then specify a further limitation of the subject matter claimed. A claim in dependent form shall be construed to incorporate by reference all the limitations of the claim to which it refers.

A claim in multiple dependent form shall contain a reference, in the alternative only, to more than one claim previously set forth and then specify a further limitation of the subject matter claimed. A multiple dependent claim shall not serve as a basis for any other multiple dependent claim. A multiple dependent claim shall be construed to incorporate by reference all the limitations of the particular claim in relation to which it is being considered.

An element in a claim for a combination may be expressed as a means or step for performing a specified function without the recital of structure, material, or acts in support thereof, and such claim shall be construed to cover the corresponding structure, material, or acts described in the specification and equivalents thereof.

With respect to an invention involving biological material, the Commissioner may accept a deposit of biological material to satisfy any requirement of this section if made accessible under such conditions as the Commissioner may require.

*　　*　　*　　*　　*　　*　　*

PART III—PATENTS AND PROTECTION OF PATENT RIGHTS

*　　*　　*　　*　　*　　*　　*

CHAPTER 28—INFRINGEMENT OF PATENTS

*　　*　　*　　*　　*　　*　　*

§ 271. Infringement of patent

(a) * * *

* * * * * * *

(g)(1) It shall not be an act of infringement for a person whose occupation is farming to reproduce a patented transgenic farm animal through breeding, use such animal in the farming operation, or sell such animal or the offspring of such animal.

(2) Notwithstanding the provisions of paragraph (1), it shall be an act of infringement for a person to sell the germ cells, semen, or embryos of a patented transgenic farm animal.

(3) For purposes of paragraphs (1) and (2)—

(A) the term "transgenic farm animal" means a farm animal whose germ cells contain genetic material originally derived from another animal other than the parent of the farm animal; and

(B) the term "farm animal" means any animal used or intended for use as food or fiber.

* * * * * * *

XV. Agency Views

General Counsel of the
U.S. Department of Commerce,
Washington, DC, August 1, 1988.

Hon. Robert W. Kastenmeier,
Chairman, Subcommittee on Courts, Civil Liberties and the Administration of Justice, Committee on the Judiciary, House of Representatives, Washington, DC.

Dear Mr. Chairman: During the Subcommittee's session to mark up legislation concerning animal patents, the Subcommittee considered and rejected Mr. Rose's proposed moratorium on patenting animals, both as a separate proposal and as an amendment to H.R. 4970, your proposal that we commented on earlier. Inasmuch as this moratorium may be proposed again during consideration by the full Committee, we would like to take this opportunity to reiterate our strong opposition to establishing a moratorium in any form.

In 1988, sales revenues for the biotechnology industry are estimated at $900 million, up from $60 million in 1984. By 2000, annual revenues are roughly estimated to be between $15 and $40 billion. At present, U.S. firms are the leaders in this area of technology and create new products and markets both here and abroad. This leadership, however, is challenged by the Japanese who have targeted it as a major growth sector and the Europeans who have invested heavily in creation and development of biotechnological inventions.

The availability of patent protection will be a key factor for U.S. companies maintaining leadership in the global arena. While the lack of patent protection in the U.S. will not eliminate research and development in the biotechnology area, a moratorium will discourage and decrease capital investment in competitive research

78   and development. This will particularly hurt innovative small businesses.

Internationally, only a few countries provide patent protection for man-made plants and animals. Unless patent protection is made available throughout the world, foreign competitors will be able to copy innovative products created by U.S. firms without having to undertake expensive research and without compensating our companies, as our competitors do now in the pharmaceutical and agrichemical areas. Our negotiators in the Uruguay Round and in the World Intellectual Property Organization are trying to correct these shortcomings. However, enactment of a moratorium would completely undercut their ability to achieve results. Not only the biotechnology industry, but other industries such as the pharmaceutical and agrichemical industries will suffer.

Research in the biotechnology area has the potential of providing great benefits to the human race through new methods for controlling disease and through more efficient plant and animal strains. We recognize that it may also raise environmental and ethical issues. While it is entirely appropriate for the Congress to consider these issues and to regulate this area of technology, such regulation is more appropriately carried out by agencies such as the Food and Drug Administration, the Environmental Protection Agency, the U.S. Department of Agriculture, the National Institutes of Health, or the National Science Foundation.

Such regulation should not be affected through a moratorium on issuing patents. One purpose of the patent system is to publicize innovative activity so that society is informed. A moratorium would encourage inventors in this area to keep their activities secret. It may even make it more difficult to regulate their activities where there are legitimate environmental or safety concerns.

A moratorium is simply not in the national interest. It would slow down the development of new methods for treating diseases and for increasing the food supply that will benefit our society. It would substantially harm the competitive position of U.S. industry in this area, and it would encourage secret research.

The Office of Management and Budget has advised us that there is no objection to the submission of this report from the standpoint of the Administration's program.

Sincerely,

ROBERT H. BRUMLEY,
General Counsel.

EXECUTIVE OFFICE OF THE PRESIDENT,
OFFICE OF SCIENCE AND TECHNOLOGY POLICY,
Washington, DC, August 1, 1988.

Hon. PETER W. RODINO, Jr.,
Chairman, House Judiciary Committee, House of Representatives, Washington, DC.

DEAR MR. CHAIRMAN: I would like to forward my views to you regarding H.R. 4970, the "Transgenic Animal Patent Reform Act." The assumption contained in the bill that genetically altered animals meet the requirements for the granting of patents is of great

importance to the United States in developing a competitive posi-   79
tion for new and innovative technologies in the world market
place. Extension of patent protection to transgenic animals is a logical and consistent step in administering patent law.

Animal biotechnology will contribute substantial benefits to
health and agriculture by providing models for research on human
diseases, genetically improved farm animals, and animals genetically modified to produce pharmaceutical products. The economic
benefits, also, of this technology have considerable potential that
will be lost to the United States if it is not protected. Ten countries
now permit animal patents, including Japan and Canada, while another 53 have not prohibited the granting of patents.

I am deeply concerned that a moratorium on animal patents may
be introduced as an amendment to H.R. 4970 at the hearings.
Patent protection is essential to maintain U.S. advances in animal
biotechnology and to encourage investment in this highly competitive area. Any attempt to prevent the full protection of innovative
advances in biotechnology is not in the best interests of the United
States.

Opposition to the granting of animal patents appears, in most instances, to be based on either the perceived need for animal regulation or the desire to stop all research using animals. The moratorium on animal patents, however, would not satisfy these objectives.
Patents are designed as a means of promoting public disclosure and
carry no approval of the invention. By not issuing patents, dissemination of both information and animals could be sharply curtailed.
This could result in a negative impact on research and increased
secrecy of the innovative methods and animals being developed,
making regulation more difficult.

In conclusion, I strongly urge you to support passage of this or
other legislation that provides patent protection for genetically altered animals and to strongly oppose any moratorium. I look forward to continuing to work with you to ensure that the highest
quality science and innovative research is conducted in the interest
of the United States.

    Sincerely,

WILLIAM R. GRAHAM,
Director.

XVI. ADDITIONAL VIEWS OF CARLOS J. MOORHEAD

I support the enactment of H.R. 4970. The Committee worked long and hard on the drafting of this complicated legislation. However, I am concerned that we may have gone too far in drafting the "farmers exemption." I can support in principle a limited exemption for farmers, but I believe the provision contained in H.R. 4970 is too broad. It is important to preserve the economic incentive for the biotech industry to develop genetically improved animals for farmers. If a farmer can purchase a single transgenic animal and then reproduce and sell that animal in perpetuity then we may well have diminished the value of patents for farm animals and established a precedent for weakening other parts of our patent law.

An exemption for farmers should be limited to use and sale for non-reproductive purposes of the first generation offspring of lawfully purchased, patented animals and should contain safeguards against diversion to reproductive use.

Aside from the broad "farmers exemption", H.R. 4970 is a good bill. Our technology is such that we can create things never before thought possible. In so doing we are advancing through uncharted waters. I understand why animal rights groups are concerned, they do not want to see more abuse and misuse directed toward animals. Although there is no indication that there will be any more abuse towards animals, however, we can't guarantee that. I also understand the concern of our church groups. They too are concerned with where this type of research may lead. But even the church groups are hard pressed to give reasons for their opposition. We are tinkering with the very concept of creation. And to be honest, that makes me a little nervous too. However, if we were to ban this research, if we were to declare a moratorium, I don't believe it would stop it because this research is worldwide. All we would accomplish is to make such development more difficult in this country and hurt our industry and put them at a serious disadvantage.

Our hearings and research have not produced any information that would indicate that this type of research and experimentation is dangerous, or that it's unethical or evil. That's not to say that some day it might take a turn in the wrong direction. Congress has the ability to monitor research and development in this area and as soon as we detect abuse we can move in and remedy the situation—What we are talking about here is genetically improved farm animals for food and genetically altered laboratory animals for research and treatment of human diseases. In the area of human medicine, the goal is the development of model animals for pharmaceuticals and medical research. For example, a Japanese company has genetically engineered silkworms to produce a hepatitis vaccine. American scientists are presently engineering strains of laboratory mice that can be affected with the AIDS virus, so that cures for the disease can be tested in mice, instead of primates because

(80)

chimps and humans are the only known species that are suscepti- 81
ble to AIDS. On April 12, 1988, the U.S. Patent Office awarded
Harvard University a patent for a genetically engineered mouse,
the first patent ever for an animal. The Harvard research was financed by the DuPont Company, who hold the licensing rights for
the patent. This special mouse would involve inserting a gene from
another animal into the house embryo in order to give the mouse
characteristics that mice don't naturally have. These mice are extremely sensitive to cancer causing chemicals and will develop
tumors quickly if exposed to even small amounts. This research is
thought to be extremely helpful in early detection of breast cancer
in women. In the food area, research is directed at producing
leaner meat, more productive cows, and disease resistant animals.
The same type of gains that breeders have been working on for
10,000 years.

Improved source of food and medical research to combat the
human hunger and disease in the world are so important, I think it
would be a mistake for Congress to declare a moratorium on such a
vitally important area of research. If we are ever to find the cure
for cancer and other dreaded diseases we must support this research.

CARLOS J. MOORHEAD.

O

DEPARTMENT OF COMMERCE*

Patent and Trademark Office

37 CFR Part 1

[Docket No. 70635–7135]

Deposit of Biological Materials for Patent Purposes

AGENCY: Patent and Trademark Office, Commerce.

ACTION: Advance notice of proposed rulemaking.

SUMMARY: This advanced notice of proposed rulemaking sets forth proposed rules and guidelines that the Patent and Trademark Office (PTO) is considering to govern the deposit of biological materials for patent purposes.

Every patent must contain a written description of the invention adequate to instruct a person skilled in the art to which the invention pertains how to make and use the invention. In certain instances, such as with some biotechnological inventions, the written description of the invention may not in itself be adequate to permit reproduction of the invention. In these cases, the written description must be supplemented by a deposit of the biological material which constitutes the invention or on which the invention depends if the biological material is not otherwise known and readily available to those skilled in the art. The deposited material becomes unconditionally available to the public at the time the patent is granted.

The rules being considered for proposal by the PTO prescribe the conditions under which a deposit must be made, the kinds of materials that may be deposited, the type of depository which is acceptable to the Office, the time for making an original deposit, the procedures and obligations applicable to the making and maintaining of a deposit and its possible replacement, the term of a deposit and other matters relating to the deposit of a biological material. In general, the rules being considered by the PTO would continue and clarify both long-standing practices of the Patent and Trademark Office and judicially developed principles of patent law. The explanations associated with the rules that are ultimately adopted along with the substantive content of the comments and responses will be incorporated into a set of guidelines that will be published in the Manual of Patent Examining Procedure.

In response to a draft policy statement on the deposit of biological materials for patent purposes, which was circulated among interested bar and industry groups and published in the BNA-Patent, Trademark and Copyright Journal on May 22, 1986, the PTO received twenty-five (25) written comments directed to that draft statement. This advance notice addresses the comments received. Interested persons are invited to comment on the rules being considered for proposal. A proposed rulemaking could be made as early as January 1988. A hearing could be held as early as March 1988.

DATE: Comments must be received on or before November 30, 1987 to insure consideration.

ADDRESS: Address written comments to: Commissioner of Patents and Trademarks, Box 4, Washington, DC 20231.

Mark to the attention of Stanley D. Schlosser (703) 557–3065. All comments received will be publicly available for inspection in the PTO in

---

* This article appeared first in the Federal Register Vol. 52 No. 174, Wednesday September 9 1987

room 11C28, Crystal Plaza Building 3 (2021 Jefferson Davis Highway, Arlington, Virginia).

FOR FURTHER INFORMATION CONTACT: Mr. Stanley D. Schlosser by telephone at (703) 557–3065.

SUPPLEMENTARY INFORMATION: An applicant for a patent involving biological material must meet the same requirements for disclosing the invention as apply to other kinds of technology. These requirements are set forth in the first paragraph of § 112 of the patent law (Title 35, United States Code). The invention must be described in such full, clear, concise and exact terms as to enable a person skilled in the relevant technology to make and use the invention. The best mode contemplated by the inventor for carrying out the invention must also be disclosed. The statutory requirements for claiming inventions set forth in the second paragraph of 35 U.S.C. 112 also apply to inventions involving biological material. That is, claims must particularly point out and distinctly claim that which applicants for patent regard as their invention.

Where the invention involves a biological material and words alone are not sufficient to describe the invention adequately to meet the requirements of 35 U.S.C. 112, the required biological material completing the written description must either already be known and readily available and likely to continue to be available or be deposited into a suitable depository. Samples of the deposited material must be publicly and unconditionally available upon issuance of the patent. The deposit will be considered part of the patent disclosure and taken into account in determining the scope of the invention and related questions of infringement. As indicated above, the requirement for making a deposit only applies in situations where the biological material is essential to a complete disclosure and either is not known and readily available to the public, or cannot be readily produced from publicly available material according to the information contained in the patent.

A new chapter of rules of practice devoted exclusively to biological inventions, entitled "Deposit of Biological Materials for Patent Purposes", would be added, beginning with proposed new rule 1.200. This new chapter would specifically incorporate into patent practice judicially developed principles applicable to the deposit of biological materials and would be consistent with the duties and responsibilities of the United States as a signatory country to the Budapest Treaty on the International Recognition of the Deposit of Microorganisms for the Purposes of Patent Procedure. It must be recognized, however, that a comprehensive body of patent law has not yet been developed by the courts dealing with the treatment of inventions relating to biological material. In situations where the courts have not provided specific guidance, appropriate rules and procedures are extracted or implied as far as possible from available decisions and existing practices.

The rules being considered for proposal are intended to apply to patent rights pursued under section 101 of the patent law (Title 35, United States Code). Patent applications filed under the Plant Patent Act (35 U.S.C. 161–164) would be unaffected by this advanced notice. However, comments are solicited on the question of whether the Office should consider requiring a deposit of plants in appropriate circumstances where it is clear that a deposit is possible and is necessary to complete the description of an invention under 35 U.S.C. 162, first paragraph.

New rule 1.200 would be proposed to define the nature of biological material that falls within the scope of the rules. The definition is not intended to provide an exhaustive list of materials which may be deposited in accordance with these procedures. Rather, the need for a deposit and the types of material which must be deposited will be developed through experience and judicial decisions. Meanwhile, some guidelines can be provided.

First, biological material includes material that is capable of self-replication, either directly or after insertion into a host. Assuming the continued viability of the samples deposited, this should provide a reproducible supply of the biological material for the term of the deposit.

Chemical compounds, no matter how important or defined their biological activity, are not regarded as biological material within the scope of these regulations. Chemical compounds are capable of description at least through the identification of starting materials and explanation of appropriate procedures used in making the compounds. It must not require undue experimentation in order to make or use the chemical compound from the written description in the patent application. Thus, materials such as proteins, enzymes, or other complex organic materials need not be deposited where the written description alone is adequate to enable those skilled in the art to make and use the claimed invention.

Plant material must be deposited when the patent application is filed outside the Plant Patent Act if needed to meet the requirements of 35 U.S.C. 112. As with other biological material, the deposit of plant material together with the written specification must enable those skilled in the art to make and use the claimed invention. Thus, if a plant itself is claimed, deposit of plant cells can be accepted only if the deposited cells will develop into the plant for which a patent is sought through the exercise of procedures either known in the art or taught in the application disclosure. Seeds may be deposited, but must be deposited in sufficient quantity to insure an adequate and timely supply once a patent is granted. The PTO solicits comments on the setting of an appropriate minimum number of seeds to ensure availability of the seed through the enforceable life of the patent. The replacement provisions of proposed rule 1.204 would also apply to replenishing the supply of seeds but may require special provisions because of the time required to provide new seeds—e.g. the replacement provision could be coupled with a terminal disclaimer provision for appropriate reasons. If a hybrid variety is claimed, the PTO will take a position that applicant must deposit the parent lines of the hybrid variety unless applicant is able to establish that propagation of the variety can be achieved by micropropagation or other techniques from the hybridized seed or plants grown from such seed. In the latter case, the deposit of the hybrid seed itself would make an adequate deposit.

While the proposed rules under consideration would be applicable to multicellular living organisms other than plants, including animals, it is anticipated that inventions relating to the development of animals having new and otherwise patentable characteristics will rely on the identification and description of a known and readily available animal that will be treated in a reproducible process to obtain the new animal variety. The PTO is presently not aware of any organization that is willing and able to undertake the responsibility of a suitable depository for live animals.

Rule 1.201 would be proposed to provide an operative definition of when a deposit is required and also define when a biological material would be considered to be known and readily available to the public so that a separate deposit would not be required. The third paragraph of this rule would provide that there is no presumption that a specific biological material is required for the practice of an invention simply because it is mentioned in an application disclosure. The need to make a deposit of a biological material in accordance with these rules is necessitated only where the biological material is essential to meet one or more of the requirements of 35 U.S.C. 112 and is not known and readily available and cannot be obtained through procedures known in the art or described in the application from known and readily available materials.

If a biological material is known and readily available at the time the patent is granted, and there is no reasonable basis to believe that the biological material will cease to be available during the life of the patent, no requirement for a separate deposit would be made.

While it is not possible to list all circumstances under which a biological material may be considered to be known and readily available to the public, it is clear that the written description in the specification should be sufficient to allow one of ordinary skill in the art to identify and to obtain the known and readily available material. The present commercial availability of the biological material through normal commercial suppliers, particularly suppliers not under the control of those relying on the availability of the biological material, would make the material known and readily available. The mere fact that the biological material is commercially available only through the patent holder or the patent holder's agents or assigns shall not by itself justify a finding of non-availability, absent a reason to believe that access to the biological material would later be improperly restricted. Since the public has a continuing interest in the availability of information and materials necessary to make and use an invention claimed in a patent, regardless of the patent holder's interest, actual distribution of the biological matter in the marketplace may be required if commercial availability is to be relied on to establish that a specific biological material is known and readily available to the public.

Evidence that a biological material is known and readily available may also take the form of a reference in printed publications or a declaration of accessibility by those working in the field to which the invention relates which establishes wide distribution and ready availability of the biological material. The probative value of this type of evidence will depend on whether the evidence establishes that the biological materials are known and accessible without restriction to those who desire to obtain and test the biological material.

Evidence that a biological material is known and readily available may take the form of a statement showing that it is readily identifiable and available in nature in useful form or that it is available in nature coupled with the existence of a reliable screening test or procedure defined in the specification disclosure or known to those skilled in the art that could be used to isolate the required biological material with reasonable predictability from an identified genus of biological material. See *Tabuchi v. Nubel*, 194 USPQ 521 (CCPA 1977). A deposit made of a biological material that was known and accessible without restriction to those who desired to obtain and test the biological material would also satisfy the definition of being known and readily available to the public. However, since a mere reference to a biological material deposit in a patent would not necessarily mean that it was accessible without restriction to the public the burden would be on the applicant to establish its ready availability without restriction as through a statement from the depository.

New rule 1.202 would be proposed to define an acceptable depository for the deposit of biological materials for patent purposes for applications before the United States Patent and Trademark Office. This rule states that a deposit may be made either in an International Depositary Authority (IDA) as established under the Budapest Treaty or a depository recognized to be suitable by the Patent and Trademark Office. The depository may be domestic or foreign to the United States, public or private. While it would be administratively convenient for the Patent and Trademark Office to limit acceptable depositories to an IDA, such a restricted policy would not provide a patent applicant with the type of flexibility and availability necessary in the event no available IDA would accept a deposit of a particular biological material. Nevertheless, a depository other than an IDA would be called upon to essentially establish compliance with the administrative and technical requirements set forth in the Budapest Treaty for IDAs in order to establish suitability of the depository

to the Office. While there is a desire to provide flexibility to a patent applicant in selecting an appropriate depository, these guidelines are not intended to permit each patent applicant to become its own depository since both the patent owner and the public have an interest in the continued availability and accessibility of the deposit during the enforceable life of a patent and the public has a continuing interest in its availability when the patent is no longer enforceable.

Paragraph (c) of new rule 1.202 indicates that the Office will recognize the transfer of a sample to a suitable depository from a depository which either defaults or discontinues the performance of any of the tasks it should perform. Where such a transfer takes place after a patent issues, a suitable Certificate of Correction would be acceptable to identify the new depository and/or accession number. An appropriate amendment to a pending application to identify the new depository and/or accession number would not constitute new matter. Cf. *In re Lundak, 277 USPQ 90 (Fed. Cir. 1985).*

Paragraph (d) of new rule 1.202 sets forth the procedure for notifying the Commissioner of the intent to be recognized as a suitable depository by the Patent and Trademark Office. The depositories recognized as suitable by the Office will be published in the Official Gazette of the Patent and Trademark Office as will the identity of a depository which has defaulted or discontinued its performance under these rules.

New rule 1.203 would be proposed to set forth the time for making an original deposit. An original deposit may be made at any time before the application is filed or during pendency pursuant to a requirement that will be made no later than the date the Notice of

Allowance and Issue Fee Due is mailed. The decision in *Lundak* indicated that a specification disclosure need not be enabling until such time as a patent is granted. Unless the examiner and applicant agree on whether a deposit is required, what must be deposited and the appropriate conditions, the deposit issues will be resolved pursuant to a rejection under 35 U.S.C. 112. The time specified in this particular rule for making a suitable deposit is the last practical moment that the Office can insure that a deposit has been made in accordance with these regulations before a patent is granted. After the issue fee is paid in an application the application undergoes preparation for printing for a period of 8 to 10 weeks so that all the information necessary for printing should be in the application file and should have been approved by the examiner as conforming to these regulations at the time the issue fee is paid. Where a deposit is made after the Notice of Allowance and Issue Fee Due is mailed, applicant would be required to file an amendment under 37 CFR 1.312 to add a description of the accession number and depository together with any required statement.

Unless the regular deposit is made before the effective filing date of an application for patent in the United States, a verified statement will be required from a person in a position to corroborate that the biological material described in the application as filed is the same biological material which is deposited in a suitable depository. The nature of this corroboration will depend on the circumstances in the particular application under consideration including the length of time between the application filing date and the date of deposit.

New rule 1.204 would be proposed to define the circumstances and procedures for replacing a deposit which is necessary for patent purposes. Failure to replace a deposit within three (3) months after learning or receiving notice from a depository that a replacement is needed may cause the application or patent involved to be treated by the PTO as if no deposit were made. The Patent and Trademark Office will apply a rebuttable presumption of an identity between the original and the replaced sample in the event a deposit is replaced where the application or patent making reference to the deposit is relied upon during any Patent and Trademark Office proceeding.

New rule 1.205 would be proposed to define the term of a deposit to be a minimum of 5 years after the most recent request for the furnishing of a sample of the deposited biological material and at least 30 years after the date of deposit. Any deposit which is made pursuant to the Budapest Treaty will be for a term acceptable to the Office. However, where a deposit is not made under the Budapest Treaty, samples must be stored under an agreement that would make them available for at least the term specified in the Budapest Treaty so long as it extended beyond the enforceable life of the patent for which a deposit was made. The enforceable life of a patent includes the original term of seventeen years, shortened by any terminal disclaimer or lengthened by any patent term extension, plus six (6) years to cover the statute of limitations and any additional time beyond this period where the enforceability of the patent remains in litigation.

The period for storing a deposit as literally stated in the Budapest Treaty is likely to cover almost all of the circumstances before the Patent and Trademark Office. However, in the event that the period of storage would expire before the earliest possible expiration date of the enforceable life of the patent, one of the basic intents of Congress to insure that the public can practice the invention claimed in an expired patent may be frustrated, and it is not believed that the period set forth in the Budapest Treaty intended for such a situation to arise. The availability of the deposited biological material which is essential for making and/or using the subject matter claimed in the patent is a legitimate ground for concern on the part of the Patent and Trademark Office. *Ex parte Lundak* (decided August 21, 1984, reversed on other grounds *In re Lundak, 227* USPQ 90 (Fed. Cir. 1985)). The Board of Patent Appeals considered the possibility that an initially enabling disclosure might become non-enabling over a period of time. *In re Metcalfe*, 410 F2d. 1378, 161 USPQ 789 (CCPA 1969). Suggesting that a rule of reason approach similar to that applied by the Court in *Metcalfe* should continue to inhere in the deposit procedure of the Patent and Trademark Office, the Board suggested that it was appropriate to insist that the depository be contractually obligated to maintain the deposit for at least a reasonable time after expiration of the patent rights. In determining whether the period is sufficient to extend beyond the enforceable life of the patent, neither the possibility of patent term extension nor the possibility of protracted litigation will be considered. Where the minimum period of storage would not extend beyond the enforceable life of the patent, as where there is prolonged pendency of an application or continuation or divisional applications are involved, one approach would be to require applicant to undertake to request a sample every five years beyond the 30 years measured from the date of deposit so that the deposit would be stored for a period beyond the

enforceable life of the patent.

A non-viable deposit cannot be relied upon to supplement a written description in a patent application. Experience has shown that as many as 10% of the deposits made with American Type Culture Collection (ATCC) on which a viability test was conducted were not viable when received at the depository. The requirement for verification of the viability of deposits is consistent with the Budapest Treaty and is a subject of proposed new rule 1.206.

The viability of a deposit made under the Budapest Treaty is a requirement. Thus, a mere statement by applicant, an authorized representative of applicant or assignee that the deposit has been accepted under the Budapest Treaty would satisfy this rule. Otherwise, viability may be tested by the depository or any other entity provided that the material tested is received from the depository. The viability test must conclude that the deposited biological material is capable of reproduction directly or indirectly and no evidence will be required to satisfy the deposit requirement relative to the ability of the deposited material to perform any function described in the application. However, as with any other issue of description or enablement, if the examiner has evidence or reason to question the objective statements made in the application, applicants may be required to demonstrate that the deposited biological material will perform in the manner described.

A viability statement for each deposit which is not made under the Budapest Treaty must be filed in the patent application and contain the information identified in paragraph (b) of proposed new rule 1.206. The examiner shall not question the conclusion in a viability statement issued by a depository recognized under either proposed new rule 1.202 (a) or (b). If the viability test indicates that the deposit is not viable upon receipt, or the examiner cannot for scientific or other valid reasons accept a statement of viability received from the applicant, the examiner shall so notify the applicant stating the reasons for not accepting the statement and proceed with the examination process as if no deposit had been made.

New rule 1.207 would be proposed to address the conditions under which a deposit must be made in order to satisfy access to the deposit. First, access during the pendency of an application to a deposit must be available to one determined by the Commissioner to be entitled thereto under 37 CFR 1.14 and 35 U.S.C. 122. A deposit pursuant to the Budapest Treaty meets this requirement. Secondly, the deposit must be made under conditions that all restrictions on the availability to the public of the deposited biological material will be irrevocably removed upon the granting of the patent. Conditions on the release of a deposited biological material such as identifying the ultimate recipient of the material, or a provision on the further transfer of the material, or any other stipulation that acts as a precondition to the release of the biological material referenced in an issued patent will be considered to be a prohibited restriction on the availability to the public of the biological material so deposited. The depository may be asked to provide to the depositor such information as the identity of sample recipients but not as a precondition to release after the patent is granted.

Since the mere description of a deposit or identity of a deposit in a patent specification is not necessarily an indication that a requirement for deposit or compliance with these rules has been made, the Office will certify whether a deposit was stated as having been made under conditions which make it available to the public provided the request contains the information set forth in Paragraph (c) of proposed new rule 1.207.

New rule 1.208 would be proposed to set forth the procedures which would be followed by an examiner once the examiner determines that a specific biological material is both essential to make and use the claimed invention and is not known and readily available within the meaning of rule 1.201(b). It is only when the examiner has made these determinations based on the record in the application being considered that the need for a deposit of the identified biological material must be considered. A deposit accepted by an IDA under the Budapest Treaty shall be accepted for patent purposes by the PTO if additional statements are made that all restrictions on the availability to the public of the deposited material will be irrevocably removed upon the granting of the patent, and the deposit will be replaced if viable samples cannot be dispensed by the depository.

A deposit under the Budapest Treaty would mean that a viable deposit has been made (Budapest Rule 10) in an acceptable depository (IDA) for a period of five years after the most recent request and at least 30 years from the date of deposit (Budapest Rule 9) under conditions that access to the deposit will be available during pendency of the patent application to one determined by the Commissioner to be entitled thereto under 37 CFR 1.14 and 35 U.S.C. 122 (Budapest Rule 11.1). Assurance of reasonably permanent availability of the deposited material through the depository is reasonably assured through the deposit of a viable culture under the Budapest Treaty and the requirement to make a new deposit in § 1.204(a). It is sufficient if a written statement is made by applicant, an attorney or agent prosecuting the application or a person representing the assignee that a deposit has been accepted by an IDA under the Budapest Treaty under conditions that all restrictions on the availability to the public of the deposit will be irrevocably removed upon the granting of the patent. A suitable statement would be as follows:

(1) I am (relationship to application)
(2) Viable samples of—
Material:
Accesssion Number:
Deposit Date:
were deposited and will be maintained with
(3) (Name and Address of Depository)
(4) Under terms which are in accordance with the provisions of the Budapest Treaty.
(5) Upon issuance of a patent on this application, all restrictions on the availability of the deposited material to the public will be irrevocably removed.

Date _____
Name _____

If the examiner determines that a deposit is required and has not been made in compliance with these rules, the examiner shall reject all the affected claims in the application under the appropriate provision of 35 U.S.C. 112, explaining why a deposit is needed or why a deposit which was made cannot be accepted for patent purposes. Although the Court in *Lundak* indicated that the enablement requirement of 35 U.S.C. 112 need not be satisfied until the patent issues, the only way the Office can efficiently and effectively address the deposit issue is during the examination of the application. After the examiner has determined that a deposit is required, and until a deposit in accordance with

these rules is made, or until the Office is assured in writing that a deposit in accordance with these rules will be made up to and including the date the issue fee is paid, or the examiner is convinced that a deposit is not required under the circumstances of the application being considered, the rejection will be made and maintained by the examiner. Written assurance may take the form that an identified specimen will be deposited and maintained in an IDA under the Budapest Treaty before the issue fee is paid under conditions that all restrictions on the availability to the public of the deposited material will be irrevocably removed upon the granting of the patent, or any other specific assurance that the examiner can recognize and accept that there are no outstanding issues to be resolved on the deposit question.

In the circumstances where the Office has received written assurance that an acceptable deposit will be made before or on the date of payment of the issue fee, and there are no other outstanding matters to be considered relative to the patentability of the claims, the Office will mail to the applicant a Notice of Allowance and Issue Fee Due together with a requirement that the required deposit be made within three (3) months. The period for satisfying the requirement for deposit will be extendable under 37 CFR 1.136(a), as is the case with a requirement for drawing corrections made at the time the Notice of Allowance and Issue Fee Due is mailed. In appropriate circumstances, relief also may be available under 37 CFR 1.136(b) if sufficient cause is shown for an extension of time in order to make the appropriate deposit. Sufficient cause would be decided by the appropriate Group Director. Failure to make the required deposit in accordance with the requirement will result in abandonment of the application for failure to prosecute. Since the opportunity exists to request extensions of time under 37 CFR 1.136 to make a viable deposit, no application should go abandoned for failure to make a viable deposit. However, the Office reserves the right to require the filing of a terminal disclaimer where the time required to make a viable deposit unreasonably delays the issuance of a patent.

The contents of the specification regarding any deposit made are specified in new rule 1.208(d). In addition to such identifying criteria as accession number for the deposit and the name and address of the depository, the specification should include the date of deposit (i.e. the date from which the term of deposit specified in new rule 1.205 is to be measured) and a taxonomic description of the deposit. This written description is that required by 35 U.S.C. 112, first paragraph and should be sufficient to characterize and distinguish the biological material deposited. This written description will serve to inform the public of the essential characteristics of the deposited material once the patent is granted, and will facilitate the examination process which necessarily involves comparisons with prior art biological material.

Other Considerations

The rule change being considered for proposal is in conformity with the requirements of the Regulatory Flexibility Act (Pub. L. 96–354), Executive Order 12291 and the Paperwork Reduction Act of 1980, 44 U.S.C. 3501 et seq.

The rule changes being considered for proposal are not expected to have a significant adverse economic impact on a substantial number of small entities (Regulatory Flexibility Act, Pub. L. 96–354). The proposed deposit practice will not impose extra work on patent applicants (whether small or large businesses or individuals).

The Patent and Trademark Office has determined that this rule change being considered for proposal is not a major rule under Executive Order 12291. The annual effect on the economy will be less than $100 million. There will be no major increases in costs or prices for consumers, individual industries, Federal, State or local government agencies, or geographic regions. There will be no adverse effects on competition, employment, investment, productivity, innovation, or on the ability of United States based enterprises to compete with foreign-based enterprises in domestic or export markets.

Any information collection requirements that may be contained in the proposed rulemaking resulting from proceedings under this advance notice will be submitted for OMB approval at the time the proposed rulemaking is announced.

List of Subjects in 37 CFR Part 1

Administrative practice and procedure, Courts, Inventions and patents.

For the reasons set out, 37 CFR Part 1 is being considered for proposed amendment as follows:

PART 1—RULES OF PRACTICE IN PATENT CASES

1. The authority citation for 37 CFR Part 1 would continue to read as follows:

Authority: 35 U.S.C. 6 unless otherwise noted.

2. Centered heading and new §§ 1.200 to 1.208 are added as set forth below:

*   *   *

Deposit of Biological Material

Deposit of Biological Material

§ 1.200   Biological material.

For the purposes of these regulations pertaining to the deposit of biological material for patent purposes, the term biological material shall include material that is capable of self-replication either directly or after insertion into a host. Representative examples include bacteria, fungi including yeast, algae, protozoa, cell lines, plant tissue cells and seeds. Viruses, vectors, cell organelles and other non-living material existing in and reproducible from a living cell may be deposited by deposit of the host cell capable of reproducing the non-living material. Materials analogous to conventional chemical compounds such as proteins and enzymes are not subject to these regulations.

§ 1.201   Need to make a deposit.

(a) Where a claimed invention is, or relies on, a biological material, the requirements of the first and second paragraphs of 35 U.S.C. 112 apply. Applicant is required to comply with these requirements in the written description of the invention, which may include reference to known and readily available biological material. If the written description does not meet the requirements of 35 U.S.C. 112, the specification may be supplemented by a deposit of samples of the biological material necessary to meet those requirements in a depository and under conditions complying with these regulations.

(b) Biological material need not be deposited if it is known and readily available to the public or can be made or isolated in a reproducible manner from known and readily available materials. Biological material will be considered to be known and readily available to the public if samples of the biological material are known and accessible without restriction to those who desire to obtain and test the biological material. Samples will be considered to be accessible even though some requirement of law or regulation of the United States or of the country in which the depository institution is located permits access to the material only under conditions imposed for safety, public health or similar reasons.

(c) The reference to a specific organism or other biological material in a specification disclosure does not create any presumption that the specific material is necessary to satisfy one or more requirements of 35 U.S.C. 112 or that a deposit in accordance with these regulations is required.

§ 1.202   Acceptable depository.

(a) A deposit may be made in any International Depositary Authority (IDA) as established under the Budapest Treaty on the International Recognition of the Deposit of Microorganisms for the Purposes of Patent Procedure.

(b) A deposit may be made in any depository recognized to be suitable by the Office. Suitability will be determined by the Commissioner on the basis of the administrative and technical competence, and agreement of the depository to comply with the terms and conditions applicable to deposits for patent purposes. The Commissioner may seek the advice of impartial consultants from the biotechnology industry on the suitability of a depository. The depository must:

(1) Have a continuous existence;

(2) Exist independent of the control of the depositor;

(3) Possess the staff and facilities sufficient to enable it to examine the viability of a deposit and store it in a manner which ensures that it is kept viable and uncontaminated;

(4) Provide for sufficient safety measures to minimize the risk of losing biological material deposited with it;

(5) Be impartial and objective; and

(6) Furnish samples of the deposited material in an expeditious and proper manner.

(c) If any depository under (a) or (b) defaults or discontinues the performance of any of the tasks it should perform, the Office will recognize as a substitute in any pending application or patent a viable deposit made with an IDA or depository recognized to be suitable by the Office which is transferred to said depository from the defaulting depository in the manner required for replacing a deposit under § 1.204.

(d) A depository seeking status under paragraph (b) of this section must direct a communication to the Commissioner which shall:

(1) Indicate the name and address of the depository to which the communication relates;

(2) Contain detailed information as to the capacity of the depository to comply with the requirements of paragraph (b) of this section, including information on its legal status, scientific standing, staff and facilities;

(3) Indicate that the depository intends to be available, for the purposes

of deposit, to any depositor under these same conditions;

(4) Where the depository intends to accept for deposit only certain kinds of biological material, specify such kinds;

(5) Indicate the amount of any fees that the said depository will, upon acquiring the status of suitable depository under paragraph (b) of this section, charge for storage, viability statements and furnishing of samples of the deposit.

(e) Once a depository is recognized to be suitable by the Commissioner or has defaulted or discontinued its performance under this section, notice thereof will be published in the Official Gazette of the Patent and Trademark Office.

§ 1.203 Time of making an original deposit.

(a) An original deposit may be made at any time before filing an application for patent or during pendency of the application for patent pursuant to a requirement that will be made by the examiner no later than the date the Notice of Allowance and Issue Fee Due is mailed.

(b) When the original deposit is made in a depository defined in §§ 1.202 (a) or (b) after the effective filing date of an application for patent, a verified statement will be required from a person in a position to corroborate the fact that the biological material described in the application as filed is the same biological material which is deposited in the depository defined in §§ 1.202 (a) or (b).

§ 1.204 Replacement of deposit.

(a) Where a depository possessing the original deposit cannot furnish samples of the deposit for any reason, the depository shall, promptly after having noted its inability to furnish samples, notify the depositor of such inability, indicating the cause thereof, and the depositor shall be required to make a new deposit of the biological material which was originally deposited within three months of receiving notification that the depository cannot furnish samples. The replacement shall be made in the same depository as the original deposit except:

(1) Where the original depository has lost it status under §§ 1.202 (a) or (b) or no longer carries out its obligations applicable to the involved deposit; or

(2) Where the depository for health or other legitimate reasons is unable to provide samples to requesters outside of the jurisdiction where the depository is located.

(b) An applicant or patent owner shall notify the Office in writing as soon as reasonably possible after a replacement deposit is made in each application or patent affected. This notification shall state the name and address of the depository, the accession number for the deposit, the date of making the deposit, the results of a viability test (as provided for in § 1.206), the reason for making the replacement deposit, and a statement that the replacement deposit is to the best of the depositor's knowledge identical to the original deposit. The notification shall be placed in each application or patent file.

(c) A depositor's failure to replace a deposit within three months after learning or after receiving written notice from a depository that a replacement is needed may cause the application or patent involved to be treated in any Office proceeding as if no deposit were made.

(d) In the event a deposit is replaced, the PTO will apply a rebuttable presumption of an identity between the original and the replaced sample where the application or patent making reference to the deposit is relied upon during any Office proceeding.

§ 1.205 Term of deposit.

A deposit shall be made for a term of at least thirty (30) years after the date of a viable deposit and at least five (5) years after the most recent request for the furnishing of a sample of the deposited biological material was received by the depository. In any case, samples must be stored under agreements that would make them available beyond the enforceable life of the patent for which the deposit was made.

§ 1.206 Viability of deposit.

(a) A deposit of biological material must be viable at the time of deposit and during the term of deposit. Viability may be tested by the depository or by another provided the material tested is received from the depository. The test must conclude only that the deposited material is capable of reproduction. No evidence is necessarily required relative to the ability of the deposited material to perform by function described in the patent application.

(b) A viability statement for each deposit not made under the Budapest Treaty must be filed in the application and must contain:

(1) Name and address of the depository;

(2) Name and address of the depositor;

(3) The date of deposit;

(4) The identity of the deposit and the accession number given by the depository;

(5) The date of the viability test;

(6) The procedures used to obtain a sample if the test is not done by the depository; and

(7) A statement that the deposit is capable of reproduction.

(c) If a viability test indicates that the

279

deposit is not viable upon receipt, or the examiner cannot, for scientific or other valid reasons, accept the statement of viability received from the applicant, the examiner shall proceed as if no deposit has been made. The examiner will accept the conclusion set forth in a viability statement issued by a depository recognized under §§ 1.202 (a) or (b).

§ 1.207   Furnishing of samples.

The deposit must be made under conditions that assure that:

(a) Access to the deposit will be available during pendency of the patent application making reference to the deposit to one determined by the Commissioner to be entitled thereto under § 1.14 and 35 U.S.C. 122, and

(b) All restrictions imposed by the depositor on the availability to the public of the deposited material will be irrevocably removed upon the granting of the patent.

(c) Upon request, the Office will certify whether a deposit has been stated to have been made under conditions which make it available to the public as of the issue date of the patent grant provided the request contains:

(1) The name and address of the depository;

(2) The accession number given to the deposit;

(3) The patent number and issue date of the patent referring to the deposit; and

(4) The name and address of the requesting party.

§ 1.208   Examination procedures.

(a) The examiner shall determine in each application for an invention if a deposit is needed, in case one has not been made, or if a deposit actually made is acceptable for patent purposes. A deposit accepted in any depository under the Budapest Treaty shall be accepted for patent purposes if made under conditions complying with § 1.207(b). If a deposit is required and has not been made in accordance with these regulations, the examiner shall in an Office action reject the affected claims in the application under the appropriate provision of 35 U.S.C. 112, explaining why a deposit is needed and/or why a deposit actually made cannot be accepted.

(b) The applicant shall respond to a rejection under paragraph (a) of this section by—

(1) making an acceptable deposit or assuring the Office in writing that an acceptable deposit will be made on or before the date of payment of the issue fee or;

(2) Establishing that the involved biological material is known and readily available to the public or;

(3) Arguing why a deposit is not required under the circumstances of the application considered.

Other replies to the examiner's action shall be considered non-responsive. The rejection will be repeated until either paragraph (b)(1) or (b)(2) of this section is satisfied or the examiner is convinced that a deposit is not required.

(c) If an application is otherwise in condition for allowance except for the required deposit and the Office has received a written assurance that an acceptable deposit will be made on or before payment of the issue fee, the Office will mail to the applicant a Notice of Allowance and Issue Fee Due together with a requirement that the required deposit be made within three months. The period for satisfying this requirement is extendable under 37 CFR 1.136. Failure to make the required deposit in accordance with this requirement will result in abandonment of the application for failure to prosecute.

(d) For each deposit made pursuant to these regulations, the specification shall contain:

(1) Accession number for the deposit;

(2) Date of the deposit;

(3) Taxonomic description of the deposit; and

(4) Name and address of the depository.

Comments and Responses:

(**Editorial Note.**—These comments and responses will not appear in the Code of Federal Regulations)

The following responses are directed to the comments received in response to the draft policy statement on the deposit of biological materials for patent purposes. The comments are arranged to generally correspond to the order of topics addressed in the draft guidelines.

Comment: The guidelines should make explicit that it is the examiner's, not the applicant's, burden to show that a written description is not adequate to describe the invention as claimed. This has been a real problem in that simply because a microorganism or other biological material is involved in a particular claimed invention, it is automatically assumed that a deposit should be required. This is, of course, quite out of touch with reality especially when it comes to inventions relating to recombinant technology.

Response: This suggestion has been in effect, since the PTO clearly has the initial burden of giving reasons, supported by the record as a whole, as to why the written description is not sufficient to enable one skilled in the art to make and use the claimed invention in the absence of a particular microorganism or other biological material. All assertions that the written

description is not enabling without a deposit must be supported by the examiner with (1) evidence or (2) reasons to support the conclusion of noncompliance. New rule 1.201(c) being considered for proposal also provides explicitly that there is no presumption that a specific material is required simply because it is described in the specification.

Comment: If enablement and description requirements can be met with a written description, is a deposit required solely for compliance with the best mode requirement?

Response: The best mode requirement of the first paragraph of 35 U.S.C. 112 is a separate and distinct requirement from the enabling requirement. In re Newton, 414 F2d 1400, 163 USPQ 34 (CCPA 1969). The best mode requirement is a safeguard against the possible selfish desire on the part of some people to obtain patent protection without making a full disclosure. The requirement does not permit an inventor to disclose only what is known to be the second-best embodiment, retaining the best as a trade secret. The fundamental issue that should be addressed is whether there was evidence to show that the quality of an applicant's best mode disclosure is so poor as to effectively result in concealment. In re Sherwood, 615 F2d 809, 204 USPQ 537 (CCPA 1980). If a deposit is the only way to comply with the best mode requirement then the deposit must be made.

Comment: We regret that the PTO has not attempted to provide some guidance as to the circumstances under which a biotechnology invention will be deemed to be reproducible from the written description alone. One such circumstance would appear to be where sequence data for the transcriptional unit of rDNA vector is available either directly from the specification, or from the published literature.

Response: While such guidance may be of some assistance, it may be of momentary value because of the changing nature and development of technology. In addition, useful guidelines would be difficult in view of the tremendous variety of factual circumstances that play a role in determining whether the claimed invention can be practiced without undue experimentation. Some guidance is available in *Ex Parte Forman*, 230 USPQ 546 (BPAI 1986) where the Board of Patent Appeals and Interferences summarized eight (8) factors to be considered in a determination of "undue experimentation."

Comment: Please consider replacing the word "define" in the phrase "define the metes and bounds of the claimed invention" with the word—support— because applicant should be allowed to select representative biological samples to place on deposit which support rather than define the "metes and bounds" of the claimed invention.

Moreover, the deposited biological sample which applicant demonstrates, by the description in the application, to be operable should be deemed sufficient by the PTO to satisfy the deposit requirement and provide adequate basis for applicant to claim variants of the deposited material. Another comment expressed concern that limiting claims to the deposited material (*Ex parte Jackson*) may become the norm in patent examination practice if such language is included.

Response: Claims are required to set out and circumscribe a particular area with a reasonable degree of precision and particularity. 35 U.S.C. 122, second paragraph. This requirement is separate and distinct from the requirement of the first paragraph of 35 U.S.C. 112 that the specification disclosure enable one skilled in the art to make and use the invention to a degree commensurate in scope with the claims. Under appropriate circumstances, it may be necessary to specially recite and limit the claims to the deposited biological material in order to adequately define the metes and bounds of the claimed invention. *Ex parte* Jackson, 217 USPQ 804 (Bd. App. 1982). However, the mere facts that a claimed invention requires the use of a living organism or that samples of a living organism that may be used in the claimed invention have been deposited are *never alone* sufficient to require applicant to comply with the deposit guidelines or limit any claim to the deposited material.

Comment: There is some interest that the Patent and Trademark Office be requested to print deposit information on the front page of the issued patent—analogous to the cited references rather than buried in the general text.

Response: At the last meeting of the WIPO Permanent Committee on Patent Information, a revised standard was approved recommending use of INID (Internationally agreed Numbers for The Identification of Data) codes to identify bibliographic data on the front page of patent documents. A new INID Code (83) has been approved to identify information concerning the deposit of microorganisms, e.g., under the Budapest Treaty.

The PTO is not considering the publication of deposit information on the front page of an issued patent because of the substantial administrative burden that would be involved for a relatively small number of patents. No compelling need or rationale is apparent that would justify the cost for the rare case where such a format may be more convenient.

Comment: The practice of presenting a microorganism for deposit in connection with a patent application was initially adopted as a means for complying with the requirements of section 112. The PTO's current proposal would make a deposit mandatory under administrative rulemaking, for compliance with the requirements of 35 U.S.C. 112 in an invention which "depends on the use of biological material".

Response: The PTO proposal does not make a deposit mandatory for an invention which depends on the use of biological material. The PTO policy and deposit requirements are intended to provide guidance in those situations when it is determined that a deposit is necessary to satisfy one or more requirements of 35 U.S.C. 112. The proposed rules concern the requirements and procedures for making a suitable deposit if it is determined that a deposit is required before a patent can be granted. The guidelines associated with the proposed rules recognize that the specification may properly rely on information which is publicly available.

Comment: Some recognized culture collections do not make their strains readily available. What can a requester do if it is found that the biological material is not readily available. Most of us do not have access to legal recourse.

Response: The PTO will assume that any deposit made according to these regulations will be readily available upon the granting of the patent. This is a rebuttable presumption that could be overcome only by evidence of the nature which would show that the patent relied upon is inoperative. Since every patent is presumed valid and since that presumption includes the presumption of operability, the burden of proof is high. The PTO does not have the resources to police the depositories such that the depositor must assume the risk that the depository selected will preserve and maintain the deposit made.

Comment: It was suggested that the statement that the availability of the biological material must be such that there is no reasonable basis to question the continued availability of the biological material beyond the enforceable life of a patent was overly stringent. Citing In re Metcalfe, 410 F.2d 1378, 161 USPQ 789 (CCPA 1969).

Response: The suggestion that the proper perspective should be whether there is reasonable basis to believe that the biological material will cease to be available during the life of the patent has been adopted.

Comment: The draft guidelines indicated that a material would be considered to be known and readily available to the public even though some requirement of law or regulation restricted access to material for safety, public health or similar reasons. It has been suggested that the term "national security" be specifically defined in the list of exceptions since this constitutes the basis which precludes making available to the public significant amounts of governmental information. It was further suggested that the phrase "of either of the United States or of the state in which the depositor or the depository institution is located" be added after regulation in the acknowledgment of the fact that biotechnology is an international industry. Finally, it was noted that companies my find it advisable to restrict access even in the absence of any formal legal requirement for product liability reasons so that the PTO should regard more leniently restrictions which are fully imposed for public health reasons even if not required by law or regulation, and particularly if they are required by an insurer.

Response: First, the PTO has not seen fit to add national security as a specific item which would permit restriction on access to a biological material which would still be considered to be known and readily available. It is difficult to determine with any degree of certainty what any country may consider to be national security. Further, an invention which involved national security matters would not be published before the restrictions on access to that invention involving national security were removed.

Secondly, while the international scope of the biotechnology industry is clearly recognized, the proposal to include the country or state in which the depositor is located would appear to be unnecessary so long as the requirement of law or regulation would apply to the depository institution where the deposit is located. Accordingly, the suggestion has been adopted to this extent.

Finally, it is believed inappropriate for the PTO to accept a biological material to be known and readily available to the public on the basis of what some private insurer may require of the depositor. Unless the restriction is based on some requirement of law or regulation which restricts access to the material for safety, public health or similar reasons, the PTO will not consider that a biological material is known and readily available to the public.

Comment: It was suggested that a biological material should not have to be deposited if it could be readily reproduced from materials known and available to the public based on the description of how to make and use

found in the disclosure.

Response: The suggestion has been adopted in the first sentence of new rule 1.201(b) being considered for proposal which includes the statement that the biological material need not be deposited if it can be made or isolated in a reproducible manner from known and readily available material.

Comment: The guidelines had stated that the fact that the biological material had multiple known uses would tend to provide assurance that the required biological material would continue to be available. It was noted that this might be construed to mean that a recitation of multiple uses in applicant's disclosure is evidence that the biological material would be readily available to the public which clearly it is not.

Response: The person making the comment accurately noted that the two have no bearing one to the other. However, if there was evidence that the biological material had been put to use for more than one purpose by a variety of people, it would be considered to constitute at least an indication that the biological material in question was known and accessible to those who desire to obtain at least a sample of the subject biological material. It would have been evidence of distribution in commerce, consistent with the idea that it was known and readily available.

Comment: With respect to biological material that is known and readily available, the initial guidelines indicated that the written description in the specification should contain information on the biological material to the extent available. This, according to the comment, could be construed as requiring an enormous amount of information.

Response: This comment is well taken. Accordingly, new rule 1.201(b) would be proposed to require that the written description of the biological material should be sufficient to allow one of ordinary skill in the art to identify and obtain the publicly available material.

Comment: The initial guidelines stated that material would be considered to be known and readily available if the biological material was known and accessible to those who would desire a sample to practice the invention. The comment indicated that the word "practice" implies a right to utilize the deposited materials and thus the invention. This right does not exist absent a license if the material is protected by a patent. Experimental use is not a right but rather an exception to a finding of infringement and thus subject to different burdens of proof. It was suggested that the word "test" be substituted for practice.

Response: This suggestion would be adopted in new rule 1.201(b) since the concept of whether a biological material is known and readily available to the public is not determined on the basis of whether or not its manufacture, use or sale would infringe an existing patent.

Comment: There is no statutory basis in U.S. law for supporting the position that availability of the biological material must extend beyond the enforceable life of a patent. To require otherwise is to inequitably place a patentee in a position that amounts to guaranteeing a supply of the "manufacturing facilities" to competitors at little or no cost and at a time when the competitors are free to use the deposited material without an accompanying benefit to the ex-patentee.

Response: This provision finds specific basis in the decision of Ex parte Lundak, and is based on one of the basic principles of the patent system—i.e. that a patent is an exclusionary right granted for a "limited" time and that the public is not excluded from practicing the invention once the patent expires. This does not mean that the patentee must be a perpetual supplier of the biological materials that may be necessary to practice the invention. However, it does mean that the patentee should not be permitted to place a limitation on the accessibility of the necessary biological material once the patent expires. As noted by the Court in In re Metcalfe, 410 F2d. 1378, 161 USPQ 789 (CCPA 1969) it is always possible that the practice of a given patented invention may become impossible because an essential material becomes unavailable due to a lack of raw materials, public disaster, or other occurrence not within the control of the patentee. The proposed regulations contemplate that the patentee would not control the availability of the biological material once the patent has expired.

Comment: The phrase "known and readily available' should be in the disjunctive. There is no case regarding regular chemical inventions that chemicals used by an applicant need to be both known and readily available.

Response: The phrase "known and readily available" was selected to indicate public accessibility to those wishing to test the biological material. A material may be known in the sense that its existence has been published, but is not available to those who wish to test that particular known biological material. In addition, a biological material may be available in the sense that those having possession of it would make it available upon request, but no one has been informed of its existence. Consequently, the concept of known and readily available is considered to accurately define the level of public accessibility to the biological material intended.

Comment: An examination of the PTO policy statement on the deposit of biological materials suggests that the only safe procedure for satisfying the requirements of 35 U.S.C. 112 would be to require a deposit or to establish that the biological material is readily available in nature or can be obtained by some type of screening procedure. The other criteria set forth pertaining to "known and readily available to the public" did not appear to have sufficient safeguards for access during the term of the patent and after its expiration date.

Response: While there is clearly an element of risk involved in trying to preserve living matter over an extended period of time even with a deposit, the Office believes that where there is a sufficient indication that the biological material has reached a sufficient level of accessibility and availability for distribution which is intended to be captured by the concept of "known and readily available" the public interest has been served as necessary to support a patent grant. The incentives provided by the patent system should not be constrained by the possibility that a disclosure that was once enabling would become non-enabling over a period of time through no fault of the patentee. *In re Metcalfe.*

Comment: Several people made comments relative to the commercial availability of the biological material being an indicator that the material was known and readily available. Suggestions were made to substitute "applicant or applicant's assignee" for those relying on the availability of the biological material and to clarify the "patent holder's agent".

Response: The PTO does not want to guess or be constrained by any particular business relationship that may be created to control accessibility of the biological material to the public. The concept was intended to embrace the situation where an applicant or a patentee before the Patent and Trademark Office relying on the public availability of the biological material through a commercial supplier is not likely to restrict access once the patent is granted.

Comment: While some characterize the PTO's concern for commercial suppliers under the control of those relying on the availability of the biological material as almost insulting, others indicated that they could appreciate the PTO's concern when the patent holder controls commercial availability. One person suggested that a patent owner who tried to restrict access after a decision was made not to enforce the patent would run the risk that a disgruntled requester would seek treble damages anti-trust action based on patent misuse, or a requester might file a complaint with the FTC or the anti-trust division of the U.S. Department of Justice. Moreover, it was suggested that a disappointed requester could certainly notify the PTO of the incident which might result in a disciplinary proceeding against the patent counsel, and would certainly discredit subsequent attempts by the same patent owner to rely on an allegation of commercial availability. It was also suggested that it would be appropriate for the PTO to suggest one or more means by which a patent owner could provide acceptable assurance that the biological materials would remain available such as by deposit of a performance bond which would be forfeited if the biological material is not provided to a lawful customer upon tender of payment.

Response: The PTO does not have the resources or expertise to engage in the type of enforcement procedures suggested in these comments. Further, there is clearly no evidence at this point in time to provide for the mere possibility that a commercial supplier may be motivated to eliminate or otherwise restrict access to the biological material once the patent is no longer enforceable or a decision is made not to enforce the patent.

The PTO will accept commercial availability as evidence that a biological material is known and readily available only when the evidence is clear and convincing that the public has unrestricted access to the material. A product could be commercially available but only at a price which effectively eliminates its accessibility to those desiring to obtain a sample. The relationship between an applicant relying on a biological material and the commercial supplier relied upon is simply one factor that would be considered in determining whether the biological material was known and readily available. However, the mere fact that the biological material is commercially available only through the patent holder or the patent holder's agents or assigns shall not by itself justify a finding of non-availability, absent reason to believe that access to the biological material would later be improperly restricted.

Comment: Several comments were received directed to the use of printed publications providing evidence that the biological material is known and available to the public. It was suggested that the probative value of this type of evidence should depend not only on the number of publications but also the character and institutional affiliation of the publications. It was also suggested that foreign applicants would rightfully object to consideration of whether the publications are domestic or foreign. One comment stated that the concept of peer review should be eliminated and

that inquiry be made into whether the publication policy of the journal makes references to the availability of cited material, and whether that policy is in fact enforced. Finally, it was indicated that it was impractical to expect an applicant to provide a tally or comprehensive search of technical journals and patent literature to establish availability of biological materials.

Response: The PTO does not believe that it is possible to list all the possible factors that might be considered relevant or how they would be weighed under any particular factual circumstances to determine whether a biological material is known and readily available to the public. However, it is considered appropriate to list exemplary factors that might be considered in determining the probative value of this type of evidence. There was no intent to discriminate between domestic and/or foreign applicants or publications, but the reference to domestic and foreign publications could be an indication of the scope of distribution of the biological material in question. Thus publications in a single country, whether it be domestic or foreign to the United States, would suggest more limited distribution than references and publications of both domestic and foreign origin. Finally, there is no requirement to demonstrate that a biological material is known and readily available by any particular set of facts, but the PTO has provided some guidance in proposed rule 1.201(b) and associated text as to the variety of circumstances that an applicant may use to establish that a biological material is known and readily available to the public.

Comment: The language pertaining to declarations of accessibility which indicate a preference for those who are not members of the same organization as applicants in the application should be deleted because it suggests a higher level of credibility attaches to the declaration of such an individual.

Response: While it is recognized that the declaration executed by any declarant is subject to the same penalties under § 1001 of Title 18 of United States Code, it can be agreed that the evaluation of declarations should be based solely on their merit and not the organizational relationship between the inventor and the declarant. However, the preference was directed not to the credibility of the declarant but whether accessibility was known beyond the confines of the organization of which both the applicant and the declarant were members. The knowledge might be compared to an uncataloged manuscript in a library that was distributed among the staff of an organization which included that library but was unknown to people outside that organization. Again, the mere fact that applicant and declarant were members of the same organization should not by itself justify a finding that the biological material in question is not known and readily available. Other factors such as the nature of the organization, distribution of the biological material, and procedures or mechanisms for access would also be considered.

Comment: The meaning of the term "abundantly" as modifying the availability in nature of the biological material was not understood. It was pointed out that a rare microorganism might be readily obtained if a good screening procedure was available. It was also pointed out that it was not understood what is meant by evidence of being available in nature since a description in the patent of a precise geographic location should be sufficient because this is an instance

when a deposit is not required.

Response: These suggestions have been essentially adopted. As noted in one of the comments, the decision by the PTO Board of Patent Appeals and Interferences (Reinhardt, US Patent 4,548,814) held that a description of the precise geographic location of Marine Tunicates used in the patent was adequate to satisfy the enablement requirement. However, use of the term "readily" to define availability is considered appropriate to define that degree of availability which would be reasonable under the circumstances. For example, when an applicant tried to rely on patent applications which had been opened for public inspection in Rhodesia, Panama and Luxembourg to fulfill the enabling requirement, the Court held that when no guide at all has been given in the application, an applicant must show that anyone skilled in the art would actually possess the requisite knowledge or would reasonably be expected to check the source which the applicant relies upon to complete his disclosure and would be able to locate the information with no more than reasonable diligence. In re *Howarth*, 210 USPQ 689 (CCPA 1981).

Comment: It was suggested that there is no good reason why a previous deposit can be relied upon only when it is referred to in a United States patent or statutory invention registration as opposed to a foreign patent. One person went so far as to suggest that any reference to a microorganism deposited in one of the recognized depositories should be sufficient in and of itself.

Response: Since the arrangement made with the depository is one between the depository and the depositor, the simple deposit of a biological material in a recognized depository is not sufficient in and of itself to satisfy the requirement of the biological material to be known and readily available. However, if the deposit has been accepted under the Budapest Treaty and made under conditions that all restrictions on its accessibility will be irrevocably removed upon the granting of the patent, whether the deposit is referenced in a United States or foreign patent document would not make any difference. However, there may be limitations on release of the biological materials that are permitted in other countries but which are not within the scope of the conditions accepted in the United States once the patent has been granted. Consequently, the mere reference in any document, be it a United States patent or a patent in a country foreign to the United States is not in and of itself sufficient to establish that it is known and readily available unless the deposit has been made under conditions which are consistent with those specified in these proposed rules.

Comment: It would be very helpful if you included a statement to the effect that if a deposit meets the requirement of the Budapest Treaty, the Office will accept the deposit.

Response: An explicit provision to this affect would be included in new rule 1.208(a). It would state that a deposit accepted in any depository under the Budapest Treaty shall be accepted for patent purposes if made under the conditions complying with 1.207(b) – that all restrictions on the availability to the public of the deposited material will be irrevocably removed upon the granting of the patent. The additional requirement of 1.207(b) must be stated since the Budapest Treaty leaves to the national laws the specific provisions to obtain access to a sample after the patent has issued. The requirement to maintain a viable deposit of the biological material

(1.204a) recognizes the public interest in the availability of the information and materials to make and use the claimed invention.

Comment: The inventor of a biological invention should not be hostilely discriminated against by satisfying a higher burden to prove enablement but should instead be treated on the same basis as are all other applicants. The proposed guidelines should allow for and recognize that in many instances a deposit simply is not required.

Response: There was no intent in the proposed guidelines nor in the proposed rules to alter in any way the standard of enablement required by 35 U.S.C. 112, first paragraph. The rules being considered by the PTO specifically indicate that a biological material need not be deposited if the written description is sufficient to meet the requirements of 35 U.S.C. 112 or if the biological material is known and readily available to the public or can be made or isolated in a reproducible manner from known and readily available materials. See new rules 1.202(a) and (b) being considered for proposal. In addition, it is specifically stated that the mere reference to a specific organism for other biological material in a specification disclosure does not create any presumption that the specific material is necessary to satisfy one or more requirements of 35 U.S.C. 112 or that a deposit is required to be made. See new rule 1.201(c) being considered for proposal.

Comment: Requiring that the deposits be made in an IDA is excessively burdensome, particularly to a small inventor and those academic institutions which generate in the course of a typical research program dozens or even hundreds of hybridomas which must then be deposited if the institution is to comply with PTO deposit guidelines. Depositing of biological materials (when required) at any location should be sufficient providing that the averments for appropriate access and supply of viable material can be made. The patentee has the most at stake in insuring that the deposit is maintained and available during the life of the patent. If the deposit is permanently lost, the patent will be lost also. The entire rationale for requiring an independent depositor is to remove the responsibility from the patentee and place it in the hands of an independent third party. If the depository is required to replace a strain if it becomes non-viable, it would appear that double depositing is necessary. The logical thing, according to one comment, is either to have the third party depository entirely responsible for the culture or to permit the depositor to maintain his own cultures.

Response: The concept of an independent depository or an IDA as an acceptable depository is based on the need and desire to ensure the safe and reliable storage of a deposited biological material under circumstances that are free of the opportunity for intentional or negligent handling of the deposited material. The use of an independent depository or an internationally recognized depository will tend to preserve the integrity of the deposit process against those that may accidently alter the deposited material, may wish to tamper with the deposited material or may wish to resume control of its availability when the patent is no longer enforceable, and to preserve the interest of the public in the free access to the biological material for any purpose once the term of the patent expires. Further, while the PTO is constrained to approve independent depositories other than an IDA, the PTO has neither the resources nor

capability to assess the individual capability of any party that wishes to act as its own depository. The rules under consideration are intended to minimize depositories that will be found acceptable.

The concept of having an independent depository in addition to the requirement of the depositor to replace a culture which is no longer viable is based on the premise that the patent owner has an interest in maintaining the accessibility of the deposit during the enforceable life of the patent for its own protection, and has an obligation to the public to ensure access to that deposit during the period of enforceability so that a third party could test the biological material, and availability to the public after the patent expires. A patentee should not be able to intentionally convert a patented biological material to a trade secret merely because it was no longer interested or able to enforce the patent.

Comment: A depository does not normally notify the depositor when his strains are supplied to third parties except under the Budapest Treaty. Does this mean we must now change our policy.

Response: No.

Comment: Several comments were received to the effect that due to the nature of deposits, and the ease with which harmful infringing acts can be practiced following access to deposited material, it is reasonable to require that minimum restrictions be made before a request for access to a deposit is satisfied. Such minimum restrictions should include (1) identification of the ultimate recipient and (2) an averment that the ultimate recipient will not use the deposited materials for any uses which would infringe a valid claim and (3) a prohibition against transfer to third parties. The thrust of these arguments is that a patentee has a definite interest in knowing to whom the deposited material is being released and such restrictions would provide the patentee with some measure of protection against those who would unfairly profit from the required deposit. It was concluded that these provisions would not in any substantive way interfere with the purpose of a deposit under 35 U.S.C. 112 or the public disclosure function served by the patent system.

Response: While the unique nature of a deposit in satisfying the enabling or other requirements of 35 U.S.C. 112 is recognized, every patent is required to place in the hands of those skilled in the art to which the invention pertains the information required to make and use the invention without undue experimentation. The PTO does not restrict or otherwise monitor the sale of other patent documents containing an enabling disclosure nor place any limits on the further disposition of patents that it sells. Consequently, there is no basis in the law for treating a patent directed to an invention requiring the use of a deposited biological material in any manner different from a patent which does not require a deposit. Patents not requiring a deposit may involve subject matter which is just as difficult to detect infringement as it may be where no deposit is required.

The PTO recognizes the unique nature of an invention which requires the deposit of a sample of a biological material as part of the disclosure, particularly as it relates to the attendant risks that the sample may be used in a way or location that would avoid infringement of the patent. The PTO, however, solicits comments on the advisability of and rationale for seeking a provision in the law that would permit the type of restrictions on access to a deposit after the patent issued that

are recommended in the April 8, 1987 WIPO report on the Industrial Property Protection of Biotechnological Inventions. These recommendations, on which we are seeking comment, were as follows:

Samples shall be furnished only if the requesting party has undertaken vis-a-vis the owner of the patent on which the request is based, for the period during which the patent is in force:

(1) Not to make the deposited biological material or any biological material derived therefrom available to any third party;

(ii) To use the deposited biological material or any biological material derived therefrom only for experimental purposes concerning the invention;

(iii) Not to export the deposited biological material or any biological material derived therefrom to any other country or, if the sample was obtained in the country where the depository institution is located and that country is not the country in or for which the patent on which the request was based has been granted, to any other country than the country in or for which the relevant patent has been granted;

(iv) The requesting party shall have the burden of proof concerning compliance with the undertakings referred to in subparagraphs (i–iii); and

(v) For the purposes above, any biological material shall be deemed to be derived from the deposited biological material if it is derived therefrom by culturing or in any other way of replication, provided that the derived matter still exhibits those characteristics of the deposited biological which are essential for the carrying out of the invention.

Comment: The guidelines appear to ignore that the identification of ultimate recipient and limitations on further transfer are required in many cases under the export control laws administered by the Commerce Department. Depositories such as the ATCC regularly apply for licenses before releasing strains. It would appear entirely consistent, therefore, to allow depositors to require that requesters comply with the export control laws since the depository must do so in any event.

Response: The rules being considered by the PTO require only that the depositor make the deposit under such conditions that all restrictions made by the depositor on the availability to the public of the deposited material will be irrevocably removed upon the granting of the patent. This condition does not affect laws or regulations that restrict access for public health or safety reasons.

Comment: The requirement for the patentee to notify the depository promptly after issuance of the patent is unwise and unnecessary. One comment suggested that the use of the word "promptly" is vague and presents the opportunity for problems to arise. The provision was considered unnecessary because the depository releases the deposit when the requester provides the depository with a copy of the issued patent.

Response: This provision has been removed from the rules being considered by the PTO. However, it should be noted (new rule 1.201(c) being considered for proposal) that the mere reference to a specific biological material in the specification disclosure does not create any presumption that the specific material is necessary to satisfy one or more requirements of 35 U.S.C. 112 or that a deposit in accordance with Office policy has been made. A procedure is defined in new rule 1.207(c) being considered for proposal whereby the Office would

certify whether a deposit has been made under conditions which make it available to the public as of the issue date of the patent grant.

Comment: Some of the comments received on the requirement for a viability statement provide an adequate response to other comments received. For example, some comments indicated that there should be a presumption that the microorganism is alive and that such testing should not be required. On the other hand, one comment was received to the effect that we should be aware of the problem that material shipped to depositories which, presumably, was viable when shipped, is received and when tested is not viable. This is not uncommon at the ATCC. Another comment indicated that if a viability statement is required it should be done by the depository if the biological material is deposited in a public depository. Another comment indicated that this person was pleased that we have included the third party competent to test for viability option. In some cases tests for viability can require expertise which might not be available at a depository. This option could be very helpful.

Response: Based on the evidence and comments received to date, the PTO is convinced that the requirement for a viability test is appropriate.

Comment: A deposit for either the enforceable life of the patent or for the 30/5 years of the Budapest Treaty should be considered acceptable. While the Budapest Treaty is an executive agreement, and therefore cannot override any clear dictate of 35 U.S.C. 112, it seems presumptuous for an office of an executive department to adopt a policy which is contrary to that embodied in an executive agreement.

Response: The period literally defined in the Budapest Treaty is considered acceptable for a deposit made under that Treaty. However, it is not difficult to imagine a situation where the period defined in the Budapest Treaty would not necessarily extend beyond the enforceable life of the patent. In the Board's decision in Ex Parte *Lundok*, it was noted that one of the basic principles of the patent system was that the public would not be prohibited from practicing the invention after the enforceable life of the patent. Implicit in that basic principle is the logic that a depositor should not be able to make a deposit under conditions that do not provide for storage beyond the enforceable life of the patent. Nor do we believe that the Budapest Treaty contemplated that the deposit would not be available while the patent is in force. The patentee need not be a guarantor of the availability of the deposited material after the enforceable life of the patent, but neither should the patentee be permitted to provide for storage only up to the date the patent expires.

Comment: The requirement for corroboration goes beyond the holding in *Lundak*. The requirement is unprecedented in ex parte prosecution. The PTO has regularly accepted Rule 131 declarations without corroboration, and to require it in the deposit situation would be completely inconsistent. The guidelines also fail to address what would be sufficient corroboration.

Response: The degree of corroboration required would depend on circumstances in the individual application. For a situation such as *Lundak* where a mistake was made relative to the presence of a deposit at the time of filing followed by a deposit within a week to ten days, a verified statement tracing the steps undertaken to deposit the biological material from the point of time of the filing date of the application to the actual deposit would

be sufficient. It is the function of the description requirement to ensure that the subject matter that is later claimed in the patent was described in the application as originally filed. Consequently, an applicant who waits to make the deposit until sometime after the filing date of the application has the burden of showing that which is later deposited was the same biological material as existed and was described in the application as originally filed. Corroboration can take any form which is suitable to establish the fact, as opposed to a bare statement made on information and belief, that the deposited material is the same as that which existed as of the filing date of the application. If the material was viable and capable of reproduction as of the time of deposit the verified statement should indicate that the material was viable and capable of reproduction as of the filing date.

Comment: It would seem that the two month formalities notice under Ex Parte *Quayle* would be appropriately used in instances where an application is allowable but assurance of public accessibility has not yet been made. There is no statutory authority for setting a three month period for response which would not be extendable upon payment of the appropriate fee.

Response: The PTO believes that once the issue of deposits has been either resolved or is in dispute, no additional time should be necessary. The basic concern is an adverse impact on pendency and disclosure to the public for no apparent reason. If an applicant is going to dispute the necessity of a deposit or the conditions under which it is made, then an appropriate appeal can be taken on that issue. If applicant agrees that a deposit is necessary, the three month period to pay the issue fee is considered adequate to get that job done. Nevertheless, provision has been made in new rule 1.208(c) being considered for proposal for an extension of time under 37 CFR 1.136.

Comment: There should be more specific guidelines as to the form of assurances that will be accepted for making an appropriate deposit. An averment by the applicant, assignee or attorney, in papers submitted during pendency of the application should be acceptable to the PTO. Deceit by such applicant, attorney or assignee should be dealt with in the same manner as deceit in conventional chemical cases.

Response: The Office will accept any assurance made in the record with the intent that the PTO rely on applicant to fulfill the deposit requirement as set forth in these proposed rules. The PTO will ensure that applicants have filed a statement that all conditions have been satisfied before the application is allowed to become a patent.

Comment: The PTO policy and guidelines should not make statements or predictions as to burden of proof during enforcement or other actions in a court of law. The indication that the burden of proof to establish an identity between the replaced sample and the original deposit may be on those seeking to enforce the patent outside the PTO goes against a statutory presumption of validity.

Response: The rules being considered by the PTO are limited to the presumption that the PTO will make in any proceeding involving the patent before the PTO.

Comment: It has been suggested that the procedure to be followed when biological material becomes unavailable be separate from the rest of the paragraph dealing with replacement deposits so that these separate situations are not viewed as one. For example, cessation of availability of biological material not previously deposited can result from, for example, the bankruptcy of the sole commercial supplier of the material. Under such circumstance, a deposit of no longer readily available material would be required.

Response: Since the necessity or desirability of replacing a deposit may arise from a number of circumstances, the PTO does not consider it appropriate to define separate rules or procedures for making a replacement under each circumstance. The rules being considered by the PTO are limited to a replacement right only for the original depositor. As one comment observed, the law on property rights in biological materials is somewhat unclear at this time and redeposit by a party other than the original depositor might be considered an act of conversion, depending on the precise circumstances. Moreover, the PTO has indicated an intention of applying a rebuttable presumption that once a biological material has been deposited for the term and under conditions specified in these rules under consideration by the PTO, the biological material deposited would be considered to be known and readily available to the public.

Comment: The guidelines are unclear as to the ability to obtain the benefit of a foreign priority date. Apparently, the PTO is aware that *Lundak* held that 35 U.S.C. 112 requires that a deposit be made and a reference added to the specification before the U.S. patent issues. Thus, 35 U.S.C. 119 affords the benefit of the priority date even if the priority document fails to mention a deposit and even if a deposit had not been made.

Response: The PTO will follow the same procedures for handling a claim for foreign priority in all applications. The examiner will acknowledge a claim for foreign priority when all formal requirements are met and will not consider the merits of an applicant's claim of priority unless a reference is found with an effective date between the date of foreign filing and the date of filing in the United States or when an interference situation is under consideration. Where the merits of a claim for priority need to be determined, the examiner will follow the guidelines in § 201.15 of the Manual of Patent Examining Procedure in making that determination. It must also be emphasized that applicants may not be granted priority in applications filed in countries foreign to the United States if they fail to make a deposit in a permanent depository acceptable to that foreign country before the filing date of the application in the Untied States.

Comment: If a deposit is found to be contaminated, what option does a depositor have? Can the deposit be replaced and the original deposit date be retained?

Response: If a deposit can still be considered to be viable, even though contaminated, the rules being considered by the PTO would not permit replacement of the original deposit. While there may be an appropriate mechanism for substitution of a deposit number in an existing application, the original deposit, even though contaminated, would provide the best evidence of whatever it was that was originally deposited and should be preserved.

Comment: If a deposit does not produce the product for which it was deposited (antibiotic, for instance), what option does a depositor have? Can the deposit be replaced and the original date retained?

Response: Any deposit which is made in accordance with the rules being considered by the PTO would have only a viability statement associated with it. There is absolutely no proof that the material originally deposited was capable of producing the product for which it was deposited. While it's clearly in the interest of the public to have a deposit available to it which is capable of making the product for which it was deposited, the destruction or replacement of the best evidence of what was originally deposited should not be lost if made in association with an existing patent. Perhaps the depositories should consider preservation of samples of the original deposit in conjunction with a deposit which is neither contaminated nor incapable of producing the product for which it was deposited.

Dated: June 19. 1987.

Donald J. Quigg,
Assistant Secretcry and Commissioner of Patents and Trademarks.
[FR Doc. 87-20528 Filed 9-8-87; 8:45 am]
BILLING CODE 3510-16-M

Livestock and Related Statistics for the United Kingdom and the European Community

(a) Structure of Livestock Production in the European Community

These figures are provided to offer a contrast with livestock agriculture in the USA, as described in the text.

In general, farm sizes in Europe are far smaller than the US, whether size be measured in acres or in herd size (Tables 1, 4–6). This difference is due both to variations in the land resource base and in government policy which can help preserve small farms in the face of substantial size economies in production. Like the US, a small percentage of large farms are disproportionally important as suppliers of food. For example, the two percent of farms classified as "very large" provide 15 percent of total output (Table 2). Larger (100+ cows) dairy farms in the UK hold more than 42 percent of all cows even though they constitute but 18 percent of total dairy farms.

The most extreme example is with pigs where in Ireland more than two thirds are concentrated in less than five percent of the farms. That suggests extreme specialization in a relatively minor crop for that country.

While these disparities between the two areas exist, they are narrowing. The major agricultural nations in the EC, the EC-9, have been undergoing a rapid consolidation in livestock farms (Table 8). Dairy and egg operations have lost 40 percent of their numbers from 1975–85 while breeding sow farms are down 50 percent. Indeed, consolidation in egg production is largely underway with 85 percent of laying hens held in 5,000 bird and above operations. This suggests that, while the situation is more advanced in the U.S., the pressures for farm consolidation are similar in the EC. Concerns about the implications of animal patents for further farm number consolidation are likely to be expressed in Europe as they have been in the U.S.

Mr. D. E. Bradbury, Head of Statistics for the U.K. Ministry of Agriculture, Fisheries and Food, assisted in the compilation of these figures.

Table 1 Average farm size, all agriculture, U.S. and EC-10, 1984

	EC-10	U.S.
Number of farms (millions)	6.8	2.3
Av. hectors/farm	17	177

Source: Newman, Fulton and Glaser, Table 4

Table 2 Average farm size by size class, EC-11, 1985/86

Size class	Very small	Small	Lower medium	Upper medium	Large	Very large
% in class	19	19	21	27	12	2
% total output	3	5	11	33	33	15
Av. hectors	5.1	7.5	15.7	30.6	54.0	151.7

Source: Comm. European Communities, Table H

Table 3 Livestock numbers by species and country, 1987

Country	Beef cattle 1000 head	%	Dairy cattle 1000 head	%	Pigs 1000 head	%	Sheep 1000 head	%
EC 12	79,441	100	24,663	100	103,976	100	89,883	100
EC 10	73,037	91.9	22,495	91.2	84,302	81.1	66,549	74.0
Belgium	2,950	3.7	918	3.7	5,970	5.7	133	.1
Denmark	2,323	2.9	807	3.3	9,048	8.7	77	.1
FR Germany	14,887	18.8	5,077	20.6	23,670	22.8	1,414	1.6
Greece	741	.9	232	.9	1,139	1.1	10,816	12.0
Spain	5,071	6.4	1,778	7.2	17,221	16.6	20,297	22.6
France	21,052	26.5	5,841	23.7	11,915	11.5	10,360	11.5
Ireland	5,580	7.1	1,444	5.8	960	.9	3,252	3.6
Italy	8,898	11.2	3,024	12.3	9,383	9.0	11,457	12.7
Luxembourg	209	.3	64	.3	77	.1	7	0.0
Netherlands	4,459	5.7	2,038	8.2	14,226	13.7	1,215	1.4
Portugal	1,332	1.7	388	1.6	2,452	2.3	3,035	3.4
UK	11,849	14.9	3,052	12.4	7,915	7.6	27,820	31.0

Source: Comm. European Communities, T/112–113

Table 4 Cattle farms by herd size and country, 1987

Country	Av.No./ Cattle/Farms	1–9		10–39		40–59		60–99		100–199		200–299		>300	
		% Cattle	% Farms	% Cattle	% Farms	% Cattle	% Farms	% Cattle	% Farms	% Cattle	% Farms	% Cattle	% Farms	% Cattle	% Farms
EC-10	37.9	3.7	31.5	20.9	37.1	14.4	11.2	24.0	11.9	23.4	6.7	6.7	1.1	6.9	.6
Belgium	48.2	2.0	20.6	16.0	33.7	15.6	15.4	29.5	18.6	27.1	10.1	4.8	1.0	4.9	.4
Denmark	57.7	1.5	19.1	11.8	30.1	10.8	12.7	25.4	18.8	38.7	16.8	8.6	2.1	3.2	.5
FR Germany	35.5	3.5	25.0	26.1	42.3	19.2	14.0	27.3	12.8	19.4	5.3	2.8	.4	1.6	.1
Greece	9.5	30.7	79.1	29.8	16.4	10.0	2.0	12.5	1.6	11.9	.8	3.0	.1	2.1	0
Spain	—	—	—	—	—	—	—	—	—	—	—	—	—	—	—
France	42.3	2.3	19.3	21.4	40.3	17.2	14.9	30.6	17.1	23.3	7.6	3.6	.7	1.6	.2
Ireland	32.9	3.9	23.3	32.0	50.5	16.6	11.4	21.4	9.3	18.6	4.7	4.2	.6	3.1	.2
Italy	19.7	11.5	57.2	31.7	32.6	10.4	4.4	11.7	3.1	11.9	1.7	8.0	.7	14.9	.5
Luxembourg	71.1	1.0	11.9	7.4	23.0	8.3	12.1	27.9	25.2	46.6	25.2	7.5	2.3	1.5	.3
Netherlands	69.6	1.0	12.8	8.8	26.6	10.8	15.3	27.7	24.8	31.7	16.9	6.7	2.0	13.3	1.8
Portugal	6.3	42.7	88.0	27.4	9.8	6.8	.9	6.5	.6	8.1	.4	2.9	.1	5.5	.1
UK	80.7	3.7	13.7	8.1	29.3	7.4	12.2	15.7	16.4	32.6	18.9	17.6	6.0	17.9	3.4

Note: Read across table. For example, in Belgium 31.5% of cattle farms have fewer than 9 cattle but they in total constitute only 3.7 percent of the total number of cattle in that country.

Source: Comm. European Communities, T/114

Table 5 Dairy farms by herd size and country, 1987

Country	Av. No./ Cattle/Farms	1-9		10-29		30-59		60-99		>100	
		% Cattle	% Farms	% Cattle	% Farms	% Cattle	% Farms	% Cattle	% Farms	% Cattle	% Farms
EC-10	18.4	9.1	44.4	34.4	35.6	33.1	15.2	14.0	3.5	9.4	1.2
Belgium	24.2	4.0	20.4	36.7	48.3	43.0	26.2	13.5	4.6	2.8	0.6
Denmark	30.4	2.5	16.3	24.6	39.3	46.9	34.5	19.6	8.4	6.3	1.5
FR Germany	16.0	12.1	40.3	50.0	45.6	30.9	12.7	6.1	1.4	0.8	0.1
Greece	3.7	64.8	93.6	22.0	5.3	8.7	0.9	3.6	0.2	0.9	0.0
Spain	—	—	—	—	—	—	—	—	—	—	—
France	20.0	6.2	28.6	44.3	48.1	41.2	21.0	7.1	2.0	1.1	0.2
Ireland	20.9	6.5	34.8	33.7	40.9	34.6	18.2	17.7	5.2	7.6	1.2
Italy	9.7	23.5	72.6	34.5	20.4	20.2	4.8	10.7	1.4	11.1	0.7
Luxembourg	31.8	1.4	9.4	24.4	14.5	59.7	46.3	13.1	5.9	1.4	0.4
Netherlands	37.6	1.6	16.6	37.9	27.3	42.8	37.2	30.6	15.7	10.6	3.1
Portugal	3.6	58.1	92.5	27.1	6.5	8.7	0.8	2.8	0.1	3.3	0.1
UK	63.2	0.4	7.8	5.6	17.8	21.4	31.2	30.4	25.3	42.4	18.0

Note: Read across table. As an example, small Belgium dairy farms (less than 10 cows) constitute 20.4 percent of all dairy farms but include only 4 percent of all dairy cattle.

Source: Comm. European Communities, T/117

Table 6 Pig farms by herd size and country, 1987

Country	Av. No./ Pigs/Farms	1–9 % Pigs	1–9 % Farms	10–49 % Pigs	10–49 % Farms	50–99 % Pigs	50–99 % Farms	100–199 % Pigs	100–199 % Farms	200–399 % Pigs	200–399 % Farms	400–999 % Pigs	400–999 % Farms	>1000 % Pigs	>1000 % Farms
EC-10	76.7	2.2	63.6	5.0	16.4	5.4	5.8	9.0	4.9	15.7	4.2	30.7	3.8	32.0	1.2
Belgium	221.1	0.4	22.4	2.5	20.8	4.2	12.9	9.2	14.3	17.3	13.5	34.0	12.2	32.5	3.9
Denmark	245.9	0.2	9.1	2.8	25.7	4.7	16.1	9.0	15.5	16.9	14.5	36.5	14.5	29.9	4.5
FR Germany	62.4	2.8	47.7	10.3	26.9	11.0	9.7	16.2	7.2	22.7	5.0	31.5	3.3	5.6	0.2
Greece	31.5	4.7	81.0	9.7	12.0	9.2	3.6	5.6	1.3	6.9	0.8	17.4	0.8	46.5	0.5
Spain	—	—	—	—	—	—	—	—	—	—	—	—	—	—	—
France	175.7	0.9	37.0	3.0	22.7	3.2	7.8	7.1	8.6	16.6	9.9	38.3	10.8	31.0	3.3
Ireland	200.0	0.7	56.3	2.8	25.0	1.7	4.2	1.7	2.1	3.7	2.1	11.4	4.2	77.9	4.2
Italy	19.3	10.4	91.2	6.0	6.4	2.8	0.8	2.3	0.3	6.6	0.4	18.0	0.5	53.8	0.4
Luxembourg	53.8	3.5	54.0	11.0	23.2	12.4	9.7	16.0	6.3	19.7	4.0	25.1	2.2	12.3	0.6
Netherlands	405.9	0.0	5.4	0.7	10.9	2.3	12.9	6.8	19.0	13.7	19.5	34.9	22.2	41.5	10.1
Portugal	9.3	20.9	90.6	14.2	7.3	5.9	0.8	10.0	0.7	7.9	0.3	12.0	0.2	29.1	0.1
UK	382.8	0.2	24.9	1.6	25.4	1.8	9.6	3.1	8.3	7.4	10.0	19.3	11.2	66.5	10.4

Note: Read across table. In Belgium, for example, a large portion of pig farms (22.4%) are small (10 or fewer pigs) but in total contain less than 0.5% of all pigs in Belgium.

Source: Comm. European Communities, T/120

Table 7　Poultry Numbers by class and country, 1986

Country	Broiler Chicks hatched	Laying Hens
EC-10	2,260,125	292.766
Belgium	—	10.719
Denmark	82,893	4.224
FR Germany	212,223	49.700
Greece	67,687	16.784
Spain	469,001	—
France	622,333	68.600
Ireland	32,192	3.281
Italy	330,040	48.035
Netherlands	297,339	39.291
Portugal	94,897	—
UK	529,600	52,041

Source: Comm. European Communities, T/271, T/275

Table 8　Trends in livestock farm size by species, EC-9, 1975–85, selected years

	1975	1979/80	1985
DAIRY COWS			
no. farms (thousands)	2,164	1,655	1,287
av. herd size	11.6	14.9	18.7
Herds 50 cows or more (thousands)	53	75	99
% total farms	2.4	4.5	7.7
% total cows	16.3	23.4	31.4
BREEDING SOWS			
no. farms (thousands)	733	511	358
av. herd size	10.4	16.9	25.9
Herds with 50 or more (thousands)	26	41	50
% total farms	3.5	8.0	13.9
% total sows	33.0	49.4	65.0
SHEEP			
no. farms (thousands)	588	573	533
av. flock size	85.4	95.6	113.9
Flocks of 500 or more (thousands)	26	31	36
% total farms	4.5	5.4	6.7
% total sheep	44.8	49.1	55.0
LAYING HENS			
no. farms (thousands)	3,052	2,416	1,820
av. flock size	90.8	136.7	170.7
Flocks of 5000 or more (thousands)	11.3	12.5	10.8
% total farms	.4%	.5%	.6%
% total hens	64.5	79.6	84.1

Source: Statistical Office of the European Communities, MAFF
　　　　Compiled by D. E. Bradbury, Head of Statistics, MAFF

Sources of Additional Information

Livestock breeders and stock raisers

European Association for Animal Production (EAAP). Corso Trieste 67, I–00198 Rome. *Tel.:* (06) 86 07 85.

Belgium:

Association Nationale des Eleveurs et Déténteurs de Bétai Bovin/Nationale Vereniging van Kwekers en Houders van Rundvee. 49 avenue du Souffrage Universel, B–1030 Brussels. *Tel.:* (02) 242 19 87.

Fédération Nationale des Associations Provinciales des Eleveurs de Moutons à Viande/Nationaal Verbond der Provinciale Verenigingen van Kwekers van Vleesschapen. c/o W. Nijs, 3 Gilainstraat, B–3300 Tienen. *Tel.:* (016) 81 18 44.

Fédération Nationale des Eleveurs de Porcs asbl (FBEP)/Landsbond van de Belgische Varkensstamboeken (BEVA). 49 avenue du Souffrage Universel, B–1030 Brussels. *Tel.:* (02) 242 27 39.

Fédération Nationale des Fédérations Provinciales des Syndicats d'Eleveurs de Chèvres et de Moutons Laitiers/Nationale Verbond der Provinciale Verbonden der Geiten-en Melkschapenkweek-syndikaten. c/o J. Notez, 32 Fr. Schollaerstraat, B–3200 Kessel-Lo (Louvain).

Denmark:

Danmarks Kaninavlerforening. Engblommevej 32, DK–3390 Hundested. *Tel.:* (03) 33 84 24.

Dansk Pelsyravlerforening. Langagervej 60, DK–2600 Glostrup. *Tel.:* (02) 96 71 22.

Landsforeningen 'Dansk Faareavl'. c/o Fr Andersen, Bægebakken 5, Lillering, DK–8462 Harlev J. *Tel.:* (06) 94 12 43.

France:

Association Française des Eleveurs de Visons, 28 rue Rocher, F–75008 Paris. *Tel.:* (1) 45 22 62 40.

Association Française de Zootechnie. 16 rue Claude Bernard, F–75231 Paris Cedex 12.

Confédération Nationale de l'Elevage (CNE). 149 rue de Bercy, F–75579 Paris Cedex 12. *Tel.:* (1) 43 46 12 20.

Fédération Nationale Bovine. 149 rue de Bercy. F–75579 Paris Cedex 12. *Tel.:* (1) 43 46 12 20.

Fédération Nationale Chevaline (FNC). 149 rue de Bercy, F–75579 Paris Cedex 12. *Tel.:* (1) 43 46 12 20.

Fédération Nationale des Eleveurs de Chèvres (FNEC). 149 rue de Bercy, F–75579 Paris Cedex 12. *Tel.:* (1) 43 46 12 20.

Fédération Nationale Porcine (FNP). 149 rue de Bercy, F–75579 Paris Cedex 12. *Tel.:* (1) 43 46 12 20.

Fédération Nationale Ovine. 149 rue de Bercy, F–75579 Paris Cedex 12. *Tel.:* (1) 43 46 12 20.

Union Nationale des Eleveurs de Porcs. 29 rue Fortuny, F–75017 Paris. *Tel.:* (1) 42 67 41 83/96.

Union Nationale Interprofessionnelle du Cheval (UNIC). 51 rue Dumont d'Urville, F–75116 Paris. *Tel.:* (1) 45 00 03 10.

Germany:

Arbeitsgemeinschaft der Landesverbände Deutscher Ziegenzüchter eV. c/o Dr Carl Roesch, Thomas Mann Strasse 12, D–7012 Fellbach bei Stuttgart. *Tel.:* (0711) 58 28 92.

Arbeitsgemeinschaft Deutscher Rinderzüchter eV. Adenauerallee 174, D–5300 Bonn 1. *Tel.:* (0228) 21 20 71. *Telex:* 886807.

Arbeitsgemeinschaft Deutscher Schweineerzeuger eV (ADS). Adenauerallee 174, D–5300 Bonn 1. *Tel.:* (0228) 21 10 69.

Arbeitsgemeinschaft Deutscher Tierzüchter eV. Adenauerallee 174, D–5300 Bonn 1. *Tel.:* (0228) 21 20 71.

Arbeitskreis Deutscher Klein- und Pelztier-Züchter (ADKPZ) Goethestrasse 5/1, D–7450 Hechingen. *Tel.:* (07471) 4740.

Deutsche Gesellschaft für Züchtungskunde eV (DGfZ). Adenauerallee 174, D–5300 Bonn 1. *Tel.:* (0228) 21 34 11.

Deutsche Reiterlich Vereinigung eV – Hauptverband für Zuch: und Prüfung Deutscher Pferde. PO box 640, Freiherr von Langen Strasse 13, D–4410 Warendorf. *Tel.:* (02581) 8041. *Telex:* 89950.

Vereinigung Deutscher Landesschaftzuchtverbände eV (VDL). Godesberger Allee 142–148, D–5300 Bonn 2. *Tel.:* (0228) 37 53 51.

Zentralverband Deutscher Kaninchenzüchter eV (ZDK). Langenburger Strasse 62. D–7000 Stuttgart (Zuffenhausen). *Tel.:* (0711) 85 90 51.

Zentralverband Deutscher Pelztierzüchter. Johannssenstrrasse 10, D–3000 Hannover. *Tel.:* (0511) 166 54 82.

Greece:

Enosis Krinotrofiki Ellados. Ag. Konstantinou – Vilara, Athens. *Telex:* 5249858.

Ireland:

Irish Grassland & Animal Production Association. c/o Agricultural Institute, Belclare, Tuam, Co. Galway. *Tel.:* (01) 25455.

Irish Pedigree Pig Breeders Society. 3 Sydney Parade Avenue, Dublin 4. *Tel.:* (01) 692334.

Italy:

Associazione Italiana Allevatori (AIA). Via Tomassetti 9, I–00161 Rome. *Tel.:* (06) 85 95 41. *Telex:* 613440.

Associazione Nazionale Allevatori Bovini Italiani da Carne (ANABIC). Via Antonio Bosio 22, I–00161 Rome. *Tel.:* (06) 86 42 45; 844 13 93.

Associazione Nazionale Allevatori Cavalli Puro Sangue. Via del Caravaggio 3, Rome. *Tel.:* (02) 498 13 04.

Associazione Nationale Allevatori di Suini. Via G.B. di Ross: 3, I–00161 Rome. *Tel.:* (06) 844 9106.

Associazione Nazionale Coninglicoltori Italiani (ANCI-AIA). Via A. Torlonia 19, I–00161 Rome. *Tel.:* (06) 85 49 03.

Associazione Nazionale della Pastorizia (ASSONAPA). Via Ravenna 9/c, I–00161 Rome. *Tel.:* (06) 42 21 03.

Netherlands:

Central Bureau voor de Varkensfokkerij (CBV). PO box 1159, Oranjesingel 74, NL–6501 BD Nijmegen. *Tel.:* (080) 22 63 55.

Landelijke Organisatie van Fokkers. Groest 93, NL–1211 EB Hilversum. *Tel.:* (035) 19941.

Nederlandse Organisatie voor de Geitenfokkerij (NOG). Looydijk 67, NL–3612 BE Tienhoven. *Tel.:* (03469) 338.

Nederlandse Vereniging van Fokkers van Edelpelsdieren (NFE). PO box 12, Kommerdijk 2, Gendt OB. *Tel.:* (08812) 1504.

Nederlandse Zöotechnische Vereniging. Kerkstraat 22, NL–3972 EL Driebergen.

Spain:

Asociación Nacionale de Criadores de Ganado Porcino Selecto. Goya 115, Madrid. *Tel.:* (1) 401 08 00/50.

Unión de Almacenistas de Hierros de España. Principe de Vergara 74, Madrid 6. *Tel.:* (1) 411 18 34.

United Kingdom:

British Rabbit Council (BRC). 7 Kirkgate, Newark on Trent NG24 1AD. *Tel.:* (0636) 76042.

British Society of Animal Production (BSAP). PO box 47, Bridgets EHF, Martyr Worthy, Winchester, Hampshire SO21 1AL. *Tel.:* (096278) 220.

Commercial Rabbit Association (CRA). Tyning House, Shurdington, Cheltenham GL51 5XF. *Tel.:* (0242) 862387.

Council of Quality Pig Producers' Association (CQPPA). Agriculture House, 25–31 Knightsbridge, London SW1X 7NJ. *Tel.:* (01) 235 5077.

Fur Breeders Association of the United Kingdom (FBA). 67 Upper Thames Street, London EC4V 3AB. *Tel.:* (01) 248 9095.

National Cattle Breeders' Association (NCBA). Cholesbury, nr Tring, Hertfordshire HP23 6PD. *Tel.:* (024029) 544; 622.

National Pig Breeders' Association (NPBA). 7 Rickmansworth Road, Watford, Hertfordshire WD1 7HE. *Tel.:* (0923) 34377.

National Pony Society (NPS). 7 Cross & Pillory Lane, Alton, Hampshire GU34 1HL. *Tel.:* (0420) 88333.

National Sheep Association (NSA). Cholesbury, nr Tring, Hertfordshire HP23 6PD. *Tel.:* (024029) 544. *Telex.* 826715 AERO G.

Poultry breeders and egg producers

Denmark:

Dansk Erhvervsfjerkræ. Steløsevej 361, DK–5260 Odense S. *Tel.:* (09) 96 13 72.

France:

Confédération Française de l'Aviculture (CFA). 28 rue du Rocher, F–75008 Paris. *Tel.:* (1) 45 22 62 40.

Germany:

Zentralverband der Deutschen Geflügelwirtschaft eV. Niebuhrstrasse 53, D–5300 Bonn. *Tel.:* (0228) 21 50 11.

Italy:

Unione Nazionale dell'Avicoltura (UNA). Via Pasubio 4, I–00195 Rome. *Tel.:* (06) 31 63 97.

Netherlands:

Landelijke Organisatie van Vermeerderaars (LOV). Covert Flinckstraat 16, NL–3351 VH Papendrecht. *Tel.:* (078) 55486.
Nederlandse Organisatie van Plumveehouders (NOP). PO box 506, Utrechtseweg 31, NL–3700 AM Zeist. *Tel.:* (03404) 10909.

Portugal:

Associação Portuguesa dos Aviários de Multiplicação (APAM). Avenida Columbano Bordalo Pinheiro 71–3°–E, P–1000 Lisbon. *Tel.:* (19) 73 02 82.

United Kingdom:

British Egg Association (BEA). 52–54 High Holborn, London WC1V 6SX. *Tel.:* (01) 242 4683/4. *Telex:* 28479.
British Poultry Breeders & Hatcheries Association Ltd (BPBHA). 52–54 High Holborn, London WC1V 6SX. *Tel.:* (01) 242 4683. *Telex:* 28479.
British Poultry Federation (BPF) 52–54 High Holborn, London WC1V 6SX. *Tel.:* (01) 242 4683. *Telex:* 28479.
British Turkey Federation (BTF). 52–54 High Holborn, London WC1V 6SX. *Tel.:* (01) 242 4683. *Telex:* 28479.
Duck Producers Association Ltd (DPA). 52–54 High Holborn, London WC1V 6SX. *Tel.:* (01) 242 4683. *Telex:* 28479.

Sources

Morris, B. and K. Boehm, *The European Community, A Practical Director and Guide.* London: Macmillan Publishers, 2nd Ed., 1986.
Newman, M., T. Fulton and L. Glaser, "A Comparison of the United States and European Community." U.S. Dept. Agr., Econ. Res. Service Foreign Ag. Econ. Rpt. 233, Oct. 1987.
Commission of the European Communities, *The Agricultural Situation in the Community, 1988 Report*, Luxembourg, 1989.

(b) Livestock Statistics for the United Kingdom and the European Community*

Table 1   Selected livestock data for the United Kingdom (in thousands) at June each year: from the Agricultural Census

	1975	1976	1977	1978	1979	1980
Total Cattle and Calves	14,717	14,069	13,899	13,670	13,589	13,426
dairy cows	3,242	3,228	3,269	3,290	3,292	3,228
beef cows	1,899	1,764	1,688	1,588	1,543	1,478
heifers in calf	903	939	824	859	864	838
Total Sheep and Lambs	28,270	28,265	28,190	29,772	29,946	31,446
breeding ewes	13,750	13,666	13,741	14,199	14,578	14,923
Total Pigs	7,532	7,947	7,756	7,728	7,864	7,815
breeding sows	814	884	832	845	851	831
Total Fowls	130,260	134,917	128,453	131,116	127,433	127,063
: laying flock	49,360	49,085	49,616	50,985	48,120	46,012
: pullets not in lay	18,195	18,383	16,411	17,343	15,504	14,457
: breeding fowls	5,997	6,125	6,252	6,447	6,657	6,678
: table fowls	56,708	61,325	56,174	56,340	57,153	59,917

Source: Agricultural Statistics UK, annual volumes

Definitions:
: dairy and beef cows include both those in milk and those not in milk
: heifers in calf, all ages, include those intended for dairy or for beef
: breeding ewes include—
     ewes kept for breeding, and shearlings put to the ram
: breeding sows include—
     sows in pig, gilts in pig, other sows suckled or kept for breeding
: the laying flock consists of birds laying eggs for eating
: pullets not in lay are intended for the laying flock
: breeding fowls are for producing eggs for hatching

*Supplied by the Ministry of Agriculture, Fisheries and Food.

(*continued*)

1981	1982	1983	1984	1985	1986	1987	1988
13,138	13,244	12,290	13,213	12,911	12,534	12,158	11,872
3,191	3,250	3,333	3,281	3,150	3,138	3,042	2,911
1,420	1,390	1,358	1,351	1,333	1,308	1,343	1,373
863	851	847	811	874	879	774	834
32,097	33,067	34,069	34,802	35,628	37,016	38,701	40,942
15,271	15,780	16,243	16,540	16,878	17,398	18,068	19,017
7,828	8,023	8,174	7,689	7,865	7,937	7,942	7,980
836	864	856	800	828	824	820	805
122,639	126,091	117,855	118,846	119,456	120,740	128,628	130,809
44,473	44,792	41,127	40,573	39,538	38,056	38,498	37,389
14,219	14,767	11,828	12,536	12,503	12,502	12,230	11,236
6,117	6,457	6,012	6,396	6,104	6,324	7,146	6,879
57,830	60,075	58,888	59,341	61,311	63,808	70,754	75,305

Table 2 Livestock: selected size analyses: United Kingdom
at June each year: from the Agricultural Census
(in thousands—except head and percentages where shown)

	1975	1980	1985
Holdings with DAIRY COWS			
: number of holdings	81.0	63.1	54.0
: number of dairy cows	3,241.7	3,223.6	3,146.7
: average herd size (HEAD)	40.0	51.1	58.3
: herds of 60 or more			
: number of holdings	18.0	20.3	21.1
: as per cent of total	22.2%	32.2%	39.1%
: number of dairy cows	1,747.8	2,065.3	2,191.3
: as per cent of total	53.9%	64.1%	69.6%
Holdings with BREEDING EWES			
: number of holdings	80.6	78.6	83.6
: number of breeding ewes	13,188.9	14,308.0	16,020.3
: average flock size (HEAD)	163.6	182.0	191.6
: flocks of 500 or more			
: number of holdings	5.6	6.6	7.9
: as per cent of total	6.9%	8.4%	9.4%
: number of breeding ewes	4,958.0	5,872.4	7,014.4
: as per cent of total	37.6%	41.0%	43.8%
Holdings with BREEDING SOWS			
: number of holdings	35.6	22.4	17.5
: number of breeding sows	814.0	828.5	823.2
: average herd size (HEAD)	22.9	37.0	47.1
: herds of 50 or more			
: number of holdings	4.4	4.5	4.2
: as per cent of total	12.4%	20.1%	24.1%
: number of breeding sows	517.7	641.4	552.0
: as per cent of total	63.6%	77.4%	67.1%
Holdings with LAYING FLOCK			
: number of holdings	84.1	59.2	46.4
: number in laying flock	49,360	45,574	39,268
: average flock size (HEAD)	586.9	770.3	846.5
: flocks of 5,000 or more			
: number of holdings	2.0	1.7	1.3
: as per cent of total	2.4%	2.8%	2.8%
: number in laying flock	38,403	39,176	34,731
: as per cent of total	77.8%	86.0%	88.4%

Source: MAFF

Definitions:
: dairy cows include those in milk and those not in milk
: breeding ewes include—
    ewes kept for breeding and shearlings put to the ram
: breeding sows include—
    sows and gilts in pig, other sows suckled or kept for breeding
: the laying flock consists of birds laying eggs for eating—
    excluding pullets not in lay

310

Table 3   Selected livestock data for the European Community,
Euro-9: from the Community Farm Structure Survey

	1975	1979/80	1985
TOTAL BOVINES	80,400	78,170	78,354
dairy cows	25,020	24,664	24,091
heifers	6,016	5,907	5,545
TOTAL SHEEP	50,182	54,738	60,688
TOTAL PIGS	66,242	74,791	78,958
breeding sows	7,623	8,627	9,264
TOTAL POULTRY	568,405	704,584	703,903
: laying hens	277,041	330,182	310,651
: table fowls	240,553	298,630	314,266

Sources: Statistical Office of the European Communities; MAFF

Definitions:
: bovines include buffaloes
: heifers—all females over 2 years old not yet calved
: sheep cover all ages
: breeding sows include—
      sows in pig, gilts in pig,
      other sows suckled or kept for breeding,
      gilts over 50 kg intended for breeding
: poultry include—
      all fowls, ducks, geese, turkeys, guinea-fowl
: laying hens include—
      all fowls laying eggs (for eating or hatching)
      growing pullets, not in lay
      breeding cocks

Table 4 Livestock: selected size analyses: European Community Euro-9:
from the Community Farm Structure Surveys
(in thousands—except HEAD or percentages where shown)

	1975	1979/80	1985
Holdings with DAIRY COWS			
: number of holdings	2,164	1,655	1,287
: number of dairy cows	25,020	24,664	24,091
: average herd size (HEAD)	11.6	14.9	18.7
: herds of 50 or more			
: number of holdings	53	75	99
: as per cent of total	2.4%	4.5%	7.7%
: number of dairy cows	4,089	5,774	7,557
: as per cent of total	16.3%	23.4%	31.4%
Holdings with SHEEP			
: number of holdings	588	573	533
: number of sheep	50,182	54,738	60,688
: average flock size (HEAD)	85.4	95.6	113.9
: flocks of 400 or more			
: number of holdings	26	31	36
: as per cent of total	4.5%	5.4%	6.7%
: number of sheep	22,475	26,897	33,368
: as per cent of total	44.8%	49.1%	55.0%
Holdings with BREEDING SOWS			
: number of holdings	733	511	358
: number of breeding sows	7,623	8,627	9,264
: average herd size (HEAD)	10.4	16.9	25.9
: herds of 50 or more			
: number of holdings	26	41	50
: as per cent of total	3.5%	8.0%	13.9%
: number of breeding sows	2,515	4,262	6,019
: as per cent of total	33.0%	49.4%	65.0%
Holdings with LAYING HENS			
: number of holdings	3,052	2,416	1,820
: number of laying hens	277,041	330,183	310,651
: average flock size (HEAD)	90.8	136.7	170.7
: flocks of 5,000 or more			
: number of holdings	11.3	12.5	10.8
: as per cent of total	.4%	.5%	.6%
: number of laying hens	178,706	262,975	261,332
: as per cent of total	64.5%	79.6%	84.1%

Sources: Statistical Office of the European Communities; MAFF

Definitions:
: breeding sows include—
    sows in pig; gilts in pig
    other sows suckled or kept for breeding
    gilts over 50 kg intended for breeding
: laying hens include—
    all fowls laying eggs (for eating or hatching)
    growing pullets, not in lay; breeding cocks

Table 5 Milk and egg yields

	MILK YIELDS (kg per head)			EGG YIELD eggs per bird
	UK	EC-9	EC-10	UK
1977	4,571	3,845		241
1978	4,800	4,010		242
1979	4,685	4,040	4,004	247
1980	4,757	4,107	4,093	248
1981	4,831	4,182	4,172	250
1982	5,078	4,328	4,314	251
1983	5,138		4,398	258
1984	4,721		4,222	250
1985	4,834		4,338	251
1986	4,958		4,505	251
1987				253

Sources:
Annual Review of Agriculture (MAFF)
Agriculture in the UK 1988 (MAFF)
Agricultural Situation in the Community (EC Commission)

COMMISSION OF THE EUROPEAN COMMUNITIES

COM(88) 496 final – SYN 159
Brussels, 17 October 1988

Proposal for a Council Directive on the Legal Protection of Biotechnological Inventions

(presented by the Commission)

(EXTRACTS)

Purpose and Scope of the Proposed Directive

8. The main purpose of this proposal for a Directive is to establish harmonised, clear and improved standards for protecting biotechnological inventions in order to foster the overall innovatory potential and competitiveness of Community science and industry in this important field of modern technology. The previsions of the Directive systematically adapt existing patent law principles to the field of biotechnology with the aim of securing the application of patent laws in this important area as effective as possible.

9. By providing improved possibilities to protect biotechnological inventions and greater certainty regarding the scope of protection available, the Directive should allow inventors and investors in the Member States to benefit from patent protection as effective as that in the competitive markets of Japan and the United States of America (USA). This will result in a greater willingness to invest labour and capital in research and development and in exploiting the results thereof in spite of the high risks involved.

10. Establishing a harmonised system of patent law in this area will facilitate the development of Community industry in biotechnology, trade in biotechnological products and the establishment of a common market in this field. Moreover, it will enable Community industry to keep pace with leading nations in biotechnology and to close or narrow existing gaps.

11. The primary purpose of the modern patent system is to promote technical innovation as the major factor of economic growth by encouraging inventive activity through rewarding inventors for their creative efforts. The patent system thus secures costly investment in research and development and industrial exploitation of research results. Simultaneously, the patent system encourages an early and beneficial dissemination of knowledge in the field of activity involved which, without such protection, might be kept secret. The patent system also offers the necessary incentives for exploiting the results of publicly funded research. Such exploitation itself requires costly investment.

12. Biotechnological research and development and industry making use of developments in this field are rapidly evolving and expanding on the international level. Biotechnology is likely to influence and modify the lives of many people through its ultimate impact on human and animal health care, agriculture, the food and chemical industries, energy resources and the environment. It has evolved dramatically through

315

the advance of various genetic engineering techniques in recent years, particularly so in the USA and Japan. It is, therefore, of particular urgency for patent protection to play its important part in these fields in the European Communities.

13. The patent system, when applied to biotechnology, encounters a number of particular problems. A reason for this is that biotechnology, as the name says, is related to living matter, which poses problems in relation to ethics as well as in relation to the traditional patent law concepts of patentable subject matter, discovery, novelty, sufficient written disclosure, industrial applicability and the extent and exhaustion of patent protection.

14. These particular problems have been handled in some respects in a different manner in different Member States and, even where Member States have unilaterally introduced into their laws provisions similar to those of the European Patent Convention, these provisions do not provide for specific rules which relate to and are necessary for resolving the particular problems of biotechnological inventions. In fact, the legal situation suffers from deficiencies as well as discrepancies in statutory law, regulations and their interpretation and a general shortage of case law.

15. The problem is particularly acute in the European Communities, where the existence of a harmonised and adequate body of law, rules and practices is of major importance to the proper functioning of the internal market and the competitive vigour of industry.

$$* \qquad * \qquad *$$

The Need for Approximation of Laws

(i) Existing Legal Framework in the Member States

21. The existing legal framework for protecting biotechnological innovation in the Member States has been strongly influenced by two international conventions, conceived in the late fifties and early sixties on the basis of the-then state of the art in biological sciences: The "International Convention for the Protection of New Varieties of Plants", established in 1961 in Paris (the UPOV Convention), and the "Convention on the Unification of Certain Points of Substantive Law on Patents for Invention", signed in 1963 (the Strasbourg Convention).

22. The current patent laws of most of the Member States were adopted and introduced in the late seventies and early eighties as a direct result of the more recent 1973 "Convention on the Grant of European Patents" (the European Patent Convention – EPC) and the "Convention for the European Patent for the Common Market" (Community Patent Convention – CPC), signed in Luxembourg in 1975, but not yet in force. With regard to biotechnological innovation, they follow the basic principles of the UPOV and Strasbourg Conventions, which were introduced into the EPC without seriously reconsidering developments which in the meantime had taken place in various areas of biotechnology.

23. The key assumptions of the UPOV and the Strasbourg Conventions, which were taken over into the EPC and the harmonised national patent laws of all the Member States, except Ireland and Portugal[8], are, firstly, the belief that the traditional concept of "technical invention" renders biological inventions only in rare cases capable of

---

[8]   These Member States have not yet brought their national patent laws into line with EPC.

complying with the usual requirements of patentability; and, secondly, that inventions in the field of living matter could be divided into those of microbiology and those of (macro-) biology.

Based on these premises and taking into account certain known needs of traditional plant breeders, the 1961 UPOV Convention established a tailor-made type of protection for new varieties of plants.

Subsequently, the Strasbourg Convention, in view of the long history of patenting microbiological processes and their products in several States party to it, made it mandatory as early as 1963 to protect microbiological processes and their resulting products, but left the signatory States a free hand as regards the protection of new plant or animal varieties and essentially biological processes employed in their production.

The EPC, when adopted in 1973, expressly excluded from patent protection plant and animal varieties and essentially biological processes for the production of plants and animals but allowed patenting of microbiological processes and their products (Article 53b).

24. It should also be mentioned that in 1977, under the auspices of WIPO, the Budapest "Treaty on the International Recognition of the Deposit of Microorganisms for the Purposes of Patent Procedure" was concluded to which twenty-one States have adhered[9]. The States party to this Treaty, which allow or require the deposit of microorganisms for the purpose of patent procedure, are obliged to recognise, for such purposes, the deposit of a microorganism with any recognised international depository authority. Although this Treaty facilitates applications for patent protection of biotechnological inventions abroad, it does not influence the substantive patent law of the "Contracting States". Its influence on patent laws of the Contracting States is limited to purely technical provisions regarding the depositing and redepositing of microorganisms, as demonstrated by Rule 28a EPC, which was inserted into the EPC Regulations as a result of the conclusion of the Budapest Treaty.

25. Achievements in biotechnology reached during the period of time necessary to bring into force this international legal framework at the national level demonstrate that the distinction between micro- and macrobiology, which serves as the dividing line between patentable and non-patentable inventions, is artificial and no longer tenable. Developments originating in microbiology, either as processes or products, are likely to have a direct effect on the macrobiological sector, giving rise similarly to visible changes in the plant or animal world. They should, therefore, enjoy legal treatment according to the same principles as other inventions in microbiology.

26. One major consequence of micro- and biotechnological developments is that "Agriculture has moved from a resource-based to a science-based industry as science and technology have been substituted for land and labor"[10]. A greatly improved understanding and mastery of basic biological mechanisms have given rise to a change in the concept of what may be considered "technical" for purposes of patent law. Beginning in the late sixties, the courts of at least one Member State have held

---

[9]   As of April 1987. From the Community Member States Greece, Ireland, Luxembourg and Portugal are not yet party to this Treaty.

[10]   Committee on a National Strategy for Biotechnology in Agriculture—Board on Agriculture—National Research Council, Agricultural Biotechnology—Strategies for National Competitiveness, Washington, D.C., 1987, 1, 2. According to the Executive Summary of this report, it is true even for USA that "Yet current political and economic policies governing agriculture neither fully recognize nor take these changes into account".

that the general field of biology may be included in the notion of what is "technical"[11]. This changed appreciation from that represented by the existing international legal framework, however, has only partially been incorporated into statutory law and into patent practice, at both the national and the international level.

27. Due to its underlying assumptions, outdated by scientific and technological developments, the present legal framework for protecting biotechnological inventions in the Member States is unable to satisfy either the needs of science and industry in this field or the needs of patent granting authorities and courts. Apart from the now rather questionable explicit exclusions from patentability, only in part resulting from the prohibition of double protection established in Art. 2 (1) UPOV Convention, the main and decisive deficiency of the system is to be seen in its almost complete lack of any reliable legislative guidance on such essential questions as:

Patentability of Living Matter, that is, what are the criteria to patent natural material in view of the existing exlusion of discoveries from patent protection and also in view of the novelty requirement; what is to be understood by the terms "microbiological" and "essentially biological process"; can a microorganism *per se* be regarded as a product of a "microbiological process";

What are the effects of the exclusion from patentability of plant and animal varieties upon the patenting of microorganisms or taxonomic units different from plant or animal varieties or upon the patenting of parts of plant or animal varieties or their uses?;

What is the Scope of Patent Protection for Living Matter, in view of the fact that living matter is self-replicable and, this therefore, causes particular problems in respect of further generations;

Sufficient Disclosure, which in spite of the advances in natural sciences remains a problem of major concern, for example, whether and under what conditions the written description of an invention may be completed by a deposit of a microorganism or other self-replicable matter, and what are the duties of and safeguards for the depositor.

(ii) Efforts to Improve Legal Protection for Biotechnological Inventions

28. *OECD*. Since the emergence of modern biotechnology, the ability of patent laws to offer effective protection for new biotechnological processes and products has been uncertain. The Organization for Economic Cooperation and Development (OECD) first initiated an international review on biotechnology and patent protection in 1981. Based on replies to a questionnaire from governments of 19 members[12] (out of 24), the Final Report[13] detected a great number of deficiencies in patent laws of most of the member countries regarding especially the patentability of microorganisms *per se*, naturally occurring materials, disclosure, deposit and release conditions and infringement. Moreover, it was observed in this report *inter alia*:

> In no other field of technology, old or new, do national laws vary on so many points or diverge so widely as they do in biotechnology. The answers to the OECD Questionnaire have brought a wide spectrum of varying legal opinions and practices to light which concern almost every important aspect of patent protection in biotechnology.

---

[11] Decision of March 27 1969, Federal Supreme Court, Federal Republic of Germany, 1 IIC 136 (1970) "Red Dove".
[12] Among those countries which answered the Questionnaire were the following Member States: Belgium, Denmark, Germany, France, Ireland, Italy, the Netherlands, Portugal and the United Kingdom.
[13] Biotechnology and Patent Protection—an International Review, OECD, Paris 1985.

The replies from the Member States of the Community reflected no less a divergence either in respect of varying legal opinions and practices or as to existing deficiencies of national laws. It was felt that only US and Japanese laws were on the whole adaptive and flexible in respect of new developments in biotechnology. To improve the present legal situation in the OECD countries, the report submitted a number of recommendations.

29. *WIPO*. At its fourteenth series of meetings (of September/October 1983), the Assembly of the International (Paris) Union for the Protection of Industrial Property instructed the International Bureau of the World Intellectual Property Organization (WIPO) to

> study the existing situation concerning the protection, by patents or by other means, of inventions in the field of biotechnology (including 'genetic engineering') and possible means of providing for industrial property protection for such inventions, both at the national and international level[14].

A Committee of Experts on Biotechnological Inventions and Industrial Property was established and first convened in 1984. Subsequently the International Bureau of WIPO prepared an Analysis of Certain Basic Issues in Industrial Property Protection of Biotechnological Inventions[15] and then, based on replies to two Questionnaires[16], submitted 19 suggestions for solutions concerning industrial property protection of biotechnological inventions[17]. These solutions seem to complete and supplement the recommendations of the OECD Report.

In three meetings, the Committee of Experts discussed the work done by the International Bureau and its consultants, particularly the "Suggested Solutions"[18]. It might initially have been envisaged that the ongoing work of WIPO could have produced the necessary level of harmonization for the European context. This will unlikely be the case in anything but the very long term in light of the general observation of the Director General of WIPO in the third session of the Committee of Experts, according to which

> At present, WIPO did not intend to provoke changes in national legislations; it only wanted to make governments more aware of what was happening in this field in the various countries and of what were the problems that the legislator might have to solve, so that the patent system could be fully responsive to the need for protection in this exceedingly important technological field.

Moreover, from the remarks made by a number of delegations, especially, but not exclusively from the developing countries, it may be concluded that an agreement on this topic at the universal level either in the form of a special convention or within the current work of the International Bureau of WIPO on the Draft Treaty on the Harmonisation of certain provisions in laws for the protection of inventions[19] cannot be expected for at least several more years.

30. Thus, the efforts of WIPO in this area will most likely end in no more than a recommendation addressed to the Member States of WIPO by its Director General. In view of the complexity of the issues and the interests involved, it is only realistic to note that such a recommendation could result in changes in national legislation, at

---

[14] WIPO Doc. BIOT/CE/1/2. [15] WIPO Doc. BIG 281 and WIPO Doc. BIOT/CE/II/2.
[16] WIPO Doc. BIOT/Q/1, 2. [17] WIPO Doc. BIOT/CE/III/2.
[18] The work of the Committee is reported in WIPO Docs. BIOT/CE/I/3; BIOT/CE/II/3; BIOT/CE/III/3.
[19] WIPO Doc. HL/CE/III/2.

best, in several years. Notwithstanding well founded and balanced Suggested Solutions, the WIPO initiative is unlikely to bring about a prompt, positive and harmonised response at the world or even the European level. Experience with the revision work on the Paris "Convention for the Protection of Industrial Property" confirms this appreciation.

(iii) Protection of Biotechnological Inventions under the European Patent Convention

31. The legal basis for granting European patents for biotechnological inventions is the previously mentioned Article 53 (b) EPC, which has served as a model for national patent law provisions of nine Member States of the Community. As noted earlier, this article expressly excludes from patent protection plant and animal varieties and essentially biological processes for producing plants and animals but allows patenting of microbiological processes and the products thereof. Article 53 (b), however, is not the only provision of the EPC explicitly dealing with biotechnological inventions. Because inventions concerning microbiological processes and their products incur particular difficulties with regard to the usual requirement of sufficient disclosure, the EPC from the outset introduced special provisions for compliance with this patent law requirement.

In Rule 28 of the Regulations, if an invention concerns a microbiological process or the product thereof and involves the use of a microorganism which is not available to the public and which cannot be described in such a manner as to enable the invention to be carried out by a person skilled in the art, the disclosure requirement may be satisfied by a deposit of a culture of the microorganism in a culture collection not later than the European patent application date, including with the application identifying details of the deposit. The deposited microorganism must be made available from the culture collection to any person from the date of first publication of the application. Moreover, this provision lays down detailed rules as to the release conditions of the deposited material. Rule 28 was subsequently amended to introduce the so-called "expert solution" which allows the applicant the possibility to limit the availability of the deposited material to an independent expert until the grant of the European patent.

32. To cope with problems emerging from patent applications in the field of modern biotechnology, additional guiding measures proved necessary under Article 53 (b) EPC. The European Patent Office (EPO) in its "Guidelines for Examination" therefore addressed a number of particular problems, such as, the patentability of naturally occurring substances, the demarcation between "essentially biological" and "essentially non-biological" processes and the interpretation of the terms "microbiological process", "microorganism", and "product of a microbiological process".

As to other questions, such as the effects of the exclusion from patentability of plant and animal varieties upon the patenting of taxonomic units different from plant or animal varieties or upon the patenting of parts of plant or animal varieties or their uses, the guidelines are silent.

33. Although the solutions provided for in the Examination Guidelines of the EPO offer valuable guidance for the examining organs of the EPO, and seem to meet many of the needs of applicants in an appropriate manner, they are handicapped by the fact that they are neither binding on the Board of Appeals of the EPO, deciding in final instance on patentability, nor on national courts competent in nullity procedures regarding European patents. There is no mechanism in the EPC, such as by Examination Guidelines, to provide for *mandatory* guidance on the questions arising in respect of patenting biotechnological inventions. The Boards of Appeals of the EPO and the national courts enjoy complete discretion whether to follow the practice of the EPO when interpreting the EPC. As regards the scope of protection of biotechnological inventions and the interrelation between the effects of patents and plant breeders' rights, the EPC does not regulate these issues and thus no competence of the European Patent Office exists.

34. Difficult to predict are future developments as regards the EPC. For the time being the EPO is solving problems related to the application of Article 53 (b) EPC on a case-by-case basis in addition to periodic amendment of the Guidelines for Examination. The practical effects of these Guidelines should not be underestimated. In view of their limited legal effects, however, the EPO Guidelines cannot be viewed as a suitable means to cure the deficiencies caused by the lack of legislative guidance with regard to the most essential problems of patenting biotechnological inventions under Article 53 (b) EPC.

While in theory it may be possible to introduce rules related to the interpretation of substantive patent law provisions of the EPC into the "Implementing Regulations to the Convention" (the amendment of which falls within the competence of the Administrative Council of the European Patent Organization), these Regulations so far have no binding effect on the views to be taken by the courts of the Contracting States when interpreting the EPC. The same is true even for the Boards of Appeals of the EPO: under Article 164 (2) EPC, the Implementing Regulations may be deemed to be in conflict with the wording of the Convention and the Convention may be interpreted in a different way.

Legislative guidance needed under Article 53 (b) EPC could of course be provided by a revision of the EPC. In light of the difficulties presented by the revision mechanism of Article 172 EPC, however, it appears unlikely that the EPC Contracting States would consider any revision at the present time.

(iv) Effects of the European Patent Convention upon the Protection of Biotechnological Inventions under National Patent Laws

35. When considering the possibilities of the EPC to affect the national patent laws of the Community Member States, the special legal concept of the EPC must be taken into account. Although the EPC provides for a system of law for granting European patents, these patents, in each of the Contracting States for which they are granted, have the effect of and are subject to the same conditions as a national patent granted by that State (Articles 1 and 2 EPC). A European patent is granted, defined and revoked in applying rules of the EPC, and to this extent represents a collection of "European" patents. For all other purposes, such as the scope of protection, European patents represent patents with national effects, subject to national laws, although certain minimum standards are prescribed in Articles 64(2) and 67 EPC.

In addition, it results from the design of the EPC that the Contracting States are not obliged automatically to align their national patent laws with the EPC. This has happened in the past but on a purely voluntary, unilateral, uncoordinated basis. An amendment of the EPC would probably, but not mandatorily, lead to changes in national patent laws of most of the Community Member States. Moreover, in order to secure a harmonised judicial practice on points essential to biotechnological inventions in the Contracting States, such changes of the EPC would require highly specific provisions. An additional difficulty with regard to the EPC results from its membership: whereas four EPC Contracting States are not Community Member States, Denmark, Ireland and Portugal are not yet Contracting Parties to the EPC.

(v) Effects of the Community Patent Draft Convention upon the Protection of Biotechnological Inventions under the European Patent Convention and under National Patent Laws.

The "Convention for the European Patent for the Common Market" of 1975 ("CPC") and the 1985 Agreement relating to Community Patents[20] do not themselves address questions as to patentability, but leave these issues to the EPC. The CPC will not,

[20] Cf. "Texts established by the Luxembourg Conference on the Community Patent 1985" (Council of the European Communities, Luxembourg 1986).

therefore, improve the ability to protect biotechnological inventions. It is only to the extent that the EPC provides for patent protection that the CPC will provide for instruments necessary to secure that Community patents shall have a unitary character as well as:

> have equal effects throughout the territories to which this Convention applies and may only be granted, transferred, revoked or allowed to lapse in respect of the whole of such territories . . . (Article 2 (2) CPC).

Thus, the CPC will not provide a solution to the basic issue of appropriately protecting biotechnological inventions. Even for the positive effects which the CPC may have on the unitary nature of protection, it is difficult to predict its entry into force. This is unlikely to occur before 1993 and may well come into force for less than all Member States of the Community. The possibility also exists that the CPC will leave open a permanent option between a Community patent and a European Patent. Alongside the EPC/CPC structure, national patent laws will continue to exist. Thus, even the entry into force of the CPC would by no means make superfluous amendments of national laws providing for legislative guidance as to the protection of biotechnological inventions under national patent law.

(vi) Protection of Biotechnological Inventions by the Courts

36. From past experience with the judicial practice of the courts of the Member States, it may be observed that courts would prefer, perhaps even need to have, more legislative guidance when dealing with problems of patentability in the field of biotechnology. As an example of the difficulties encountered by the courts in the Member States and of the time needed to find solutions for questions not specifically answered in the law, the case law of the German Federal Supreme Court on the repeatability requirement of biotechnological inventions may be mentioned.

This Court first demonstrated its exceptional understanding of the necessity to interpret in modern patent law the concept of invention according to the latest state of scientific knowledge in 1969 and affirmed that a method for breeding animals is eligible for patent protection, provided the procedure is repeatable, i.e. it can be readily duplicated by a person skilled in the art[21].

Six years later, when patentability of a microbiological process and of a microorganism *per se* i.e., a product claim, was at issue, the German Federal Supreme Court affirmed its position as regards the patentability of living matter in general. It also accepted the deposit of a microorganism strain in a publicly accessible depository as a valid support of the written description as far as the microbiological process was concerned, but not in respect of claims directed to the microorganism *per se*.

In the latter context it stated as follows:

> It is inconsistent with the Patent Act prerequisite of reproducibility of the invention to refer the expert to a product of the inventor according to the invention in order to reproduce his invention. Protection for a microorganism *per se* or – what amounts to the same thing – for a process of propagating a microorganism in a conventional manner without a teaching to the expert as to how to produce the microorganism is so alien to conventional patent law that it could not be obtained via a change in the conventional case law but only a change of the Patent Act.[22]

---

[21] Decision of March 27, 1969, 1 IIC 136 (1970)—"Red Dove".
[22] Decision of March 11, 1975, 6 IIC 208 (1975)—"Baker's Yeast".

After the German legislature failed to react for another eleven years, the Federal Supreme Court in 1987, in view of criticism expressed and even more so because of a different view taken on the specific issue by the European Patent Office, reversed its former case law. Since 1987, under the German Patent Act protection for a new microorganism *per se* is obtainable, if the possibility of reproducing the new breed can be substituted by the deposit and release of a reproducible sample of the micro-organism[23].

The German case law thus suggests that advances in protecting biotechnological inventions by decisions of national courts of the Member States can only be expected after long delays. Legal uncertainties and deficiencies of protection could, as a rule, be remedied only after years, perhaps even decades. Under the present patent law regime in the Community, national judicial decisions, even those of the Supreme Courts, produce legal effects only in the territory of that particular state so that favourable adaptation in one Member State results in divergent adaptation in the Community as a whole. Although case law in one Member State may eventually lead to changes in legislation or have harmonising effects on the case law of other Member States, no certainty can be offered with such an approach and much time would be lost.

(vii) Necessity for the Community to Act

37. It results from this analysis of the existing legal framework at national and international level (see (i) to (vi)) that the law for protecting biotechnological inventions is unsatisfactory and in urgent need of improvements. As a result of the work performed by OECD and WIPO, the main deficiencies have been detected and recommendations for how to improve the situation have been put forward. Particularly the "Suggested Solutions" elaborated by WIPO accord with most of the needs of inventors in modern biotechnology.

38. Having regard to the great importance of biotechnology for the future of the Community, the negative effects of the divergent adaptation resulting from the situation described above are unacceptable for the Community. Whereas the two leading nations in biotechnology, the United States of America and Japan, have been able continuously to adapt their patent protection according to the latest needs of industry, science and consumers, the Member States, representing comparable potential of intellectual manpower and capital, are immobilized by a not yet completed and, in respect of biotechnology, in part outdated legal framework. In order to preclude any further negative effects for Community science, industry and consumers arising from the present situation, it is incumbent upon the Commission to propose the necessary remedial measures.

39. The Directive is also a prerequite to eliminating barriers to the exchange of knowledge and technology transfer between Member States and to trade in the Community. By providing the same clear and improved standards of patenting in the national patent laws of Member States, the readiness to communicate technical knowledge, which in the past has suffered considerable setbacks, will grow. In parallel, harmonised protection of biotechnological inventions will not only give incentives necessary for investments in biotechnology throughout the Community but will also contribute to trade between Member States which under present conditions is hampered by the fact that export of self-reproducible biotechnological products into areas with uncertain, weak or even non-existent protection is less than attractive for obvious reasons. Also as a result of the Directive, the Community will offer investors equal possibilities for protection so that they may treat the Community as a single market with the possibility of securing reasonable returns on their investments. Community

---

[23] Decision of February 12, 1987, 18 IIC 396 (1987)—"Rabies Virus".

based industries will be attracted to repatriate their funds invested overseas in recent years in research and development in biotechnology. Investors from third countries will be more inclined to invest in the Member States.

Relationship between the Proposed Directive and the European Patent Convention

40. The proposed directive is intended to coexist, and not to interfere with, the existing international legal network in which the EPC, the UPOV Convention and the Budapest Treaty are the cornerstones. It is therefore indispensable that any proposal must be compatible with the provisions of those conventions. Therefore, the legislative guidance offered by the Directive to the Member States having in their national patent laws provisions identical or similar to that of Article 53 (b) EPC, necessarily takes the form of provisions of a more detailed nature. This represents the only realistic approach to providing solutions which meet the needs of modern biotechnology and which establish legal certainty throughout the Member States.

41. The proposed Directive does not seek to establish a Community industrial property right for biotechnological inventions. The proposed Directive has, however, methodically made use of existing legal principles in patent laws and Conventions as well as solutions developed in other fora in order to secure an application of national patent laws for biotechnological inventions which is both necessary and appropriate for the community as a whole. By harmonising national patent law standards for the patenting of biotechnological inventions and the scope of their protection, it will enable science and industry to acquire in the Member States one or more national patents tailored to their needs and the needs of the consumer. Since the EPC and the CPC do not offer the necessary legislative protection, and due to their coexistence with the national patent laws, the Directive will fulfil its tasks even after the CPC has entered into force in all Member States.

42. The proposed Directive respects the limitations existing under the pertinent provisions of the EPC and the national patent laws of the Member States. It is therefore primarily based on the following assumptions:

– discoveries as such are not regarded as patentable inventions;

– plant and animal varieties as such or essentially biological processes for the production of plants or animals are excluded from patent protection;

– microbiological processes or the products therefore are eligible for patent protection; and

– methods for treatment of the animal body by surgery or therapy and diagnostic methods practised on animal body are not regarded as inventions which are susceptible of industrial application if practised for a therapeutic purpose.

43. It is clear that the framework of the current rules on the patenting of living matter now reflects incorrect assumptions. In view of the social and economic importance which biotechnological inventions have for the Community's future, the Directive provides for principles which will ensure that such rules remain strictly limited to their original aims.

44. For this purpose the proposed solutions systematically take advantage of work performed by international organizations such as WIPO, the European Patent Organization and OECD. Particularly the approach found in the Examination Guidelines of

the EPO[24] and the "Suggested Solutions" of the International Bureau of WIPO[25] form the basis of or are even in part incorporated in the solutions of the proposed Directive.

Since the EPO patent grant practice and the Examination Guidelines are developing on a case-by-case basis, reflecting the immediate needs of the Examining Division, they do not address all problems in this area or do not so in an exhaustive manner. The provisions of the proposed Directive necessarily go further, though generally in the same direction as that originated in the EPO Examination Guidelines.

Only in some instances, for example in respect of the availability of deposited matter after the application has been refused or withdrawn or is deemed to be withdrawn, the provisions of the Directive differ slightly from those under Rule 28 of the EPC Implementing Regulations. Moreover, the Directive specifically addresses problems in respect of issues arising under national patent law only, such as the scope of protection, rights conferred, infringement related questions and the like.

45. Thus, on the whole the proposed Directive corresponds to the EPC and to the patent grant practices of the EPO. Although it will not directly or legally affect either the EPC or the practice under the EPC, the indirect effects of the proposed Directive should be substantial.

Firstly, as far as the Directive correlates with the existing patent granting practice based on the EPO Examination Guidelines, it will in fact lead to a harmonised interpretation of European and national patents.

Secondly, where provisions of the Directive clarify questions not yet answered in the Examination Guidelines of the EPO, they do so with the necessary legislative authority and closely following the solutions suggested by the International Bureau of WIPO. This will facilitate the task of the EPO in its constant efforts to improve on firm grounds its Examination Guidelines. For it is virtually excluded that national administrative or judicial authorities of the Member States, competent for example in revocation procedures, will take an approach for European patents different from that for national patents, although they would have been issued on the basis of different but analogous provisions.

As regards the differences in respect of the availability of the deposited biological materials, the proposed Directive does not interfere with the EPC. It only provides for harmonised solutions in national patent laws of the Member States, which under the present regime differ among themselves as well as with regard to EPC Rule 28.

A possible effect of the proposed provisions of the Directive which differ from EPC Rule 28 could result in an adaptation of that Rule to the Directive. Such an amendment could be provided for by agreement between the Administrative Council of the European Patent Organisation, without revising the EPC.

46. From the foregoing it is clear that the proposed Directive will not interfere with the EPC, nor will it establish any interdependence in a legal sense between the two bodies of law. The practical interaction of the two systems is nonetheless likely to be productive. On the one hand, only the Directive is in a position to secure a harmonised practice under the EPC as far as the national phase of that practice in the Member States is concerned. On the other hand, the Directive will offer the EPO firm grounds on which to develop further its patent granting practice according to the latest needs of industry and science in biotechnology.

*   *   *

---

[24] Guidelines for Examination in the European Patent Office, published by the European Patent Office, Munich 1983, as last amended in July 1987.
[25] Contained in WIPO Doc. BIOT/CE/III/2 of April 8, 1987.

PART TWO: PARTICULAR PROVISIONS

CHAPTER 1

Patentability of Living Matter

ARTICLE 1

This Article defines the aim of the Directive: to ensure that national patent laws are in compliance and accord with the terms of the Directive. The Directive will have no legal effects vis-à-vis the European Patent Convention (EPC) or any provisions thereof.

ARTICLE 2

The aim of Article 2 is to establish legislatively that the condition of being alive or of being living matter would be legally insufficient to render such material unpatentable. This principle must be explicitly recognised for biotechnological inventions. The normal criteria for patentability provide no guidance on how to determine the patentability of living matter. This article is therefore necessary even though the principle to be established is already widely recognised. Where the principle is not completely accepted, under Article 2, the argument can no longer be raised that all living matter must be excluded from patent protection on the ground that the mere fact of being alive disqualifies such inventions from being regarded as patentable, e.g., on the basis that they are natural products.

The history of industrial property protection demonstrates that inventions in newly developing technologies have always encountered difficulties in securing legal protection. Such an explicit legislative provision as is laid down in Article 2 is necessary to remedy certain difficulties and to prevent others from arising when general provisions of patent law are applied to inventions involving technology that makes use of living entities such as animals, plants and micro-organisms. As all inventive activity involves intervention by man into the processes or products of nature, there is no reason to exclude from protection inventive activity relating to living matter, other than the area of humankind (but this type of provision is already commonplace in patent law on public policy grounds as is found in Article 52(4) EPC).

Only a very few national courts of the Member States, after decades of uncertainty, have managed to develop a coherent doctrine under patent law to protect living matter. Article 2 will establish a minimum level of legal certainty without the delay caused by awaiting judicial resolutions which may not arise. Such certainty is required to foster economic and technical progress. This can only be achieved within an acceptable period of delay by requiring legislative adoption of the rule to recognise the general rule that living matter as such is no less patentable than non-living matter if the required extent of novelty, inventive activity and industrial applicabilty is present for patent law purposes.

ARTICLE 3

Although biotechnology is an old science involving the use of and deliberate selection by man of organisms which improve agriculture, animal husbandry and baking and brewing activities, research in the new areas of biotechnology is producing an even greater ability on the part of man to intervene in natural biotechnological processes. When attempt is made to determine the extent of patent protection which might be available to inventions in the field of living matter, there is the additional complication of a special system which was devised for the protection of plant varieties. The existence of this special system has generated uncertainty as to the extent to which plant matter as such can be patented.

Biological classification begins with the kingdom descending from the phylum through the genera and species. All members of genera and species possess at least some common characteristics but also usually possess other characteristics which distinguish some members from others. A variety, however, for purposes of variety protection, is defined as a group whose members possess no distinguishing characteristics one from another.

Exceptions to patentability for the categories of inventions relating to plant and animal varieties and essentially biological processes for producing plants and animals were created under certain conventions on the basis that these inventions lacked industrial applicability. It was considered preferable to provide special protection for plant varieties some of which were already patented and patentable in various countries. For animal varieties, the need for protection was less evident and therefore patent protection was not seriously considered.

It is clear today that the new biotechnological techniques, which were unknown to the authors of the relevant exclusions, have come to occupy the territory of both fields. This is demonstrated by the numerous developments which have arisen in microbiology which now lead to the development of new plant and animal characteristics. No justification appears to exist at present to continue to treat the results of different forms of research differently as to the protection which may be obtained. Thus, were patent and plant variety protection systems being formulated on the basis of current scientific developments and technology, different provisions for these systems might be adopted from those chosen thirty years ago. Nonetheless, until the international legal framework can be adapted to the new technologies, these exclusions will remain and must be addressed if greater legal clarity and certainty are to be achieved.

The exclusion of plant and animal varieties prohibits only the patenting of animals, plants and plant propagating material in the genetically fixed form of a plant or animal variety. There is no justification where an invention concerning plant or animal matter, such as plant or animal cells, cell lines, tissue cultures and larger parts, is not covered by the language of the exclusion to either withhold protection from such an invention or to give the exclusion a wider interpretation than is justified by the purpose for which it was developed. It is perfectly acceptable and appropriate for the exclusion to be limited, in conformity with its wording, to those cases in which plants are characterised precisely by their individual phenotype. Article 3 first sentence therefore provides that it is not plants and animals in general which are excluded from patentability but only plant and animal varieties as such, i.e. in the genetically fixed and stable form of a variety. Thus, Article 3 first sentence will establish the principle that patent protection is available for plant and animal material which is not a variety.

The second sentence of Article 3 is necessary as regards plants in light of the uncertainty created by Article 2(1) of the UPOV Convention which obliges contracting States to provide only one form of legal protection for the same genus or species. The principle is clear that if plant variety protection is available for a variety, patent protection would not. But if patent protection is available for plant material which is not a variety, as is required in the first sentence of this Article, the rule must be legislatively clarified as to how far the patent rights extend. Thus, this sentence acknowledges the principle that protected plant varieties must co-exist alongside patents on plants but requires the further principle to be introduced that the patent rights pertaining to such patent claims must be enforceable even in respect of finished varieties incorporating such patented inventions.

Without Article 3, the patenting of new plant characteristics, such as insect, disease and herbicide resistance, might not be given the proper legal effects which encourage economic progress via the patent system. Article 3 in no way interferes with the role or

327

the legal effects of the system of breeders' rights. However, problems of interaction between exclusive rights granted under the patent and plant breeders' system may arise where the patentability of plants, parts of plants such as genetic sequences and classifications other than varieties is recognised. The legal uncertainty which is thereby created relating to the extent of the rights which may be enforced between the two systems must be resolved. Article 3 is therefore necessary to ensure that the patent system is allowed to produce its proper effects without hindrance from or to the plant breeders' system. Article 3 is also necessary to respond to the need to determine the effect of patent rights in any invention relating to plants which is subsequently incorporated into a variety and which variety is subsequently protected by a plant breeders' right. Article 3 establishes the principle that in such a case the patent rights would remain effective as to the patented invention.

Article 2(1) of the UPOV Convention directs the contracting States that they may accord only one form of protection to any protected genera or species. This means that both variety protection and patent protection (double protection) cannot be granted to the same plant genera or species. Article 3 ensures that a clear borderline is drawn between protectable subject matter in each system. One may take as an example a genetic sequence inserted into the genetic material of a plant which renders the plant resistant to insects. The genetic sequence is patented and is subsequently incorporated into an existing variety. The new variety now possesses the new characteristic and is eligible for variety protection. There is no reason for such a new variety to be free from the effects of the patent. This would effectively deny the inventor of the legitimate scope of the right to his invention.

Such an approach neither jeopardises nor runs contrary to the principle of Article 2(1) UPOV. It is not the genetic sequence which is protected by the plant breeders' right nor is the variety protected by the patent. There is no requirement in either patent law or in plant variety law that the patent rights associated with a patented invention are extinguished simply because a variety right is also associated with the final product. Nor do any compelling policy reasons exist for such an interpretation. Quite the contrary. Future developments in biotechnology are likely to provide a valuable range of new and enhanced agricultural products incapable of being produced under traditional breeding techniques which will have a ready market demand. It is also foreseeable that new agricultural products will be developed that have new industrial applications, for example, as petrochemical substitutes and in the field of polymer chemistry.

Notwithstanding the historical context and logical inconsistency of present plant variety and patent laws, the Commission considers that it would be harmful neither to the interests of European industry engaged in biotechnological research nor to the purposes for which the directive is designed to allow a certain number of cases, likely to have applications as plant varieties, which would otherwise have been patentable, to be excluded from patentable subject matter under national patent laws when such plants have been produced by a known biotechnological process. The principle of Article 3(2) is necessary to ensure this result.

ARTICLE 4

Patent law traditionally recognises three types of protectable inventions: process inventions, product inventions and application inventions (also called "uses"). The corresponding categories of patentable biotechnological inventions would be identified as:

1) inventions relating to a process for the creation of a living organism or the production of other biological material;
2) inventions relating to an organism or material as such; and

3) inventions relating to the use of an organism or other biological material.

As most Member States have explicitly excluded from patent protection plant and animal varieties as such, the result is that plant and animal varieties as products are not eligible for patent protection. This does not, however, have the effect of excluding the other two types of inventions from protection if and as these relate to plant varieties, that is, microbiological processes and processes which are not "essentially biological" for the production of plant varieties and specific uses of plant varieties. Article 4 is needed so that these two types of inventions are expressly included in protectable subject matter under the patent laws of the Member States.

Article 4 will thus establish the principle in national patent laws that the traditional categories of patentable inventions relating to processes and uses are not affected by the exclusion of plant and animal varieties from patent protection. In light of the exclusionary provisions of many patent laws along with the principle of the prohibition of double protection in Article 2(1) of the UPOV Convention, Article 4 is necessary to establish clearly that the traditional categories of patentable inventions as these relate to biotechnological inventions constitute patentable subject matter.

ARTICLE 5

Most Member States' national patent laws mirror the language of Article 53(b) of the European Patent Convention which states that patents shall not be granted in respect of

plant or animal varieties or essentially biological processes for the production of plants or animals; this provision does not apply to microbiological processes or the products thereof.

Thus, when the exclusions for plant and animal varieties and essentially biological processes were drafted, the field of microbiology, which did not involve traditional breeding processes, was singled out as being appropriate for patent protection. Microbiological processes and products of such processes were specifically recognised as eligible for patent protection. The underlying motivation for this language was to carve out of patent law protection the results of traditional breeding processes using plants and animals. The results of such breeding processes would enjoy their own protection in the form of plant or animals variety rights.

Because inventions relating to living matter specifically resulting from microbiology are patentable in those Member States with such provisions, it is therefore of considerable importance for the application of patent law to establish what is included in the term "microbiological process". Where the determination of the patentability of a biotechnological invention rests on the criterion of whether a process is microbiological, it is vital to a proper application of patent law that this term be correctly defined. Article 5 of the Directive addresses this problem and establishes a minimum principle in this respect.

No attempt was made to specify the borderline between those areas capable of patent protection—microbiological processes and products—and those areas excluded from protection—plant and animal varieties and essentially biological processes—it being assumed that the results of traditional breeding and microbiological processes would be readily distinguishable. Had science and biotechnology not made the advances they have in the past thirty years, these distinctions would continue to be valid and the two types of protection would have wholly separate fields of application.

As many inventions in the field of biotechnology concern microorganisms, the principle of patent law in Article 5 in respect of microbiological processes corresponds best to the original intentions of the drafters of the exclusions, accords with the exclusions which have been adopted and offers an adequate incentive to potential innovators to pursue high risk and costly research.

Without this Article, it would be possible for widely varying definitions to be adopted throughout the Community of what is considered microbiological and, consequently, for very different decisions to be taken regarding the same factual patent application. Article 5 is therefore necessary to establish a minimum uniform principle of patent law and at the same time avoid an inappropriately narrow principle from being adopted in connection with the patent law concept of "a microbiological process". Thus, the rule must be established that inventions relating to processes which either use or directly operate upon or result in a microorganism should be considered microbiological and thus eligible for patent protection. Article 5 prescribes this rule. In this connection, Article 5 must be read in conjunction with Article 19 of what should be understood by the term "microorganism". Thus the principle of Article 5 should not be limited only to microorganisms as such but would apply to other microscopic animate matter as well.

ARTICLE 6

Likewise greater certainty and uniformity must be engendered into the application of the criterion in national patent laws of the patent law concept of a "microbiological process". To give optimum effect to developments in biotechnology, it must be legislatively established that neither the entire process nor every step in the process need be of a microbiological nature in order for the process as a whole to be deemed microbiological. If a necessary and important part of a complex process is microbiological, while other steps of the process are merely biological, rejections of patentability on the basis that the process is essentially biological should be prevented. Article 6 is necessary to produce this result.

The Article will make it necessary for the principle to be adopted that a multi-step process in which the essence of the invention is incorporated into a microbiological step is not deprived of its microbiological character simply because the process contains other, non-microbiological, steps. To take an example, the genetic manipulation of a plant cell may be performed which is a microbiological process. Thereafter, the entire plant may be regenerated from the single cell (a process called differentiation). This latter process may be said to be essentially biological, but the entire process should be accorded the character of microbiological because the essence of the process and the invention is a microbiological step. The process should therefore be considered patentable despite the presence of an essentially microbiological step in the overall inventive process. Without Article 6, the exclusion from patentability of essentially microbiological processes for the production of plants could result in erroneous rejections to patentability and unsystematic adaptation of national patent law principles when applied in the same factual contexts.

ARTICLE 7

Because some national patent laws exclude essentially biological processes from patentability, it is necessary to lay down a principle of patent laws which establishes the extent to which human intervention is required in order to ensure that an invention will be considered patentable subject matter. In this connection, it is important to distinguish between traditional breeding activities and other forms of human invention in biological matter. As essentially biological processes are generally agreed to refer to traditional breeding processes, it is important that the principle laid down differentiate between the use of biological material which falls into the category of essentially biological and that use which may properly be regarded as patentable subject matter.

The EPO Examination Guidelines in this regard that human intervention must play a "significant part" in determining or controlling the result it is desired to achieve and notes that the question is one of degree depending on the extent to which there is technical intervention by man in the process (C–IV, 3.4). Article 7 of the Directive, by contrast, is intended to exclude only traditional biological breeding activities based upon selection and as such may be regarded as slightly more liberal than the Guidelines.

Article 7 will ensure that both an appropriate and a consistent rule is adopted for national patent systems in situations where it needs to be determined if sufficient technical human intervention has occurred to render an invention patentable. Such a rule should reflect a liberal approach in view of the now artificial nature of the distinction between "essentially biological" and "not essentially biological" processes. Biotechnological techniques have effectively rendered this difference of little practical value. Thus, for purposes of national patent laws, human intervention of a technical nature into the natural processes of biology need not be at the same time of a drastic nature in order for a process to fall outside the scope of being "essentially biological". Any human intervention aside from selection, such as influencing the crossing procedure of the replication process, would remove the process from the field of "essentially biological" processes. The invention would, of course, thereafter fall to be considered under the criteria for patenting.

ARTICLE 8

In certain circumstances, patent law recognises the patentability of products or substances which are of natural origin. Usually this occurs in situations where a product exists in a naturally occurring mixture of substances without it having been identified in the mixture. The invention typically consists of identification of the substance and isolation for useful purposes in a usable or pure form in which it did not exist in nature.

With the new biotechnological techniques, many substances are now capable of being selected and adapted for industrial, commercial and medical uses. The possibility of legally protecting such developments in the field of biotechnology is important to ensure that the necessary investment and research are undertaken.

Not all national patent systems have recognised the patentability of naturally occurring matter which fulfils the criteria for patentability, such as that in a mixture (either natural or modified) notwithstanding the fact that the substance existed in an unidentified form prior to the recognition of its existence and utility and prior to adapting the matter for use in an industrial application. Article 8 will establish that, as long as a claimed product has not been sufficiently disclosed, it should not be considered unpatentable simply because it was part of a pre-existing natural material.

Although an invention may involve a naturally occurring substance, such as an alkaloid isolated from a plant root, or a biological factor isolated from an animal organ, there will be a considerable difference between the product as it existed in nature and the product in a useful form. As such it is different from the product as it existed in nature. The so-called natural material has been changed by human intervention and the form in which it is claimed for patent purposes is not the same as that in which it exists in nature. Such products must in any event comply with all criteria of patentability (novelty, inventive step and industrial applicability).

The EPO Examination Guidelines also recognise this rule. There, it is said that if a substance found in nature must first be isolated from its surroundings and a process for obtaining it is developed, such process is patentable. Moreover, if the substance can be properly characterised either by its structure, by the process by which it is obtained or by any other parameters, and it is "new" in the sense of having no previously recognised existence, then the substance per se may be patentable (C–IV, 2.3) unless it is specifically excluded, such as plant or animal varieties.

This Article is different from Article 2 which addresses the question of the patentability of living matter as such, whether microorganisms, plants or animals. Here, the products are likely to be other than living organisms themselves, for example, plasmids, DNA (deoxyribonucleic acid) segments, proteins, peptides, enzymes and the like.

ARTICLE 9

A basic principle of patent law is that a mere discovery is unpatentable. A discovery is defined in the Geneva "Treaty on the International Recognition of Scientific Discoveries" of 1978 as the recognition of phenomena, properties or laws of the material universe. Objections to patentability of natural substances—living or non—may be raised on the basis that such products are discoveries and therefore that they are not "new". Such objections are usually raised in the biotechnological context, as noted above, for the sole reason that the products were present in a re-existing material which itself may or may not be part of the prior art for patent law purposes. Article 9 deals with the two related issues of discovery and lack of novelty.

According to the EPO Examination Guidelines, if a new property of a known material or article is discerned, it would constitute a discovery and would be unpatentable. If, however, the new property is put to practical use, the result may be a patentable invention. If a natural substance is sought to be patented, the Guidelines note that the line of demarcation between the mere discovery of a natural substance and its patentability will depend on the degree of human technical intervention necessary to obtain it (C–IV, 2.3).

Where a substance is claimed in a form which results from human intervention in the material world, it is more than mere discovery, irrespective of whether the intervention is simple or complex. Article 9 is necessary to ensure that this distinction is correctly applied in patent law. As to the argument that such products are not "new", a product is considered "new" under the patent laws of most Member States if it does not form part of the "state of the art". The state of the art is deemed to be everything which has been made available to the public by means of a written or oral disclosure, by use or in any other way before the patent application was filed (for example, Article 54 EPC). The fact that a product may have existed in a mixture before its identification, isolation, purification and usefulness have been established does not render it part of the state of the art for purposes of patent law because it was effectively "not available" to the public by any means.

The principle required by Article 9 does not prejudge the issue of the novelty of the product. If information was available as to the existence of the particular mixture in question, and if the information available could have made the particular product foreseeable as a separate entity and would have enabled the person skilled in the art to render it into useful form, such product may be considered not to be new. In the absence of specific information, and if a product isolated from a mixture or synthesised is physically different from the mixture which was available to the public prior to the invention, novelty should be admitted as a matter of principle. Article 9 will ensure that an invention is not erroneously considered unpatentable as a discovery simply because it was once part of a pre-existing mixture.

CHAPTER 2

Scope of Protection

ARTICLE 10

Article 10 is addressed to the issue of experimental use of a patented invention involving living or self-replicable matter. The issue of experimental use in patent law is not dealt with in the EPC. Article 31(b) of the "Convention on the European Patent for the Common Market" (CPC) states only that the rights conferred by a Community patent shall not extend to:

acts done for experimental purposes relating to the subject-matter of the invention.

Under national patent laws as well, experimental use of a patented invention does not constitute patent infringement but interpretations vary of what acts constitute experimental use.

If a patented biotechnological product is employed to produce an improvement over the previous product, such use may legitimately be regarded as experimental use. If the improved product is a biotechnological product which is self-replicating, the patented starting material need only be prepared once in small quantities. To obtain commercial amounts it would not be necessary to reuse the product enjoying patent protection or to find a new way of production, avoiding the direct use of the patented product, as would be the case, for example, with a patented chemical product unable to reproduce itself. Replication of the small amount obtained in the first "experiment" with self reproducing material would suffice.

In order to safeguard the patent rights granted for the first invention and thereby place the inventor in such a case on an equal footing with inventors in other fields, Article 10 is necessary to qualify the first use of the patented product to obtain even a small amount of a new or improved product as experimental use so long as the improved product is multiplied for other experimental purposes. If multiplication were for commercial purposes, then such use of the new product would not be covered by the patent law doctrine of experimental use.

It would be irrelevant whether an improved product is obtained from a product enjoying patent protection in one or several process steps. What is essential is whether any new product obtained by using a patented product is manufactured by multiplication of the material obtained from the patented product. Article 10 establishes the minimum necessary point beyond which the use of patented self-reproducing products will not be considered experimental, that is, at commercialisation.

Article 10 is needed in part because of the variety of interpretations of what acts constitute experimental use. More importantly, it establishes a rule for patented living matter consistent with patent law doctrine applicable in other fields of patentable subject matter.

ARTICLE 11

Under traditional patent law doctrine, the purchaser of a patented product may use such product in any manner he deems fit. A purchaser may put the product to such use as is consistent with its purchase, for example, a patented machine may become part of a factory production process; a patented chemical may be used to treat plants or kill insects, etc.

It is a well-established patent law principle that a purchaser of a patented product is not allowed, unless it has been specifically agreed, to manufacture the patented product itself. The jurisprudence of the Court of Justice has recognised the patentee's right "to use the invention with a view to manufacturing industrial products and putting them into circulation for the first time" (*Centrafarm B.V. et al. v. Sterling Drug Inc. 1974 ECR 1147 at 1162*).

The Treaty's articles on the free movement of goods should not be confused with the patentee's exclusive rights to produce patented products. The principle in the Treaty of Rome in respect of the free movement of goods (Articles 30 to 36) has also resulted in the development of an exhaustion principle as applied to trade between Member States including goods covered by industrial property. Once a patented product has been placed on the market by a patentee or with his consent, no control over the further use of the product in intra-Community trade may be exerted by the patentee or a licensee.

The exhaustion of rights which applies under the Court's interpretation of these articles relates to three activities: the use, offer for sale and sale of a product covered by industrial property rights. Use in such a case relates to use of the product in commerce in intra-Community trade. It does not include the manufacture of products covered by industrial property rights. Patent rights would not be exhausted for the production of the patented product until the patent term itself expired.

The purpose of Article 11 is to establish this rule for patented living or self-replicable matter. Thus, the purchaser of, for example, patented barley may use his barley to make whisky without infringing the patent; the purchaser of patented malt or yeast, for example, may use these products to make beer without infringing the patent. Both uses involve a certain amount of multiplication (such as germination) of the product sold but such uses are clearly intended by the sale.

Where patented self-replicating material is sold for purposes of propagation, for example, seeds, the purchaser usually a farmer will have the right without patent infringement to use the products for the purpose for which he purchased such seeds, i.e. to grow a crop for harvesting even though such use unavoidably involves multiplication of his seeds. The patent rights would not be exhausted in respect of the use of the crop grown from the patented seeds as a source for the sale of new propagating material (seeds) as this would involve production for the purposes of selling the patented product itself. (Any variety rights inherent in seeds protected by plant breeders' rights would similarly be unexhausted in respect of the use of the crop grown from the seeds as a source for the sale of new propagating material).

Article 11 will ensure that the use which is intended in a sale of patented self-reproducing material is not confused with a use which involves patent infringement. The provisions of Article 11 are needed because the issue of the extent of patent rights in respect of patented living or self-replicating material has not been dealt with in any national patent system and the provisions of the EPC do not address this question, save that the rights conferred by a European patent are said to be the same as would be conferred by a national patent (Article 64(1) EPC). Infringement of European patents is considered under national law principles taking account of EPC requirements regarding claim interpretation. The issue which is addressed in Article 11 therefore is not regulated by any specific provision of the EPC.

The CPC, of which seven out of the nine original signatories have adopted laws ratifying this Convention, at Article 32, provides that the rights conferred by a Community patent shall not extend to acts concerning a patented product within the territories of the contracting States after the product has been put on the market in any State by or with the consent of the proprietor of the patent unless there are grounds under Community law which would justify the extension of the patent rights to such acts. Article 81 of the CPC provides the same principle in respect of national patents.

The intention of the drafters of these provisions was to incorporate into the provisions of the CPC the prior and future jurisprudence of the Court of Justice dealing with the interpretation of Articles 30 and 36 of the Treaty of Rome. These provisions, as has been demonstrated above, relate to different principles of Community law than those dealt with in Article 11 of the Directive.

Article 11 is necessary therefore to distinguish between the meaning of "use" for different purposes of national patent law, the EPC and the CPC. For national patent laws, it needs to be legislatively established that use which involves propagation solely for the purpose of obtaining additional propagative or self-replicating material does not come within the scope of intended use which would be exhausted upon the sale of a patented product. The patent rights inherent in the use of material such as seeds are not exhausted for a use which consists of multiplying such material solely to obtain more thereof. Without Article 11, the relationship of the exhaustion principle under Articles 30 to 36 of the Treaty of Rome and exhaustion of patent rights for self-replicating material under national patent laws might have remained unclear.

*   *   *

ARTICLE 13

As a result of the Directive greater possibilities will exist for patenting products consisting of or containing genetic information, such as a particular DNA segment. Where such biological products are incorporated into a more complex product, such as where the DNA is incorporated into a host microorganism which may be multiplied, the patent protection enjoyed by such products should extend to all products in which the particular genetic information which was essential for the invention remains of essential importance for the products concerned.

Where the patented material is incorporated into a plant or animal variety, such variety may legitimately be subject to the rights granted in the patent. Article 13 will establish this principle for national patent rights. Two arguments have been advanced to suggest that this result would be inappropriate: first, because manufacturing steps were required to obtain the variety from the patented product; and secondly, because plant varieties are excluded from patentability.

As to the first argument, if the particular industrial applicability or usefulness of a variety directly results from an invention which has been patented, then such a variety owes its unique characteristics to the effects of the invention and should therefore come within the scope of protection accorded by the patent. Where an invention is of no commercial importance for the variety, then a different issue would be raised. This situation is not addressed in the Directive because Article 13 specifically stipulates that the patented invention must be of essential importance for the utility or industrial applicability of the final product.

As to the second argument, an exclusion of varieties from patentability is not synonymous with being free from the scope of a relevant patent. In future there are likely to be inventions capable of application in many different plant varieties. For example, resistance to disease or herbicide tolerance may be genetically incorporated into a broad range of plants covering many different varieties. Thus, to be excluded from patentability does not mean that a variety should be free from the effects of a patent granted in a case where an invention in the field of plants concerns a genetic concept which is characterised by new generic information and which can be realised in a multitude of different varieties.

Article 13 is necessary so that this important principle of patent law is explicitly recognised for inventions which do not permit their direct exploitation but which must become part of another entity in order to be used effectively. It would be an insufficient incentive for ensuring that necessary research is undertaken to accord patent protection only to material which on its own has no commercial value. Patent rights must be legislatively prescribed for any final product whose utility, commercial value or industrial applicability depends on a patented invention. The rule must be legislatively mandated in light of the variety of views on this issue for which existing patent laws provide no solution. Without Article 13, it might be considered that the patent protection of a biological product would be lost if such product becomes part of a more complex final product even though such biological product is of essential importance for commercialising the final product.

CHAPTER 3

Dependency License for Plant and Animal Varieties

ARTICLE 14

It is foreseeable that if patents are granted to genetic material, to products containing such material and to biological classifications of plants or animals different from varieties, the situation will arise that new varieties will be bred incorporating such material which will fall under the scope of one or more patents. Commercialisation of such new varieties without authorization by the patentee could constitute patent infringement.

The implications for granting such patents require that a balancing of interests be made as regards the value for society of promoting new technologies and as regards the public interest in maintaining a reasonable limitation on exclusive rights in sensitive areas. This is particularly true in the agricultural sector where the interests of breeders, growers, farmers, science-based industry, the environment, tax payers and the consumer must be taken into account.

Article 14 is necessary to provide for the possibility commercially to exploit new varieties which represent significant technical progress under a non-exclusive license as of right, provided the patentee enjoys the right to receive fair renumeration for the exploitation of his invention. Provision must also made for the patentee to be granted a non-exclusive royalty-paying license from the variety rightholder because in some cases the inventor himself may not be able to exploit his invention in a commercially usable form unless he can commercialise the results obtained by his licensee.

The basic principle provided for in this article is needed in order to give effect to the public interest in promoting further developments of agricultural inventions through breeding activities and to recognise the interests of the patentee to enjoy his exclusive rights which rights provide the incentive for engaging in innovatory activities.

The patent laws of some Member States already provide for a dependency or compulsory license in the event that a subsequent patentable invention cannot be worked without infringement of an earlier patent. This article is similar in that a variety could not be commercially exploited without a license granted by the patentee if such variety came within the scope of relevant patent rights. The provisions of Article 14 differ from existing national patent law provisions in according a license of right, not to a subsequent patentee, but to a subsequent rightholder of a variety developed using the patented invention.

There is no principle of compulsory licensing between patent and plant variety rights which exists in any patent or plant variety law. Article 14 is crucial therefore to an effective exploitation of patented biotechnological inventions in the plant field. Without Article 14, a plant variety rightholder would have to rely on the willingness of the patentee to enter into voluntary bilateral agreements for the use of the patented invention, which agreements the patentee otherwise may or may not be willing to enter into, on terms the breeder may or may not be willing to agree.

To benefit from the provisions of Article 14(1), a variety must represent significant technical progress compared with the teaching of the patent. The significance of the technical progress required for this purpose is a different notion from that of distinctness as currently used in plant variety protection law. This provision ensures that licenses of right would only be available where the new variety represents a genuine agricultural achievement in the first instance, for example, in successfully introducing a genetic sequence into an existing variety. This requirement would preclude licenses from being issued for only minor improvements to varieties which had been initially bred by incorporating patented inventions.

Article 14(2) provides that an application for compulsory licenses may only be made after the expiration of a certain period of time. This period is a reasonable measure to ensure that a patent applicant will have a limited opportunity to make exclusive use of or even to develop for commercial marketing his invention prior to encountering competitors and competition in the market place. In normal circumstances, competitors would be required to await the expiration of the full patent itself i.e., twenty years from the date of filing of the patent application, before being able to use the invention as of right (albeit without the payment of royalties).

Article 14(3) anticipates the situation where the original patentee would like to exploit his invention in the form of a plant variety into which it has been developed by a breeder. This provision of the Article would accord the patentee the right to obtain a non-exclusive license from the breeder to exploit on a commercial basis any variety into which his invention may have been incorporated, upon payment of reasonable royalties. This provision is necessary, for example, to give an inventor who is not a breeder the possibility of commercially exploiting his invention in cases where such exploitation may only be possible in the form of a variety.

Article 14(4) allocates to a national tribunal the task of resolving disputes between patentees and holders of breeders' rights as to the significance of the technical progress or whether the royalties are reasonable. This is both a reasonable safeguard and a necessary measure as it may be expected that disagreements could arise over these issues in the same manner as they may arise over whether a plant variety development falls within the claims of a patent, especially in the context of exploiting new and commercially superior products in the plant field. A neutral adjudicating body having the power to enforce its judgements will be necessary for the effective implementation of the principles in Article 14. Paragraph 4 of Article 14 is therefore necessary to direct that the resolution of disputes concerning the application of the principles prescribed in this article should be determined by a court of competent jurisdiction. This would normally be a court seised of a patent infringement case.

CHAPTER 4

Deposit, Access and Re-deposit

ARTICLE 15

Deposit

It is a fundamental requirement of all patent laws that an enabling disclosure must be made with an application for a patent. All Member States have enacted a similar standard in this regard. An enabling disclosure is one which enables a person skilled in the art to carry out the invention. This principle also appears in the EPC (Article 83). It is a requirement whose purpose is justified by the grant of exclusive rights to an inventor in exchange for disclosure the invention. This in turn contributes to technical progress for the general public and to an advance in the technical state of the art. Once the patent has expired the enabling disclosure provides a description of how the invention may be reproduced for those who wish to capitalise on the no longer patented invention.

In the case of biotechnological inventions, the complexity of biological material generally makes it impossible either to describe in a written fashion the living material itself or to describe in a written fashion all the steps and parameters involved to reach the result which is sought to be patented. It is therefore impossible in many cases for the inventor to state how a person skilled in the art could successfully repeat his invention.

The unique aspect of inventions dealing with biological matter is that they usually self-reproduce themselves under appropriate conditions. In such a case, reproduction by a person not the inventor of the steps and parameters originally employed to develop the invention ceases to be important because the result desired can be obtained much more simply and reliably by self-replication of the material.

Although the patent laws require an enabling disclosure, there is no legislative requirement that such disclosure be in written form. The fact that product inventions in traditional fields of technology could only be disclosed in the required manner by a complete written description of how to make the product must not have as a logical consequence that, in a new technological field, the legal requirement cannot be satisfied in another manner, namely through a reference to a deposit. It is therefore possible and desirable, in order to secure the patentability of biotechnological inventions which cannot be described in a written form, to require that a system of deposit be established for all national patent systems not unlike that which already exists for the EPC. Many Member States already, as a practical matter, permit but do not require deposit while at least one requires that patent applications for living matter be supplemented by reference to a deposited sample of the animate material.

Several Member States are already parties to the Budapest "Treaty on the International Recognition of the Deposit of Microorganisms for the Purposes of Patent Procedure of 1977". This Treaty establishes accepted procedures for deposits to be made for patent purposes. It regulates the technical and legal aspects of the depository institution and of the deposit and binds the signatories who require or admit such deposits for patent purposes to accept, for purposes of their national patent procedure, a deposit made in accordance with the Treaty in any depository institution provided by the Treaty. This Treaty does not oblige the signatories to accept a deposit for purposes of national patent law procedures.

Article 15 of the Directive requires the principle to be adopted that the deposit mechanism will be recognised in all national examining offices for patent application purposes both for process and product patents. Such a principle is necessary in light of the differences in national practices and requirements. Without the principle that a deposit may suffice as an enabling disclosure, the patentability of many important inventions, for example, in the field of new hybridoma cells for the production of antibodies, vaccines or other biological factors, or of microorganisms isolated from their environment which may be valuable agents in the fields of ecology or agriculture or as a means of producing antibiotics or biological factors, could be jeopardised or rendered less certain.

The EPC regulations have established rules for deposit of living matter in connection with applications for European patents. The provisions of Article 15 of the Directive correspond to these rules (Rule 28) for depositing living matter in connection with European patent applications with one exception and three differences. EPC Rule 28 applies to inventions whose claims relate to microbiological processes or products thereof. The rule in Article 15 is not limited to inventions involving a microbiological process but could apply to virtually any invention which involved the use of either a microorganism or other self-reproducing material, which might be claimed in any form (i.e. product, process or use claims). In practice, the rule of Article 15(1) should provide a clearer, but not substantively different, rule than that found in Rule 28 EPC.

Unless such a clear statement of the principle of the extent to which a deposit may complete or replace a traditional written description of the invention is adopted legislatively, considerable difficulties would be encountered in patent enforcement procedures in determining the validity of a patent, such as occurred in the German Federal Supreme Court decision in the "Tollwutvirus" case which endorsed a similar deposit rule for product claims in Germany but which had to overrule longstanding prior jurisprudence to do so.

Access/Release

The Budapest Treaty does not regulate the question of the release of samples of deposited material to the public. Issues such as the time at which release is required, to whom and under what conditions such release should take place were left to national and international laws – with the exception of the minimum requirement that, generally, release is only made if the patent application has been published (Rule 11, Regulations of the Budapest Treaty).

Unlike a traditional written description of an invention which always requires a third party seeking to work the invention to invest a perhaps substantial amount of time, effort and expense, access to deposited living matter enables competitors and would-be users of the invention to obtain instantly and without cost the results of the applicant's research. A single sample may, under appropriate conditions, be sufficient to begin commercial activities. In some cases, a microorganism will represent an entire factory. Unless the issues of the time and conditions of release are satisfactorily resolved, inventors will be tempted to refrain from disclosing their inventions to the detriment of the public and of technical progress in this field, and at considerable risk to the inventor whose invention may be re-invented by another or may lose its confidential nature.

For these reasons a standardised deposit system with sufficient safeguards for the applicant as to the time and conditions of release needs to be established for national patent laws so that equal possibilities will exist for protecting inventions in this field.

The practice of early publication of a patent application in Europe came about as a result of the introduction of deferred examination of such applications because most patent offices had thousands of pending, unexamined, applications on file at any given moment. Publication of the patent application alerted the public of the existence of the claims in pending applications which otherwise would have remained unknown for several more years. This avoided duplication of research and production in fields covered by others. The adoption of a system of publication and deferred examination was not initially intended to provide industry with a source of valuable technical information on the relevant state of the art. Rather, it was more of a practical necessity. The importance and use of the publication of patent applications as a source of technical, commercial and industrial information for interested circles developed subsequently.

Thus, the purpose for which the publication of patent applications was adopted was to give notice to the interested public of areas likely to be covered by future exclusive rights. There was no intention or desire to create the capability of exploiting the invention for commercial purposes although, even with a written disclosure, such a possibility was not excluded. For this reason, a system of compensation was devised for the use of an invention prior to patent grant following publication.

Since a written disclosure in a patent application is open to the public in Europe at the date of first publication, it has been argued that the same criterion should apply to a deposit and that deposits should likewise be open to the public. This problem does not arise in the USA where no publication of the application is made prior to the grant of a patent. If a patent is not granted, no release is made of deposited material. An applicant could then make use of his invention as a trade secret. In Japan, a distinction is made between the initial publication of the application and third party access to deposited material, so that samples are only made available to the public during the period allocated for the opposition procedure after the second publication indicating the notice of patent grant.

In European countries with an early publication system, a rule imposing public access rights to deposits from the date of first publication could produce considerable disadvantages for the inventor of a biotechnological invention. If release to the public of deposited material is made before patent grant, an inventor whose application is withdrawn or denied would not have the possibility of using his invention as a trade secret. Release of such material to third parties could enable them, in some cases, to begin commercial activities. While the possibility of losing the confidential nature of an invention exists for all published but subsequently unsuccessful patent applications, the release of material which greatly facilitates the use of an invention distorts the disclosure rule to the unwarranted advantage of a competitor because of the greater immediate value of a sample of the deposited material than that of a written description.

In respect of deposited animate matter, therefore, it is necessary to separate the desired notice function of the early publication from the undesirable effects of providing the capability for the public to employ the invention for other than verification or experimental purposes. Thus, restrictions and conditions on access to and transmission of any samples of matter deposited in connection with patent application procedures must be established.

Patent applicants who have considered making or have made deposits in connection with their applications have expressed dissatisfaction with certain aspects of the EPC deposit rules (Rule 28 EPC) and similar provisions of national patent systems. Under the EPC rules, where a deposit has been made pursuant to a patent application, a party requesting a sample must undertake not to make it available to third parties and to make use of the sample only for experimental purposes. These undertakings expire if the patent application is unsuccessful, is withdrawn or is deemed to be withdrawn, or if the patent has expired in all designated States.

The undertaking to restrict the use of samples of deposited matter to experimental uses prescribed in EPC Rule 28 expires as soon as the application is refused or withdrawn and at the moment a patent is granted. In cases where the patent is granted, the patent rights themselves would prevent other than experimental use of such samples. In the cases where no patent is granted, an applicant not only is obliged to allow samples of his material to be delivered to third parties without any compensation he also loses the confidential nature of his work and the possibility of exploiting the invention as a trade secret.

Rule 28 EPC was amended in 1979 following wide-scale dissatisfaction with this aspect of the release conditions to contain mainly two improvements:

(1) adoption of the expert solution; and
(2) an extension of the undertaking required from the requesting party to include cultures derived from the sample.

The expert solution is an option which an applicant may elect which provides for release of a sample up to the moment of patent grant or refusal thereof or of withdrawal of the application if a third party requests a sample of the deposit. Release is made to an independent expert who is himself bound to use the sample only for experimental purposes and not to transmit it to others including the third party. The expert is free, however, to report the results of his experiments and verification of the sample to the third party. The expert solution has been introduced into the national patent practices of Denmark, France and Italy. The Italian practice is a variant of the EPC rule in that the expert solution is not optional and applies for the entire patent term.

The expert solution of EPC Rule 28 does not protect the applicant in a situation where an application is withdrawn, not pursued or refused. In addition, it has been questioned whether the rule is compatible with the requirement that an application must disclose an invention in a manner sufficiently clear and complete for it to be carried out by a person skilled in the art (Article 83 EPC). There have as yet been no judicial decisions on this question and thus on the issue of the sufficiency of the disclosure for purposes of the EPC. Both difficulties need to be addressed in the context of national patent laws.

The obligation for a patent disclosure to enable the public to carry out an invention applies to the public in the jurisdiction of the patent right involved. According to the accepted theory of patent law, whereby the granting authority and the inventor effectively enter into a contract to the effect that the inventor is accorded exclusive rights in exchange for disclosing his invention, there is an absence of the quid pro quo between the patentee and the grantor where disclosure in the form of a sample of self-replicating material is provided to the public of a jurisdiction where no patent has been granted or applied for.

There is no legal requirement in patent law that an applicant must enable the public or other countries to exploit his invention nor is there any interest on the part of a State which has granted exclusive rights in respect of an invention to make samples available to another jurisdiction where no protection exists. Transmission of a sample of the deposit to another jurisdiction where release has been requested, despite the absence of rights associated with a patent application or a patent, serves no genuine purpose of the patent system. Such a possibility should be minimised for inventions in the field of living matter.

It has been suggested that to eliminate the possibility of inappropriate release of samples, the rule would need to be adopted that samples of the deposit may only be delivered to parties residing in a country for which or in which a patent application had been filed or where a patent had been granted. Such an approach is unlikely to meet with much support in light of the well-established principle of open disclosure in all patent laws. A similar result can be achieved, as is done in Article 15(3)(b)(iii), by imposing an undertaking on a requesting party that the sample will be used only for experimental purposes irrespective of the countries to which such samples may ultimately be brought or transmitted. This restriction, along with the undertaking not to transmit a sample to any third parties, will enable an applicant to monitor whether undertakings have been respected as well as to ensure the effectiveness of the undertakings given.

For some inventions, patent applications will concern biotechnological inventions starting from living material which was previously deposited in connection with another patent application by either the same or another person. If such an earlier deposit had legally become available to the public not later than the time of the new patent application, it would belong to the relevant state of the art for all patent law purposes. The patent law concept of the state of the art comprises everything which has been made available in some form to the public prior to the filing of a patent application. The novelty of an invention, as is its inventive step, and its disclosure are judged against the standard of the state of the art of the relevant technical field concerned. If a microorganism had become available to the public and thus formed part of the state of the art at the time of a subsequent application, there would be no need for the applicant to re-deposit this material or to maintain such earlier deposit. This result follows from the fact that the microorganism forms part of the state of the art and would be the same in any other technical field for purposes of patent application procedures.

Any restriction on the release of samples of a deposit which was made for purposes of patent procedures which prevents the public in the country of the patent right from having access to the deposit after first publication may put into question the loss of novelty normally accompanying the initial publication, that is, it may be queried whether or not such material is deemed to be part of the state of the art. If a microorganism or other deposited animate matter has become part of the state of the art, which occurs in all technical fields upon publication of the patent application, such matter should be regarded as available to the public within the meaning of novelty or disclosure for national patent law purposes. In consequence, samples could cease to be available to the public from the depositary institution without affecting the novelty-destroying or disclosure effect of the published application. In as much as public was provided with access to the technical details of an invention either directly or through an expert and in view of the fact that such access will be considered to constitute an adequate disclosure of the invention, it follows that a published application becomes part of the prior art independent of the outcome of the application. Article 15(10) establishes this principle.

Such a principle needs to be established particularly for those cases involving living or self-reproducing matter where an application does not result in the grant of a patent and where the application is published so that one or more samples could have been released either to the public or to an expert. The application of such a principle in these cases is analogous to the situation where a product has been exhibited for a time at a public trade fair and has consequently become part of the state of the art for all time and is thus considered as being available to the public. No obligation exists to provide another enabling disclosure to the public.

The system of early publication and deferred examination of patent applications is unlikely to be changed in Europe in the foreseeable future. The requirements for disclosure of inventions are closely similar in all Member States both for European and national patent applications. In view of the works already done and the consensus already achieved in respect of EPC Rules 28 and 28a, any harmonisation of the provisions of national patent laws regulating the conditions of access, release and re-deposit should parallel those of the EPC taking into account the shortcomings from which the EPC rules are thought to suffer.

Thus, the differences between Article 15 of the Directive and EPC Rule 28 may be summarised as follows:

1. The undertaking required in Article 15 paragraph 3(b) (i)—that a party requesting a sample of deposited material will not make it available to third parties—does not expire while the undertaking in EPC Rule 28 expires if "the application has been refused or withdrawn or is deemed to be withdrawn or, if a patent is granted, before the expiry of the patent in the designated State in which it last expires" (Rule 28(3)(a)).

2. The undertaking required in paragraph 3(b) (ii)—to use the sample for experimental purposes only—will expire only in those countries where a patent right comes into existence. Once a patent right is created, the patent laws themselves would limit a third party to the use of a patented invention for experimental purposes. This rule permits those who have received samples to use the material in other countries for experimental purposes. Under EPC Rule 28, if a patent is refused or an application is withdrawn, this undertaking would expire, enabling third parties to commercialise the deposited material. This is an undesirable consequence resulting from a misconstrued application of the system of early publication wherein physical access to deposited material is equated with the notice function of the publication.

3. The sample would no longer be available to the public or to an expert if the application fails or otherwise does not lead to the grant of a patent where the application had been published and the deposit was available either to the public or to an expert.

Related Articles on the Economic Implications of Patented Livestock

(a) Applying Animal Patents in Agriculture: Lessons for Farmers and the Patent Office for Self-Reproducible Animals*

William Lesser

Just two months ago, on April 3, 1987, the Board of Patent Appeals and Interferences of the U.S. Patent and Trademark Office, in a decisive decision, declared higher animal life to be patentable subject matter (*Ex parte Allen*, Appeal No. 86–1790). This was not an entirely unexpected position following, as it does, the pathbreaking 1980 Supreme Court decision in *Chakrabarty* (447, U.S. 303, 206 U.S.P.Q. 193, 1980) and a similar extension of patent protection to open-pollinated seeds in September 1985 (*Ex parte Hibberd*, Appeal No. 645–91, 1985). Indeed, the Canadian Patent Appeal Board has recognized animal varieties as potentially patentable subject matter, notwithstanding the rather limited scope of the Canadian patent law at this time (Straus, p. 75).

Yet the important fact remains that animal varieties may now be patented in the U.S. According to internal sources, 15 applications are currently awaiting processing (U.S. Dept. Commerce, p. 2). The deposit issue as a technical matter requires clarification, a process which will likely take a year or longer (Figg). Several years from now, in all likelihood, there will be a patented, multi-celled animal. The question is, how will this situation "play" in Peoria? Here my concern is not with the political and social image issues which will arise—and indeed are already arising—but with the impacts of this new policy. My objective then is to identify how property rights for this class of products is likely to be applied and the implications for users, for PTO, and for the policy itself. Emphasis shall be on agricultural applications. This is done at the exclusion of laboratory specimens, purebred dogs and cats, and thoroughbred horses, to mention a few of the more obvious other animal classes where patents might be sought and effectively used. By implication, attention is placed on animals which are largely self-reproducible as this class presents far more complex legal and economic issues than do sterile animals. I begin by describing the domestic livestock sector and dividing it into classes.

THE U.S LIVESTOCK SECTOR

Livestock is the single largest agricultural sector in the United States, measured both in terms of sales and geographic scope. Major contributors are beef cattle, hogs and dairy cattle with sheep and goats constituting relatively insignificant proportions. Geographically each of the 50 states has some commercial livestock activity, although concentrations exist in the Upper Midwest—hogs, High Plains—cattle feeding, New

---

* This paper was first presented at the World Intellectual Property Organization and Cornell University Symposium on the Protection of Biotechnological Inventors, Ithaca, New York, June 4–5, 1987.

York, Wisconsin, Minnesota and California—dairy, and the Southeast—poultry, including eggs. Annually, animal agriculture contributed, in 1982, $64.9 billion valued at farm level (Bureau Census, p. VIII). Total animal numbers on farms, as of January, 1986, was 168 million red meat animals and 647 million chickens (Ag. Stat. Board, a and b). Together this vast source permits per capita domestic meat consumption of 223 pounds (retail weight) (101 kilograms), of which 31% is poultry and 69% red meats in 1985. Egg disappearance is around 255 per capita (Bunch, Tables 2 and 8). Imports and exports are a modest component of this total.

Farm numbers in aggregate are equally staggering—some 1.2 million according to the 1982 Census of Agriculture (Bureau Census, Table 15). But like other agricultural commodities produced in this country, much of total supply is provided by a small proportion of large, specialized farms. For example, only 35 percent of these livestock farms had sales above $10,000 annually, and less than a half percent fit in the largest size category (more than 5,000 hogs or 2,500 cattle sold) Bureau Census, p. VIII, Tables 23 and 30).

Breeding Practices

At this point it is convenient to limit attention to the major red meat species of cattle and hogs, while recognizing a fundamental distinction in cattle between those intended for meat and those used for milk production. Cows if properly managed produce one calf a year while sows should have two litters averaging 7–8 pigs. Based on economic considerations, dairy and hog producers typically provide their own replacement cows/sows. Beef cattle, however, are reared in two quite different stages, many calves on grasslands heavily in the West and fattened cattle near feed supplies in the Midwest and High Plains. Very different production practices and owners are involved with these two stages.

Dairy

In 1984 the national mean production per cow was 12,500 pounds (5,700 kilograms), a level which has been increasing at an average rate of one percent over the past generation (Crop Rpt. Board). One source of this improvement is genetic potential with some cows in commercial production able to yield 20,000 or even 24,000 pounds a year. Such supercows are scarce and expensive, but dairy farmers have available to them another source of improved genes, those from the male. For over half of dairy farmers in the latter 1980s, this is delivered through artificial insemination (AI) with the remainder using a bull. AI use is facilitated by the regular milkings needed, which makes identifying estrus ("heat") relatively easy. Several kits are available to assist in this process.

Supplying the semen is a large and sophisticated international industry, of which several of the largest firms are cooperatives. One very substantial cooperative with an international market, Eastern AI Cooperative, is located here in Ithaca. In brief the selection process followed by Eastern and similar firms is to identify top-producing cows and mate them with bulls with high producing daughters. The selection process for these matings is elaborate and involves not a small amount of judgment. Promising looking bulls are reared, mated and the production of their daughters monitored. Fathers of daughters with high yields in commercial herds, plus other desirable health and handling attributes, are retained for semen donation purposes. The semen is preserved in liquid nitrogen and generally administered by a staff of technicians.

Beef Cattle and Hogs

The situation for these species and classes of animals is quite different because they are typically kept in large lots making AI use difficult. This is especially true for beef cows which are often maintained on the range, although materials are available which stimulate ovulation and hence make group breeding possible. Yet the use of AI is low, about two percent for cattle and equally low for hogs in 1980–81 (Gilliam, Table 15; Van Arsdale and Nelson, p. 22). Instead, most producers rely on natural breeding, giving rise to an industry which produces breeding boars and bulls. Many of these are purebreds which producers use to gain the efficiency or heterosis, from cross-breeding or hybridization.

Figure 1 shows the approximate utilization of the sires and dams of beef and dairy cattle and hogs in three age groups. In general, all female dairy calves are reared for milk production while the males are slaughtered, mostly for veal. Male meat animals are typically castrated and fattened prior to slaughter. Females may be fed or held for breeding. The actual proportions of breeding and feeding use depends on the stage of the livestock cycle (see Beale, et al.). These use factors are important because of their possible influence on how patented animals will be utilized in these major branches of the livestock sector. As significant is the recognition of the complex coordination relationships in the sector, especially among the several vertical market levels. It is evident that patented animals must adapt to this system, not vice versa.

POSSIBLE PATENTABLE INNOVATIONS AND INHERITABILITY

As a final preliminary step, it is helpful to identify the kinds of "new" animals for agricultural uses which may be patented in the future. At the present time, the introduction of the ability to produce higher levels of growth hormone is being experimented with in hogs (Hammer, et al., 1986; Hammer, et al. 1985). Experience with *administered* Porcine growth hormone has shown that the animals convert feed more efficiently while producing a leaner, more marketable carcass (Boyd, et al.; Meltzer; Etherton, et al.; Fabry, et al.). Such an attribute, if it indeed can be introduced into the gene base of hogs and cattle, would be commercially attractive as well as seemingly eligible for the grant of a patent. A number of related production attributes providing stress resistance and/or productivity enhancement would seem to be equally desirable and patentable.

Figure 1 Use of males and females by species, class and age, U.S. red meat livestock sector, mid 1980s

SPECIES/ CLASS	FEMALE			MALE		
	calf	*heifer*[1]	*cow*	*calf*	*steer*[2]	*bull*
Dairy Cattle	100% raise	95% raise	95% milk and calf production	90% slaughter for veal	9% slaughter for beef	1% breeding
Beef Cattle	100% raise	50%[3] fatten and slaughter	50% breeding	100% raise	98% fatten and slaughter	2% breeding
Hogs	*pig*	*barrow*[4]	*sow*	*pig*	*gilt*[5]	*boar*
	100% raise	50%[3] fatten and slaughter	50% breeding	100% raise	98% fatten and slaughter	2% breeding

[1] Female cattle which have not calved
[2] Castrated male cattle
[3] Proportion bred and slaughtered varies over time in relation to the cattle cycle
[4] Female hog which have not littered
[5] Castrated male hog

As a practical consideration, the reduction to practice of these modified animals is in its early stage. For single gene attributes, like growth hormone, the principal limiting factors are the low efficiency on the inoculation of the eggs (on the order of .2 per cent) as well as the imperfect control over the secretion of the hormone throughout the growth cycle. According to one leading researcher, "We're still at the Orville Wright stage of this research." (quoted in Miller). Attributes dependent on the interaction of numerous (perhaps hundreds) of genes are quite distant in production as the controlling genes and interactions among them have yet to be identified (Wahl).

The inheritability of the traits also depends on the controlling genes. Single gene-based attributes, like growth hormone, will be inherited by half the progeny of one gene-carrying parent. However, even if both parents have the trait (unless they are brother and sister), less than all the offspring will inherit it due to the varied location of the coding of the gene. Many generations will be needed before the inheritance factor can be stabilized near 100 percent. For multiple gene-controlled attributes the inheritability will be far lower, probably on the order of the inheritance of major characteristics. Experimental evidence on naturally occurring traits shows these to be inherited on the order of 5 to 60 percent (Table 1).

Table 1 Approximate heritability rates for selected characteristics in livestock and poultry

Characteristic	Percentage			
	Dairy Cattle	Beef Cattle	Hogs	Poultry
Number born	—	5	10	—
Birth weight	60	40	5	—
Weight at weaning	—	25	10	—
Mature weight	60	—	—	50
Milk production	25	—	—	—
Egg production	—	—	—	35
Feed efficiency	—	40	30	—
Percent lean meat	—	40	35	—

Source: Compiled by Acker, Table 18-1

Inheritability is not an issue for the PTO beyond the effect it has on disclosure. For the patent holder it has major considerations for the extension of control to progeny. Patent holders are likely to wish to strengthen rights to offspring through the use of a contract, drawn at the time of sale, which specifies rights over succeeding generations. This would be a more secure approach than the use of the uncertainly defined "implied use" stipulation which passes with the sale of a patented product. Probably the stipulation will require a royalty to be paid on the birth of a calf or pig. Rights to subsequent generations may be sought as part of the same agreement, but would likely require that the customer serve as an enforcer of patent rights, as a collector of royalties and/or presenter of a contract to his/her buyer. One and more generations from the parent stock the likelihood the patented trait will be inherited can be expected to be quite low. Under these conditions the buyer will be hesitant to accede to a royalty payment without the assurance that the animal does indeed have the patented trait. Some traits may be readily observable, but many will require a confirmation test of some form. To be practical, these tests will have to be simple and very inexpensive.

While the inheritance of traits will create a patent-right enforcement problem, low inheritability would be even less desirable (see Miller). Low inheritance will require a regular purchase of trait-carrying sires whenever AI is not used. And the sires must be

346

produced directly using genetic manipulation techniques, or selected from among a large number of potential breeding animals which do not carry the trait. Both approaches are costly as well as limiting on the sires which can enter the breeding pool, at the likely cost of reduced ability to select for other desirable attributes.

APPLICATIONS OF ANIMAL PATENTS BY LIVESTOCK SECTOR

Dairy

Dairy cows are relatively small in number and are handled frequently on an individual basis. This environment makes it conceivable that patent holders' rights to calves born to a patented cow could be enforced within a reasonable and economical system. Indeed, purebred production herds now exist which are registered on an ongoing basis. The system in its basis works this way for holsteins. The breeder registers the sire and dam number with the national association, which checks a random sample using a blood sample from the calf to verify parentage. Both parents must be registered; "upgrading" is not permitted for holsteins. Other breed associations function in much the same manner with the exclusion of the requirement for having both parents registered purebreds.

Ensuring rights over progeny would, as mentioned, likely require the patent holder to exercise a license and royalty agreement at the time of initial sale. This arrangement would further protect the patent owner in cases where a cow is used as a source of eggs for transplanting, becoming in the process the biological dam for multiple offspring. The licensing agreement would have to specify that equivalent conditions be placed on subsequent buyers—again roughly equivalent to the purebred registration system.

For dairy cows, the system is possibly workable. For bull calves, the prospects dim rapidly. Most dairy bull calves as noted are sold for veal, some for immediate slaughter, some after feeding for "white veal," while a very small portion is retained for breeding purposes. Conceptually, each use could have a different fee arrangement. In practice, it is inconceivable that a dairyman would permit a patent agreement to dictate how bull calves are to be handled. Male calves are treated as byproducts of the main enterprise, milk production, and are accorded little attention or value. The complexity in enforcing patent rights arises from the maintenance of identity and use through numerous changes of ownership. At a minimum, bull calves typically pass through an auction market where they are purchased by an order (commission) buyer who later resells to feeders or packers. The maintenance of a structured fee system, with covenants on subsequent purchasers, through this system seems highly suspect. It is done with purebreds and thoroughbred horses, but they are much less numerous and far more valuable, justifying individual treatment. For example, roughly 500,000 holstein calves are registered annually. Bull dairy calves, on the other hand, number some five million annually and their value is low; the market value is between $60 and $100.

Maintaining control through the first round sire lineage would be simpler, at least for those bulls used in AI. The artificial insemination firms maintain careful records and could easily pay a royalty to the patent holder for each "straw" of semen from a patented bull. Control of the dispersion of the resultant calves raises those problems as described above.

Hogs

The combination in most hog operations of activities from breeding through feeding within a single enterprise greatly facilitates the enforcement of patent rights for this species. Moreover, as breeding is internalized the producer has information about the genetic makeup of the stock. The multiplication rate for the breeding stock into marketable animals may be collected from farm records or based on national average litter size and periodicity data. Thus, a measure of the flow is relatively simple, the count of animals shipped, and may be used to assess a royalty. Barrows (castrated males) present no further problems following sale as they have been neutered. What is potentially complex is the dispersion of gilts, young females, and cull sows, both of which are capable of reproducing. The majority of these animals—about 85 percent in 1985 (P&SA, Table 9)—are sold direct to pork packers permitting a relatively easy tracing of possible diversions to breeding. The remainder moves through a multiplicity of markets, including auctions and order buyers. Control of patent rights through these channels will be very difficult.

Beef Cattle

The imposition of patent rights on the U.S. beef cattle industry will be the most complex undertaking, due largely to the ownership/geographic split between calf producers and cattle feeders and the nature of calf production. In brief, the so-called cow calf operators maintain the cow herds, raising the calves on grass to about 600 pounds. From that point they are sold to a feedlot for final finishing prior to slaughter. Many cow-calf operations are land-extensive, operating in areas of sparse vegetation which can support one brood cow or less per acre. Breeding is done naturally with bulls wandering with the cows. In such an environment, there is great uncertainty about which bull mated with which cow and hence what property rights exist over the calves when mixed bulls are used. Typically, operators will vary bull breeds as a means of controlling the genetic mix of the calves.

If control is difficult for the first generation, it is more so for succeeding ones. This does not apply to males (steers) as they are castrated. Heifers, however, may be retained for replacement breeding cows, sold for breeding purposes, or sold for finishing and slaughter. The proportion moving to each market varies, depending in a large part on the cattle cycle. Again, the marketing of heifers moves through multiple channels and often over great distances. Maintaining identity through these channels will be difficult.

A second complexity affecting the utilization of these calves is the information exchange on the genetic basis and production potential. Cattle feeders buy calves largely by sight, selecting on certain visual characteristics like frame (skeletal) size. Official U.S. Department of Agriculture grade standards are of limited value in this selection process, and feeders generally prefer to purchase from a known calf producer as a means of identifying better the weight gain potential of the calves. As Van Arsdall and Nelson note for hogs, "the current marketing system seldom retains the identity of pigs between producer and finisher" (p. 23).

Marketing patented calves in this environment raises the information problem for cattle feeders unless the results are visually apparent, such as a larger calf at a younger age. Without visual confirmation, buyers must rely on the integrity of the seller, a problematic arrangement when calves from different sources are typically mixed by middlemen. Reputation of the calf producer and/or dealer can substitute for product information, but the process is a slower one and will likely reduce the adoption rate of patented animals in this sector.

IMPLICATIONS FOR THE LIVESTOCK SECTOR

Patented animals will introduce a new organizational component in this large and complex sector. If the patented trait disappears rapidly after the first generation—that is, has a low inheritability level—then as a practical matter the trait must be introduced through the sire. This could be done alternatively through AI or natural breeding. The patent holder would sell the stock as breed animals either for a one-time charge (probably for hogs and beef bulls used in natural breeding) or a per-calf fee (especially applicable to breed animals used in AI). Incumbent on the patent holder will be the introduction of the patentable attribute into a number of breeds, especially for beef cattle and hogs. Only this will permit livestock producers to maintain some cross breeding programs which have been so successful in maintaining hybrid vigor, or heterosis. This could well be a protracted process which will delay the adoption process and reduce the value of the invention.

An inheritable trait would be far more efficient in a biological sense and would be disbursed far more rapidly. Yet the ability of the patent holder to capture the benefits would be reduced. Among seed breeders, a similar situation exists with farmer saved seed. But as farmers typically purchase new seed every two to three years anyway, it is possible to anticipate the production potential value of the patented variety over that period and incorporate it into the initial sale price (see Lesser). The small share of seeds of total crop production cost—around three percent—makes this practice acceptable to producers. This marketing approach would obviate the need to enforce rights to prevent farmers from reusing seed. For livestock breeders the situation is quite different. Traits which can be inherited may be introduced into the entire herd through on-farm breeding, while the relatively high cost of livestock would make it infeasible to "front load" the value of the patented attribute on the initial sales. Hence it is highly likely that animal patent holders will attempt to enforce patent rights over subsequent generations. Rather than rely on the uncertain interpretations of the "implied use" doctrine, a specific sales agreement is likely to be included with each sale. To be effective, this agreement must be extended to subsequent purchasers of progeny.

Such a royalty agreement signed at the time of sale makes the livestock producer a defacto component in the system of enforcing patent rights. This responsibility will not sit well with producers, nor is it clear they have sufficient control to be effective. Problems arise when animals are sold through multiple middlemen where maintaining identity is problematic and diversion from, say, slaughter to breeding possible at any stage. Compliance/enforcement becomes highly complex and questionable even with a single patented trait. Introducing multiple traits with separate ownership into a single animal—say the ability in a dairy cow to produce more milk and resist mastitis infection, a widespread bacterial infection in the udder—would create a far more difficult and complex system.

Roughly comparable post-sale conditions exist in the livestock sector for the registration of purebred animals, but these are sufficiently different in two respects so as not to be a clear indicator of the transferability to patents. Registration procedures are based on *voluntary* compliance, with the benefit the ability to register an animal as a purebred. Thus there is a positive incentive structure. The number of animals involved is a small portion of the total herd—probably much less than 10%. What may be successful on a relatively small scale may not be extendable potentially to the entire population. Conversely, precedence does exist for mandating that certain animals when sold go to slaughter (or export) rather than being diverted for production or breeding purposes. This was the case under the recent "Dairy Termination Program" established by the U.S. Department of Agriculture. Farmers electing this system were paid a premium to withdraw from dairying for five years, including disposing of their milking herd (see Kaiser and Novakovic). While this plan shows it is *possible* to maintain control of farm animals following sale, the circumstances may not apply to the entire sector. Cows sold under the buyout program were limited in number—about 15 percent of the national herd of eleven million, or 1.6 million head—and were granted a substantial premium making special marketing arrangements feasible. For routine sales of hogs and cattle, neither of these special conditions apply.

When examining the impact of animal patents on the U.S. livestock sector it is also important to recognize the narrow margins farmers operate within. Cost of production and profitability estimates are always difficult to estimate and vary over time with price changes among other factors, but in recent years they have been no higher than $33 for hogs and barely profitable for fed cattle. Marketing costs are presently a small percentage of total production costs, on the order of $1.14 (hogs) or $3.35 (cattle) (Econ. Res. Service, Tables 12, 27 and 28). What this says is that a patent enforcement system which imposes substantial extra costs on farmers will not be viable except in certain limited aspects of the livestock sector. Indeed, volume is such that any patent enforcement system which imposes any costs on the purchaser/farmer will seemingly not be viable unless the potential net profit increase is large indeed. Overall then it is possible to say that animal patents for agricultural applications will indeed not play at all well in Peoria.

Nor will they likely play well in the remainder of the country, and not for ethical reasons alone. Patents in this subject area will have high enforcement (excludability) costs for regaining private investment. While such an approach is required in a free enterprise economy, it is not efficient in an economic sense, and hence will be subject to much public criticism. An economist would say this is an appropriate area for public investment (see discussion of public goods in e.g. Asch and Seneca), but that is not a feasible solution in an era of burgeoning public budget deficits. Moreover, even if substantial public investment were possible, there is reason to believe private involvement would speed the realization of an invention. Wherever the outcome of research is uncertain, and the result in part of chance, multiple independent efforts increase the likelihood that a successful outcome is discovered (see Lesser and Masson, pp. 35–37). Thus enforcement costs for private property returns must be accepted as a necessary evil, but much of the public will focus on the "evil,"and not the "necessary."

Animal patents appear to provide but another and largely overlapping means of protecting a genetic transformation. Biotechnology companies now appear to have the option of patenting the altered genes directly *or* the animals which contain those altered genes (but not both simultaneously). This too is similar to seeds where the benefit of patenting the seed, as opposed to the altered genome, is debatable and seemingly dependent on how courts would interpret a patented gene in case of any challenge (see Lesser). With animals, to my mind, the enforcement of rights over a patented gene within the vast domestic cattle or hog herd would be essentially impossible. Enforcement over progeny to be effective must be tied to the offspring at the time of sale. Thus higher animal patents provide an important, and likely popular, means of protecting research developments in this expanding area.

The PTO does not have any direct responsibility for, nor control of, these matters related to commercialization of patents. Yet two factors fall within its jurisdiction and must be handled in an optimal fashion if patents are to serve the public interest as they are intended. First it is necessary that these patents be processed in an expeditious manner. The commercial life of an animal "variety" is brief, and much can be consumed while the patent application is in process. Delays serve no one's benefit, not the researcher nor the public. If the patent examination period is unduly long, then only very major advancements will be patented. As a result, a stream of useful but individually less important improvements in breed characteristics will not receive the research and development attention they otherwise might. Studies have shown that patents serve a highly important role in stimulating routine research activity directed to noteworthy but nonetheless minor embellishments in existing products (Jewkes, Sauers and Stillerman). At the same time, it is essential that the PTO does not allow too broad a scope of patent protection. This applies also during the first applications in this new subject area. Broad patents could in time encompass much of the livestock sector causing major and costly changes in coordination procedures.

These points relate to future action by the PTO in which we all have the utmost confidence in the methods and judgments used. Where judgment was lacking, in my personal opinion, was announcing on April 3rd the status of multi-celled animals as patentable subject matter. Technically this decision is unassailable, but as a public relations effort it was seriously lacking. Experience with public response following the *Chakrabarty* decision and, subsequently, the proposed amendments to the Plant Variety Protection Act should have left no doubt but that there would be an outcry. To my thinking there was a gentler approach which could have been followed, especially since the deposit arrangements needed for the actual issuance of an animal patent are far from complete. Perhaps the Board of Patent Appeals and Interferences could have identified animals as patentable subject matter contingent on the acceptance of a deposit system. Ideally that would have been enough forewarning to begin public debate while not implying that the means of patenting animals was already established and largely beyond public influence. What is being proposed is something approaching the European system where matters of patent law are treated as public policy with a period of public reply allowed before the law is finalized. While that method does not fit directly within the U.S. common law tradition, the concept of public involvement is certainly applicable.

If the role of the PTO is rapidly approaching that of administration of this new directive, the role of the Congress remains incomplete. In my judgment there is a need for some form of intellectual property protection for sexually propagated animal "varieties." The products of traditional crossbreeding serve a useful role yet are probably unpatentable due to obviousness and the problem of satisfying disclosure requirements under the Patent Act. What is required is a separate body of law intended to protect this class of products. A direct parallel may be drawn between the forms of protection allowed for sexually-propagated seeds by the Plant Variety Protection Act and the Patent Act. But this is a separate topic which exceeds my purposes here today.

REFERENCES

Ackers, D. 1983. *Animal Science and Industry*, 3rd ed. Englewood Cliffs, NJ: Prentice-Hall.

Asch, P. and R. Seneca. 1985. *Government and the Marketplace*. New York: Dryden Press.

Beale, T., P. R. Hasbargen, J. E. Ikerd, D. E. Murfield and D. C. Petritz. 1983, "Cattle cycles: How to profit from them." USDA, Extension Service, Mis. Pub. 1430 (March).

Boyd, R. D., D. E. Bauman, D. H. Beerman, A. F. Neergaard, L. Sauza and W. R. Butler. 1986. "Titration of the porcine growth hormone dose which maximizes growth performance and lean deposition in swine." Abstract of paper presented at the Annual Meeting of the American Society of Animal Science, Kansas State University (July–August).

Bunch, K. L. 1987. "Food Consumption, Prices and Expenditures 1985." USDA, Econ. Res. Service, Stat. Bul. 749 (January).

Etherton, T. D., C. M. Evock, C. S. Chung, P. E. Walton, M. N. Sillence, K. A. Magri and R. E. Ivy. 1986. "Stimulation of pig growth performance by long-term treatment with pituitary porcine growth hormone [pGH] and a recombinant pGH." *J. Animal Science*, 63:219 (suppl. 1).

Fabry, J., L. Ruelle, V. Claes and E. Ettaib. 1986. "Efficacy of exogenous bovine growth hormone for increased weight gains, feed efficiency and carcass quality in beef heifers." *J. Animal Science* 61:261–62 (suppl. 1).

Figg, Tony. 1987. Memo to members of the American Bar Association/Patent and Trademark Committee, 110 (April 9).

Gilliam, H. C. Jr. 1984. "The U.S. beef cow-calf industry." USDA, Econ. Res. Service, Ag. Econ. Rpt. 515 (September).

Hammer, R. E., D. G. Pursel, C. E. Rexrood Jr., R. J. Wall, D. J. Bolt, C. M. Ebert, R. D. Palmiter and R. L. Brinster. 1985. "Trans-genetic production of rabbits, sheep and pigs by micro engineering." *Nature* 315:680–83.

Hammer, R. E., D. G. Pursel, C. E. Rexrood Jr., R. J. Wall, D. J. Bolt, R. D. Palmiter and R. L. Brinster. 1986. "Genetic engineering of mamallian embryos." *J. Animal Science*, 63:269–78.

Jewkes, J., D. Sawers and R. Stillerman. 1969. *The Sources of Invention*, 2nd ed. New York: Norton.

Kaiser, H. M. and A. M. Novakovic. 1986. "Results of the dairy termination program and implications for New York milk production." Cornello Univ., Dept. Agr. Econ., A. E. Ext. 86–20 (June).

Lesser, W. 1986. "Patenting seeds in the United States of America." *Industrial Property*, 9:360–67 (September).

Lesser, W. H. and R. T. Masson. 1985. *An Economic Analysis of the Plant Variety Protection Act.* Washington, DC: American Seed Trade Assoc.

Meltzer, M. I. 1987. *Reportitioning agents in livestock: Economic impact of porcine growth hormone.* Master's thesis, Cornell University.

Miller, C. 1987. "Growth hormone genes bring super pigs closer to market." *Genetic Eng. News*, p. 7 (May).

Packers and Stockyards' Adm., USDA. 1986. "Statistical Report, 1985 Reporting Year." P&SA Stat. Rpt. 86–2 (December 1).

Straus, J. 1985. "Industrial property protection of biotechnological inventions: Analysis of certain basic issues." World Intellectual Property Org., BIG/281 (July).

USDA, Economic Research Service, 1987. "Livestock and Poultry: Situation and Outlook Report." LPS–23 (February).

USDA, Nat. Ag. Stat. Service, Ag. Statistics Board. 1987(a) "Eggs, Chickens and Turkeys." Pou 1–1 (April).

USDA, Nat. Ag. Stat. Service, Ag. Statistics Board. 1987(b). "Meat Animals Production, Disposition and Income, 1986 Summary." MtAn 1–1 (April).

USDA, Statistical Reporting Service, Crop Rpt. Board. 1985. "Milk Production, Disposition and Income, 1984 Summary." Da 1–2.

U.S. Dept. Commerce, Patent and Trademark Office. 1987. "News." (April 17).

U.S. Dept. Commerce, Bureau Census, 1983. *1982 Census of Agriculture.* Vol. 1, Part 51, US-Summary and State Data, AC82–A–51 (October).

Van Arsdall, R. N. and K. E. Nelson. 1984. "U.S. Hog Industry." USDA, Econ, Res. Service, Ag. Econ Rpt. 511 (June).

Wahl, R. USDA Beltsville Research Center, personal communication.

(b) Animal Patents in the USA: Are the Concerns Justified?*

William Lesser

INTRODUCTION

Many people around the world were shocked when on April 3, 1987 the Board of Patent Appeals and Interferences of the U.S. Patent and Trademark Office (PTO) declared higher animals patentable subject matter (*Ex parte Allen* Appeal No. 86–1790) In the previous decision in *Re Merat* (Court of Customs and Patent Appeals, 1975) the court had let stand without comment the contention that animals were not patentable subject matter. Following *Chakrabarty* (447 U.S. 303, 206, USPQ 193 (1980)), the patentability of multi-celled animals was widely anticipated, but the decision came much sooner than many had expected.

It was soon the turn of the PTO, for wholly different reasons, to be surprised. The PTO initially agreed to a voluntary eight-month moratorium on animal patenting. From that point events accelerated. In April 1988, the first animal patent was granted, for a laboratory mouse genetically susceptible of contracting breast cancer. An additional 21 applications were reported to be in process (Schneider). Three bills were earlier introduced into Congress. One, S.2111, would ban animal patents outright and HR3119 would impose a two-year moratorium, while HR4970 would make animal patents more akin to Plant Breeders' Rights with a limited farmer exemption from royalty payment. HR3119 was voted down in committee, but HR4970 passed the House of Representatives only to die in the Senate following adjournment. Its fate in the new term is unknown.

The issue I shall attempt to address here is if all this concern is justified. There are many bases for concern and I shall limit myself to but one major one, concerns about the impact on business and particularly farm business. Major work is being done on other "animal models" for medical research similar to the previously patented mouse. These developments present great potential benefits to human and animal health care. But medical research is an enormous undertaking and no one seriously doubts but that the U.S. National Institutes of Health and major research facilities can hold their own with patented laboratory specimens. What does concern a number of people is how the livestock farmer will fare in all of this, especially the hard-pressed small farmer.

Unlike some parts of the world, the U.S. uses the free entry and exit of farms to regulate supplies. Total U.S. farm numbers declined almost 60 percent from 1950–84 during which time the average acreage per farm more than doubled, but total land in farming remained nearly constant (U.S. Dept. of Agriculture). The major reason seems to be economic efficiency associated with larger farms (see e.g., Stanton), but farmers are scared and oppose much new technology that in their view could further destabilize their position. It is no accident that HR4970 was proposed by Representative Kastenmeier from Wisconsin, with its leading "save the family farm" advocacy.

Despite the newness of animals as patentable subject matter, and indeed the

* This paper was first presented at the World Intellectual Property Organization Worldwide Forum on the Impact of Emerging Technologies on the Law of Intellectual Property, Geneva, Switzerland, September 14–16, 1988.

complete lack of a patented animal with an agriculture application, it is possible to say a great deal about the likely impacts of patents on U.S. livestock farming. I pursue that subject first and then step back and assess what that knowledge tells us about animal patent law in the United States and the rest of the world.

POTENTIAL DEVELOPMENTS IN AGRICULTURE

There are three likely sources of patentable animals for agriculture: 1) naturally occurring, 2) products of traditional breeding, and 3) products of genetic engineering. Naturally occurring organisms are unlikely to be patented ". . . unless given a new form, quality, properties or combination not present in the original article existing in nature . . ." (Quigg letter). As Tegtmeyer notes, (p. 11), "A naturally occurring article, that is substantially unaltered, is not a 'manufacture'". One accepted means of creating a manufacture from a naturally occurring product is to purify it (Van Horn). That method has been used for microorganisms, but its application to higher animals is unclear. Thus naturally occurring animals are unlikely to be patentable.

The products of "traditional breeding" too are problematic for generational change is slow (see e.g. Campbell in Lasley). Due to this factor, the achievable changes over a few generations may be "obvious" and hence unpatentable. Cross-bred animals have a further reproductability problem, at least using traditional methods, as was pointed out in *Re Merat* (Court of Customs and Patent Appeals, 1975). Thus there is nothing **inherent** about traditional breeding practices which would preclude patenting the products, but the practical realities are such that this approach is unlikely to be a major source of patentable animals.

Patented farm animals then are likely to be derived largely through the process of biotechnology in which a novel gene or genes are inserted into the new host. These practices have achieved success in the laboratory with large animals, but are limited by several factors in commercial applications:

1) Complex characteristics are controlled by multiple, interacting genes. These interactions are poorly understood at this time and current procedures are limited in the amount of genetic material that can be transferred (Dr Noden, Biotechnology Inst., Cornell Univ., personal communication).

2) The proper location and regulation of the transferred genes is a highly complex matter that is but poorly understood (Gordon, et al., Habers, et al., Dr. Pursel, U.S. Dept. Agr., Ag. Res. Service, Reproduction Lab, personal communication).

3) The success rate of introducing new genetic material is very low, on the order of .2 to 1 percent, raising costs and slowing progress (Drs. Wall and Pursel, U.S. Dept. Agr., Ag. Res. Service, Reproduction Lab, personal communication).

Due to these factors, major developments in patentable farm animals are expected to be a decade or more away (U.S. Congress, 1988, Hansel, p.9). Current research is generally limited to federal and university projects or to government-sponsored firms in the U.S., Japan and Western Europe, especially the U.K. Developing countries like India are not expected to be far behind (Dr. Chakrabarty, personal communication). Financial support in the U.S. is up to $50 million annually.

Despite these limitations, major advances have been made in the areas of accelerated weight gain (Schwarz testimony; *Bio/Technology*, 6(1988):179), disease resistance (DeQuattro; *Biotechnology Newswatch*, 8(1988):8), and production of pharmaceuticals by animals (Gordon, et al.; *Nature*, 329(1987):447).

At this point in time, prior to the development of any commercial trans-genetic farm animals, it is not possible to be at all specific about their impacts. Research on **injected** products which are being bred into chicken, cattle and hogs may nonetheless give a broad indication of the degree of impacts of genetically engineered animals on the agricultural sector. Disease resistance is cost savings for producers; the control of Marek's disease in poultry was estimated to save $178.4 million, but when the resistance is too narrow its values might not be great (Acker; Walsh and Sundquist).

Of greater potential impact is enhancements to weight gain for meat animals and greater milk production potential for dairy stock. Table 1 indicates the potential level of impact in these areas, for the major livestock species. These efficiency gains will lead to the need for fewer head on feed and, at least in U.S. probably contribute to a continuing decline in farm **numbers.** The impact on farm **size** is less clear, but these changes will put a higher premium on management quality. Experience suggests strongly that better managed farms tend to grow more rapidly so bioengineered animals will probably contribute to larger, as well as fewer, farms.

Table 1 Impacts of biotechnology products on livestock production costs

Species/Class	Product	Projected Impacts	References
Dairy Cows	Injected Somatotropin (growth hormone)	6–25% increase in production 5–26% return @ current prices potential 20% reduction farm numbers; scale neutral	Kalter et al., U.S. Congress, 1986
Hogs	Injected Somatotropin	Gain efficiency +10%, backfat −32%, production costs −8.5%	Shagam. Kalter and Milligan
Cattle	Injected Somatotropin	Gain efficiency +21% production costs −7%	Kalter and Milligan
Poultry	Disease Resistance	Savings from Marek's disease $178.4 million (2% costs)	in Acker

IMPLICATIONS FOR AGRICULTURE

The first issue in examining the likely impacts of animal patents on agriculture is forming a judgment on the incentive effect of patents on inventors. This matter can never be resolved to everyone's satisfaction because in a dynamic world it is not possible to say absolutely what would have happened without patents (Machlup). The passage of the Plant Variety Protection Act of 1970, the U.S. version of Plant Breeders' Rights, nonetheless provides a convenient vantage point for examining how inventors respond to intellectual property protection for a new class of products. A review of the retrospective analysis for that law suggests strongly that private investment in plant breeding research did indeed increase, providing more productive varieties for farmers (see Butler and Marion; Brim; Cooper quotes some corollary evidence for the U.K.). It is then reasonable to expect that the opportunity to patent animals will increase private research expenditures in this area **provided** the inventor has the opportunity to recover the investment. That is, can the inventor collect royalties?

Some livestock producer groups have called for a ban on royalties, and the bill recently approved by the House of Representatives would prohibit royalties for the sale of offspring (but not semen and embryos) (HR4970). At least one author has predicted that inventors would not choose to exercise the right to a royalty (Raines). In my earlier work on seeds I argued the same point, that royalties were not essential. But in that case the deterioration of seed quality along with ongoing improvements necessitated the purchase of new seed every three years or so (Lesser 1986). With livestock, once a desirable, inheritable trait enters the gene pool, it is passed along from generation to generation by farmers who produce their own replacement animals with no need to return to the original stock.

To understand better this point it is helpful to examine how the U.S. livestock sector functions. For this purpose the four major species and classes will be included: dairy

355

cattle, beef cattle, hogs and poultry. The beef cattle sector is notable because calf production is separated geographically and in ownership from the growing/fattening stage. These two enterprises require very different land resources so that it is far more economical to move the cattle to the feed than feed to the cattle. For the remaining species/classes, the production of replacements and the ultimate product, whether that be eggs, milk or pork, is typically done on the same farm, at least for all but the smallest.

Breeding, the production of new, more productive varieties, including both purebreds and cross-breds, is typically done in separate operations. Here too there is a difference between the species, with many thousands of beef and dairy cattle breeders but only a handful of poultry breeders and producers of cross-bred and "synthetic" bred hogs. These and other relevant characteristics of the US livestock sector are summarized in Table 2.

Table 2   U.S. Livestock Production and Marketing Arrangements.

Beef Cattle

- Calf production – is done in remote grasslands on multiple (1 + million) small farms – many with less than 20 cows.

- Cattle feeding – is carried out in grain rich areas. Increased specialization on larger farms with capacities of 32,000 head +.

- Breeding – is done on multiple (10's of thousands) farms with some 80 breeds common.

- Sales – made from breeder to calf producer, calf producer to feeder and feeder to packer. Independent ownership dominates.

Hogs

- Pork production – three quarters of 315,000 (1982) farms combine pig production with feeding. A few very large farms – some owned by non-farming interests – contribute a substantial amount of total production.

- Breeding – a large number (10,000+) of purebred breeders exist but only 4–5 supplying cross-bred stock to largest producers.

- Sales – from breeder to producer and producer to packer.

Dairy Cattle

- Milk production – milk production and replacements produced on same farm. Large number of farms in all 50 states; a very few milk 2,000 head.

- Breeding – some half done with artificial insemination. Breeding bulls produced on multiple small farms.

- Sales – livestock sales are by-products to milk production accounting for less than 10 per cent of resources.

Eggs

- Chick production – done by hatcheries, integrated into larger operations.

- Egg production – production widespread but less than five percent are "commercial size," above .5 million birds in production. Size extends up to 5 million birds.

- Breeding – but five breeders dominate the sector.

- Sales – Breeders sell to hatcheries with some contracted limitations on the release of breeding stock. Eggs are sold in a variety of ways including integrated producer/processors and contract production.

Broilers

- Production – farmers combine hatcheries with feeding, bringing birds to market in seven weeks. About 17,000 farms (in 1982) produced 80 percent of output. Size varies up to 100,000 birds at one time.

- Breeding – a total of seven firms (three for females and four for males) control the sector, selling to large hatcheries.

- Sales – about 11 integrators own the broilers which are raised under contract by farmers. These large integrators sell directly to supermarkets and other outlets.

From the material in Table 2 it is evident that there are major differences among the species/classes. What follows is an attempt to determine the incentive impact of patents on each of these species/classes, including an exploration of alternative protection mechanisms such as secrecy. Subsequently the expected impacts on livestock production is addressed. For that discussion it is instructive to divide the species/ classes along somewhat different lines, as follows:
1) high-valued, low reproduction rate animals for producing pharmaceuticals, such as proteins in milk,
2) low-valued but high reproduction rate, eg., poultry, and
3) low-valued, low reproduction rate animals, especially cattle (one calf a year per cow) and hogs (16 pigs a year per sow).
CLASS 1 (production of pharmaceuticals): This class of products appears to require few animals, possibly only 100 cows for products excreted into milk. As a result, the maintenance of control of the invention through secrecy seems plausible as ownership can be controlled through retention or through a small number of contracts. Alternatively, the trait can be made non-inheritable (as with so-called mosaic animals). The costs of retention of control would be relatively small compared to the productive value of each animal.
CLASS 2 (poultry): Secrecy is not a viable option as there are numerous hatcheries (often operating as part of a production operation) which require both males and females to produce chicks. Contracting nonetheless appears viable and, indeed, has a precedent in the industry in the laying hen sector where breeders release "parent" and "grandparent" breeding stock to hatcheries under the contractual stipulation that only commercial cross-breds be sold. A similar procedure could be used to control release of varieties carrying a patented gene. Alternatively, inheritance through the male line only could be employed as a protection mechanism since only females are used in egg production.
For broiler (chicken meat) production contracts would have to be used as both male and female chicks are required in production. Contracting would be facilitated by the small number – about 11 – or "integrators" who own the vast bulk of broilers in the U.S. (Table 2). Finally, a relatively low inheritance rate for the trait would be acceptable because of the high reproduction rate and low value per chick. The text for the presence of the trait would have to be very inexpensive due to the very high volumes.
CLASS 3 (livestock): This group of animals presents the most complex case under patent law. The red meat species are numerous, scattered geographically, slow to reproduce yet yield a low average net margin. (The average net margin for cattle feeding is on the order of $30 for an animal with a selling price of around $750). These characteristics mean that the engineered traits on which a patent is based must be inheritable at a high level and be stable over time. Substantial prior work or livestock has shown that complex traits, those controlled by multiple genes, are inheritable in only 5 to 60 percent of cases (Acker, Table 18–1).
Among dairy cattle, where the practice is currently used in 50 percent of breeding, artificial insemination (AI) could be used to disseminate the invention relatively

357

rapidly. AI is far less practical for cattle and hogs, meaning a bull or boar can service far fewer females. Recognizing Mendellian inheritance norms, when but one parent carries a trait, this means that a very large number of trait-carrying males would be needed to disseminate the trait. Alternatively, and probably preferably, if both the males and females have the trait, it will be disseminated far more rapidly. Together this says that secrecy is not practical with the red meat animals although contracts could possibly be used with a limited number of larger farms.

Considered overall, it is apparent that patents will function quite differently for each of the animal "classes" identified above and hence provide varying levels of incentive effects. Developments among the red meat species seem the most in need of patent protection for the recovery of research and development expenditures, while pharmaceutical production applications would seem to depend the least on patents. These aspects are summarized in Table 3.

Table 3 Classification of animals by impacts of patents

	Class 1 Production of pharmaceuticals	Class 2 Poultry	Class 3 Livestock
Examples	cows (in milk), hamsters, caterpillars	chicken, turkeys	cattle, pigs, sheep
Economically feasible transfer	male only possible	male only possible	trait must be carried by both males and females, high inheritance rate
Ramifications for technology	attribute may be relatively unstable as need not be passed across generations	intergeneration transfer not required	must transfer stably across multiple generations
Testing for trait	yes—discard non-trait bearing animals	yes—discard non-trait carrying animals	yes—discard non-trait carrying will be fed and/or handled differently
Means of protecting investment	secrecy, contracts, patents	contracting possible, patents	contracting possible, only with small number of large farms, patents
Incentive impacts of patents	low	moderate	high

Transgenic animals will have different production attributes and hence require some changes in management practices. The major impact of animal patents on the livestock farmer, however, will likely be associated with the collection of royalties. As stated earlier, I feel royalties will be an essential component of any significant work on animal genetics.

Royalty collection would seem to fit relatively easily in the vertically and horizontally concentrated poultry sector, at least for broilers. There the dozen or so major integrators own the birds from birth to slaughter and can be monitored relatively easily.

Cattle and hogs present an entirely different situation, especially cattle. Beef cattle are born on the range and sold several times before slaughter. This makes it extremely difficult to follow ownership of trait-carrying individuals and to prevent diversion to breeding programs. Hogs and dairy cattle are less complex for "farrowing and finishing" are done in the same location, and often in extremely large operations. To me, these factors taken together suggest three things:

1) only very major developments will be economically viable when the costs of royalty collection are considered, and

2) there is a great likelihood that patent rights will be clarified or extended through the use of supplementary contracts, and

3) many inventors will choose to limit the release of their inventions to a smaller number of farms, which will be the largest ones.

This scenario will become more complex once multiple patented genes, such as ones for disease resistance and growth efficiency, are incorporated into the same animal. One can speculate on organizational arrangements to carry out such a task, but that exceeds our scope here.

Those individuals who fear that patented animals will lead to the loss of farms, and small farms in particular, have some basis for their concerns. While genetically altered animals are not inherently biased to large size farms, as are many mechanical inventions, the effect nonetheless is likely to be increased concentration of production and loss in farm numbers. This, if it occurred, would be an individual and social problem, but would not pose a real economic threat for the U.S.

What the critics of animal patents have not considered is the implications of *not* allowing patents. That would slow, but not halt, research in this area. Developments when they did come along would be protectable only through secrecy or contract. In my judgment, such a case would be certain to limit access to these inventions by small farms, no matter how efficient. Overall this could make the structural implications of animal patents **more**, not less, pronounced. The underlying destabilizing factor is the emergence of a major new technology which, if it proceeds in accordance with current work, will change the livestock sector. Patents are a facilitating, but by no means necessary, component of that technological process.

IMPLICATIONS FOR U.S. PATENT LAW

The rather abrupt emergence of animals as patentable subject matter in the U.S. presents some intriguing issues for patent law. Perhaps most significant of these is the approach taken and the sharp and ongoing public response. The threat of HR4970 and similar legislation suggests a major breach of the traditionally independent operation of the PTO. This says Patent and Trademark Office officials need to become better political scientists than has been necessary in the past. Public reaction must be recognized in any major policy decision of this type. Acting as if that is not the domain of the PTO is unrealistic and in my view damaging to the long term interests of the patent system. In Europe and other countries following that legal system, public comment is incorporated into the process of revising patent law. In the U.S. it is not presently, but that seems to be changing.

On a more technical level, I see it as essential that the "experimental use" doctrine be clarified to allow access to the genetic material in patented animals for the purpose of improving those strains. A generally accepted principal is that "scientific" research is permitted. In *Roche Products v. Bolar Pharmaceutical Co.* (733 F.2d. 858(Fed. Cir. at 863)), the court recognized, as counterdistinctions to business reasons, scientific uses undertaken for "... amusement, to satisfy idle curiosity, or for strictly philosophical inquiry." Interpreted narrowly, this decision would seem to foreclose patented products from any use which might have an intended practical application.

Goldstein distinguishes between experimentation *on* a patented product and experimentation *with* it. The former – which would seem to include animal breeding – is in his judgment generally permitted while the latter is not (p. 15). His interpretation is nonetheless not universally accepted, necessitating a clarification of this significant issue.

On an even more technical level, the PTO to my thinking must redraft its policy on disclosure requirements for this new class of patentable subject matter. While deposits are now widely required for microorganisms, to the degree that a major international treaty governs some aspects of their use, the recent PTO statement on this subject treats all patentable animals as reproducible through a describable process (U.S. Dept. of Commerce). This seems unlikely and indeed is contrary to the issue raised in *Re Merat*. Today, with technology existing for preserving embryos over long periods of time, it is appropriate to evaluate those procedures and establish appropriate guidelines for their use when replication indeed requires "undue experimentation" (see Van Horn). HR 4970 in fact calls for the use of deposits to satisfy the disclosure requirement (35 USC sec. 112).

In summary then, animal patents raise some intriguing legal and economic issues. Ethical considerations aside, there is no clear implication that patents will be a necessary component in fostering investment in genetic engineering of farm animals. Patents will likely provide important private research incentives, especially for the red meat species, but are not necessary for this work. In fact, while transgenic animals will certainly change the composition of the U.S. livestock sector, it is not clear if the change will be greater with rather than without patents.

Critics appear to overstate the role of patents, treating them as the causal factor they are not. For their part, officials of the Patent and Trademark Office seem to have misjudged, or disregarded, public comment, setting the stage for a dangerous legislative battle over the form of patents in this area. Moreover, some technical adjustments remain regarding the administration of animal patents. Hopefully, if approached properly in the U.S., other countries will not be far behind in this extension of patent law, for many countries are potential users, and producers, of this significant new technology.

BIBLIOGRAPHY

Acker, D., *Animal Science and Industry,* Englewood Cliffs, NJ: Prentice-Hall, Ed., 1983.

Brim, C., "Plant Breeding and Biotechnology in the United States of America: Changing Needs for Protection of Plant Varieties. In World Intellectual Property Organization Proceedings, Symposium on the Protection of Biotechnological Inventions, June 4–5, 1987, Ithaca, NY, pp. 117–34.

Bureau of National Affairs, *Patent, Trademark and Copyright Journal,* Vol. 36, Sept. 15, 1988, pp. 449–452.

Butler, L. J. and B. W. Marion, *The Impacts of Patent Protection on the U.S. Seed Industry and Public Plant Breeding.* U. of Wisconsin, NC–117, Monograph 16, Sept. 1985.

Campbell, J. R. and J. F. Lasley, *The Science of Animals that Serve Humanity.* New York: McGraw-Hill Book Co., 3rd Ed., 1985.

Cooper, P., "Plant Breeders' Rights: Some Economic Considerations." Agriculture Canada, Economic Working Papers, March 1984.

deQuattro, J., "Bioengineered Chickens for the Future," U.S. Department of Agriculture, *Agricultural Research.* March 1987, p. 10.

Goldstein, J., "Legal and Administrative Developments in Depository Practice – U.S. and Abroad." In *The World Biotech Report,* Vol. 2, USA. New York: Online International, 1985, pp. 9–16.

Gordon, K., E. Lee, J. A. Vitale, A. E. Smith, H. Westphal and L. Hennighavsen, "Production of Human Tissue Plasminogen Activator in Transgenic Mouse Milk." *Bio/Technology,* 5(1987):

Hansel, W., "Animal Agriculture for the Year 2000 and Beyond." W. H. Hatch Memorial Lecture, Phoenix, Arizona, Nov. 10, 1986.

Harbers, K. D., D. Johner and R. Jaenisch, "Microinjection of cloned retroviral genomes into mouse zygotes: Integration and expression in the animal." *Nature,* 293(1981):540–42.

Kalter, R. J. and R. A. Milligan, "Emerging Agricultural Technologies: Economic and Political Implications for Animal Production." Paper presented in the Symposium on Food Animal Research, Lexington, KY, Nov. 2–4, 1986.

Kalter, R. J., R. Milligan, W. Lesser, W. Magrath, L. Tauer and D. Bauman, "Biotechnology and the Dairy Industry: Production Costs, Commercial Potential and Economic Impact of the Bovine Growth Hormone." Dept. Agr. Econ., Cornell U., AE Res 35–20, Dec. 1985.

Lesser, W., "Patenting Seeds in the United States of America." *Industrial Property.* 25,(1986):360–67.

Machlup, F., *An Economic Review of the Patent System.* Study No. 15. of U.S. Congress, Senate, Subcommittee on Patents, Trademarks and Copyright, 85th Cong., 2nd session, 1958.

Quigg, D. T., Patent and Trademark Office, News Release, April 7, 1987.

Raines, L. J., "The Mouse that Roared," *Issues in Science and Technology.* Summer 1988, pp. 64–70.

Schneider, K., "Mouse Patent is Issued to Harvard, World's First for Higher Life Form." *N.Y. Times*, April 13, 1988, pp. A1, A22.

Shagam, S. D., "Growth Promoting Agents and the U.S. Hog Sector – Current Research and Economic Implications." *Livestock and Poultry: Situation and Outlook Report*, USDA, Econ. Res. Service, LPS-27, Jan. 1988.

Schwaze, D., Testimony before the Committee on the Judiciary, House of Representatives. In *Patents and the Constitution: Transgenic Animals.* June 11, July 22, August 21, and November 5, 1987, Washington, D.C., Serial No. 23.

Stanton, B. F., "Perspective on Farm Size," *American Journal of Agricultural Economics*, 60(1978):727–37.

Tegtmeyer, R., Testimony before the Committee on the Judiciary, House of Representatives. In *Patents and the Constitution: Transgenic Animals.* June 11, July 22, August 21, and November 5, 1987, Washington, D.C., Serial No. 23.

U.S. Dept. of Agriculture, "Crop Production Summary," Crop Reporting Board, Statistical Reporting Service, Various years.

U.S. Dept. Commerce, Patent and Trademark Office, "Deposit of Biological Materials for Patent Purposes." 37 CFR Pat. 1, *Federal Register*, Vol. 52, No. 174, Sept. 9, 1987, pp. 34080–093.

U.S. Congress, Office of Technology Assessment, "Technology, Public Policy, and the Changing Structure of American Agriculture." OTA-F-285, March 1986.

U.S. Congress, Office of Technology Assessment, "Transgenic Animals." Staff paper, Biological Applications Program, Feb. 1988.

Van Horn, C., "Recent Developments in the Patenting of Biotechnology in the United States." In World Intellectual Property Organizations Proceedings, Symposium on the Protection of Biotechnological Inventions, June 4–5, 1987, Ithaca, NY, pp. 73–86.

Walsh, M. E. and W. B. Sundquist, "A Case Study of Genecol–99: Possible Implications for Other Single-Use Agricultural Biotechnology Products," *North Central Journal of Agricultural Economics*, 10(1988):25–34.

INDEXES

Index of Subjects

References to the Appendices appear in **bold** type.

Index of Authors

Index of Cases